P9-AGE-277

Browning's Characters

A Study in Poetic Technique

LIBRARY
NOV 5 1970

Browning's Characters

A STUDY IN POETIC TECHNIQUE

by Park Honan

ARCHON BOOKS 1969

227030

© Copyright 1961 by Yale University Press, Inc.
Reprinted 1969 with permission

SBN: 208 00793 8
Library of Congress Catalog Card Number: 69-19215
Printed in the United States of America

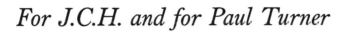

For J.C.H. and for Paul Turner

Acknowledgments

I am most deeply indebted to Mr. Paul Turner, of University College, who stimulated and criticized all of my efforts—both grandly and minutely—during the entire time that this study was being prepared in London. I am greatly obliged, as well, to Professor James R. Sutherland of University College for helpful criticism and advice over a long period; to Professor Geoffrey Tillotson of Birkbeck College for pointed comments after his reading of the manuscript; to Dr. Hilda Hulme and Dr. Mohammed Aslam of London for much good counsel; to Dean Noyes of Connecticut College for a close perusal; to Dean DeVane of Yale University and Professor Rosemond Tuve of Connecticut College for several gracious kindnesses; and to Mr. and Mrs. Geoffrey Musset in London for favors too diverse to mention. One's incalculable debts are not to be absolved, nor would one wish them to be. And J.C.H. knows of my gratitude.

I should also like to thank several editors and publishers for privileges kindly granted. I am grateful to the editors of *Modern Philology* and *English Studies* for allowing me to use material on *Sordello* and on punctuation that originally appeared in their journals. I am obliged to Harcourt, Brace, and Company for permission to quote from I. A. Richards' *Principles of Literary Criticism;* to The University of Michigan Press for permission to quote from Roma A. King, Jr.'s *The Bow and the Lyre: The Art of Robert Browning;* and to Random House, Inc., for permitting me to quote from Robert Langbaum's *The Poetry of Experience: The Dramatic Monologue in Modern Literary Tradition.*

Publication of the book has been assisted by a grant from the Ford Foundation, to whom I am very grateful.

P.H.

New London, Connecticut
November 1960

Texts

THE conventions of reference follow a difference between Browning's development as it may be traced in first editions of the plays and early poems, and his mature achievement as it may be seen in the revised texts that represent the best that Browning left us.

Thus in Chapters 1–3 my citations from Browning are to first editions, or, for the "Madhouse Cell" poems, to the *Monthly Repository* for January 1836. In every case I have indicated the pertinent text in the footnote that follows my first quotation from the poem or play concerned. I have supplied line numbers (which do not occur in the early editions) as nearly as possible on the basis of the numbering system in *The Works of Robert Browning*, ed. F. G. Kenyon, London, 1912.

In Chapters 5–9 I have sought to examine Browning's techniques of portrayal as they appear in twenty mature dramatic monologues —including ten from *The Ring and the Book*. In these chapters I have used not first editions but the revised texts of the poems as they appear in Kenyon's Centenary Edition, except that I have used the one-volume Oxford Edition of *The Ring and the Book*, London, 1912—an accurate reprint of the first edition—partly because it preserves Browning's more convenient earlier system of numbering half-lines and partly because the text seems to be artistically better than either of the slightly revised texts that Browning brought out in 1872 and 1888—when he was, in fact, well past the peak of his poetic powers.

DeVane, *Handbook*	William Clyde DeVane, *A Browning Handbook*, 2d ed. New York, 1955.
Griffin and Minchin, *Life*	W. Hall Griffin and Harry Christopher Minchin, *The Life of Robert Browning, with Notices of His Writings, His Family, & His Friends*, 3d ed. London, 1938.
Letters, ed. Hood	*Letters of Robert Browning Collected by Thomas J. Wise*, ed. Thurman L. Hood, New Haven, 1933.
Letters of R.B. and E.B.B.	*The Letters of Robert Browning and Elizabeth Barrett Barrett, 1845–1846*, 2 vols. London, 1899.
Macready, *Diaries*, ed. Toynbee	*The Diaries of William Charles Macready, 1833–1851*, ed. William Toynbee, 2 vols. London, 1912.
New Letters, ed. DeVane and Knickerbocker	*New Letters of Robert Browning*, ed. William Clyde DeVane and Kenneth Leslie Knickerbocker, New Haven, 1950.
Orr, *Life*	Mrs. Sutherland Orr, *Life and Letters of Robert Browning*, ed. Frederic G. Kenyon, London, 1908.

Special abbreviations for the titles of twenty dramatic monologues of Browning have been adopted in the line references in Chapters 5–9:

AdS   *Andrea del Sarto (Called "The Faultless Painter")*
BBA   *Bishop Blougram's Apology*
BSP   *The Bishop Orders his Tomb at St. Praxed's Church*
C   *Cleon*
CGF   *Count Guido Franceschini*
CUS   *Caliban upon Setebos; or, Natural Theology in the Island*
DD   *A Death in the Desert*
EK   *An Epistle containing the Strange Medical Experience of Karshish, the Arab Physician*
FLL   *Fra Lippo Lippi*
G   *Guido*
GC   *Giuseppe Caponsacchi*
HdA   *Dominus Hyacinthus de Archangelis, Pauperum Procurator*

H-R   *Half-Rome*
JDB   *Juris Doctor Johannes-Baptista Bottinius, Fisci et Rev.*
        Cam. Apostol. Advocatus
MSM   *Mr. Sludge, "The Medium"*
OH-R   *The Other Half-Rome*
P   *Pompilia*
PH-S   *Prince Hohenstiel-Schwangau, Saviour of Society*
TQ   *Tertium Quid*
TP   *The Pope*

To avoid footnotes, in Chapters 5–9, which are devoted almost exclusively to a consideration of the above twenty monologues, I have specified the poem and line number after the first verse quoted and again after any verse following an omission of one or more lines in a passage.

Errata

p. 76, line 26: for "Valance" read "Valence".
p. 77, line 5: for "gutterals" read "gutturals".
p. 119, line 10: for "lies" read "lie".
p. 130, note 5: for "Tyrannt" read "Tyrant".
p. 165, throughout: for "Tyrannt" read "Tyrant".
p. 266, note 25, line 1: for "gives" read "give".

Contents

Introduction

BROWNING'S reputation is not very high today. Literary reputations are always difficult to assess and still harder to explain, but when that of a major poet is so low that his letters appear to be more widely read than his poems,[1] we may well ask ourselves who is to blame: have even serious critics of the past overrated his art, or have we failed to see in his art enduring qualities that are truly there?

In their "own era," Lionel Stevenson has said, "the Victorian poets were glorified by so many devout enthusiasts that the modern reader with critical intelligence hesitates to express himself in their favour." [2] This is an attractive explanation of Browning's decline, because we remember the Browning societies, and we can credit what DeVane has called "the natural and inevitable failure of sympathy between contiguous or near generations." [3] Edith Sitwell has despaired of those "swollen, inflated boomings and roarings about the Soul of Man" that marked fashionable Edwardian verse,[4] and perhaps our own age feels that Browning, too, boomed and roared a little too much.

But when we turn to Browning's present-day detractors—those critics who would save us the trouble of reading Browning, or

1. See, for example, reviews of the recent *Letters of the Brownings to George Barrett*, ed. Paul Landis and Ronald E. Freeman (Urbana, 1958) which contain statements such as: "Mr. Landis is certainly right that the Brownings' poems are of late less generally read than their letters" (William Irvine in *Victorian Studies*, 2, Sept. 1958, 85); or: "It [i.e. *Letters*, ed. Landis and Freeman] is also a moving record of two inspiring lives . . . For, as Mr. Landis writes, 'Volumes of the Brownings' letters accumulate as interest in their poetry wanes'" (Frances Winwar in *New York Times Book Review*, July 6, 1958).

2. "The Pertinacious Victorian Poets," *University of Toronto Quarterly*, 21 (1952), 232.

3. "Robert Browning," *The Victorian Poets* . . . , ed. Frederic E. Faverty (Cambridge, Mass., 1956), p. 59.

4. *Alexander Pope* (London, 1930), p. 3.

much of Browning, and direct us to more worth-while poets—we find that only very rarely are we warned away from Browning because of his faulty psychology, philosophy, or theology. Browning, we are told, was a crude poet: "He is indeed one of those writers who treat language not as a musical instrument, needing delicacy no less than power in its handling, but rather as an iron bar which they are to twist and tangle in an exhibition of their prowess as professional strong men." [5]

Even when his "profundity" is called into question, bad or false technique is usually cited as well.[6] It might be supposed that these criticisms have been offset by a host of detailed and appreciative studies of Browning's technique, that they only reflect the prejudices of those still blinded by antipathy to the Victorians. But the very reverse is true: few close studies of his poetic technique exist, and those that do exist almost uniformly substantiate the charge that Browning was "rugged," "careless," or "insensitive" to the finer tones of rhythm, diction, or other elements of verse. Thus the work that we still acknowledge as the "standard book upon Browning's meters" [7] tells us that Browning's verse reflects his own "rugged personality," and that the poet "composed with such ease and agility that he was not fastidious in selecting his phrases, and he never took what a poet like Tennyson would call scrupulous pains with his versification." [8] Santayana's rather devastating criticism, that "we are [with Browning] in the presence of a barbaric genius, of a truncated imagination, of a thought and an art inchoate and ill-digested, of a volcanic eruption that tosses itself quite blindly and ineffectually into the sky" [9] not only has not been answered by close students of the poetry but has been echoed by

5. F. L. Lucas, *Ten Victorian Poets* (Cambridge, England, 1940), p. 34.

6. E.g. "Browning exemplifies the poet who appreciated and indulged the popular weakness for profundity, appearing to be profound without really being so, keeping the required illusion by various technical devices such as unnecessarily protracted sentences and an over-clipped grammar." Robert Graves, *The Common Asphodel* . . . (London, 1949), p. 128.

7. See DeVane, *Handbook*, p. 586.

8. Harlan Henthorne Hatcher, *The Versification of Robert Browning* (Columbus, 1928), p. 25. See also, e.g., the remarks upon Browning's diction in Bernard Groom, *On the Diction of Tennyson, Browning and Arnold.* SPE Tract 53, Oxford, 1939.

9. George Santayana, "The Poetry of Barbarism," in *Interpretations of Poetry and Religion* (London, 1900), p. 189.

those upon whom we must still rely for information about the technical elements of Browning's art. If a steady little note of praise has been sounded for the poetry since the days of F. J. Furnivall and the Browning societies, and a number of excellent studies of individual poems have appeared in the last thirty or forty years, and in the present century a vast amount of Browning scholarship has accumulated—all of this has not managed to outweigh the critical objections to his technique that continue to be cited. Our own age is reluctant to acknowledge Browning's significance not because he was one of the worshiped Victorians, but because we suspect that he lacked precision, concentration, and subtlety—and few voices have been heard to deny the charge.

The aim of this study is not to provide a new and systematic analysis of Browning's poetic technique. It is rather to suggest that we have so far failed to understand his poetic technique because we have not examined his finest work closely in the light of his own evident intention, and to show that, when we begin to consider at least twenty of the dramatic monologues strictly as portraits of character, and certain poems and plays written before these monologues as experiments in which Browning perfected his character-portraying techniques, a rich and enormous vista opens up before us: Browning then appears to have written with notable precision, concentration, and subtlety, and to be a poet who has indeed much to teach us about the potentialities of verse itself. Members of the London Browning Society long ago recognized Browning's interest in character and we are still sometimes told that the dramatic monologues are primarily character portraits. But whether it is because we cannot bear to think that anything members of the London Browning Society said was valid, or because we instinctively react against simple explanations, we have failed to inspect his verse closely in the light of character.[10] This

10. To some extent, Roma A. King, Jr.'s *The Bow and the Lyre: The Art of Robert Browning* (Ann Arbor, 1957) represents a departure from Browning criticism of the past in that King inspects four blank-verse dramatic monologues quite closely for what he calls *"matter, structure, and meaning"* (p. 9) and, in the process, sometimes seems to treat the poems as character portraits. King's work will be discussed below, pp. 117–18. In the same year as King's study, 1957, Robert Langbaum published his *The Poetry of Experience: The Dramatic Monologue in Modern Literary Tradition*, London and New York. Langbaum's approach is decidedly different

is the more remarkable, as few English poets, in their letters, prefaces, or other recorded remarks, have made their central artistic intentions more explicit than did Browning.[11] "Now, could we shoot / Liquidity into a mould," he wrote in old age, summing up a lifelong wish and aim in the *Parleying with Charles Avison* (1887),

>   —some way
> Arrest Soul's evanescent moods, and keep
> Unalterably still the forms that leap
> To life for once by help of Art!—which yearns
> To save its capture: Poetry discerns,
> Painting is 'ware of passion's rise and fall,
>
> . . . .
>
>   . . . Each Art a-strain
> Would stay the apparition,—nor in vain:
> The Poet's word-mesh, Painter's sure and swift
> Colour-and-line-throw—proud the prize they lift!
> Thus felt Man and thus looked Man.[12]

The character-revealing dramatic monologue was developed through numerous experiments with the "Poet's word-mesh"; by 1845, the year of *Dramatic Romances and Lyrics,* Browning had perfected a kind of mesh for catching character that consisted of a remarkably intricate set of dramatic, prosodic, and verbal techniques, and these he fully exploited in at least twenty of his finest poems.

Our first object will be to see how these techniques were developed in the early long poems and in his plays (Chapters 1–3). We shall consider briefly certain problems involved in classifying and defining the dramatic monologue and the relationship between character portrayal and the monologue form (Chapter 4), and then

---

from my own, but it also demonstrates an interest in looking at technique in the monologues rather more closely than critics have in the past, and I shall have more to say about this work in Chap. 4 as well.

11. Evidence of Browning's interest in and emphasis upon character will be discussed below, Chaps. 1–3.

12. Lines 209–15, 217–21. My citation is to the unnumbered text in *Parleyings with Certain People of Importance* . . . London, 1887; line numbers are to the Centenary Edition.

isolate and examine different character-revealing techniques as they appear in twenty of the mature poems (Chapters 5–8). Lastly, we shall take up two passages from related monologues—*Count Guido Franceschini* and *Guido*—and examine them quite closely for all of the character portrayal that seems to go on in them (Chapter 9). Our object in this case will be to suggest the complexity, intensity, and unity that Browning's finest dramatic verse appears to have just when we approach it in the light of its character-revealing effects, and with some background information about the operation of individual character-revealing techniques in the dramatic monologues.

1. Experiments and Self-Portraits

THE TWOFOLD SEARCH: FORM AND TECHNIQUE

IN 1840 Robert Browning was twenty-eight years old—the same age as Wordsworth when he published the *Lyrical Ballads*. He could look back on a youth well spent in the service of poetry. In sheer bulk of verses produced, the young poet had kept pace with the English poets and playwrights of almost any era. His 20,000 lines of verse [1] greatly outnumbered those that Wordsworth had written by the *Lyrical Ballads* year of 1798; they stood up well, at least numerically, against the precocious and prolific output of Byron and Shelley. If one included the hybrid drama *Paracelsus*, Browning's dramatic poetry in print or in manuscript by the end of 1840 —about 12,800 lines [2]—would approach the amount that Shakespeare had probably written by 1592 at the age of twenty-eight.

One might object that there was no *Tintern Abbey* among these first twenty thousand lines, no *Ode to the West Wind,* and certainly no *Love's Labour's Lost.* But there were lines even in the earliest of the Browning poems, *Pauline,* which compared favorably with the best of Shelley and Wordsworth. Those which the twenty-year-old poet had addressed to Shelley were Shelleyan not only in tone but in quality:

---

1. It seems likely that MS versions of *Pippa Passes, King Victor and King Charles, The Return of the Druses,* and *A Blot in the 'Scutcheon* were in existence by the end of 1840; see DeVane, *Handbook,* pp. 91, 98–99, 132, 137. *Pauline, Paracelsus, Strafford,* and *Sordello* were already in print. Exclusive of juvenilia, at least ten other shorter poems had been written by the end of this year. These known works, with *The First-Born of Egypt* and *The Dance of Death,* total about 19,900 verses—if we take the line totals for the later published versions of the works then in manuscript. Still other boyish writings had existed.

2. *Paracelsus* (4,152) and five dramas (8,652) would total 12,804 lines.

Sun-treader—life and light be thine for ever;
Thou art gone from us—years go by—and spring
Gladdens, and the young earth is beautiful,
Yet thy songs come not—other bards arise,
But none like thee . . .[3]

While there may be a certain innocence about these lines—an innocence of syntax and punctuation, at any rate—that lends them a special charm, their unmistakable quality is no mere fluke of inspiration. The same degree of lyric intensity and technical perfection can be found in parts of *Paracelsus* ("Over the sea our galleys went," for example, in Part IV, or Paracelsus' dying speech in Part V), in the descriptive passages of *Sordello,* and in sections of the plays—notably the Ottima and Sebald sequence in *Pippa Passes,* which combines dramatic with lyric excellence.

Browning had demonstrated by 1840 that he could write very good—and even great—bits of poetry. But unlike the twenty-eight-year-old Shakespeare, he had not written a memorable play. And unlike Wordsworth and Shelley at the same age, he had not written a great poem.

Unless a young poet discovers that the poetic forms already in use at the time that he is writing give full and free scope to his own natural talent, he must invent new forms. If he cannot do that, he must revive old ones—modifying them where needed to suit the peculiar requirements of his own vision.

The ordeal of Robert Browning's early years was partly a search for form. Partly, too, it was a search for the techniques which would fully exploit the complex and exceedingly difficult form that he was tending toward. Despite a vast expenditure of energy, steady labor, glowing faith in himself, and a magnificent lyric gift, which manifested itself early, the search kept Browning from writing a truly individual and successful poem for twelve years after the publication of *Pauline.* The first poem of Browning's that can be placed beside *Ode to the West Wind* or *Tintern Abbey* is really a blank-verse dramatic monologue, one of the first that Browning

3. *Pauline,* 151–55. My citations from *Pauline* are to the numbered 1833 text in *Pauline by Robert Browning. The Text of 1833, Compared with that of 1867 and 1888,* ed. N. Hardy Wallis, London, 1931.

wrote.[4] But *The Bishop Orders his Tomb at St. Praxed's Church* was composed at the age of 32, an age which Shelley never even lived to see and an age at which much of Wordsworth's finest work was already done. Artistry in the poetry of human character came late for Browning, and the search for it was arduous.

Incondita, Pauline, AND SHELLEY

In 1826 the publisher William Benbow, of 252 High Holborn, London, brought out a small, squarish volume in light drab boards entitled *Miscellaneous Poems.* The author of these poems was Percy Bysshe Shelley, and the book was a literary piracy.[5] James Silverthorne, the eldest son of a Peckham Road brewer, purchased a copy of the *Poems* soon after its publication and presented it to his good friend and fourteen-year-old cousin, who was interested in poetry.[6]

As students of Browning's early verse are now very careful to point out, the influence of Silverthorne's gift upon its recipient was prodigious. But it is surely doing an injustice to the young Browning to say that Shelley took him by storm; in fact, it may well be that the ways in which Shelley did not impress Browning were more important than the ways in which he did. For one thing, Browning evidently had been writing poetry before Silverthorne introduced Benbow's book to the house in Camberwell. Shortly after seeing Shelley's verse for the first time he completed a group of poems which he named *Incondita.* This was the juvenile collection which, according to the Flower sisters, fourteen-and-a-half-year-old Browning was "mad to publish"; his parents could find no publisher for it, however, and as Mrs. Orr conjectures, Browning probably destroyed the manuscript in a fit of "disappointment and disgust"—but not before Sarah Flower had copied out two of the poems in a letter dated May 31, 1827, to her friend W. J. Fox.[7]

---

4. *Pauline* is hardly a dramatic monologue, as I shall attempt to show; and *My Last Duchess,* composed two years before *The Bishop at St. Praxed,* is not in blank verse. The term "dramatic monologue" itself will be examined below, Chap. 4.

5. Frederick A. Pottle, *Shelley and Browning: A Myth and Some Facts* (Chicago, 1923), appendix A.

6. Ibid., and Griffin and Minchin, *Life,* pp. 52, 54–55.

7. See *New Poems by Robert Browning and Elizabeth Barrett Browning,* ed. Sir

The letter was discovered among other papers at the sale of the Browning Collections in 1913, and Browning's *The First-Born of Egypt* and *The Dance of Death* from the *Incondita* volume eventually appeared in print—some eighty-eight years after they were written.[8]

It is not possible to tell whether these hardy survivors of the *Incondita* were composed before or after the appearance of Benbow's pirated Shelley; it is only known that they were in existence in May 1827.[9] They show extraordinary skill, a feeling for musical flow in verse, and a fondness for the Romantic vocabulary. The adjectives in the first eight lines of *The First-Born of Egypt,* for example, are *gorgeous, pale, liquid, shadowy, soft, purple,* and *care-worn;* [10] but the Romantic elements of the poem may have been derived from Coleridge or even Shakespeare. In fact, Coleridge's *Fire, Famine, and Slaughter* seems to have suggested *The Dance of Death,* although Browning's poem is certainly no "direct imitation" of Coleridge, as Mrs. Orr reports that someone who had seen the poem before "its destruction" told her it was.[11]

Apart from their clear demonstration of poetic skill, the most remarkable fact about both poems is that they are, in a very rudimentary sense, "dramatic" monologues. It is true that the monologist of *The First-Born of Egypt* can hardly be said to exist; one is aware of no voice save the poet's own until a third of the way through the poem, when one is jolted by the narrator's telling what he has *seen* of the biblical events reported in the eleventh

---

Frederic G. Kenyon (London, 1914), pp. 16–18; Orr, *Life,* pp. 31–32; and DeVane, *Handbook,* p. 554.

8. *New Poems,* ed. Kenyon, pp. 3–12, 18.

9. That is, by the time of Sarah Flower's letter to W. J. Fox. According to Browning himself, "a bookful" of his verses was "written at the ripe age of twelve and thirteen." See his undated letter to Fanny Haworth in Orr, *Life,* p. 96. This seems to be the *Incondita* volume, because he mentions it as the collection shown to Fox; but as Fox did not see *Incondita* before the month of Sarah Flower's letter—May 1827— when Browning turned fifteen, the two surviving poems may have been written (and presumably added to the volume) even as late as the winter of 1826–27, or the spring of 1827, well after Browning's first sight of Shelley's poems.

10. Not all the adjectives here are more typical of the Romantics than, say, of the Augustans—e.g. *purple* is not. But they seem a Romantic grouping. Citations from *The First-Born of Egypt* are to the unnumbered text in *New Poems,* ed. Kenyon, pp. 3–7.

11. Orr, *Life,* p. 32.

and twelfth chapters of Exodus. But hazy as the speaker's identity is, one believes in him as an eyewitness, and Browning's descriptions of the Egyptian tragedy gain some immediacy by being reported in the first person:

> I marked one old man with his only son
> Lifeless within his arms—his withered hand
> Wandering o'er the features of his child
> Bidding him [wake] from that long dreary sleep,
> And lead his old blind father from the crowd
> To the green meadows . . .[12]

In some ways *The Dance of Death* is an even more impressive performance; it consists of five highly rhythmic, chanting speeches by Fever, Pestilence, Ague, Madness, and Consumption. Yet its charm is mainly musical; each of the five spirits in turn boasts of its special claim on mankind, but is not otherwise characterized. The device of the monologue in this poem, just as in *The First-Born of Egypt*, had been used merely to heighten lyrical effects by casting them in a kind of semidramatic framework. Literally scores of English poets, ranging in time and in quality from Chaucer to Mrs. Felicia Dorothea Hemans, had written poems in the monologue form before this, and Browning may have picked up the trick from any one of a number of them: the idea of the poetic monologue itself is neither a profound nor a complex one; it could even have been suggested to Browning by Shakespeare, although it is more likely that it came by way of Coleridge, Wordsworth, or Byron.[13] Probably, too, not every poem in the *Incondita* collection was a monologue—the experimenting boy must have tried his hand at other types of the lyric. All that is definitely known about the rest of the volume was that it impressed Fox as showing "too great splendour of language and too little wealth of thought." [14] But it is worth noting that the two poems Sarah Flower evidently thought were

12. *The First-Born of Egypt*, 70–75. Kenyon indicates that these lines were italicized by Sarah Flower; see *New Poems*, ed. Kenyon, p. 6.

13. All three of these poets used the monologue form on occasion and were almost certainly read by Browning at an early age. For Coleridge, see the discussion of *The Dance of Death* above, and Mrs. Orr, *Life*, p. 32. Mrs. Orr states that she was "told" the "Byronic influence was predominant" in the *Incondita* collection, and that "Byron was his chief master in those early poetic days" (*Life*, p. 31).

14. Orr, *Life*, p. 33.

the best of *Incondita*—the ones that she first copied out for Fox
and that have been accidentally preserved in her letter—were cast
in a form which foreshadowed that of Browning's greatest verse
and one that not even the impact of Shelley would prevent him
from using in his first serious bid for recognition.

Shelley composed *Alastor; or, The Spirit of Solitude* in the late
summer of 1815 when he was twenty-three years old.[15] It is probably his first wholly characteristic and successful effort and doubtless owes much of its relative serenity and control (in contrast with
Queen Mab and the other juvenile efforts) to the influence of
Wordsworth. Browning was impressed by it. Five or six years after
his first glimpse of the poem, when he was writing his own *Pauline*
between October 22, 1832 and January 1833,[16] the rhythms, the
diction, the imagery, and the subject matter of *Alastor* were in his
mind.

There is probably no better way to demonstrate (and perhaps to
exaggerate) the over-all importance of Shelley to Browning than
by comparing the technical aspects of *Alastor* with those of
Pauline.[17] Similarities in diction and syntax occur throughout the
two works. One need only take the first few lines of Browning's
poem,

> Pauline, mine own, bend o'er me—thy soft breast
> Shall pant to mine—bend o'er me—thy sweet eyes,
> And loosened hair, and breathing lips, and arms
> Drawing me to thee—these build up a screen
> To shut me in with thee, and from all fear,[18]

15. See Mary Shelley's note in *The Complete Poetical Works of Shelley,* ed.
Thomas Hutchinson (Oxford, 1904), p. 32.

16. DeVane, *Handbook,* p. 41. *Alastor* was not contained in Benbow's pirated
Miscellaneous Poems of 1826, although it was contained in a second pirated collection of Shelley called *Posthumous and Miscellaneous Poems, Vol. I,* brought out
by Benbow in the same year (see BM Cat. No. C. 117 a 74). Browning read *Alastor*
very soon after reading *Miscellaneous Poems,* presumably, although exactly when—
and in what edition—we do not know. See Frederick A. Pottle's discussion in *Shelley
and Browning . . .* (Chicago, 1923), pp. 23–27, 76–77.

17. Pottle, pp. 36–55, has listed a number of parallel passages from both poems
and Hatcher has found rhythmic correspondences, which I shall mention, but we
do not have, so far, a close analysis of *Pauline's* many-sided technical indebtedness
to *Alastor.*

18. *Pauline,* 1–5.

to see that *Alastor* supplied significant details:

> [He] spread his arms to meet
> Her panting bosom: . . . she drew back a while,
> Then, yielding to the irresistible joy,
> With frantic gesture and short breathless cry
> Folded his frame in her dissolving arms.[19]

From the latter passage it is apparent that Browning not only took for his opening lines some of Shelley's words (*pant*[ing], *breath*-[less], *arms*) but imitated participial constructions (*breathing lips* after *panting bosom* and *dissolving arms*) and furthermore physically characterized Pauline with the nouns *breast, eyes, hair, lips, arms,* used in close succession, after Shelley's *arms, bosom, frame, arms* in this passage—a kind of enumerative technique that Shelley makes significant use of in *Alastor*. Prosodically the influence of *Alastor* on *Pauline* is even more striking. According to Hatcher, Shelley's characteristic iambic-pentameter line—"*Made paler the pale moon, to her cold home,*" where "the important adjectives are emphasized by making monosyllabic measures of them preceding their nouns"—occurs in twenty percent of the verses of *Alastor;* it also occurs in twenty percent of the verses of *Pauline* [20]—a rather impressive correspondence. Hatcher also finds what he calls "arresting evidences of an embryo Browning who delights in smashing the regularity of the metrical pattern" [21] in *Pauline,* but cites only five lines that could not, for their scansion, have been written by Shelley, and it is very doubtful if a tenth of the lines in the poem fall into this category; the "embryo Browning" hardly makes itself known in a prosodic sense. Most important, nothing whatever is done metrically in *Pauline* to create the illusion of a human being speaking—or even writing, if the poem is to be taken as a kind of epistolary monologue. The only "voice" one hears is the voice of Shelley himself, a lovely voice indeed, metrically the voice of *Alastor:*

19. *Alastor,* 183–87. My citations from *Alastor* are to the numbered text in *The Complete Poetical Works of Shelley,* ed. Thomas Hutchinson, Oxford, 1904.

20. Harlan Henthorne Hatcher, *The Versification of Robert Browning* (Columbus, 1928), p. 35.

21. Ibid., p. 36.

> Thou wilt remember one warm morn, when Winter
> Crept aged from the earth, and Spring's first breath
> Blew soft from the moist hills . . .[22]

So closely does Browning follow his predecessor's style that even
Shelley's eccentricities are copied. There is an apparent looseness
of grammatical structure and particularly of punctuation in *Pauline,* which is reminiscent of all Shelley's work—at least before
editors began to go to work on his text. As Hutchinson remarks,

> Shelley recked little of the jots and tittles of literary craftsman-
> ship; he committed many a small sin against the rules of gram-
> mar, and certainly played but a halting attention to the nice
> distinctions of punctuation. Thus in the early editions . . .
> the dash itself becomes a point of all work, replacing indiffer-
> ently commas, colons, semicolons or periods.[23]

True to the text of *Alastor,* Browning uses the dash for every
imaginable purpose in *Pauline;* it welds together fragments and
sentences, substitutes for at least four of the common stops, and
indicates ellipsis. Still, it may not be so easy to edit out the dashes
of *Pauline* as it is those of *Alastor.* Browning "recked" a good deal
of the "jots and tittles of literary craftsmanship" and at the age of
twenty seems to have written sentences of high tensile strength:
the dashes are integral to some of Pauline's loveliest effects (as,
for example, in the lines to Shelley quoted at the beginning of this
chapter) and one could not replace them without doing subtle
damage to the verse.[24]

However, in almost every way the technical indebtedness of
Pauline to *Alastor* is clear. It is only when one turns to the elements
of form and character in both poems that something else appears.

In *Alastor* Shelley tells the mournful story of a poet, doomed
from the start, who, upon reaching early manhood, wanders over

22. *Pauline,* 55–57.
23. *Works,* p. iv.
24. Apparently the only editor who has tampered with the 1833 text has been
Browning himself; see the revisions of *Pauline* in the collected editions of his works
in 1868 and 1888. While these later texts are grammatically more respectable, they
do much to destroy the charm of the original *Pauline.* Browning himself looked
upon the poem with revulsion in later years and corrected some of its technical
peculiarities—I think—brutally.

half the world under the evil influence of the κακοδαίμων, Solitude.[25] When he reaches Kashmir he experiences a dream in which a beautiful, idealized woman appears. He wakes up in despair at having lost her, and spends the rest of his short life in a vain attempt to find her. "Blasted by his disappointment," as Shelley declares in his preface, "he descends to an untimely grave." [26] The Poet's dream in Kashmir is, of course, the climax of the poem; until this point the Poet has wandered from the ruins of one ancient civilization to the next, driven by "high thoughts," but with little real aim; after the dream his only aim is to catch up with his vision, which he fails to do, and dies. The dream-vision, then, dominates *Alastor;* it organizes the narrative; and in spite of the vaguely cloying terms in which it is described, the vision is a powerful and suggestive one. One may fairly say that apart from its being a Shelleyan symbol for human love ("spirit of sweet human love," 203), it is, for the Poet, an individual lover-image ("[He] sickened with excess / Of love," 181–82), a kind of protection- or mother-image ("[She] Folded his frame in her dissolving arms," 187) and an image of the Poet's alter-ego, or ideal self ("Knowledge and truth and virtue were her theme, / And lofty hopes of divine liberty, / Thoughts the most dear to him, and poesy, / Herself a poet," 158–61; see also 153).

The hero—that is, the speaker, or supposed "author"—of Browning's *Pauline* is also a poet. His relationship to Pauline is also threefold: he looks upon Pauline as his lover, his "own," as the opening lines of the poem make clear; he looks to her as at least a temporary source of motherly protection, as one who will draw him to her and screen him from the frightening things of the world; and lastly, he talks to her as he might talk to himself—an alter-ego (indeed, as her footnote after line 811 strongly suggests, Pauline herself is either a poet, like the hero, or an amateur literary critic [27]). She is

25. ". . . I proposed that [i.e. the title of Shelley's poem] which he adopted. . . . The Greek word Ἀλάστωρ is an evil genius, κακοδαίμων . . . The poem treated the spirit of solitude as a spirit of evil." Thomas Love Peacock, *Memoirs of Shelley,* in *The Life of Percy Bysshe Shelley,* ed. Humbert Wolfe (London, 1933), 2, 341.

26. *Works,* ed. Hutchinson, p. 15.

27. As when Browning has her say: "—Je n'en crois pas moins au grand principe de toute composition . . . d'où il suit que la concentration des idées est dûe bien plus à leur conception, qu'à leur mise en execution . . . j'ai tout lieu de craindre

every bit as cloudily characterized as the dream-vision of *Alastor,*
and but for the footnote four-fifths of the way through the poem,
one would be tempted to look upon Pauline as nothing more than
a product of the speaker's imagination—in that sense, too, the
perfect counterpart of the vision in *Alastor.* Yet, like that vision,
Pauline, too, is essential to the organization of the poem in which
she appears. Browning introduces her at once, as the occasion of his
own poet's "Fragment of a Confession." She is the one person in
whom the poet may safely confide; her very beauty takes the poet
out of his "aimless, hopeless state" (50) and reminds him of his
older, better self, his ideals and struggles; he bares his soul to her
in order that he may win her love, and his own salvation. Without
the dim, scarcely created figure of Pauline, Browning's poem would
lack an organizing center—just as Shelley's would without the
equally dim dream-vision of the Poet. So far the indebtedness of
Pauline to *Alastor* on the level of character seems complete. In
each case, a dim female figure is related to a poet-hero in three
ways: as a lover, as a source of protection, and as an alter-ego. In
each case the female figure organizes and suffuses the poem. However, in Browning's poem this figure is presented dramatically,
instead of narratively as in Shelley's case, and this fact indicates a
considerable gulf between the two poems, and in fact between
their creators.

The hard core of subject matter in both *Alastor* and *Pauline* has
a past existence, for both poems recount the history of spiritual experiences that are now over. *Alastor's* hero has been killed by his
ordeal, and so an impartial poet-narrator (Shelley) must tell his
story. *Pauline's* hero, on the other hand, has just managed to survive his ordeal intact, and so he himself may be permitted to
narrate. But this alone would indicate only a relatively trivial difference between the two poems—a difference between first and
third person narratives with similar heroes and roughly similar
spiritual preoccupations. Browning's significant innovation was
the introduction of a living audience for his hero's story in the
shape of Pauline, who, hazy as she is, has two vital functions in the
poem. She motivates the narrator's self-revelations, and she is in

que la première de ces qualités ne soit encore étrangère à mon ami—et je doute fort
qu'un redoublement de travail lui fasse acquérir la seconde."

herself part of the narrator's spiritual dilemma, a prolongation of
that dilemma into the present. Through Pauline, Browning's poet-
hero becomes not only a narrator of past events, but a dramatic
figure of the present, struggling with the very real and immediate
problem of human love as represented by the woman to whom he
addresses himself. It is this added dimension that distinguishes
Pauline from *Alastor* and incidentally puts Browning's poem in a
strange class of its own: it is not simply a narrative poem in the first
person, because some of its psychological action takes place in the
present; and it is not a typical dramatic monologue, either, because
its primary intention is plainly to recount struggles that took place
in the past.[28]

No doubt whatever nomenclature one decides to attach to it,
Pauline must be considered an absolute failure of form. For example, the opening lines imply that Pauline is physically present,
listening to her lover; not until line 870 does a reference occur to
"this lay," followed by "this verse" (992) and "this song" (1004),
and one realizes that the poem is, after all, not a speech but a
written testimony. Further astonishing intelligence comes with
Pauline's 340-word footnote in French, which treats the poem
merely as a literary exercise. Apart from being uncertain as to
whether the poem is intended to be a speech, a letter, or, indeed,
a poem (supposedly written by someone other than the poet who
did, in fact, write it), the reader has no real clue as to whether the
poet-hero is old or young, sad or gay, in sickness or in health, about
to perish or simply to write another poem. These are grave shortcomings in *Pauline:* not so very grave, perhaps, coming as they do
from the pen of a twenty-year-old author, but grave enough to have
won for the poet fairly harsh critical treatment at the start of his
career.[29] Had Browning imitated his mentor more exactly in the

28. If the term "dramatic monologue," in its poetic sense, may be taken to mean
"a single discourse by one whose presence is indicated by the poet but who is not the
poet himself" (see below, p. 122), then *Pauline* is either a very weak dramatic monologue or not a dramatic monologue at all, for the "presence" of its central figure is
not firmly established, and it is, perhaps, difficult to suspend one's awareness of
Browning's own "presence" in many passages of the poem—as, for example, in all
of the verses to Shelley.

29. Of the six reviews of *Pauline* that are known to have appeared in 1833, two
were favorable and one was middling; but one of the favorable notices was by
Browning's "literary father," Fox, who no doubt took special care with the poem.

matter of form and character presentation, a poem more nearly like Shelley's *Alastor* might have resulted and it would not have had these defects. But then it is just in the incongruities of *Pauline* that one sees the young Browning and not the young Shelley: a young Browning willing and able to imitate the lyricism of his Romantic predecessor, but consciously or unconsciously disposed to do more with character, to heighten it, above all to dramatize it.

Paracelsus

Paracelsus was begun in October 1834 and finished five months later.[30] A week after its publication a review of the poem appeared in the *Athenaeum* for August 22, 1835, which Browning did not quickly forget. "Writers would do well to remember," it said in part, ". . . that though it is not difficult to imitate the mysticism and vagueness of Shelley, we love him and have taken him to our hearts as a poet, not *because* of these characteristics—but in *spite* of them."[31] Ten years later Elizabeth Barrett could fume over this review: "An imitation of Shelley!—when if 'Paracelsus' was anything it was the expression of a new mind, as all might see—as *I* saw, let me be proud to remember . . ."[32] Although much criticism of the poem seems to have taken its cue from this letter, it has slowly become clear that though *Paracelsus* was in many respects "the expression of a new mind" it was also one more tribute to the young Browning's "Sun treader." It would be curious if the poem were not at all Shelleyan: begun nineteen months after the publication of *Pauline*, when Browning was still only 22, *Paracelsus* could scarcely be expected to display an entirely new, fully-matured poetic technique of its own. Nor, considering Browning's apparent indebtedness to the dream-vision in *Alastor* for his own equally ethereal Pauline, could one expect to find complete independence from Shelley in the matter of character. As Griffin pointed out in

Against these, were three other reviews that totally condemned *Pauline*. See Leslie Nathan Broughton, Clark Sutherland Northup, and Robert Pearsall, *Robert Browning: A Bibliography, 1830–1950* (Ithaca, 1953), pp. 83–84.

30. DeVane, *Handbook*, p. 50.

31. Quoted in DeVane, *Handbook*, p. 56. For Browning's recollection of the review as late as 1845 see *Letters of R.B and E.B.B.*, *1*, 323; RB to EBB, December 9, 1845.

32. *Letters of R.B. and E.B.B.*, *1*, 327; EBB to RB, December 10, 1845.

1910, the preface to *Alastor* supplied Browning with an over-all attitude toward the historical Paracelsus: Browning would view him, in Shelley's words, as "one who drinks deep of the fountain of knowledge and is still insatiate," and also as one who keeps apart from others and then, at last, vividly realizes the need for human love; it is also possible that Shelley's treatment of Prometheus influenced Browning at this point; W. O. Raymond has made the simple but ingenious suggestion that Shelley's own personality provided the model for Aprile in the poem, and it is clear that bits of physical description—that of the young Paracelsus as a withered old man, in Part IV, for example—derive from the older poet.[33]

It is, once again, when one turns to form and to the relationship between form and character in *Paracelsus,* just as in the case of *Pauline,* that one sees something strikingly new and different. In these matters the young Browning strides beyond Shelley, strides beyond his own accomplishment in *Pauline,* and unmistakably presents to the world an "expression of a new mind."

It will be important to discover what these innovations in form and character consisted of in *Paracelsus;* then to estimate how successful they were; and lastly to see to what extent, at the age of twenty-three, Browning had liberated himself from the spell of Shelley in the manipulation of the blank-verse line. No one can expect to prove that *Paracelsus* is not a very Shelleyan poem; but Browning's progress by 1835 toward poetic techniques and a form which would above all things present and reveal character should become clear.

In the manner of Shelley, who was much given to introducing his longer works with a short prose "Advertisement" or longer "Preface," Browning had prefaced *Pauline* in 1833 with a lengthy Latin quotation from Cornelius Agrippa; [34] it had the effect (for those who could and would take the trouble to read it) of rather haughtily begging the reader's pardon for offering him a frank work by an immature author. Browning introduced *Paracelsus* two years later with a very different sort of preface. It is a polite but

33. See Griffin and Minchin, *Life,* pp. 66–69, and William O. Raymond, *The Infinite Moment and Other Essays in Robert Browning* (Toronto, 1950), pp. 164–65.
34. See *Pauline by Robert Browning. The Text of 1833* . . . , ed. N. Hardy Wallis (London, 1931), p. 3.

urgent appeal to the reader not to mistake the poet's intention in the work that follows; in it Browning tells what he was trying to do in *Paracelsus:*

> it is an attempt, probably more novel than happy, to reverse the method usually adopted by writers whose aim it is to set forth any phenomenon of the mind or the passions, by the operation of persons and events; and . . . , instead of having recourse to an external machinery of incidents to create and evolve the crisis I desire to produce, I have ventured to display somewhat minutely the mood itself in its rise and progress, and have suffered the agency by which it is influenced and determined, to be generally discernible in its effects alone, and subordinate throughout, if not altogether excluded: and this for a reason. I have endeavoured to write a poem, not a drama . . .[35]

The preface was necessary in the first place because the unwarned reader, opening *Paracelsus* for the first time, would almost certainly feel himself to be in the presence of a drama, not a poem:

PARACELSUS.

I.—PARACELSUS ASPIRES.

SCENE, *Würzburg—a garden in the environs.* 1507.

FESTUS, PARACELSUS, MICHAL.

Par. Come close to me, dear friends; still closer—thus;[36]

Only reading on would he discover the striking fact that the very slight action implied in Paracelsus' opening line, namely, the drawing "close" and "still closer" of Festus and Michal to Paracelsus as he speaks, is, in fact, almost the major action in Part I of this peculiar drama; for the rest, none of the characters seem to do anything or get anywhere; nothing, in the ordinary dramatic sense of the term, "happens." But even this is not the worst criti-

---

35. *Paracelsus,* preface, pp. vii-viii. My citations from *Paracelsus* are to the unnumbered text in Robert Browning, *Paracelsus,* London, 1835.
36. Ibid., p. 1.

cism that could be made of *Paracelsus* viewed as any ordinary sort of dramatic production: assuming 854 lines of unrelieved dialogue to be the necessary groundwork for a later crisis, the reader might ask himself to what degree character had been portrayed in the figures of Michal, Festus, and Paracelsus; and here a second striking fact would come to light: Paracelsus, who speaks nearly two-thirds of these lines, could just as well have been given the other third. Festus and Michal hardly exist, except perhaps as feeble foils to the loquacious hero—but their objections might have occurred to Paracelsus without their mentioning them at all, without either being present. Part I, then, is virtually a soliloquy, unrelieved by dramatic action or even the convincing verbal interplay of character.

With this in mind it is a bit surprising that Browning omitted his preface in later editions of the poem, unless he felt by 1849 that his methods no longer needed an explanation. The form of *Paracelsus* was novel and asked much of the reader. Browning had retained certain trappings of the dramatic play (a cast of characters, five "acts," terse scene and stage directions) but he had left out any "external machinery of incidents" and totally excluded from his poem the representation of dramatic action—either action which brings about a crisis in character, or action that is a result of it. He had by no means picked a dull historical personality or an actionless career for his subject. The wandering, reforming, erratic, brilliant Renaissance figure of Paracelsus was a hero in Browning's home; Robert Browning, Sr., knew of his exploits and Browning must have heard of them at an early age; the *Biographie universelle* and the two older volumes in his father's library which the poet used as biographical sources certainly suggested more than enough action in Paracelsus' life for an ordinary play.[37] But the dramatic events that shaped Paracelsus' career, and acted upon his personality, twenty-two-year-old Browning would not show for the reason that they were not important. What was important in a man's life was not, in fact, what happened to him but how he was inwardly changed by what happened: not the events of Paracelsus' career but Paracelsus' "mood itself," the state of his being, "in its rise and progress." An assumption about dramatic writing in gen-

37. Griffin and Minchin, *Life*, pp. 65, 69–72, and DeVane, *Handbook*, p. 53.

eral appears almost between the lines in the 1835 preface. Browning would "reverse the method usually adopted by writers whose aim it is to set forth any phenomenon of the mind or the passions, by the operation of persons and events . . ." As it appears in context, this statement suggests that writers of ordinary drama use subsidiary characters and action ("the operation of persons and events") primarily to reveal the mental state of a single central character ("to set forth [a] phenomenon of the mind or the passions"), and that the revelation of this central character's state of being is the reason for a writer's using action at all, or, indeed, for writing a drama. Thus: *Othello* was written for Othello's sake alone; if the change in Othello's nature from that of a calm, capable military leader in Act I to that of an insanely jealous murderer in Act V could have been shown without recourse to Desdemona, Iago, Emilia, and Cassio, and without recourse to the presentation of an action—in other words, without recourse to the drama—so much the better for Shakespeare: the "phenomenon of the mind or the passions" of Othello is the object of interest. Browning is not certain that his particular method (suppression of action and minor characters, and concentration upon the hero's mood) is altogether feasible; his work is only "an attempt, probably more novel than happy" to get more directly to the essence of what is most important in any drama or dramatic poem. But *Paracelsus,* as it turned out, was never to be considered a real failure in Browning's opinion, as *Pauline* was,[38] and the idea of the central importance of character revelation to dramatic and semidramatic writing would remain with the poet from now on.

True to its preface, *Paracelsus* presents a "phenomenon of the mind" in a unique way. The poem opens at the outset of Paracelsus' career, in 1507, when he is fourteen years old, and ends with his death thirty-four years later in 1541. The events of these thirty-four years are only sketchily mentioned in the course of the text. Instead, the reader views what may be called five psychic portraits of Paracelsus: that is, Paracelsus' frame of mind is sketched at five important intervals during his lifetime. The nature of these intervals, or moments, is significant. The first takes place in "a garden in the environs" of Würzburg, when Paracelsus is seen on

38. Griffin and Minchin, *Life,* pp. 56–60, 78.

the verge of early manhood, full of hope and ready for adventure; he explains to his childhood friends, Festus and Michal, why it is important for him to leave Würzburg at last and follow his God-directed path; he aspires "to know," to find truth mystically, to avoid human love; Festus raises a few objections, which are easily defeated. The second portrait occurs fourteen years later: Paracelsus, now in Constantinople, feels that he has failed so far in his quest, but a chance meeting with the rather Shelleyan poet, Aprile, convinces him that his mistake has been in failing to unite his knowledge with love; Aprile has failed to unite his own love with knowledge; realizing the necessity for this union, Paracelsus for the moment "attains." The third glimpse occurs five years later in the city of Basil, where he is now a professor at the University and, outwardly, very successful; he expresses his deep spiritual dissatisfaction to Festus and tells him why he has "failed utterly." The fourth glimpse is in Colmar in Alsatia, this time only two years later; Paracelsus dismisses his secretary, Oporinus, and reveals to Festus his feelings about losing the Basil professorship; he sees the need for "joy" (rather than Aprile's "love"), yet his profound discouragement is evident; learning of Michal's death at the end of this interview, he expresses a gladiatorial indifference to life. The last view of Paracelsus comes thirteen years later, in a hospital cell in Salzburg; Festus listens to his friend's final grand summation of life (a 300-line speech), after which Paracelsus dies.

To some extent these are five "successive crises," as Frederick S. Boas has called them.[39] However, not one of the exact moments presented—with the apparent exception of the last—is *in itself* a highly critical moment. That is, one does not sense dramatic urgency at any point in the poem. Paracelsus is seen among friends: with Festus and Michal, with Aprile, with Festus alone. He is never under pressure. The scenes contain no physical movement (other than, say, Oporinus' getting up and leaving the room in Part IV, or Paracelsus' rising to speak in Part V). In each case action has already occurred, or will occur in the convenient future. So absolutely is dramatic tension missing from the poem that it is not even possible to take Paracelsus' dying speech as extraordinary; it

39. "Robert Browning's 'Paracelsus', 1835–1935," *Quarterly Review*, 265 (1935), 287.

has almost no dramatic context, and 300 vigorous lines from a man about to die do not really astonish the reader; it is evident that Paracelsus will talk until he has exhausted his doctrines—and not his body. The moments in which one sees Paracelsus are like flat troughs between waves of action and event—times of calm, each one near to some crisis, but not so near as to show Paracelsus urgently involved in any of them. The moments are not idly chosen, Browning would say, for it is at such times that men are most likely to review their careers, to see themselves, to talk candidly—and so to reveal themselves. He will display his hero only when the reader is apt to get the most out of him—when Paracelsus is relaxed, talking to an old friend, unconsciously ready to reveal the most pertinent changes in his outlook and, more subtly, in his character. The "moments" of the mature dramatic monologues are more complex than these. But it is in *Paracelsus* that Browning takes his first significant step in the development of complex situations whose prime purpose will be to aid in the revelation of character.

In treating his theme this way, then, Browning hoped to offer five clear, direct, uncluttered views of Paracelsus' soul. From hints in the scenes, and especially from an intelligent understanding of Paracelsus' mental condition as it was presented each time, the reader would be able to sketch in for himself the significant events of Paracelsus' life: "indeed," as Browning continues in his preface, "were my scenes stars it must be his [i.e., the reader's] co-operating fancy which, supplying all chasms, shall connect the scattered lights into one constellation . . ." [40]

But the difficulties of such a method were enormous in practice. No doubt it is a tribute to the twenty-two-year-old poet's rare lyric gift that *Paracelsus* is as readable as it is. The gaps between the "stars" or the five glimpses of Paracelsus amount to thirty-four eventful years, and the exposition necessary to suggest them is simply not contained in Browning's poem. No doubt it would be a prodigious amount, and Browning's method did not permit him time for exposition. Paracelsus, intent on expressing his *Weltanschauung,* or on outlining his relationship to Death, or on weighing the merits of Knowledge and Love, rarely refers in concrete

40. *Paracelsus,* preface, p. ix.

terms to the events of his life; the result is that the reader is hardly ever certain what has been happening in the stellar "chasms" and finds it nearly impossible to account for Paracelsus' state of mind at any time. More than that, he is confused by the constant absence of any sense of time and place: the scenes contain so few references to events that they seem unreal. Part IV might equally well be unfolding on a cloud bank, as in *A House at Colmar, in Alsatia. 1528*. The slight and nebulous shapes of Michal, Festus, and Aprile do little to impart reality to the poem; each subordinate character stands for no more than an idea—or an alternate attitude—in Paracelsus' head. If the poem is "eine Sammlung von Monologen," as a German student of Browning once put it,[41] then the monologues are almost entirely those of Paracelsus, and they are collected on a very frail string.

It is for its lyrical qualities, surely, and not for its dramatic ones that *Paracelsus* deserves to be read. "The blank verse here," Saintsbury stated in *A History of English Prosody*, "is still of the *Pauline* or Shelleyan type"; [42] Hatcher, too, found something approximating the old Shelleyan smoothness: "The verse is calm, monotonously uniform if the later verse sets the standard, and without the compression of the more vigorous monologues." [43] But if one is searching for signs of Browning's development of a blank-verse line capable of expressing dramatically the idiosyncrasies of character, the verse of *Paracelsus* seems to suffer for the most part from the same failing as that of *Pauline*: it does not reproduce the cadences of human speech, but the cadences of the lyric, as in Aprile's rather lovely:

> Knowing ourselves, our world, our task so great,
> Our time so brief; 't is clear if we refuse
> The means so limited, the tools so rude
> To execute our purpose, life will fleet,
> And we shall fade, and nothing will be done.[44]

41. Karl Bleier, *Die Technik Robert Brownings in seinen "dramatischen Monologen"* (diss., Marburg, 1910), p. 8.
42. George Saintsbury, *A History of English Prosody* (2d ed., London, 1923), *3*, 219.
43. *The Versification of Robert Browning*, p. 36.
44. *Paracelsus*, II, 497–501.

Just as in the case of Shelley's "Lyrical Drama," *Prometheus Unbound,* one feels that speech in *Paracelsus* may break into song at any time—and in fact it does, with Aprile's "Lost, lost! yet come," Paracelsus' "Heap cassia, sandal-buds, and stripes" and "Over the sea our galleys went," and Festus' "Thus the Mayne glideth." At rare intervals there is a departure from Shelley, however. Paracelsus' outburst in Part V is emotionally charged, and the blank verse momentarily adopts the rhythm of genuine anger and despair:

> Hell-spawn! I am glad, most glad, that thus I fail!
> Your cunning has o'ershot its aim. One year,
> One month, perhaps, and I had served your turn:
> You should have curb'd your spite awhile. But now,
> Who will believe 't was you that held me back?
> Listen: there's shame, and hissing, and contempt,
> And none but laughs who names me—none but spits
> Measureless scorn upon me, 't is on *me,*
> The quack, the liar, the arch-cheat—all on *me.*[45]

The cadence of this passage is dramatic and not chiefly lyrical; a human voice seems to make itself heard for almost the first time in the poem; but this is a rare occurrence in *Paracelsus.*

The imagery in the poem is most often "superfluous adornment," as W. H. Clemen calls the imagery of the young Shakespeare,[46] and one feels again and again its almost total irrelevance to character. Very often it is lyrically apt, as in Festus' lines:

> Best ope the casement: see
> The night, late strewn with clouds and flying stars,
> Is blank and motionless: how peaceful sleep
> The tree-tops all together! like an asp
> The wind slips whispering from bough to bough.[47]

45. Ibid., V, 194–4⒉
46. *The Development of Shakespeare's Imagery* (London, 1951), p. 33. Browning, like Shakespeare, learned to use imagery later on "as a direct form of expression." Cf. p. 34.
47. *Paracelsus,* III, 999–1003.

The "asp" no doubt effectually suggests the progress of the wind, but it has no relation to the passage as a whole, and certainly no bearing on the character of Festus. The most vivid and memorable images and sounds in the poem really exist for their own sakes; Paracelsus' metaphor of the spent hurricane (V, 471–91) or his lines beginning, "The wroth sea's waves are edged / With foam" (V, 659–65), remarkable as they are, do not throw light on their speaker; Paracelsus' whole death-bed speech is, in fact, more effective as a 300-line lyric than as a revelation of thought.

On the level of diction, Browning breaks away from Shelley to a greater extent, although words in *Paracelsus* that would have seemed impermissible to the poet two years before are by no means common. There is a small but interesting strain of earthy, colloquial usages in the poem, such as *blinkers, carcass, gout, stench, stunk, zany*. These certainly point to a departure from the typical Romantic vocabulary. Too few of these words are used to aid in characterization, but they suggest radical innovations to come and foreshadow Browning's whole development of a poetic diction broad and versatile enough to assist in characterization. The expanding range in diction is also indicated by the presence of less common terms such as *arch-genethliac, cassia, furfair, labdanum, malachite, morphew,* and *suffumigation,* which help to suggest the professional background of the scholarly medical figure who utters them. Browning's addiction to heaped and tortured comparatives and superlatives is indicated in phrases like, "Of the meanest, earthliest, sensualest delight" (IV, 244); and a fondness for, or at least a boldness with, long "unpoetic" words of Latin derivation is first noticeable in *Paracelsus,* which contains *exterminate, impracticable, inextricable, inexplicable, inexhaustible, inscrutable, intelligible,* and *unexceptionable,* among others. Diction seems to miss fire occasionally; in Paracelsus' echo of Martin Luther,

Here I am
And here I stay, be sure, till forced to flit (III, 603–4),

as in Festus' lament over his dying friend,

He will drowse into death without a groan! (V, 11),

the mood is shattered by what seem, in the contexts, rather over-ebullient terms: *flit* (used in the older sense of "to die") and *groan*. It is in the lyrical passages of the poem that one feels the young poet's diction is surest—partly because in those passages Browning is aided by the congenial example of Shelley. His dramatic diction is feebler and less certain; for example, Paracelsus, who is always articulate when speaking leisuredly and metaphorically, usually seems to be at a loss for words when he has some strong emotion to express; when the least bit aroused, he simply repeats himself—as in Part V: *Stay, stay* (107); *Aprile, Aprile!* (121); *Lost, lost!* (272); *none, none!* (273); *men, men* (312); *Spare, spare* (315); *for a purpose—for a purpose* (458); *Well; / Well* (470–71). So infectious is this habit that Festus picks it up by Part V as well. It should be added, incidentally, that repetition as a lyrical and rhetorical element in Browning's mature poetry is in other ways successfully foreshadowed in *Paracelsus.* Later Browning will use repetition as a distinct means of character expression, but even here it is rather deftly employed to enhance rhythm and to tie together argument, as in Festus':

> . . . 'tis doubtless need
> That he appoint no less the way of praise
> Than the desire to praise; for, though I hold
> With you, the setting forth such praise to be
> The natural end and service of a man—
> And that such praise seems best attain'd when he
> Attains the general welfare of his kind—
> Yet, *that,* the *instrument,* is not the *end.*[48]

But the felicities of *Paracelsus,* on the whole, are lyrical and not dramatic. It is impossible not to feel boundless admiration for the technical accomplishments of the twenty-two-year-old lyric poet who produced such a work. The cadences, the sounds, the imagery in this poem are lovely in their own right, for their own sake. Diction is on the whole mellifluous and, with a few striking exceptions, neither difficult nor very precise; Browning is still not far from the diction of Shelley, with its vagueness and sonority;

48. *Ibid.,* I, 298–305.

most of the words in *Paracelsus* are more important for music than meaning. The truth is that *Paracelsus,* like *Pauline,* is more interesting and significant for the ways in which it abjectly fails as a work of art than for the charming ways in which it succeeds. It cannot be taken seriously as any kind of dramatic poem; it is almost incomprehensible as a portrait of the historical Paracelsus; it is too vague, too abstract, too greatly lacking in concrete references and details of any sort to "set forth [a] phenomenon of the mind or the passions"; it suffers moreover from the almost total absence not only of action in the ordinary sense, but of dramatic tension—and this fact makes it difficult to appreciate as an entirety. Lastly, it is disjointed; the five glimpses that one has of Paracelsus are separated by gaps which Browning's form did not permit him the opportunity to fill in: gaps of background, action and event which only the reader who comes to the poem with an intimate knowledge of Paracelsus' life can supply. But in its very failure of form, a form which had been designed by Browning explicitly to present and to emphasize a "phenomenon of the mind," *Paracelsus* stated an aim, and it provided a point of departure for experiments leading to a new poetry which would adequately deal with the problem of character revelation. Technically it would be a poetry that would show few traces of the old Shelleyan influence: the vagueness, the allusiveness, the sonority, the easy and unhurried flow of Shelley were lyrically effective, but they would not do for the presentation of character, and *Paracelsus* was to be Browning's last Shelleyan poem.

Early Lyrics

Between October 1832, when he began to write *Pauline,* and the end of the year 1840, when he was still twenty-eight years old, Browning wrote eight long works, which occupied almost all of his creative time and effort. These were *Pauline, Paracelsus* and *Sordello,* and the five dramas, *Strafford, King Victor and King Charles, The Return of the Druses, Pippa Passes,* and *A Blot in the 'Scutcheon.* It is rather surprising that during these eight years fewer than a dozen surviving short poems [49] were produced, al-

49. Probably including the following works: *Lines to the Memory of his*

though the figure is a little higher if one includes the lyrics imbedded in *Paracelsus* and *Pippa Passes*. With the exception of the dramatic monologues in *The Ring and the Book* and the grand outpouring of Bishop Blougram, the finest poems of Browning's maturity were never to contain more than four hundred lines; Browning may be said to have discovered and perfected the techniques of his great, relatively short dramatic monologues by writing a series of long and definitely inferior poems and plays.

But during the first eight years of his apprenticeship he did write at least six short poems, all in the form of the poetic monologue, which are partly valuable as gauges of his progress in the development of a poetry of human character. The first two of these, Griffin asserts (without saying where he obtained the information), Browning wrote in April or May 1834, while he was traveling in Russia, [50] if Griffin is right, then Browning composed *Johannes Agricola* and *Porphyria* a year after publishing *Pauline* and six months before starting *Paracelsus;* even if Griffin is wrong, the two poems must have been written before the end of 1835—that is, around the time *Paracelsus* was published—because they were both printed in the first issue of the *Monthly Repository* for 1836. [51]

In form and general appearance *Porphyria* and *Johannes Agricola* seem at first glance to be nearer the mature dramatic monologues than either *Pauline* or *Paracelsus.* They are short, 60-line poetic speeches, each delivered by a single character who provides a definite psychological interest. The Antinomian Agricola and the murderer of Porphyria are unusual and striking figures, and they seem to have been chosen largely because they would stand out as extraordinary men; Browning's early grouping of the two poems under the heading *Madhouse Cells* indicates the extent to

---

Parents, *Johannes Agricola, Porphyria,* "Eyes calm beside thee . . . ," "Still ailing, Wind . . . ," "A king lived long ago . . ." (revised and included in *Pippa Passes*), *A Forest Thought, Rudel to the Lady of Tripoli, Soliloquy of the Spanish Cloister, Artemis Prologizes,* and possibly *Cristina.* See the discussion of likely composition dates after each title in DeVane, *Handbook.*

50. Griffin and Minchin, *Life,* p. 73.

51. My citations from both poems are to this issue of the journal, new ser. *10* (Jan. 1836), 43–46. Browning grouped the two poems under the general title, *Madhouse Cells* in 1842, and lengthened the titles to *Johannes Agricola in Meditation* and *Porphyria's Lover* in 1849.

which he considered both speakers unusual. But a closer inspection reveals the fact that human character is, at best, only of secondary interest and importance in these poems and that they hardly comprise "advances" over either *Paracelsus* or *Pauline* in Browning's treatment of character. After nearly a century of generally favorable criticism, *Porphyria* was brushed aside as "that juvenile and unrepresentative horror poem" by J. M. Cohen in his study of Browning in 1952; [52] while this may have irritated some readers, there is truth in such a judgment. Character is no more revealed in *Porphyria* than in the average tale of Poe; the horror story itself is the thing, and in the case of this poem the tight lyrical telling of an extremely good anecdote accounts for the main effect. Strangely, one of the aptest parallels for *Porphyria* in Browning's poetry may be his even more juvenile work, *The First-Born of Egypt;* for in this poem a past (and rather horrible) happening is given dramatic immediacy through the account of an eyewitness; the lover of Porphyria is an eyewitness admittedly more involved with the event; but both speakers "speak" lyrically about what has happened and not dramatically: both poems are more effective as lyrics than as character-revealing monologues. This is not to imply that *Porphyria* is merely a trivial juvenile poem, or that Mr. Cohen's curtness is altogether justified, for as a work of art it succeeds precisely where *Pauline* and *Paracelsus* fail. Here Shelleyan lyricism and vague characterization are wholly adequate to the poet's purpose; one does not demand that human character reveal itself through speech, for the poem proclaims itself as a lyrical monologue from the start; its meter (iambic tetrameter), its high degree of rhyme (in the scheme A-B-A-B-B) and even its visual appearance reinforce the manifest lyricism of its diction and adequately compensate for what is missing in character revelation.

Johannes Agricola substitutes for a horror story the presentation of what might be called a "horror" doctrine. It is identical to its companion poem not only in length, meter, rhyme and appearance, but also in an equally scanty and vague treatment of character. Agricola tells what any Antinomian believer might think of God and predestination (and this in itself has a certain

52. *Robert Browning* (London, 1952), p. 1.

psychological interest) but he reveals nothing about himself as an individual, and his language and cadences are precisely those of Porphyria's murderer. But for their actual meaning, the lines,

> And having thus created me,
> Thus rooted me, he bade me grow—
> Guiltless for ever, like a tree
> That buds and blooms, nor seeks to know
> A law by which it prospers so: [53]

might have been uttered by the same voice that is made to say:

> Murmuring how she loved me—she
> Too weak, for all her heart's endeavour,
> To set its struggling passion free
> From pride, and vainer ties dissever,
> And give herself to me for ever: [54]

The speakers of both poems no doubt would have proved exciting subjects for blank verse dramatic monologues, but Browning in 1834 and 1835, at the time of *Paracelsus,* was only beginning on that search which would take him from the lovely but monotone lyricism of Shelley to the mastery of a complex blank-verse line such as appears in *The Bishop at St. Praxed*—a line which could express human character dramatically, with economy, subtlety, and vigor. The *Madhouse Cell* poems are successful because, unlike *Paracelsus,* they attempt nothing the twenty-two-year-old Browning could not adequately handle; they suggest no new form, no new techniques; they are not experimental; they do not begin to utilize any of the special attributes of verse to "betray" the characters of their speakers.

As marks of his progress from Shelley, and also as indications of an increasing tendency to write lyric verse that would reflect character, the four other poetic monologues produced before 1840 are significant. But the "Still ailing, Wind" stanzas, *Rudel to the Lady of Tripoli, Cristina,* and the *Soliloquy of the Spanish Cloister* were not proving grounds for Browning; they only display evi-

---

53. *Johannes Agricola,* 21–25. (The indention of line 25 in the *Monthly Repository* text is probably a compositor's error.)
54. *Porphyria,* 21–25.

dence of his progress—revealing, especially in the case of the
Soliloquy (which was probably composed in 1839,[55] four years
after *Paracelsus*), giant strides in the direction of the mature dramatic monologues. But these short poems were on the whole too
few-and-far-between to have been of much assistance in themselves; it was not in the *Soliloquy of the Spanish Cloister* that
Browning wrestled with the failures of *Pauline* and *Paracelsus,*
liberated himself from Shelley, and perfected the techniques of
dramatic character revelation, but rather in his series of unsuccessful plays (as we shall presently see), and in that magnificent 6,000-
line experiment and failure—*Sordello*.

Sordello

It is possible that *Sordello* is the most difficult literary work of
the nineteenth century. Perhaps one must turn ahead to the novels
of James Joyce to find anything equally demanding in the English
language. But if one does that—and compares critical literature
that has arisen around *Sordello* and around the novel *Ulysses,* for
example—one finds that, even among obscure works, *Sordello* is
in a class of its own, for it has been categorically and almost uni-
versally damned. Condemnation of it as a work of art has come
not only through witty observations directed against it (those
of Tennyson, Lowell, Mrs. Carlyle, Douglas Jerrold, Chesterton,
Lounsbury, and others) but through patient, balanced, and informed criticism. Perhaps Sir Henry Jones best sums up judicious
opinion of *Sordello* when he says:

> It is uncompromisingly and irretrievably difficult reading. No
> historical account of the conflicts of Ghibelline and Guelph,
> no expository annotation of any kind, not even its own wealth
> of luminous ideas or splendour of Italian city scenes and
> solitudes, can justify it entirely as a work of art.[56]

55. In the month of May, "when Browning was studying Elizabethan plays," according to DeVane's estimate; see *Handbook,* p. 114.

56. "Robert Browning and Elizabeth Barrett Browning," *Cambridge History of
English Literature,* ed. Sir A. W. Ward and A. R. Waller (Cambridge, England,
1916), *13,* 59.

If the poem is so clearly a failure, one of the more fascinating questions that suggest themselves in relation to it is why Robert Browning devoted seven years to it (from March 1833 to March 1840)—why, in fact, did he write *Sordello* at all? This question has been answered—unsatisfactorily, I think—in a number of ways. In 1863 Browning himself supplied a hint in his well-known dedicatory letter to Milsand: "The historical decoration was purposely of no more importance than a background requires; and my stress lay on the incidents in the development of a soul: little else is worth study." [57] But as an explanation of the poem's being, this fails in several ways: "the historical decoration" is so complex and elaborate that it almost totally—and, as it were, intentionally—shrouds "the incidents"; also, if "the development of a soul" was what Browning chiefly wanted to show, why was it not shown more simply and straightforwardly? It is not enough to say that Browning's techniques utterly failed him in *Sordello,* because he proved himself, again and again through these seven years, capable of carrying out his artistic intentions with at least some degree of success. Arthur Symons, Edward Dowden, and others have treated *Sordello* in passing as a study of character; but if this represents its object, then the poem is an almost unbelievable and nightmarish failure for Browning, an immense regression, from which he profited little. Nor can one claim that the object was to tell "Sordello's story"—unless one is ready to admit that Browning's story-telling powers at this point were either severely paralyzed or nonexistent.

In recent years, Stewart Walker Holmes has related *Sordello* to Carl Jung's "Theory of Types"; Holmes finds that the poem was written for its psychotherapeutic effect on Robert Browning himself.[58] C. Willard Smith also finds that the poem was partly produced "in the excitement of self-revelation." [59] Perhaps these psychological approaches at least point to a different line of inquiry for literary criticism—that is, assuming that the failure of

57. *Works* (1863), *3,* 251.

58. "Browning's *Sordello* and Jung: Browning's *Sordello* in the Light of Jung's Theory of Types," *PMLA,* *56* (Sept. 1941), 758–96.

59. *Browning's Star-Imagery: The Study of a Detail in Poetic Design* (Princeton, 1941), p. 88.

Sordello as a work of art is settled, the question becomes: To what
extent was the poem useful to Browning as a poet? It is in answering this deceptively simple question, I believe, that the ultimate
reason for Browning's writing *Sordello*—and, in fact, the complex
significance of the poem itself—becomes clear.

In Book II of *Sordello*, Browning's dreamy and vaguely love-
struck hero wanders into Mantua in search of the lady Palma and
success. He finds himself at the Court of Love. There he outplays
"the best Troubadour of Boniface," Eglamor, on the lute, and
Eglamor, apparently mortified by this defeat, promptly dies. Sordello is then elevated to Eglamor's old position—that is, Palma
chooses him to be her minstrel—and for the moment Sordello is
supremely happy. He finds that by exerting himself he has the
power to charm multitudes of people; yet soon he is dissatisfied.
He wishes to achieve even greater perfection in the art of song.

At this point in Browning's narrative a significant passage occurs.
It is a long passage, but it is worth quoting in full and attempting briefly to analyze for the light that it sheds on Browning's
own position at the time of *Sordello*. "Give thyself," Sordello ad-
vises himself in a moment of reflection, when he is musing about
his art (his "slave"),

> To the day's task; compel thy slave provide
> Its utmost at the soonest; turn the leaf
> Thoroughly conned; these lays of thine, in brief—
> Cannot men bear, now, somewhat better?—fly
> A pitch beyond this unreal pageantry
> Of essences? the period sure has ceased
> For such: present us with ourselves, at least,
> Not portions of ourselves, mere loves and hates
> Made flesh: wait not! [60]

One does not attempt an explication of any part of *Sordello* in
perfect confidence, but these lines seem to suggest that Sordello
feels he has not asked enough of his art. Men can "bear" better.
He has been presenting an "unreal pageantry of essences" or disembodied feelings in his songs and so far has not presented whole,

---

60. *Sordello*, II, 560–68. My citations from *Sordello* are to the unnumbered text
in Robert Browning, *Sordello*, London, 1840.

living men and women, as it were. If this reading is correct, is it
not true that Browning after *Pauline, Paracelsus,* and short poems
such as *Porphyria* and *Johannes Agricola* had also failed to present
whole characters in his poems—even though the presentation of
character had been his avowed intention in his most ambitious
work before *Sordello?* Like Sordello, Browning had presented a
disembodied, unreal, Shelleyan pageantry. It was time for something better: wait not! Yet:

> Awhile the poet waits
> However. The first trial was enough:
> He left imagining, to try the stuff
> That held the imaged thing and, let it writhe
> Never so fiercely, scarce allowed a tithe
> To reach the light—his Language. How he sought
> The cause, conceived a cure, and slow re-wrought
> That Language, welding words into the crude
> Mass from the new speech round him, till a rude
> Armour was hammered out, in time to be
> Approved beyond the Roman panoply
> Melted to make it, boots not. This obtained
> With some ado, no obstacle remained
> To using it; . . .

> .   .   .   .

> . . . Fond essay!
> Piece after piece that armour broke away
> Because perceptions whole, like that he sought
> To clothe, reject so pure a work of thought
> As language: Thought may take Perception's place
> But hardly co-exist in any case,
> Being its mere presentment—of the Whole
> By Parts, the Simultaneous and the Sole
> By the Successive and the Many. Lacks
> The crowd perceptions? painfully it tacks
> Together thoughts Sordello, needing such,
> Has rent perception into: it's to clutch
> And reconstruct—his office to diffuse,

Destroy: as difficult obtain a Muse
In short, as be Apollo . . .

.   .   .   .

. . . be content
Both parties, rather: they with the old verse,
And I with the old praise—far go, fare worse! [61]

Sordello leaves "imagining" in order "to try the stuff that held
the imaged thing," his language; for the very means of his expression had to be improved before he could change from presenting
unreal essences to presenting real men and women. In time, he
developed a language even better than the one "melted to make
it." This he put to use. But the experiment was unsuccessful, for
perceptions or inspired ideas were of a different nature altogether
from man-made (or thought-produced) language. Thought can
take the place of perception, but one is not the other, and one
really cannot convey the other. Sordello's only recourse was to
tear apart his perceptions into smaller, unsatisfactory bits of
thought; the crowd, receiving these, had the terrible task of tack-
ing them back together again to get Sordello's whole intended
perception. Naturally, this was too hard for the crowd. Perhaps it
would be better to go back to the old style, anyway. The crowd
would then be content with the old verse—and Sordello with his
old praise.

It seems fairly clear that the poem *Sordello* itself represented
for Browning not precisely a leaving of "imagining" but a lessen-
ing of concern for form and aesthetic effect—and even for character—and, on the other hand, an intense effort "to try the stuff
that held the imaged thing." [62] The rest of the passage quoted

61. Ibid., II, 568–81, 587–601, 608–10.
62. This view is partly reflected in the evidence of Browning's own changing attitude toward *Sordello* between 1835 and 1840. In his April 16, 1835, letter to W. J.
Fox, he speaks of it as an affair "of a more popular nature"—presumably, at this
point, a straightforward dramatic or narrative poem. Two years later in his preface
to *Strafford* (April 23, 1837), he confesses that his efforts on it have "jaded" his mind.
On December 23 of this year, an entry in Harriet Martineau's diary indicates that
Browning's chief interest has been diverted to the historical details of the poem:
"Browning called. 'Sordello' will soon be done now. Denies himself preface and
notes. He must choose between being historian and poet. Cannot split interest . . ."

might seem to have its parallel in the absolute failure of the poem *Sordello* to reach its readers. But this is extending the parallel too far, for *Sordello* is not the *product* of Browning's linguistic and prosodic experiments: it is really those experiments themselves— a considerable laboratory of them. Lines 587–610 almost certainly amount to a pessimistic expression of the difficulties that Browning felt himself to be facing in these experiments—his own pessimistic view, at the time, of language itself.

In almost every technical respect *Sordello* is boldly experimental. Purposely or not, Browning chose a mode of discourse that would give him the broadest range, for the narrative mode (which he explains to the reader he has adopted, against his own wish, because of the uniqueness of his theme and characters—see I, 11–31) could also include both the dramatic and the expository; and, indeed, all three alternate throughout the poem. A *Sordello* in dramatic form would have proved a much more cramped poetic laboratory. The only essence that Browning will not have on hand is Shelley (I, 60–79); for Shelley represents the old way of singing, and the "unreal pageantry of essences" in *Pauline* and *Paracelsus*. It is significant that while the very character of Sordello is somewhat Shelleyan and reminiscent of both *Pauline's* poet-hero and the character of Aprile in *Paracelsus*, Browning's technical experiments in *Sordello*—his rhythms, imagery, diction, sound, and, above all, syntax—are ruthlessly individual and un-Shelleyan. This is not the place for an exhaustive analysis of these technical elements in the poem, but several remarks may be made here which have a particular bearing on Browning's use of the "laboratory" of *Sordello* to work out techniques which would be of use in the

---

Then, weary of the poem thematically, Browning seems to have turned it into a laboratory for technical experiments. The last lines of *Sordello* (VI, 871–85) acknowledge the poem's difficulty for the reader; and in August 1840 (after *Sordello's* unfavorable reception), Browning is able to write Macready: "tomorrow will I betimes break new ground with So and So . . . let it but do me half the good 'Sordello' has done—be praised by the units, cursed by the tens, and unmeddled with by the hundreds!" No defense of *Sordello* as a work of art is heard from the poet until 1863, in the dedication to Milsand; in 1840 Browning can only speak of the "good" the poem has done him—surely a technical, artistic "good." Cf. W. C. DeVane's account of the poem's composition, "*Sordello's* Story Retold," *Studies in Philology*, 27 (Jan. 1930), 1–24.

blank-verse dramatic monologues that followed the poem in the decade of the 1840's.

In *Sordello* Browning not only worked himself out of the lyric style of Shelley but made great strides in developing a blank-verse line that could "imitate" or suggest human speech. Partly this was done through an experimental extension of diction to include colloquial and familiar terms of all kinds: *chew the cud, leave in the lurch, hanker after, egging on, like enough, chuckle, a-glimmer.* Partly it was done through numerous experiments with ellipses and inversions that normally occur in speech; in many of the syntactical experiments of *Sordello,* Browning achieves not only poetic compression but patterns of character expression. Partly, too, the blank-verse line of the dramatic monologues was perfected through radical experiments in rhythm; these experiments are never quite so obvious as those in syntax, but they are almost as plentiful. In this passage, for example, the combination of first-foot inversions and early caesuras creates a very different rhythm from anything in Shelley, an experimental speech-rhythm:

> As patiently perform till Song produced
> Acts, by thoughts only, for the mind: divest
> Mind of e'en Thought, and, lo, God's unexpressed
> Will dawns above us. But so much to win
> Ere that! A lesser round of steps within
> The last. About me, faces! and they flock,
> The earnest faces. What shall I unlock
> By song? behold me prompt, whate'er it be,
> To minister: how much can mortals see
> Of Life? [63]

Experiments are performed in the use of sound patterns to suggest character in *Sordello,* as in the lines:

> . . . the thin
> Grey wizened dwarfish devil Ecelin,
> And massy-muscled big-boned Alberic
> (Mere man, alas).[64]

63. *Sordello,* V, 574–83.
64. Ibid., VI, 763–66.

If *Sordello* is a failure as a work of art, it is partly due to the boldness of many of these technical experiments, particularly those with syntax and diction. The overabundance of historical detail in the poem, which clutters many passages hopelessly, is the very reverse of the Shelleyan vagueness and dreamy timelessness of *Paracelsus* (the scenes of which critically lack in references to place and event), and in this sense, too, *Sordello* may be said to be radically experimental. An equally concrete but more selective use of detail will be a distinct feature of the mature monologues. Perhaps the surest evidence of *Sordello's* use to Browning and its direct relationship to those monologues is the presence, in the poem, of what are, in effect, short dramatic monologues very nearly in Browning's mature manner. For example:

> . . . Why to be sure
> Yours is one sort of heart—but I mean theirs,
> Ours, every one's, the healthy heart one cares
> To build on! Central peace, mother of strength,
> That's father of . . . nay, go yourself that length,
> Ask those calm-hearted doers what they do
> When they have got their calm! Nay, is it true
> Fire rankles at the heart of every globe?
> Perhaps! But these are matters one may probe
> Too deeply for poetic purposes:
> Rather select a theory that . . . yes
> Laugh! what does that prove? . . . stations you midway
> And saves some little o'er-refining. Nay,
> That's rank injustice done me! I restrict
> The poet? Don't I hold the poet picked
> Out of a host of warriors, statesmen—did
> I tell you? Very like! as well you hid
> That sense of power you have! True bards believe
> Us able to achieve what they achieve—
> That is, just nothing—in one point abide
> Profounder simpletons than all beside:
> Oh ay! The knowledge that you are a bard
> Must constitute your prime, nay sole, reward! [65]

65. Ibid., II, 798–820.

Naddo's prattling speech in Book II is a bit obscure; it is difficult to follow; it is barely motivated; but in its rhythms, vocabulary, and syntax it is strongly reminiscent of a more distinguished prattler—Fra Lippo Lippi.

2. Character for the Stage

THE THEATER

PERHAPS it was fortunate for the young Browning that *Sordello's* appearance was delayed for so long; had the poem appeared in 1835 instead of 1840, and in its present form, it is very doubtful whether Browning would have enjoyed a theatrical career at all. It is inconceivable, for example, that John Forster would have found "Evidences of a New Genius for Dramatic Poetry" [1] in *Sordello's* six thousand tortured lines, or that William Macready after reading it would have asked Browning to write him a tragedy and thus save him from going to America.[2] *Paracelsus,* for all its vagueness of setting, meagerness of plot, and absolute lack of action and dramatic tension was the poem that caused Macready and others to think in 1836 that a new saviour had materialized for the English theater.[3]

Two days after Macready's well-known proposal at Talfourd's dinner party, Browning took up the challenge to write a play; the second paragraph of his letter to Macready on May 28, 1836, is revealing of his attitude toward the task:

> I allow myself a month to complete [*Sordello*]: from the first of July I shall be free: if, before then, any subject shall sug-

1. Forster used these words in the title of an article praising *Paracelsus* and ranking Browning's genius with that of Shelley, Coleridge and Wordsworth. See [John Forster,] "Evidences of a New Genius for Dramatic Poetry, No. I," *New Monthly Magazine and Literary Journal, 46* (March 1836), 289–308.

2. Edmund Gosse, *Robert Browning, Personalia* (London, 1890), p. 43.

3. That the theater was in some need of serious talent may be seen from Allardyce Nicoll's account of what he calls "the dramatic debility" of this period; see *A History of Early Nineteenth Century Drama, 1800–1850* (Cambridge, England, 1930), *I,* 155–216 and p. 58. It would seem that the lyrical qualities of *Paracelsus* impressed Macready more strongly than the lack of ordinary dramatic ones—a lack

gest itself to you—I will give you my whole heart and soul to
the writing a Tragedy on it to be ready by the first of November next: should I be unequal to the task, the excitement and
extreme effort will have been their own reward:—should I
succeed, my way of life will be very certain, and my name
pronounced along with yours.[4]

A more reserved expression of this attitude, for the public, appears a year later in the published preface to *Strafford* dated April
23, 1837:

While a trifling success [with *Strafford*] would much gratify,
failure will not wholly discourage me from another effort: experience is to come, and earnest endeavour may yet remove
many disadvantages.[5]

The challenge of the theater to Browning in the 1830's is not
that of an amusing, momentarily intriguing diversion, nor is it in
any way a potential threat to his central poetic purpose; it is a
grave summons. Browning sees human destiny in Macready's offer,
for if he succeeds his "way of life will be very certain"; his first
tragedy will have his "whole heart and soul," will elicit an "extreme effort"; and a year later he can speak of "earnest endeavour"
to come in the writing of drama, even though his first play may
fail. From what is known of Browning's personality, one might
say that this was his characteristic and lifelong approach to almost
any affair of consequence: "whole heart and soul" were in almost
everything that he did. But at no other time in Browning's life
is his dedication to an artistic goal more apparent. At the age of
twenty-four he had been called upon to save the English stage.
With self-conscious idealism, perhaps, and with a few passing
doubts as to his own ability, Browning threw himself into the
task.

---

which had, of course, been accounted for to some degree by Browning in his 1835
preface.

4. *New Letters,* ed. DeVane and Knickerbocker, p. 12.

5. My citations from *Strafford* are to the unnumbered text in Robert Browning,
Strafford: An Historical Tragedy, London, 1837. See p. iii for the preface.

In the last sixty years scholarly opinion of Browning as a playwright has been united in at least one conclusion: that he failed in his task. An inaccurate entry of nine lines follows his name in the latest edition of *The Oxford Companion to the Theatre* (there are longer entries for Coleridge, Byron, Shelley, Tennyson, and even Arnold), and it would seem that Browning is of interest to students of the theater *per se* only as a sad example of "the great cleavage between poetry and the stage in the nineteenth century." [6] Almost every commentator upon Browning's early poetry has offered an explanation for his theatrical failure, however. Briefly these explanations might be grouped under four headings: circumstantial, philosophical, psychological, and technical. Browning himself, in a letter written in old age to Lawrence Barrett, provides the best evidence for explanations of the first category: "When I look back to the circumstances under which the piece [i.e. *A Blot in the 'Scutcheon*] was brought out in London—forty-two years ago—I may well wonder whether,—if my inclination for dramatic writing had met with half so much encouragement and assistance as you have really gratuitously bestowed on it,—I might not have gone on, for better or worse, play-writing to the end of my days . . ." [7] Browning's quarrel with Macready over the production of *A Blot* in 1843 [8] probably dampened his enthusiasm for the theater, but he went on to write at least one more stage play after that (*Colombe* [9]), and it seems unlikely that the quarrel

6. The entry is as follows: "BROWNING, Robert (1812–89), English poet, two of whose verse-plays were seen on the stage: *Strafford* (1837), written for Macready, and *A Blot on the 'Scutcheon* [sic] (1843). Neither of these was particularly successful, and they serve only to mark the great cleavage between poetry and the stage in the nineteenth century. His other plays were written to be read, and are part of English literature rather than drama." In point of fact, *King Victor and King Charles, The Return of the Druses* and *Colombe's Birthday* were all written for the stage. *Colombe* was produced seven times at the Haymarket Theatre in April 1853 by Helen Faucit and was well received; later productions followed in Manchester and in Boston. On November 28, 1884, *In a Balcony* was presented by the London Browning Society with Miss Alma Murray playing the part of Constance. See De-Vane, *Handbook*, pp. 98–99, 132–33, 146–47, 149, 254. For its treatment of Browning see *The Oxford Companion to the Theatre*, ed. Phyllis Hartnoll (2d ed. London, 1957), p. 102, and cf. entries for "Arnold," p. 36, "Byron," p. 107, "Coleridge," p. 137, "Shelley," p. 736, and "Tennyson," p. 785.

7. Letter dated February 3, 1885, in *Letters*, ed. Hood, p. 235.

8. See Griffin and Minchin, *Life*, pp. 113–19.

9. Ibid., p. 119. *Colombe's Birthday* was composed in 1843 and 1844.

—or almost any other circumstance—would have stopped Browning from writing a successful play if he had been able to write one; even a casual reading of the biographies reveals the fact that Browning was seldom influenced one way or another by the critical reception of his work. Arthur Symons was among the first to suggest that Browning's philosophical view of character was wrong for the stage in that Browning chose to reveal character not through depicting action but through states of mind.[10] Since Symons, most students of the dramas have attributed Browning's failure to reasons beyond the poet's control—to certain psychological and technical shortcomings. Dowden classified Browning's genius as "static" (versus "dynamic") and found his sympathy with action defective.[11] Stopford Brooke [12] and later Frances Russell developed the notion of there being two types of poetic mind, "one," as Dr. Russell has written, "gifted with observation and constructive fancy, and the other with reflection and sympathetic imagination" [13]—and Browning apparently did not possess the former, necessary for the theater. Technical explanations began during Browning's lifetime, the most frequent being that as Browning's characters spoke exactly alike, in "Browningese," the plays were dull, lacked variety, and were in essence one-character pieces.[14] While this explanation has wilted, perhaps, under the simple rejoinder that even Shakespeare's characters in the same sense seem to "talk like Shakespeare," [15] more recent critics have developed the idea that Browning's failure may be traced partly

10. *An Introduction to the Study of Browning* (London, 1906), pp. 3–7.

11. Edward Dowden, *The Life of Robert Browning* (London, 1915), pp. 53–54.

12. See *Tennyson: His Art and Relation to Modern Life* (London, 1894), pp. 411–15.

13. Frances Theresa Russell, *One Word More on Browning* (Stanford, 1927), p. 94.

14. "Many critics have pointed out that whoever the speaker may be, he speaks in the voice of Browning; and the fact is too obvious to require much discussion. No dramatist ever possessed a style less flexible. The simple mill-girl Pippa and the magnificent Ottima use the English language in the same way. Thorold, Luria, Djabal, Valence, all speak Browningese. . . . And this perhaps is one reason for the fact that Browning's plays tend so often to become one-character plays." Hugh Walker, *The Literature of the Victorian Era* (Cambridge, England, 1910), p. 320. See also the criticisms of Browning's diction cited below, pp. 207–8.

15. C. Willard Smith, *Browning's Star-Imagery: The Study of a Detail in Poetic Design* (Princeton, 1941), p. 112.

to matters of syntax and diction. In his excellent essay on the dramas, H. B. Charlton found that Browning "never manipulates verbal idiom as an instrument of characterisation," [16] and Duffin, in an echo of Lounsbury, declared: "His people talk in shapeless and endless sentences which it is impossible to follow with the ear (the long speeches in Shakespeare and Shaw are perfectly clear.)" [17] Perhaps Professor Lounsbury's account still provides the best outline of the technical failures in the dramas, however. It might be summarized as follows: (1) not one of Browning's actions gives the impression of inevitable development; (2) his human portraits are unfaithful to human nature; (3) despite powerful passages, the plays lack in sustained interest; (4) dialogue tends to be obscure; and (5) although Browning's characters speak vaguely and endlessly *about* their feelings, they do not act upon them.[18] Commentators since Lounsbury have, on the whole, developed or supported one or more of these points either through brief technical analyses of the plays or through psychological investigations of the playwright himself.

Although much of this work is impressive and undoubtedly valuable, one must conclude that Browning's relationship to the theater is a problem that has by no means been fully explained. Allardyce Nicoll has exonerated the plays from most of the usual charges leveled at the serious drama of the nineteenth century (artificial leanings toward the Elizabethans; unnatural and "poetic" language; over-chill classicism, for example [19]), and yet, despite Browning's evident uniqueness, students of the theater have noticeably neglected the plays. More important, from the point of view of the present investigation, students of Browning's poetry seem uncertain as to whether the poet's efforts in the theater were beneficial to his main line of development or not. DeVane has suggested generally that the "effect of thinking dramatically was

16. *Browning as Dramatist* (Manchester, 1939), p. 14.

17. Henry Charles Duffin, *Amphibian: A Reconsideration of Browning* (London, 1956), p. 183.

18. Thomas R. Lounsbury, *The Early Literary Career of Robert Browning* (London, 1912), pp. 62–65.

19. *A History of Early Nineteenth Century Drama, 1800–1850* (Cambridge, England, 1930), *1*, 178.

to have a profound, and in some respects excellent, influence upon his genius," [20] but C. Willard Smith, in his rather close study of Browning's star images, declared: "In no sense do Browning's plays, with the exception of those that I have classified as his original, or non-stage plays, suggest an artistic development . . . otherwise manifest from *Pauline* through the dramatic lyrics and romances to *The Ring and the Book*. In a very real sense the stage plays are a digression from the main line of the poet's development." [21] DuBois, too, found that Browning "did not grow" appreciably in the dramas.[22]

It seems likely that a study of Browning's technique in the treatment of character can, by its very nature, throw definite light upon the question of the usefulness of the stage plays to the poet in his development of the form and techniques of the dramatic monologues; for the revelation of character, as we have seen through an examination of *Pauline* and *Paracelsus*, was of paramount importance in Browning's art almost from the beginning, and, as we shall see, was to become the central theme of most of the great monologues. Between *Paracelsus*, which had stated the aim of character revelation in unmistakable terms (theoretically, in its preface; and practically, in its form and content), and *My Last Duchess*, there were, for example, mainly the narrative poem of *Sordello* and approximately five dramas, four of them written for the stage.[23] One would thus expect that the theater was an absolute necessity for Browning—granting his emergence from it with the store of techniques necessary to write the dramatic monologues; it is doubtful whether the poetic laboratory of *Sordello* and a few short lyrics alone—after *Paracelsus*—could have

20. In the entry under "Strafford" in DeVane, *Handbook*, p. 70.

21. *Browning's Star-Imagery*, p. 100.

22. Arthur E. DuBois, "Robert Browning, Dramatist," *Studies in Philology, 33* (Oct. 1936), 636.

23. Namely, *Strafford, King Victor and King Charles, The Return of the Druses, Pippa Passes*, and *A Blot in the 'Scutcheon*. For probable dates of composition see DeVane, *Handbook*, pp. 59–61, 91, 98–99, 132–33, 137–38. See also pp. 104 and 106–28 for DeVane's conjectures as to the dates of composition of the sixteen poems contained in *Dramatic Lyrics* (1842). All but two or three of these lyrics would seem to have been composed in the same year as *My Last Duchess*, so that the total number of relatively short poems Browning wrote before 1842 (and his perfection of the dramatic monologue *genre*, at least as it is exemplified in *My Last Duchess*) would seem to be fairly small.

supplied the needed artistic experience. It would also seem likely that Browning's failure in the theater taught him something about the nature of his own dramatic talent, and thus guided him toward the form and techniques of those monologues. Failure is hardest to bear when one's attempt to succeed has been serious. But when the attempt to succeed has been serious—and Browning's attempt to succeed in the theater was very serious—then failure is often particularly instructive.

Strafford

The preface to *Strafford: An Historical Tragedy* is often cited for its famous phrase, "Action in Character rather than Character in Action," [24] as Browning's declaration of a new emphasis in dramatic writing. Like the equally famous words in the dedicatory letter to Milsand prefixed to *Sordello* in 1863, "my stress lay on the incidents in the development of a soul: little else is worth study," [25] that slightly enigmatic phrase epitomizes the central intention of a good deal of Browning's poetry. Almost all of the poems in *Men and Women* (1855), for example, might be called studies of "Action in Character rather than Character in Action." But the phrase, and the preface itself, suggest nothing new in Browning's attitude toward dramatic writing in 1837. Indeed, the preface to *Strafford* prepares the reader (and spectator) for another *Paracelsus:*

> [I] am not without apprehension that my eagerness to freshen a jaded mind by diverting it to the healthy natures of a grand epoch, may have operated unfavourably on the represented play, which is one of Action in Character rather than Character in Action. To remedy this, in some degree, considerable curtailment will be necessary, and, in a few instances, the supplying details not required, I suppose, by the mere reader.[26]

"Action in Character" is almost an epigrammatic way of saying "the mood [of character] itself in its rise and progress," which,

24. *Strafford*, p. iii.
25. *Works* (1863), *3*, 251.
26. *Strafford*, p. iii.

Browning had said in the preface to *Paracelsus,* would be the central theme of that poem. In *Paracelsus* Browning would exclude "the operation of persons and events" and avoid any "external machinery of incidents to create and evolve" the crises in character that he intended to produce.[27] So in *Strafford* "Character in Action" will be avoided, and "considerable curtailment" of events will be necessary. There is one slight but interesting difference in Browning's dramatic intention as it appears in both prefaces. *Strafford* will be seen and heard, rather than simply read, and so Browning will supply for the benefit of the theater audience a few "details not required," he supposes, "by the mere reader." But in the context of the *Strafford* preface this difference is trifling. Turning from the preface to the play, one would expect to find essentially a close study of character, in the manner of *Paracelsus,* with a few details of background included in order to make the play intelligible on stage. True, the poet is now turning from the lonely, scholarly, early Renaissance world of Paracelsus to the "grand epoch," the seventeenth-century political world of Charles I; but we are not to believe that the central emphasis upon character portrayal in *Paracelsus* will be sacrificed in *Strafford.*

With this in mind, it is a surprise to turn to the play itself. Character in *Strafford* is utterly swamped in a wild and heavy sea of action and event. The contrast between Browning's stated intention in the preface and his actual handling of the materials in the play is enormous.

Perhaps the most curious aspect of this discrepancy is that Browning himself did not seem to be aware of it. The preface to *Strafford,* with its bold stress on "Action in Character," seems to have been written *after* the play—on April 23, 1837 (the date affixed to the dedication [28]); even if it had been written before *Strafford* it was allowed to go to the publisher with the play. And it is clear from an entry in Macready's diary for May 1, 1837, that Browning felt the character of his hero to be of prime importance in *Strafford* even when the play was in rehearsal; Macready, who played Strafford, jotted down:

27. *Paracelsus,* p. vii.
28. *Strafford,* p. i.

Rehearsed *Strafford*. Was gratified with the extreme delight Browning testified at the rehearsal of my part, which he said was to him full recompense for having written the play, inasmuch as he had seen his utmost hopes of character perfectly embodied.[29]

Yet, if the authorship of *Strafford* were unknown and its preface did not exist, one would be justified in thinking that its author had been interested in anything *but* the perfect embodiment of character, and that the play was as far from a study of "action in character" as any other typical early Victorian play. On the basis of the text alone, the author of *Strafford* would seem to be an inexperienced writer rather dazzled by politics (although well-read in at least one period of parliamentary history), and artistically interested mainly in the creation of striking situations, elaborate tableaux, and rather ordinary theatrical pathos.

It is still a somewhat open scholarly question as to exactly what share Browning had in the writing of John Forster's *Life of Strafford,* which was published a year before the play.[30] F. J. Furnivall, who knew Browning and talked to him often in the years preceding the poet's death, wrote a curious appendix for Sharp's *Life of Robert Browning* entitled "Corrections Etc." After the word *"Strafford"* in this appendix is the entry:

The reasons for Browning's suggesting (in May 1836) Strafford as the subject of a play, was [*sic*] that he had then just finisht, or was at work on, the prose *Life of Strafford,* which passes under the name of John Forster . . . Forster had done part (? about 4 pages) of the book, but fell ill, and couldn't get the volume out by the time he'd promist it, so Browning took away his material, and finisht Strafford's Life for him, to his great relief.[31]

DeVane, citing Furnivall's later defense of this claim in the *Forewords* to the London Browning Society's edition of the *Life of Strafford* in 1892, maintains that Browning's contribution to

29. Macready, *Diaries,* ed. Toynbee, *1,* 392.
30. On May 4, 1836. See DeVane, *Handbook,* p. 62.
31. "Corrections Etc. By F. J. Furnivall," in William Sharp, *Life of Robert Browning* (London, 1890), following p. 219.

Forster's work must have been small.[32] But it cannot be denied that Browning knew Forster's materials and that he immersed himself in the historical details of the "grand epoch" sufficiently to make some actual contribution to Strafford's biography. Thus it is reasonable to surmise that when Browning sat down to write *Strafford* the events of that statesman's career, which, artistically, Browning had set himself to minimize in a study of "Action in Character rather than Character in Action," made a pressing claim for inclusion in an historical tragedy.

Secondly, the very fact that Browning had been greatly moved by Macready's summons to write a play—the fact that he felt himself faced with a challenge that was likely to determine the course of his artistic career and that would bring certain fame if answered successfully—in all likelihood caused Browning to pay special attention to the needs of the theater.

Filled with the details of Strafford's life, then, and well aware that his first stage play would have to satisfy the theatrical standards of a man like Macready, Browning in part unconsciously abandoned the concentration upon character portrayal that had been the radical feature of *Paracelsus* and the central doctrine of his dramatic theory until this time. In fact, in *Strafford* the poet not only retreated from the aim of the *Strafford* preface and the aim of *Paracelsus,* but from his past poetic standards as well. In *Strafford* one senses a vigorous effort on Browning's part to curtail many of the usual attributes of verse: imagery is almost nonexistent, diction is simple and direct, sound—prosodically— is relatively unimportant. Syntax, rhythm, and even punctuation in *Strafford* combine to give the verse a broken, harsh, explosive movement. Sentences and fragments are short; single lines are broken by two, three, and even four pauses. The exclamation point, the dash, and the ellipsis occur so frequently in the text that they seem to have been broadcast over it like seeds. Strafford's lines in Act II are rhythmically typical:

> Do not believe—
> My liege, do not believe it! I am yours—
> Yours ever—'tis too late to think about—

32. See DeVane, *Handbook,* pp. 62–63.

To the death, yours! Elsewhere, this untoward step
Shall pass for mine—the world shall think it mine—
But, here! But, here! I am so seldom here!
Seldom with you, my King! I—soon to rush
Alone—upon a Giant—in the dark! [33]

If one considers verse technique alone, there is probably no greater disparity in all Browning's work than that between *Paracelsus* and *Strafford,* even though the play was begun a mere seventeen months after the completion of the poem. It is apparent that Browning ruthlessly sacrificed poetic qualities in *Strafford* in order to produce a text that could be successfully acted upon the stage. His aim to show "action in character" was sacrificed as well. Unfortunately, a successful stage play was not the result. Beleaguered by, on the one hand, complicated historical events and, on the other, a desire to appear theatrically correct, he produced an exceedingly poor drama, lacking in clarity, expression, and human interest. Still, *Strafford* accomplished two things for the twenty-five-year-old poet in 1837: it did not entirely alienate Macready (who considered its performance a "grand escape" [34]) and it afforded Browning new and valuable exercises in the use of blank verse to present character.

After the timelessness and vagueness of the setting in *Pauline* and *Paracelsus,* one opens the play of *Strafford* to something very different:

ACT I.

SCENE I.—A HOUSE NEAR WHITEHALL.

HAMPDEN, HOLLIS, *the younger* VANE, RUDYARD, FIENNES, *and many of the Presbyterian Party:* LOUDON *and other Scots Commissioners: some seated, some standing beside a table strewn over with papers, &c.*[35]

This stage direction suggests a tableau or even a large painted portrait in the heroic manner, with earnest parliamentarians

33. *Strafford,* II, ii, 150–56.
34. Macready, *Diaries,* ed. Toynbee, *1,* 392; entry of May 2, 1837.
35. *Strafford,* p. 1.

grouped about the uplifted, well-lit face of a Hampden or a Vane orating to the rest. But no Hampden or Vane orates, in the manner of Paracelsus, for long. The direction introduces a scene in which Vane, Rudyard, Hollis, Hampden, Fiennes, Loudon, Pym, a Puritan, "Other" Scots, a "Voice," "Voices," and "Many Voices" speak in bewildering succession, breaking each other off, often shouting and thumping. Vane, and Pym after his entrance half-way through the scene, speak a little more than the others, but they are hardly distinguished in the babble. The scene must be read several times in order to be understood; dramatically, it is a welter of confusion. However, with such a rush the real world—and a genuine setting—enters Browning's poetry for the first time.

Nothing perhaps is more indicative of Browning's lack of dramatic technique in 1837 than the way in which crowds of people are handled in *Strafford*. In *A Soul's Tragedy* (written between 1842 and 1845 [36]) crowds will be handled much more deftly, and in dramatic monologues such as *Fra Lippo Lippi* and *Half-Rome* groups of people will be brilliantly suggested—the presence of the Florentine police, for example, is distinctly felt in Lippo's opening lines. But *Strafford* taxed Browning to deal with crowds. Again and again, as the stage directions suggest, groups of people rush through the drama: *The same Party enters confusedly . . .* (II, i); *. . . as the King disappears, they turn as by one impulse to* PYM (II, ii); *Many of his Adherents enter* (III, ii); *The* PRESBY-TERIANS *prepare to dispute his passage* (III, iii); *Many groups of* SPECTATORS *of the trial* (IV, ii); *Enter* STRAFFORD, SLINGSBY *and other Secretaries,* HOLLIS, CARLISLE, MAXWELL, BALFOUR, *etc.* (IV, ii). It may be paradoxical to suggest that the necessity of coming to grips with numbers of people in a stage play helped to prepare Browning for the techniques of character portrayal in the dramatic monologues. But the settings and in particular the unheard audiences in the monologues are instrumental in helping to suggest the characters of the monologuists themselves; and *Strafford* is among other things an exercise in the handling of dramatic background. Most of the on-stage crowds in the play do not, in fact, speak; but they are there, and Browning was compelled to manipulate this often silent audience, to suggest its presence, and to

36. See DeVane, *Handbook,* pp. 190–91.

write speeches for Pym and Strafford and Vane that would be
"overheard" by an audience of other characters in the play. In
this sense *Strafford* afforded an exercise in the creation of the dramatic monologue situation, an exercise that no lyric and no dramatic poem of the *Paracelsus* type could possibly have provided.

In *Strafford's* chopped and explosive verse a second lesson of
value to the poet is evident. It will be worth-while to examine a
rather typical passage of the play—in this case an exchange between Wentworth (Strafford) and Lady Carlisle when they are
first seen in Act I:

> WENTWORTH.
>
> All the court! Evermore the Court about us!
> Savile and Holland, Hamilton and Vane
> About us,—then the King will grant me. . . . Lady,
> Will the King leave these—leave all these—and say
> "Tell me your whole mind, Wentworth!"
>
> CARLISLE.
>   But you said
> You would be calm.
>
> WENTWORTH.
>   Lucy, and I am calm!
> How else shall I do all I come to do,
> —Broken, as you may see, body and mind—
> How shall I serve the King? time wastes meanwhile,
> You have not told me half . . . His footstep! No.
> —But now, before I meet him,—(I am calm)—
> Why does the King distrust me? [37]

It is quite apparent that Wentworth's speech technically has very
little in common with that of Browning's speaker in *Pauline* or
with that of Paracelsus. It is broken speech. Hardly a single sentence is completed without the interruption of a fragment; some
of the sentences are lost and become fragments themselves. Apart
from the rhythmical disintegration of the passage, it is a very bad
one on the simple level of intelligibility; a play full of such
speeches, as *Strafford* is, must inevitably fail on stage, where even

37. *Strafford*, I, ii, 286–97.

under the best of circumstances not all of the lines that an actor speaks are comprehended by the listening audience. One has difficulty in understanding such a passage even when reading it through for the first time. But it is an interesting passage nevertheless, for what it does manage to do—clumsily to be sure—is to indicate the functioning of Wentworth's mind at work. From the smoothly flowing lyrical speech of Paracelsus, Browning turned in *Strafford* to the deliberate dramatization of psychological processes. This sort of dramatic speech had been written before, of course, and by better playwrights than Browning:

> Let me not think on 't! Frailty, thy name is woman.
> A little month; or ere those shoes were old
> With which she follow'd my poor father's body,
> Like Niobe, all tears; why she,—
> O God! a beast, that wants discourse of reason,
> Would have mourn'd longer,—married with my uncle,
> My father's brother, but no more like my father
> Than I to Hercules. Within a month. . . .[38]

In Shakespeare one may find the same type of interrupted syntactical construction, and the same interest in depicting natural processes of thought—although passages containing these features seem to occur chiefly, and significantly, in the soliloquies. The Shakespearian audience is not strained by a rapid succession of such passages, let alone a whole play full of them, and the interruptions in such passages are not so unrelated as to cloud the general meaning. In *Strafford* syntax is so broken and the meanings of the interruptions are so unrelated that the sense of many a speech is only clear after careful study and reflection. Yet a similar kind of dramatization of psychological processes will be a feature of character portrayal in the dramatic monologues. Browning uses many of the same syntactical devices in *The Bishop at St. Praxed,* for example, but with a clarity and general effectiveness that place the portrait of the Bishop on a much higher artistic level than that of Strafford; Browning's first stage play is impor-

38. *Hamlet,* I, ii, 146–53. My citations from Shakespeare in this study are to the Yale Edition.

tant in a study of the development of those techniques partly because it represents the first crude trial of them.

Very little impression of Wentworth as a character is produced on the reader of *Strafford,* moreover, because the fits and starts of his speech, while perhaps indicative of Wentworth's state of mind at any given moment, do not succeed in delivering to the reader any consistent, striking, fundamental insights about him. The syntactical peculiarities of Lippo's or the dying Bishop's speech are not only psychologically true but consistent, and the consistent impressions they deliver add meaningfully to the impression upon the reader of the other technical devices in those poems. Character is successfully revealed in Browning's blank-verse speech only when a number of character-revealing devices —syntax is one of them—produce a consistent and calculated effect. For this reason the very briefest portraits in *Strafford* tend to be the most successful. Consider that of the First Spectator in Act IV; his three-and-a-half lines open Strafford's trial scene:

FIRST SPECTATOR.
More crowd than ever! . . . Not know Hampden, man?
That's he—by Pym—Pym that is speaking now!
No, truly—if you look so high you'll see
Little enough of either! [39]

Slight as it is, this is a character-revealing speech. Its omitted grammatical elements give it a casual, colloquial air that suggests the ordinariness of the speaker. The fragmentary construction of the second line and the pauses of the first three lines to some extent help to suggest the Spectator's level of intelligence and sensitivity, too: he is a commoner, incapable of sustained utterance, who thinks as he speaks. The very simple diction of the passage and the familiar use of "man" reinforce this impression, so that the speech is in every way a consistent and revealing portrait of character. One may object that it is rather trifling; it is, for even apart from its trifling length it does not utilize sound, rhythm, and imagery to increase the intensity of its portrayal; any four lines of *Fra Lippo Lippi* tell more about Lippo's character than these lines tell about their speaker. But in its simple consistency

39. *Strafford,* IV, ii, 142–45.

a speech of this kind in *Strafford* indicates a step toward the harmonious and compact use of the techniques of character portrayal one finds in *Fra Lippo Lippi.*

Browning felt constrained in *Strafford* to sacrifice poetic imagery to the needs of Macready's stage, it would seem, and the dearth of imagery in the play is a feature that has ingratiated few readers.[40] After *Paracelsus, Strafford* seems to be a desert of talk —unrelieved by any passage that displays a charm of its own. But there is a small amount of imagery nevertheless, and its use is significant. In this respect, too, curiously enough, *Strafford* was valuable to Browning in providing an exercise in technique.

Only one of the play's characters uses imagery to any appreciable extent—and this is the Puritan, whose lines are few. But the Puritan speaks almost exclusively in biblical imagery, and his images infect the speeches that directly follow his own:

> A PURITAN (*entering*).
> —Out of the serpent's root
> Comes forth a cockatrice.
>
> FIENNES (*entering*).
> —A stinging one,
> If that's the Parliament: twelve subsidies!
> A stinging one! but, brother, where's your word
> For Strafford's other nest-egg—the Scots' War?
>
> THE PURITAN.
> His fruit shall be a fiery flying serpent.
>
> FIENNES.
> Shall be? It chips the shell, man; peeps abroad:
> Twelve subsidies!—[41]

It is as though the poet, desperately fearing to become undramatic in flights of pure, *Paracelsus*-like poetry, created one character

---

40. Arthur Symons, almost alone among twentieth-century critics of the play to date, found the chief merit of *Strafford* to be "in the language and style of the dialogue" and in the very lack of "poetical elaboration." See *An Introduction to the Study of Browning* (London, 1906), p. 42. More often critics have found the play bewilderingly obscure and in no way saved by the general barrenness of the verse.

41. *Strafford,* II, i, 3–10.

whose natural mode of talk was imagistic. The Puritan supplies most of the play's imagery. Biblical as it is, this imagery not only increases the poetic intensity of the dialogue when it appears but delineates the austere, pessimistic, religious character of the Puritan himself. It is thus an imagery of considerable relevance to character—indeed, in its small way, an instrument of characterization. In writing for the stage Browning began with an almost clean slate as far as imagery was concerned and gradually, in some measure from play to play, developed techniques in the use of imagery that were to be of enormous value in delineating character in the dramatic monologues while enriching their very texture. This is not to say that each play shows an advance upon the next in the pertinence and quality of its imagery; but it is possible to trace a general development from the early plays to the later ones, and to relate this development to the imagery of his finest work.

King Victor and King Charles

The first unmistakable reference to the existence of Browning's second stage play, *King Victor and King Charles*, contains a two-word judgment upon the play that fairly summarizes critical opinion of it in the last fifty or sixty years. On September 5, 1839, Macready wrote in his diary: "Read Browning's play on Victor, King of Sardinia—it turned out to be a *great mistake*." [42] The twentieth century has echoed this judgment. W. L. Phelps, for example, found the whole tragedy to be nothing more than a "corpse"; Symons thought it the "least interesting and valuable" of Browning's plays; Brooke pronounced it a "failure" as a drama, devoid of "any action" that could be called dramatic and filled with "stick" figures; Charlton felt that the playwright committed a kind of "dramatic suicide" in it. [43] Probably no other work of Browning's has elicited such consistently negative remarks from critics, and *King Victor* is now a neglected play. Turning to it for evidence of the poet's development of character-revealing tech-

42. Macready, *Diaries*, ed. Toynbee, 2, 23.
43. See William Lyon Phelps, *Robert Browning* (Indianapolis, 1932), p. 421; Arthur Symons, *An Introduction to the Study of Browning* (London, 1906), p. 57; Stopford A. Brooke, *The Poetry of Robert Browning* (London, 1905), 2, 20–21; and H. B. Charlton, *Browning as Dramatist* (Manchester, 1939), p. 17.

niques, one would expect to find a decline even from the level of
Strafford.

No bold declaration of an intended emphasis upon "Action in
Character rather than Character in Action" accompanied *King
Victor* when it appeared in 1842, but an Advertisement was affixed
to it, and the note is indicative of Browning's attitude toward character in the play. After discussing the sources he has used, he mentions the "knowledge" that one may obtain only from these
sources: that of

> the fiery and audacious temper, unscrupulous selfishness, pro-
> found dissimulation, and singular fertility in resources, of
> Victor—the extreme and painful sensibility, prolonged im-
> maturity of powers, earnest good purpose and vacillating will,
> of Charles—the noble and right woman's-manliness of his
> wife—and the ill-considered rascality and subsequent better-
> advised rectitude of D'Ormea.[44]

Significantly the emphasis is not upon Voltaire's "terrible event
without consequences"—which Browning simply mentions in the
note—but upon the nature of the characters who were involved
in this historical event, the four characters of *King Victor.*

In the play itself Browning fails to develop these characters
partly because the terrible event is indeed minimized. The flaw
in a dramatic theory that holds "character in action" (or, in other
words, dramatic event) to be less important than the portrayal of
character is that, of course, as far as stage plays are concerned,
character portrayal itself is severely hindered if action is not
treated as a vital element; in Shakespeare's history plays action is
implicit at once, for example, and one may say that it is just
character in action that reveals "action in character"; in *King
Victor* Browning developed no action striking enough to reveal
the "fiery and audacious temper" and the "singular fertility in re-
sources" of his Victor. He did not at this time possess the expert
techniques needed to portray character in blank verse if one
chooses to dispense with action. In the later dramas, particularly

---

44. My citations from *King Victor and King Charles* are to the unnumbered
text in Robert Browning, *Bells and Pomegranates. No. II.—King Victor and King
Charles,* London, 1842. For the "Advertisement" see p. 4.

in those not written for the stage, character is delineated without the benefit of a striking action—but Browning's blank verse at the time of *King Victor* is not supple and skilled enough to do this. Thus there is a barrenness about the play which has caused critics to think even less of it than of *Strafford*. For *Strafford* at least teemed with characters who were consistently involved in action— even if the action was developed so poorly that it could hardly be followed by spectator and reader, and even if it had the unfortunate effect of obscuring the portraits of the central characters. *King Victor,* though perhaps corpselike as a play, is a more lucid work because it dispensed with the obscuring type of action of *Strafford*. Its character portraits are very clear; the chief difficulty is that neither a prominent action nor character-revealing blank verse develops them effectively.

At the same time, the blank verse in *King Victor* does demonstrate important progress in technique. For one thing, the prosodic and imagistic elements that had been sacrificed in *Strafford* are to some extent recovered in *King Victor,* and without a return to the undramatic and rather lyrical type of speech of *Paracelsus*. It will be of interest to consider one of Victor's opening speeches rather carefully. About to abdicate in favor of his son Charles, Victor slyly urges D'Ormea to stay on as his son's First Minister:

> *Vic.*   I was about to notice, had you not
> Prevented me, that since Modovi kept
> With its chicane my D'Ormea's satchel stuffed,
> And D'Ormea's self sufficiently recluse,
> He missed a sight,—my naval armament
> When I burnt Toulon. How the skiff exults
> Upon the galliot's wave!—rises its height,
> O'ertops it even; but the great wave bursts—
> And hell-deep in the horrible profound
> Buries itself the galliot:—shall the skiff
> Think to escape the sea's black trough in turn?
> Apply this: you have been my minister
> —Next me—above me possibly;—sad post,
> Huge care, abundant lack of peace of mind;
> Who would desiderate the eminence?

You gave your soul to get it—you'd yet give
Your soul to keep it, as I mean you shall,
My D'Ormea! What if the wave ebbed with me?
Whereas it cants you to another's crest—
I toss you to my son; ride out your ride! [45]

A skillful dramatist might not have bothered with the first seventeen of these twenty lines; they slow down the dramatic movement and add little. The last three lines, in fact, contain a self-explanatory metaphor which in itself vigorously delivers Victor's message. The metaphor of the wave (Victor) ebbing, and canting D'Ormea to a new crest (Charles) is a good one, and Victor need hardly have said a word more. Browning is still far from the superb rhetorical condensation of the dramatic monologues, and the construction here is cautious. Six lines are used to introduce the naval engagement off Toulon—merely the scene, as it were, of the comparison; after describing the motions of galliot and skiff in the waves Victor must ask his audience to "apply this" to the present situation; and seven lines later one is finally led to the crux of the argument—the essential image. Imagery is thus laboriously related to character. Yet this is an advance upon *Strafford*, where none of the main characters use imagery in this manner. In *King Victor* Browning experimented with a new type of imagery, suggested by the Puritan's speeches in the first play: an imagery that would spring from the past experiences and psychological complexities of the speaker and so, at the moment of the speaker's utterance, would help to characterize him. In Victor's speech above the imagery is carefully "explained" in terms of the speaker's background; in the dramatic monologues the imagery tends to be spontaneous and self-evident: its pertinence to character and, in turn, its character-revealing quality are at once felt. But it is doubtful whether the imagery of the monologues could have come into being without the exercise afforded by such a speech, which seems to work out, step by step, the very process involved in the creation of character-revealing imagery.

Victor's lines above also indicate a return to a more judicious use of syntax and punctuation, a less explosive and self-consciously

45. *King Victor and King Charles*, "King Victor: Part II," 379–98.

"dramatic" verse rhythm, and a slightly broader range in diction—
and all without the sacrifice of an essential fidelity to the cadences
of human speech. Diction, syntax, and rhythm combine to produce, indeed, an effect in some of the lines that certainly suggests
human speech but misses the concentration of poetry.

> I was about to notice, had you not
> Prevented me . . . ,[46]

could be prose; it is loose verse, at any rate, and it does not help
to characterize Victor. But again, even such a bit points in the
direction of the monologues, for it is implicitly true to the human
voice: *in* character, even if not particularly expressive of it. Again
and again Browning seems to shatter the poetic effect of a speech
in *King Victor* in order to remain faithful to ordinary human expression:

> One called to manage kingdoms, Charles, needs heart
> To bear up under worse annoyances
> Than D'Ormea seems—to me, at least.[47]

Whatever poetic flight there may be in the first two lines is brought
to earth prosily in the last; after a series of rather resounding accented syllables the ordinary little phrase "to me, at least" is a
disappointing climax. In *Fra Lippo Lippi* the most colloquial
phrases become the material of poetry; even in the best speeches
of *King Victor* ordinary human expression seems to compete with
poetic expression. There is little fusion of the two. At times
Browning seems to be embarrassed by anything even resembling
poetry:

> For God's sake, what has night brought forth? Pronounce
> The . . what's your word?—result! [48]

Here, after a moderately forceful if melodramatic first verse, there
is a return to the mutilated syntax and rhythm of *Strafford*.

But on the whole it is plain that the verse technique of *King
Victor* is nearer to that of the dramatic monologues than is that

46. Ibid., 379–80.
47. Ibid., 440–42.
48. Ibid., 447–48.

of *Strafford.* There is no possible way to justify *King Victor* in its own right; eliminating the seething, character-obscuring action of his first play, abandoning any serious attempt to create pathos or striking situations, and, instead, concentrating on the depiction of character through realistic, "unpoetic" conversation in blank verse, Browning wrote a drama that dismayed Macready at first glance. Probably *King Victor* will always leave its readers a little cold, for, like *Sordello,* its chief importance is that it provided certain exercises. In it Browning gained some control over rhythm and syntax as implements of blank-verse speech, extended his dramatic diction from the *Strafford* level, and began to work out a type of imagery new in his poetry—an imagery springing from the imagined mental condition and past experiences of character itself.

The Return of the Druses

Among the letters that Browning wrote to Miss Fanny Haworth at the time of his stage plays is one that Mrs. Orr, in publishing, related to both *King Victor and King Charles* and *The Return of the Druses.* The letter was written before the existence of either play, on August 1, 1837,[49] but it seems fairly clear that these were the plays Browning had in mind. Having planned, or possibly having just begun *King Victor,* Browning was already thinking about the drama to follow it:

> I want a subject of the most wild and passionate love, to contrast with the one I mean to have ready in a short time. I have many half-conceptions, floating fancies: give me your notion of a thorough self-devotement, self-forgetting; should it be a woman who loves thus, or a man? What circumstances will best draw out, set forth this feeling? [50]

While remembering that this excerpt is taken from a casual letter to a close friend, one may deduce from it some evidence of Browning's attitude toward his third stage play. He is looking, it would

---

49. DeVane has dated this letter ingeniously by tracing an allusion in it; see *Handbook,* p. 132, n. 1; Mrs. Orr, who first printed the letter, supplied no date.
50. Orr, *Life,* p. 97.

seem, first of all, for a *subject* of a "wild and passionate" nature. The question of subject matter at once leads him to the question of character: "should it be a woman who loves thus, or a man?" And the question of appropriate dramatic action, the "circumstances" that will best "draw out, set forth this feeling" comes last. It is clear that Browning once again is interested not primarily in the representation of an action but in the depiction of a state of being. Circumstances will be required to set forth character, but they are not important in themselves—Browning wants Miss Haworth's aid in suggesting an action that will implement the general idea about character that he already has in mind. The sex, the individuality of the central character in the play is not yet determined: Miss Haworth can help him in this matter, too. But the emotional state of that character and also, to some extent, the nature of the new play's blank verse are clear: they are postulated in Browning's desire for "a subject of the most wild and passionate love."

Thus, on the evidence of the letter, it would seem that Browning began to write *The Return of the Druses* (or *Mansoor the Hierophant,* as the MS was called until the spring or summer of 1840) with two special objects in mind: he wished to portray a character involved in an extreme emotional state, and he wished to tax his verse technique with the new demands implicit in such a portrayal.[51]

51. That Browning's special interests in writing the play were to experiment and improvise with new techniques on the one hand, and to portray a central character in a highly-keyed emotional state successfully on the other, perhaps may be seen in his letter to Macready of August 23, 1840, as well. Browning wrote in part: ". . . I have worked from the beginning somewhat in the spirit of the cucumber-dresser in the old story (the doctor, you remember, bids such an one 'slice a platefull—salt it, pepper it, add oil, vinegar etc etc and then . . throw all behind the fire')—spite this, I *did* rather fancy that you would have 'sympathized' with Djabert [sic] in the main scenes of my play: and your failure to do so is the more decisive against it, that I really had you *here,* in this little room of mine, while I wrote bravely away—*here* were you, propping the weak, pushing the strong parts (such I thought there might be!) . . ." DeVane and Knickerbocker, *New Letters,* p. 21. The allusion to the cucumber-dresser seems to be a sprightly masking of the fact that Browning worked hard on the technicalities of the play, including the new elements of technique that may be seen in it, just as the rest of the excerpt seems to mask the fact that Browning was hurt more than anything else by Macready's failure to appreciate the portrait of the emotionally intense Djabal, his central character.

As it finally appeared in 1843, *The Return of the Druses* reveals considerable emphasis upon the portrayal of the "wild and passionate" emotion of its central character, the leader of a band of Lebanese Druses, Djabal, and considerable innovation in Browning's verse technique for the stage. Striking differences in the verse of this play from that of *Strafford* and *King Victor* are noticeable in the opening lines:

> *Kar.* The moon is carried off in purple fire:
> Day breaks at last! Break glory, with the day
> On Djabal, ready to resume his shape
> Of Hakeem, as the Khalif vanished erst
> On red Mokattam's brow—our Founder's flesh,
> As he resumes our Founder's function! [52]

Imagery begins with Karshook's first verse and occurs frequently in the speeches of the Druses; it tends to be rich, visual, and colorful. The very use of terms of color in verse is, in a broad sense, imagistic, and references to color abound: in Act I alone, after the two instances above, *purple fire* and *red Mokattam's brow,* one finds *white flame, hoar-silvered, gold fringe, White-cross Knights, silver mouth, white eyes, black white-crossed gown, blade in blue, black eyes,* along with a host of terms that suggest color: *fire, flame, spark, twinkling lights and darks, frost-work,* and so forth. Not only had Browning failed to use color to such an extent before, but he had failed to relate it to character. The rich, colorful imagery of the play helps to suggest the barbaric nature of the Druses and illustrates the feverish intensity of their feelings. It is perhaps not a subtle implement of character portrayal—as the imagery of color is in *Andrea del Sarto* or the monologues of *The Ring and the Book,* for example—for individual colors are not assigned specific tasks, and color is no more important in the speech of one Druse than another; but it is a new implement for Browning. In the cadence of the speech above something new may be seen as well. Though intended as "giving a loose to exultation" (according to the stage direction), Karshook's speech maintains a more sus-

---

52. *The Return of the Druses,* I, 1–6. My citations from this work are to the unnumbered text in Robert Browning, *Bells and Pomegranates. No. IV.—The Return of the Druses. A Tragedy. In Five Acts,* London, 1843.

tained rhythm than Strafford's exclamatory utterances or Victor's few emotionally weighted outbursts in the last play. Browning tries to suggest a "wild and passionate" feeling without the mutilation of rhythm—indeed, rhythm in the present instance seems to be the one element that holds the passage together, nearly binding it into a single exclamation. The effect only fails because the syntax is not clear. Syntactically, Karshook's opening lines—and many of Djabal's lines—are so involved that one must become rather familiar with their contexts in order to interpret them. It would seem to be this feature that caused Macready to lament in his diary of August 3, 1840, after receiving *The Return of the Druses:* "Read Browning's play, and with the deepest concern I yield to the belief that he will *never write again*—to any purpose. I fear his intellect is not quite clear." [53] Browning's intellect was probably clear, but the effort to achieve a verse rich in imagery and sustained in rhythm that would communicate the "wild and passionate" characters he had chosen as subjects brought about lapses into obscurity that condemn the work as a stage play.

The successful portraits in the tragedy are those of the Europeans—the Prefect and the Nuncio and, to some extent, Loÿs de Dreux. Rhythm, syntax, and content combine in the following lines to give an effective impression of the Prefect's character:

> —I say
> That when for the remainder of my life
> All methods of escape seemed lost—just then
> Up should a young hot-headed Loÿs spring,
> Talk very long and loud, in fine, compel
> The Knights to break their whole arrangement, have me
> Home for pure shame—from this safehold of mine
> Where but ten thousand Druses seek my life,
> To my wild place of banishment, San Gines
> By Murcia, where my three fat manors lying,
> Purchased by gains here and the Nuncio's gold,
> Are all I have to guard me,—that such fortune
> Should fall to me, I hardly could expect! [54]

53. Macready, *Diaries*, ed. Toynbee, 2, 72.
54. *The Return of the Druses*, III, 263–75.

Grammatically this sentence appears at first glance to be an ana-
coluthon, with an incongruous completion, but it is really a correct period, faithful to the intelligent and subtle character of the
corrupt Prefect. It fuses the cadence of human speech with the intensity of genuine poetry; it is clear without being prosy. And it
seems to indicate progress in the perfection of a type of blank
verse found in *Bishop Blougram's Apology:* intelligent, conversa-
tional, lucid, and subtle—although not freighted with unusual
emotion. On the other hand, when Djabal's speeches are clear
they sometimes succeed in utilizing lush imagery in sustained sentences that suggest his own romantic, intensely feeling character
expertly:

> *Dja.* (*Aside.*)   Avow the truth? I cannot! In what words
> Avow that all she loves in me is false?
> —Which yet has served that flower-like love of hers
> To climb by, like the clinging gourd, and clasp
> With its divinest wealth of leaf and bloom:
> Could I take down the prop-work, in itself
> So vile, yet interlaced and overlaid
> With painted cups and fruitage—might these still
> Bask in the sun, unconscious their own strength
> Of matted stalk and tendril had replaced
> The old support thus silently withdrawn!
> But no; the beauteous fabric crushes too.[55]

The image here is richly developed and ornamented in each successive line; in its complexity and use of nature and color it helps
to convey the passionate and complex character of the Druses'
leader. It is an example of the chief importance of the play to
Browning: the choice of a "wild and passionate" theme provided
an opportunity to weave into the matrix of dramatic verse those
poetic elements that had been sacrificed in the spare lines of *Strafford* and only partly recovered in the verse of *King Victor.*
Rhythm, sound, and especially imagery, in the best instances, are
developed as fully in *The Return of the Druses* as they are in
Paracelsus, but with the significant difference that they now im-

55. Ibid., II, 286–97.

plement verse that is dramatic and character-revealing and not primarily musical.

In the exotic speeches of Djabal and the Druses an extension in Browning's use of diction to reveal character is also evident. Diction in *Strafford* had been rather simple and direct, diction in *King Victor* more specialized but not in itself a very distinguishing feature of character portrayal. In creating the Druses, however, Browning was faced with the problem of differentiating their speech from that of the Europeans in the play so that the drama distinctly called for two different levels of diction. He met this problem in several ways: first, through the use of an unusually large number of terms having to do with color, brightness, and darkness, Browning created a kind of imagistic diction for the Druses suggestive of their barbarism and emotional intensity; second, he seems to have made the most of exotic names and titles— which the Druses are forever invoking: *Maani, Karshook, Raghib, Ayoob, Djabal,* or *Khalif, Copht, Hakeem, Biamrallah,* for example. A few specialized Eastern terms contribute to the exotic effect of these: *khandjar, tabrets, bezants.* Third, the dissimilarity in the very thought processes of the Druses from those of the Europeans is partly achieved through the use of special compounds: *Mother-mount, death-sweat, Queen-bride, yonder-columned, heart's-word, snow-swathe, saffron-vestured,* or *boy-inquirer.* One might expect to find a few of these terms in the blank-verse speech of almost any character (*heart's word* or *snow swathe*), but if such compounds occur with any real frequency they produce a distinct impression. In saying "the boy who inquired" or "the inquiring boy" one does not equalize "boy" with the act of inquiring, for example; *boy-inquirer,* on the other hand, indicates a naive equalizing in importance of the doer with the immediate act and so, in its small way, helps to suggest the operation of a less sophisticated, non-Western type of mind. Not all the compounds of the Druses are as unusual as this one, but many are of a kind not common in English—and these are noticeably missing in the speeches of the Europeans. Lastly, Browning suggests the Druses' group character through the use of archaic terms and forms. The substitution of *thou, thy, thee* and *ye* for *you* and the resulting inflection of verbs—*leav'st, bad'st, aspirest, gazest, accuseth,* and so forth—as well as the frequent appearance of words such as *ay, nay, ere, erst, lo* and *yon,* which the Prefect does not use at all, help to set the Druses apart and even to suggest their adherence to older, racial patterns of thought and conduct. Browning will use archaic diction as an instrument of character revelation more effectively in *Karshish, Cleon,* and other monologues; he will use compounds and exotic names and terms to greater effect as well; but *The Return of the Druses* is important for the poet's trying-out of much of this diction in a dramatic context for the first time.

A Blot in the 'Scutcheon

Macready lost confidence in Browning in 1840. Convinced that *King Victor* was nothing but a "great mistake," [56] appalled by the obscurity and confusion of *The Return of the Druses,* and put off by *Sordello,* he seems to have decided that the poet was not only a lost cause but a personal nuisance: "Browning came before I had finished my bath," he wrote on August 27, 1840, "and really *wearied* me with his obstinate faith in his poem of *Sordello,* and of his eventual celebrity, and also with his self-opinionated persuasions upon his *Return of the Druses.* I fear he is for ever gone." [57] It seems clear that Browning, sensing this attitude in Macready's increasing coldness, wrote his next play with the idea of pleasing Macready—at least to the extent of writing a stage-worthy drama—even if it meant sacrificing certain cherished notions about dramatic poetry that he had held since the time of *Paracelsus.*

The letter that announced *A Blot in the 'Scutcheon* to Macready is well-known, but it is worth a special examination in the present instance:

> My dear Macready,
> "The luck of the third venture" is proverbial. I have written a spick and span new Tragedy (a sort of compromise be-

56. Macready, *Diaries,* ed. Toynbee, 2, 23.
57. Ibid., p. 76.

tween my own notion and yours—as I understand it, at least)
and will send it to you if you care to be bothered so far. There
is *action* in it, drabbing, stabbing, et autres gentillesses,—who
knows but the Gods may make me good even yet? Only, make
no scruple of saying flatly that you cannot spare the time, if
engagements of which I know nothing, but fancy a great deal,
should claim every couple of hours in the course of this week.

Yours ever truly,

Robert Browning.[58]

What Browning meant by the words "my own notion" within the
parentheses, "(a sort of compromise between my own notion and
yours—as I understand it, at least)," would seem to be fairly clear:
King Victor and *The Return of the Druses* were examples of his
"notion" of tragedy, as opposed to Macready's. Browning's interest
in these plays was in portraying action in character—delineating
states of being, showing character itself in its minute particulari-
ties, and, on the other hand, in minimizing the role of dramatic
action. But it is not entirely clear what was meant by the word
"yours"—that is, one cannot be sure to what extent Browning
sympathized with and genuinely understood Macready's criticisms of his last two plays. (Neither is it wholly clear, from the
Macready *Diaries,* to what extent Macready sympathized with and
understood Browning's intention in *King Victor* and *The Return
of the Druses.* On the basis of the *Diaries* and Browning's letters
it would seem that there was, perhaps, very little understanding
on either side.) One general criticism of Macready's must have
impressed Browning strongly, however. He recommends his new
play with the words: "There is *action* in it, drabbing, stabbing, et
autres gentillesses." The absence of any single, lucid, gripping,
character-motivating action had enfeebled his past efforts. *A Blot*
will not falter, he assures Macready, in this respect, and in the
letter "action" is the one word underlined.

In the history of the work's reception, few critics have found
A Blot in the 'Scutcheon to be seriously deficient in its "action"—
to the extent that this dramatic element may be considered quite
apart from the matter of character. The action mounts swiftly and

58. *Letters,* ed. Hood, p. 5; it was written late in 1840 or very early in 1841.

clearly to its climax. There are few irrelevancies in the shape of unnecessary or trivial discussions (which are almost the substance of *King Victor*) or static bits of character analysis (which seem to account for many speeches in *The Return of the Druses*). The blank verse has the clarity of *King Victor's* verse, and more economy. For these reasons alone the play might seem to be convincing proof of Browning's ability to write for the stage and evidence of his progress toward some of the disciplines of the dramatic monologues.

It is, really, neither. The dramatic flaw in the play is so great that it almost suggests—as none of the three plays did before—that Browning did not possess the ability to write successful stage drama under any circumstances. And the blank verse of *A Blot,* for all its lucidity, seems to reveal less progress in the direction of Browning's mature technique than does that of any other stage play he wrote.

The cardinal flaw in *A Blot* is that the dramatic action bears only an arbitrary relation to character. Mildred, Thorold, and Mertoun, the characters chiefly involved in the central action, seem to become puppets at an early point in the play simply because what they do and say is unbelievable even when we make allowance for the extraordinarily severe norm of moral conduct that seems to govern their lives. It is apparent that all three characters have been forced to behave according to the dictates of a plot which requires more of them than either their circumstances or their own natures can possibly justify. A resulting falseness thus seems to infect almost every one of their speeches. In the following manner, for example, Mertoun tells Mildred that all will be well with their love, now that he has spoken to her brother (Tresham):

> *Mer.*   Oh, Mildred, have I met your brother's face,
> Compelled myself—if not to speak untruth
> Yet to disguise, to shun, to put aside
> The truth, as what had e'er prevailed on me
> Save you, to venture? Have I gained at last
> Your brother, the one scarer of your dreams,
> And waking thoughts' sole apprehension too?
> Does a new life, like a young sunrise, break

On the strange unrest of the night, confused
With rain and stormy flaw—and will you see
No dripping blossoms, no fire-tinted drops
On each live spray, no vapour steaming up,
And no expressless glory in the east? [59]

Considered in its dramatic context, this speech appears to be false in more than one respect. But the imagery of the last six lines seems hackneyed and inexact even *out* of context—the sunrise simile for Mertoun's hope of a new life could not be more commonplace; "expressless glory in the east" does not develop the image but only tritely echoes the phrase "a young sunrise." When the image is considered in the light of Mertoun and Mildred's situation it appears additionally false, for it exaggerates the position of the two lovers. There has been no "rain and stormy flaw" in their love; nothing has prevented either its existence or its lawful fulfillment in marriage. "Sunrise" seems to break upon a sky that is already brightly and serenely lit so that the effect of the image is to destroy the impression of character that Browning wishes to achieve: Mertoun himself seems to become false. In the context diction is not only trite but inexact and exaggerated: for instance, it is difficult to see why Tresham is a "scarer" of his sister's dreams, or why Mertoun should have "gained at last" access to Mildred's brother when nothing has prevented him from seeing Tresham at any time in the past. The rhythms of the passage are unfaithful to human expression for they reflect no particular emotion that Mertoun might be expected to experience as he talks to Mildred at this point. In the relative length of the sentences urgency is missing. Mertoun seems to voice his thoughts merely for the sake of hearing them—or rather, perhaps, for the sake of letting the audience hear how much more dire his predicament has been than they have been led even faintly to suspect.

Verse technique generally, in *A Blot,* is used not for the purpose of delineating character but for the purpose of justifying the impossible behavior of the principal figures. Many of Tresham's lines in Act III even seem unhappily comic in their effect:

59. *A Blot in the 'Scutcheon,* I, iii, 375–87. My citations from this work are to the unnumbered text in Robert Browning, *Bells and Pomegranates. No. V.—A Blot in the 'Scutcheon. A Tragedy. In Three Acts,* London, 1843.

> Now! Lift you the body, Gerard, and leave me
> The head.[60]
>
>   Something does weigh down
> My neck beside her weight—thanks—I should fall
> But for you, Austin, I believe!—there—there—
> 'Twill pass away soon!—ah,—I had forgotten—
> I am dying.[61]

The speeches of only one character in the play are at once life-like and revealing—and they should not be overlooked. But significantly, Guendolen is not importantly involved in the action. "Wait for me," she tells Austin, for example, in Act II.

>   Pace the gallery and think
> On the world's seemings and realities
> Until I call you.[62]

Her common sense and wit are revealed in the contrasting diction of these lines, where the simple verbs *pace, think,* and *call* heighten the satirically pompous effect of the two abstract nouns, *seemings* and *realities.* In their very excellence her lines often contrast with the absurdity of those of the other characters. In Mildred's chamber Guendolen becomes sharp with the heroine for a moment:

>   . . . Lack I ears and eyes?
> Am I perplexed which side of the rock-table
> The Conqueror dined on when he landed first,
> Lord Mertoun's ancestor was bidden take—
> The bow-hand or the arrow-hand's great meed?
> Mildred, the Earl has soft blue eyes! [63]

Rhythmically the last line is heightened through the spondee effect of "soft blue eyes" and through direct attack. The preceding four lines with their more regular iambic cadence glide over the details which Guendolen believes are irrelevant in any summing-up

60. Ibid., III, i, 183–84.
61. Ibid., III, ii, 355–59. Lines 358–59 have become notorious as an example of Browning's lack of dramatic propriety in the stage plays.
62. Ibid., II, 387–89.
63. Ibid., I, iii, 293–98.

of the Earl as a marriage partner; the abrupt trochee of "Mildred" seems to call Mildred to her senses, and the emphatic "soft blue eyes" suggests the point to be heeded—that the Earl is lovable as a human being. In so helping to make her point (and in effect deriding Mildred's preceding utterance), Guendolen's lines help to reveal her character, too. She is alert and sensible enough to oppose to the sing-song of common opinion (ideas about the Earl's ancestral qualifications) her own bold apprehension of truth (the fact that the Earl is desirable as a man). Fortunately, so far as her individual portrait is concerned, Browning gave Guendolen very few lines to say in the incredible last act of the play. Apart from a few brief exclamations, the one successful character in *A Blot* maintains a commendable silence when the action is at its very peak.

Colombe's Birthday

Colombe's Birthday was not begun until after the delayed publication of *A Blot* in February 1843. It seems to have been composed shortly after that date, although it was not presented in its final form to Charles Kean until March 9, 1844.[64] Thus Browning's last stage play was written after the appearance of the *Dramatic Lyrics* (November 1842), a volume that did not contain a character-revealing blank-verse dramatic monologue, but did contain a number of lyrics written in the monologue form (*Soliloquy of the Spanish Cloister* and the two *Madhouse Cells*, discussed in the last chapter, among others), and in particular the well-known dramatic monologue in rhymed couplets that was later to be entitled *My Last Duchess*. When *Colombe* was produced at the Haymarket Theatre in April 1853 it received a series of somewhat laudatory notices; its later productions in Manchester and in Boston were equally acclaimed.[65] The stage success of the play was modest; Mrs. Browning called it a *"succès d'estime,"* [66] but even such success is upon first consideration rather surprising. The action

---

64. See Griffin and Minchin, *Life*, p. 119, and DeVane, *Handbook*, pp. 146–47.
65. See the accounts quoted in Symons, *Introduction*, p. 76, and in *The Browning Society's Papers* (London, 1881–91), *1*, 122–25.
66. *Letters*, ed. Kenyon, *2*, 116.

of *Colombe* is negligible; Berthold, Valence, the Duchess and her court are not in tense conflict with one another; the setting is not particularly vivid or impressive; the chief issue at stake—whether Colombe will escape the petty machinations of her false courtiers and marry Valence or accept a ready solution to the duchy's political difficulties and marry Berthold—is not presented in a manner that arouses suspense or enormous interest in itself. H. B. Charlton has effectively shown that Colombe's choice is largely a matter of mere taste; there is no real struggle "between mighty moral opposites." [67] One might even add that the outcome of the play is fairly apparent at the end of the first act. In fact, in *Colombe,* dramatic action is no more important than in *King Victor* and far less developed than in *A Blot.* However, *Colombe's* characters are not warped and dehumanized by dramatic action as Mildred, Mertoun, and Tresham are on the one hand, and they are not presented in an actionless vacuum of proselike poetry as Victor, Charles, and D'Ormea are on the other. Instead, Browning's dramatic verse technique, enriched by the bold experiments of *Pippa Passes* and by those of *The Return of the Druses* (a play which had woven imagery, sound, normal blank-verse rhythm, and a much broader range in diction into the fabric of character-revealing speech) is able in *Colombe* to convey a steady, intense, economical impression of character. Even in such an introductory scrap of dialogue as this the court attendants, Guibert and Adolf, are happily struck off:

> *Gui.*   The Prince's letter; why, of all men else,
> Comes it to me?
> *Adolf.*   By virtue of your place,
> Sir Guibert! [68]

The verse seems elementary. But the lines are entirely successful. Guibert's petty self-concern is partly suggested by means of the involuted syntax and momentary pauses of his speech; Adolf's freer conscience (and his momentary triumph) are contrasted in the

---

67. *Browning as Dramatist,* p. 25.

68. *Colombe's Birthday,* I, 28–30. My citations from this work are to the unnumbered text in Robert Browning, *Bells and Pomegranates. No. VI.—Colombe's Birthday. A Play, In Five Acts,* London, 1844.

more normal word order and the use of rhythm to give force and spontaneity to his exclamation. If the instance is minor, it is, perhaps, just in the minor instance that Browning often seems to forge ahead in his treatment of character. Indeed, any one of the characters in *Colombe* might be examined for evidence of Browning's progress in character-revealing technique; but perhaps the major figure of the Duchess herself best suggests the value of the play to the poet in this respect.

Imagery in Colombe's lines is used in a new way to help characterize a speaker; it has a cumulative effect—an effect not paralleled in a monologue like *My Last Duchess* but paralleled in many of the later monologues—particularly those of *The Ring and the Book*. Colombe is associated primarily with flowers. Shortly after her first appearance, surrounded by her false courtiers, she is made to say:

> . . . I gave myself
> No more a title to your homage, no,
> Than church-flowers born this season gave the words
> In the saint's-book that sanctified them first.
> For such a flower you plucked me—well, you erred—
> Well, 'twas a weed—remove the eye-sore quick! [69]

In half a dozen lines flowers are used in at least four different ways to tell something about the Duchess: her purity, her youth, her vulnerability, and finally her modesty are suggested by her association with one of the church-flowers "born this season" that had been "plucked" by her courtiers, only to turn into "a weed." The entire image is all the more convincing as a complex figuring forth of her character because of her own final denial of its validity—she would not have the courtiers believe that she is a flower at all, only deceptively: she is the eyesore weed. In the next act she tells Valence how she is often drawn to her casement at "a bird's passage or a flower-trail's play" (III, 184), and the flower image, already well established in its pertinency to Colombe, now serves to underline her freedom of spirit. After this the image is employed by other characters in the play in reference to the Duchess: Valence would furnish "lilies for her hair" (III, 266; the lilies'

69. Ibid., II, 163–68.

beauty is Colombe's beauty); Berthold yearns to gather "this sweet
flower" (IV, 184; Colombe has the sweet flower's desirability);
Valence wants only the "withered bunch of flowers she wears—
perhaps, / One last touch of . . . [her hand]" (V, 348–49; the
essence of Colombe's beauty is transcendent, for, though Valence
is to lose her, she will remain significant to him); and at last
Berthold sees her as "Too costly a flower" (V, 362; Berthold is unable to buy Colombe even with his offer of a kingdom). With each
iteration the flower image gathers meaning, so that by the end
of the play a host of characteristics is suggested by it. Imagery thus
becomes an intense means of characterization. In the stage plays,
from *Strafford* to *Colombe*, Browning was thus able to work out
techniques in the use of imagery that would be of considerable
value in the character-revealing monologues of his maturity.

Colombe's delicacy and sensibility are partly suggested by means
of the words she uses and even the syntax of her sentences, as well.
Her statements—particularly when they involve the expression of
her own feelings—are often lightly masked in word arrangements
that are complex, but not obscure:

> . . . this was far from least
> Of much I waited for impatiently,[70]

> . . . It was not I moved there, I think:
> But one I could,—though constantly beside,
> And aye approaching,—still keep distant from,
> And so adore.[71]

Valence's statements are contrastingly more direct, energetic, un-
concealed—and never more so than when he is discussing his own
feelings. Colombe's vocabulary is rich in adverbs—some of them
polysyllabic (*impatiently, infinitely, exclusively, impetuously*), and
a few of these are slightly uncommon ones: *presagefully, oracu-
larly, opportunely*. The delicacy of the relatively rare *presagefully*
is heightened in the subtle rhythm,

> Presagefully it beats, presagefully,
> My heart—[72]

70. Ibid., II, 15–16.
71. Ibid., IV, 255–58.
72. Ibid., III, 163–64.

where the word in fact pertains directly to the state of Colombe's feelings. Many of the Duchess' lines are interesting for their use of sound, especially when one considers the sound contrasts evident in the speeches of the other characters. Berthold's opening lines, with their gutterals (two soft or voiced, in *burgh* and *good,* and four hard or unvoiced in *looks, keep, kept, Cologne*) are suggestive of his rough-and-ready manliness:

> *Berth.* A thriving little burgh this Juliers looks.
> Keep Juliers, and as good you kept Cologne . . .[73]

But Colombe's consonantal sounds more often tend to be those produced precisely with lips and teeth—the dental stops (*t* and *d*) seem to occur frequently in her speeches:

> . . . Why then cease to do it now?
> Yet this is to be calmly set aside,
> And—ere next birthday's dawn, for aught I know,
> Things change, a claimant may arrive, and I . . .
> It cannot nor it shall not be! His right?
> Well then, he has the right, I have it not . . .[74]

Again, sound would seem to implement the effect of delicacy in her character. Short of tables of statistics one must perhaps be wary of drawing conclusions about the frequency of given sounds in a fairly long work, but it is permissible to say that in *Colombe* Browning seems to use sound quality for the first time as a special means of character portrayal.

Yet, ironically, in these very felicities the poet's failure as a stage dramatist is apparent. In practice, any playwright may produce the illusion of character by showing human beings involved in events calculated to throw light upon given character traits, and he may also produce the illusion by showing character traits through the use of character-revealing speech. The alternatives are not mutually exclusive; excellent scenes usually display the use of both methods at the same time. But if the poetic dramatist should minimize character-revealing action and correspondingly perfect and enrich the texture of character-revealing speech, his work tends to become significant in its minutiae. Character is then

73. Ibid., III, 1-2.
74. Ibid., II, 61-66.

best seen when the work itself is put most carefully and intimately before its audience. Such a work becomes unsatisfactory on stage because of the physical limitations of the theater: actors must deliver verses at the swift tempo of ordinary human speech, and audiences must be able to receive the import of passages even if they miss certain words, phrases, or the effect of intricate rhythms and sound patterns. In this sense the theater is a crude medium— and certainly no play in verse has been successful on stage that depended for its chief effects upon a full and accurate reception of all its strictly poetic qualities. *Colombe's* excellence reveals the heart of Browning's failure in that it is the only stage play that fairly bears out the implications of the poet's dramatic theory: it is a fine example of action in character rather than character in action. But under the most favorable circumstances *Colombe* could never be more than a *succès d'estime* on stage, for its characters come to life through the presence of verse qualities that can be appreciated only in the study.

In the perfection of its poetic technique, in its fine use of imagery, rhythm, diction, syntax, and sound in blank-verse speech to reveal the idiosyncrasies of human character, in its dependency upon minutiae for its effects, and in the subtlety and delicacy of several of its portraits—in other words in its superb and unusual qualities—*Colombe* is the play that most perfectly embodies Browning's dramatic theory, and in so doing impressively indicates his need in the early 1840's for a new dramatic form.

3. Character for the Study

Pippa Passes

IN Part IV of *Pippa Passes* (1841), Browning's Monsignor reads a letter to his Intendant from the young foreign sculptor Jules. Introducing the letter to the Intendant, the Monsignor is scornful of it in his worldly way. Jules, he declares,

> [suddenly] notifies to me some marvellous change that has happened in his notions of art; here's his letter,—"He never had a clearly conceived Ideal within his brain till to-day. Yet since his hand could manage a chisel he has practised expressing other men's Ideals—and in the very perfection he has attained to he foresees an ultimate failure—his unconscious hand will pursue its prescribed course of old years, and will reproduce with a fatal expertness the ancient types, let the novel one appear never so palpably to his spirit: there is but one method of escape—confiding the virgin type to as chaste a hand, he will paint, not carve, its characteristics,"—strike out, I dare say, a school like Correggio: how think you Ugo? [1]

At the very least, this passage suggests an interesting theory about artistic development: the artist (Jules) begins with no "clearly conceived Ideal" of his own and instead develops technical skill through attempts to imitate the "ancient types"—the acknowledged masterpieces in his field; in time he is able to reproduce these with a "fatal expertness"—"fatal" because the "expertness" itself does not enable him to produce original, living work but

---

1. *Pippa Passes*, IV, 44–60. My citations from this work are to the unnumbered text in Robert Browning, *Bells and Pomegranates. No. I.—Pippa Passes*, London, 1841.

only praiseworthy imitations; this being the case, his one means of escaping the dilemma (so as to produce original work) is to turn boldly to a different although somewhat related form of art. If a "novel" conception has occurred to Jules it will not be expressed until he has abandoned the artistic *genre* of his training and plunged freshly into work within a new *genre*. It is, of course, risky to read autobiography in any imaginative work; but Browning appears to have used the characters of Sordello, Paracelsus, and Pauline's speaker to work out problems relating to his own career as an artist, and one may perhaps equally well claim that Jules in *Pippa Passes* expresses a view which had some pertinence to Browning's own situation in 1839.

By the late spring or early summer of that year, when Browning began *Pippa Passes,* he had already composed the two stage failures, *Strafford* and *King Victor and King Charles* (the latter a play that had not actually been performed but had been flatly rejected by Macready as being unsuitable for the stage), and had composed, or had well in mind to compose, *The Return of the Druses.*[2] In these plays he had to some extent, at least, "practised expressing other men's Ideals," for the dramatic ideal of his own as elaborated in the *Paracelsus* and *Strafford* prefaces had been compromised in his attempt to write successful stage drama. He had been working in a rather clearly defined tradition, that of the five-act poetic tragedy (only slightly departed from in the special organization of *King Victor*[3]), and had been making at least some conscious effort to please Macready on the one hand and to develop his blank-verse techniques on the other. He had certainly failed to produce a successful play. Jules' lines imply a certain rationalization of this failure and also a new hope for the future: "in the very perfection [of managing the chisel] he has attained to he foresees an ultimate failure . . . there is but one method of escape . . ." It is likely, in Browning's mind in 1839, that he will ultimately fail to produce a successful play, no matter how great

2. See DeVane's discussion of the dates of composition for *Pippa Passes, Strafford, King Victor* and *The Return of the Druses,* respectively, in *Handbook,* pp. 91, 59–60, 98, 132–33.

3. That is, the play has four acts entitled: "First Year, 1730.—King Victor. Part I"; "King Victor: Part II"; "Second Year, 1731.—King Charles. Part I"; and "King Charles: Part II."

his improvement in technique, partly because the traditional form of the five-act poetic tragedy and the existing masterpieces in that form have been of use to him in his development of technique. And yet success has really two prerequisites. Technique itself is developed through work in the old, traditional patterns. Stage writing (Jules' sculpturing) must not be abandoned until technical expertness has been achieved; and Browning continues to write for Macready's stage. At the same time this developing expertness is deemed to be "fatal" unless a distinct and radical break from the traditional form is made (Jules must turn painter instead of sculptor and "paint, not carve" the "characteristics" of his novel conceptions). In 1839, it would seem, not abandoning the stage play, the form that was so vital to the development of his blank-verse technique, Browning at the same time took a radical step to liberate himself from what he felt to be the tyranny of a traditional form that could at best only lead him into the creation of fatally expert, self-debilitating imitations. The metaphor is perhaps not too strong: in *Pippa Passes* he began to paint.

In form *Pippa Passes* does reveal certain resemblances to Browning's stage dramas of the 1830's. Its organization into parts entitled *Morning, Noon, Evening,* and *Night* is reminiscent of the four parts or acts of *King Victor;* but the resemblance is superficial the moment one considers the fundamental unrelatedness of the sections and the threadlike structural function of Pippa (who is, in fact, given a proem and an epilogue which bring the total number of sections to six); if the central parts are in themselves self-contained playlets, Pippa's stitching them together and thereby giving some meaning and unity to the drama as a whole exemplifies a structural device that would seem to have no precedent in the English theater. Browning chose a form even more radically different from that of the traditional stage play than the form of *Paracelsus* had been before. *Pippa's* form is dramatic—yet within the conceivable limits of dramatic form it is difficult to imagine a form more removed from that of the stage play unless it is that of the dramatic monologue itself. In the texture of the verse and prose of *Pippa* other differences may be seen, and it is in this respect that Browning seems most clearly to heed Jules' advice—to cease to "carve" and to begin to "paint," to abandon the attempt to write correct blank verse for tragedies that were to be appreciated mainly in Macready's theater and to begin to write less inhibitedly for the benefit of a more intimate and inevitably more discerning audience—the individual reader—and so to extend his mastery of character-revealing techniques and to move in the direction of the dramatic monologue.

When placed beside the blank verse of the stage plays that he had been working on in the 1830's, the opening lines of *Pippa* suggest a virtual declaration of independence in dramatic technique:

> Day!
> Faster and more fast
> O'er night's brim day boils at last;
> Boils, pure gold, o'er the cloud-cup's brim
> Where spurting and supprest it lay—
> For not a froth-flake touched the rim
> Of yonder gap in the solid gray
> Of eastern cloud an hour away—
> But forth one wavelet then another curled,
> Till the whole sunrise, not to be supprest,
> Rose-reddened, and its seething breast
> Flickered in bounds, grew gold, then overflowed
>   the world.[4]

In their metrical variation, rhythm, rhyme, and sound—as in their special intensity of effect—these lines are quite unlike any dramatic lines Browning had produced before 1839. Technically, their pattern is unique. The rhyme scheme (A, B, B, C, A, C, A, A, D, E, E, D), similar in effect to the rhyme through all Pippa's speeches, seems to establish a definite pattern only to break it (for example, A, B, B, *C*, or C, A, C, A, *A*) and form a unique pattern. Metrically the four-foot verse is almost established as being predominant after the first two lines, but the intrusion of a decasyllabic five-stress verse in line 9 and a hexameter verse in the concluding line produce a unique effect. Nor is an iambic rhythm

---

4. *Pippa Passes*, [Pippa's proem], 1–12. There is a typographical error in line 11, i.e. in *Rose-reddened*, which in all later editions is "Rose, reddened."

any more maintained than a trochaic; the passage derives immense
variation and energy from its spondee effect ("night's brim day
boils," "Boils, pure gold," "cloud-cup's brim," "froth-flake
touched," "forth one wave-," "bounds, grew gold") which is so
intense that the prevailing rhythm might almost be described as
spondaic, suggesting in several lines Hopkins' "sprung rhythm,"
to come. Alliteration and assonance are strong in the passage and
serve to intensify rhythm and heighten imagery. Lyrically, the
lines are intense and effective. But dramatically they are quite
effective as well, for they convey on one level Pippa's exultation
on "springing out of bed," as the direction indicates, on "New
Year's Day at Asolo" [5]—her one free day of the year; and on a
deeper level they serve to reveal the free innocence of her spirit,
all the more striking when it appears in contrast with the later
portraits in *Pippa*—Ottima's and Sebald's, for example. In the
dramatic monologues Browning is not able to suggest character
traits through the use of devices that violate the natural limitations of blank verse, of course—notwithstanding great variation
in a few instances and considerable variation in many instances
any hundred lines of a blank-verse monologue produce the effect
of a strongly prevailing iambic rhythm broken into metrical units
of five stresses—yet variations help to produce impressions of character, and they are apt to be most effective when they are radical
(without irreparably distorting the prevailing iambic pentameter
pattern), simply because radical variations, well employed, may
create telling effects. The best dramatic monologues of Browning
contain verses that depart quite radically from the rhythmic norm.
Thus one clear advantage of *Pippa* to Browning was that it provided an opportunity to work out radical variations in rhythm—
in a dramatic framework so that rhythm might be related to character, and in verse of much greater latitude than blank verse has
or can permit, so that rhythm and its relation to character might
be freely explored. In the rhythmic variations of Pippa's speeches
may be seen the technical beginnings of what are certainly the
even more character-revealing variations of, for example, Caliban's
or Karshish's verse. Not even in *Sordello* had Browning been able
to go so far in his exploration of rhythm in dramatic verse, for

5. *Pippa Passes*, p. 3.

the speeches of *Sordello* were limited to the framework of the pentameter couplet.

The freedom and energy of Pippa's lines—not alone in their rhythm but in their sound quality and imagery—seem to imbue the blank verse of *Pippa Passes* as well. This blank verse is almost entirely on a higher level of artistic accomplishment than any of Browning's blank verse before 1839. Sometimes it seems to reveal character with an intensity unsurpassed in the poet's later work. Consider, for example, Ottima's opening lines (which follow Sebald's mournful song ending with the line *"Deep into the night drink!"*):

> *Otti.*   Night? What, a Rhineland night, then? How these tall
> Naked geraniums straggle! Push the lattice—
> Behind that frame.—Nay, do I bid you?—Sebald,
> It shakes the dust down on me! Why, of course
> The slide-bolt catches—Well, are you content,
> Or must I find you something else to spoil?
> Kiss and be friends, my Sebald. Is it full morning? [6]

On a simple level these lines economically set a scene and describe an action. It is morning in Ottima's shrub-house, where she and her paramour have been sleeping. Sebald gropes his way through the potted plants to the closed shutters in order to let in the day; Ottima follows. The lattice does not open; Sebald shakes it impatiently, causing the dust along its upper ledges to fall down, and at last Ottima sees that the slide-bolt in the window frame is caught; she asks Sebald to kiss her now that the little trouble is over.

But there is a terrible meaning in these trivial details. The entire action itself images her illicit love and Luca's murder. The "tall / Naked geraniums" suggest the scene of Ottima's seduction by Sebald in the woods. Her commands "Push the lattice," "Behind that frame," and "Nay, do I bid you?" with their short length and hushed quality suggest the promptings she has given Sebald preparatory to the murder. And her cry to Sebald when he attempts to open the shutter to let in the sun but only succeeds in shaking down dust on their heads images the result of the mur-

6. Ibid., I, 4-10.

der: new light does not come into the room, bringing the murderers happiness and promise of a new life, but dust falls down upon their heads—the dust of the grave and death.

Thus a few details, vivid as images in themselves, serve to set a scene which will reveal character (the shrub-house on the morning after the murder), implement an immediate dramatic action that reveals character (Ottima's authority and presence of mind; Sebald's rough impatience), symbolize a past action that has in effect conditioned character (the murder), and, perhaps too, suggest a mental state of character that will, later in the scene, be more fully exposed (Ottima's mortal fear [7]—as when the dust falls down upon her). If the character-revealing devices in these lines may be classified as imagistic, they point to a complex, fully-wrought, many-leveled use of imagery to reveal their speaker. They exemplify Browning's ability by this time to condense his effects into a very few lines, to use details so expertly that they accomplish many things at once—condensation of effect being, of course, one of the requisites of successful character revelation in the monologue form.

The prose of the students who introduce Part II—the Jules and Phene episode of *Pippa*—follows directly after the Ottima and Sebald scene, and the contrast of the prose with the blank verse that precedes it is considerable. The prose itself is not precisely gay and sprightly: it is rather a prose of wit: apart from a few short exclamations that run through it, enlivening it, it is composed of fairly long, slightly complex, but entirely clear periods that play upon and wittily develop the thought. The first speech of the Second Student, for example, indicates something new in Browning's technique:

> 2 *Stu.* The poet's away—never having much meant to be here, moonstrike him! He was in love with himself, and had

7. Browning's later revision of this speech for the first collected edition of his works included the insertion of a verse after line 4 above that more fully suggested Ottima's state of mind at this point. She is made to see the morning light as a "blood-red beam through the shutter's chink"—the "blood-red" intimating the fact that she has Luca's murder on her mind and also, it would seem, hinting at her own fear of death. Her death, she knows, will be the consequence of her act of the day before if the world discovers the murder.

a fair prospect of thriving in his suit, when suddenly a woman fell in love with him too, and out of pure jealousy, he takes himself off to Trieste, immortal poem and all—whereto is this prophetical epitaph appended already, as Bluphocks assured me:—*"The author on the author. Here so and so, the mammoth, lies, Fouled to death by butterflies."* His own fault, the simpleton! Instead of cramp couplets, each like a knife in your entrails, he should write, says Bluphocks, both classically and intelligibly.—*Æsculapius, an epic. Catalogue of the drugs:—Hebe's plaister—One strip Cools your lip; Phœbus' emulsion—One bottle Clears your throttle; Mercury's bolus—One box Cures . . .*[8]

Typically, a conceit—in the Elizabethan sense of the word—is proposed in the first half of the second sentence; it is a good conceit, capable of witty development: "He was in love with himself . . ." The phrase that follows enriches it: "and had a fair prospect of thriving in his suit". The dependent clause offers a complication, a woman fell in love with the poet Giovacchino, which is in turn exploited in the independent clause that follows: "and out of pure jealousy he takes himself off to Trieste . . ." Then, midway in the passage, a new but related conceit is suggested by Bluphocks' epitaph, and this is similarly developed. The cadence of the passage is faithful to human speech but it is largely determined, as the syntax is, by the dictates of the twin conceits' development. That is, syntax and rhythm have two duties: first the necessary one of suggesting human speech, and second the one of underlining the progressive steps of wit. The character of the Second Student that emerges is simple but clear in its constituents: he is a witty young man wholly preoccupied with his own verbal invention, and so high-spirited that he cannot stay on one theme for long—he explodes ("His own fault, the simpleton!"), he switches from one conceit to another, he bursts into witty doggerel—possibly supplied to him by Bluphocks. The vitality and spontaneity of the passage are evident; it is a successful prose portrait of its speaker. Significantly, too, its effect is reminiscent of passages in the later monologues. In none of Browning's stage plays is there

8. *Ibid.*, I, 290–307.

a speech of such apparent fluency, and in none of the plays is any character sufficiently delineated through the use of witty, vivacious, humorous talk. Successful talk of this kind in verse depends upon the absolute mastery of rhythm and syntax for its effect, for rhythm and syntax must directly reinforce the wit and give rapidity and lightness to its expression. Browning worked out this type of speech in the prose of *Pippa Passes* and later in the prose of *A Soul's Tragedy,* where in both cases he was able to dispense with the prosodic problems of line and meter. In *Archangelis, Fra Lippo Lippi, Mr. Sludge* and other monologues the same rapidity of expression was achieved in the blank-verse framework; but these portraits owe their existence in part to the wit, the fluency, the mastery of rhythm and syntax that occur in the prose of the two antecedent works.[9]

The Jules and Phene episode of *Pippa* is developed in two long monologues of the lovers, a short intervening song of Pippa, and again in a rather lengthy concluding monologue of Jules; apart from their very length the lovers' speeches indicate progress in the direction of the dramatic monologue—and progress in the poet's ability to portray character—in their demonstrations of contrasting techniques. Jules' diction, for example, is rich in terms common to the study of sculpture and in slightly unusual, almost inventive compounds suggestive of the original and creative mind of the young artist: *swart-green, bay-filleted, thunder-free, soft-rinded, patron-ghosts.* Phene's diction is contrastingly simple; it abounds in little monosyllabic parts of speech: [10]

> —even you perhaps
> Cannot take up, now you have once let fall,
> The music's life, and me along with it?

9. The speeches of Naddo in *Sordello* (a poem which was being revised in 1839 prior to publication in March 1840) do suggest an attempt on Browning's part to achieve rapidity and wit within the framework of the pentameter line. But Naddo's wit is not of the sustained kind: he expresses himself in short syntactical bursts that reinforce his argument, as it were, from many directions, but he does not elaborate fluently and wittily on any one stated theme.

10. Statistically, of her first one hundred words (contained in her first twelve lines of speech), eighty-two are monosyllabic, and only two are words of more than two syllables—the twice occurring name of the students' intermediary, *Natalia.* See *Pippa Passes,* II, 116–27.

No—or you would . . we'll stay then as we are
Above the world—[11]

There are parallel contrasts in the syntax and imagery of the two
characters: Jules' sentences are frequently interrupted by what
amount to parenthetical descriptions and elaborations of his
thought in which he draws upon nature and his classical studies
to form vivid word pictures, whereas Phene's sentences are more
often simple ones, and her imagistic effects, as it were, unconscious, arising from her rather plain telling of the events that have
led her to Jules. Phene's portrait, technically, represents a step
in the direction of Pompilia's, and Jules' self-characterizing discussion of his art has a relationship to much of the matter and
technique of the monologues of Andrea, Lippo, and Cleon.

Modes of thought, as instruments of character revelation, are
used effectively in many instances of *Pippa*—where characters are
constantly presented as reacting to specific events in ways that contrast profoundly and ironically. The ironic contrast of two very
divergent lines of thought upon the same issue helps to reveal
Luigi and his mother in Part III, for example. The issue at hand
is Luigi's role as a would-be assassin. Luigi, in a fervor of patriotism, is certain that his attempt to kill his Italian tyrant is morally
right. Desperately anxious to save her son, the Mother attempts
to view the project through her son's eyes—and the very diver-
gence of her line of reasoning from the tenor of her feelings is
revealing of the enormous effort she makes to stop Luigi, and
thus of her love for him. Her argument is casuistical:

> *Mother.*   Well you shall go. If patriotism were not
> The easiest virtue for a selfish man
> To acquire! he loves himself—and then, the world—
> If he must love beyond, but nought between:
>
> .   .   .   .
>
> Once more, your ground for killing him!—then go![12]

And the quality of thought in Luigi's reply reveals Luigi:

> *Luigi.*   Now do you ask me, or make sport of me?
> How first the Austrians got these provinces—

11. Ibid., II, 125–29.
12. Ibid., III, 124–27, 133.

(If that is all, I'll satisfy you soon)
. . . Never by warfare but by treaty, for
That treaty whereby . . .
    Mother.   Well?
    Luigi.   (Sure he's arrived—
The tell-tale cuckoo—spring's his confidant,
And he lets out her April purposes!)
Or . . better go at once to modern times—
He has . . they have . . in fact I understand
But can't re-state the matter; that's my boast;
Others could reason it out to you, and prove
Things they have made me feel.[13]

Luigi's muddled grasp of political realities suggests his immaturity and his central motivation as well: he does not think, but he feels passionately. Even the merry note of the cuckoo distracts him from his explanation. Nevertheless, he is ingenuously clever enough to make the most of his political ignorance: the fact that he cannot "reason it out" is his "boast"—proof of the quality of his feeling, which triumphs over his mother's casuistry and (with Pippa's help later in the scene) leads him off to his martyrdom.

Part IV of *Pippa* is presented in a prose that differs markedly from the prose that has come before it. "Maffeo," the Monsignor tells his Intendant at one point,

> the sword we quiet men spurn away, you shrewd knaves pick up and commit murders with; what opportunities the virtuous forego, the villanous seize. Because, to pleasure myself, apart from other considerations, my food would be millet-cake, my dress sackcloth, and my couch straw, am I therefore to let the off-scouring of the earth seduce the ignorant by appropriating a pomp these will be sure to think lessens the abominations so unaccountably and exclusively associated with it? . . . No . . . if my cough would but allow me to speak! [14]

The Monsignor is Browning's first portrait of a type of character that was to occur often in the monologues: the intensely spiritual

13. Ibid., III, 134–45.
14. Ibid., IV, 117–31.

and intensely worldly man, whose unfailing interest lies in the conflict and uncertain adjustment of two opposing personality traits. The Monsignor's self-indulging days are largely past, for he is dying and has, as he tells Maffeo, "whole centuries of sin to redeem, and only a month or two of life to do it in." But his worldliness is still with him; it is suggested in the very lack of anger and indignation in the speech above. He understands very well the "murderer and thief" whom he addresses, half sympathizes with him (at least until Pippa sings), and the balanced and slow development of his sentences helps to express not only his cool intellectuality but, in the context above, his easy tolerance of evil—as represented by Maffeo; his ominous cough is more irritating to him than the machinations of the Intendant, and the cough alone arouses impatience. His thought tends to the abstract and universal. The Monsignor has just informed Maffeo that he will not let him have a *soldo* of his possessions—even in the face of bribery. Now a generalizing image reinforces the thought: "the sword we quiet men spurn away, you shrewd knaves pick up and commit murders with . . ." In the next balanced clause the thought is further generalized and abstracted: "what opportunities the virtuous forego, the villanous seize." With the abstraction fully developed, the Monsignor, true to the worldly element in his character, now illustrates his point through the enumeration of concrete and minute details: "millet-cake," "sackcloth," a "couch" of "straw"—he has a vivid appreciation of the humble things he would pleasure himself with, supposedly, were it not his responsibility to keep the power of his wealth from falling into evil hands. His deprecation of Maffeo, "the off-scouring of the earth," suggests a momentary glint of anger on behalf of "the ignorant" whom Maffeo would seduce; but the sentence terminates in wording and phrasing that reveal his basically cool, intellectual detachment: Maffeo would seduce the ignorant, he goes on to say, "by appropriating a pomp these will be sure to think lessens the abominations so unaccountably and exclusively associated with it." Diction and syntax combine in this case to reflect thought processes and attitudes which in turn reveal character.

The creation of figures such as Luigi, his Mother, and the

Monsignor in *Pippa* provided opportunities for Browning to work out ways of using thought and attitude in relation to character that would be of enormous use later on in the casuistical and ironical monologues.

Most importantly, the structure of *Pippa* was such that no one character in it—save the omnipresent Pippa herself—was to be presented through a succession of scenes. *Pippa* necessitated condensation of effect. Luigi, the Monsignor, Ottima, and the rest had to be fully characterized in single bursts of verse and prose. Many means of characterization—diction, syntax, imagery, rhythm, sound quality, thought—had to achieve their effects in the shortest space possible; inevitably, in *Pippa,* the minutiae of technique became vital to the success of the work. The structure of the stage plays had militated against the importance of minutiae, so that whether or not a particular rhythmic sequence or an image served to delineate character at a particular moment was of small importance in terms of many lines and scenes to be dealt with; *Colombe* was scarcely better as a play for its brilliant use of sound to help suggest the delicacy of Colombe's character. *Pippa* was a radical experiment that did not quite succeed as an entity in itself, for Pippa's function in connecting the scenes has the unfortunate effect of adding a touch of the contrived and the ridiculous whenever and wherever her miracle-effecting song is heard.[15] But

15. One cannot deny the psychological truth of the idea that casually spoken words may in some cases have an unexpected influence upon the lives of individuals. But the coincidence of Pippa's greatly altering many different lives in this manner on the same day is a considerable one. Moreover, the changes brought about by Pippa occur with unconvincing and almost ludicrous abruptness; her simple words cause character after character to see complex truth in a flash. Consider, e.g., Sebald's sudden realization:

> That little peasant's voice
> Has righted all again. Though I be lost,
> I know which is the better, never fear,
> Of vice or virtue, purity or lust,
> Nature, or trick—I see what I have done,
> Entirely now!   (*Pippa Passes,* I, 261–66)

Still, excellent commentators have defended Browning's use of Pippa in this respect. See, e.g., G. K. Chesterton, *Robert Browning* (London, 1903), pp. 43–45 for a statement of the opposite case. The usually accurate DeVane errs in concluding that Chesterton criticized the coincidence of Pippa's singing at critical moments in a number of lives; Chesterton merely criticized Browning's having the

Pippa succeeded as no other dramatic work of Browning had before; its verse and prose are highly wrought; individual lines commonly achieve many objects at once; different techniques are used coordinately to help reveal the speaking character. Portraits such as those of Ottima and Sebald and the Monsignor are fully satisfying in themselves. And yet in *Pippa's* contribution to the dramatic monologues may lie its chief significance, for in no other work before its time did Browning learn so much about the use of prosodic and linguistic techniques to portray character. In no other work had he used thought so unerringly and with such condensation that it had the immediate effect of characterizing the speaker who uttered it. And in no other work had he come closer to the form that would most truly exploit his genius: in de-emphasizing the structure of the stage play, with its many scenes and reappearing characters, in placing a premium upon the use of economically interweaving, harmonizing, mutually reinforcing techniques of character revelation, and in emphasizing in its special dramatic form the minutiae of artistry rather than the large lines of stage action, *Pippa Passes* opened up a new horizon.

A Soul's Tragedy

No present-day reader of Browning's letters to Elizabeth Barrett can fail to sympathize with Professor Lounsbury in his comment upon the poet's expressed attitude toward *A Soul's Tragedy*. Browning despised that dramatic poem and thought more of *Luria*, Lounsbury wrote, true to "the tendency he exhibited to prefer his poorest work to his best." [16]

That Browning did think little of *A Soul's Tragedy* is clear from his very first reference to it in the letters as a work that would not "do" to end the *Bells and Pomegranates* series.[17] And a year later, in February 1846, he informed Miss Barrett that it was "all

Monsignor and Maffeo in the last part discuss a plan touching the fate of Pippa. Apart from this detail, Chesterton's argument seems to be the most vigorous defense of the structural device of Pippa to date. In my own opinion it is an argument that does not stand up under the objection stated above.

16. Thomas R. Lounsbury, *The Early Literary Career of Robert Browning* (London, 1912), p. 148.

17. *Letters of R.B. and E.B.B.*, *1*, 26; RB to EBB, February 26, 1845.

sneering and *disillusion"* and that it would "not be printed but burned if you say the word." [18] In his next letter he explained in more detail his reasons for not wanting the work published right away:

> Two nights ago I read the "Soul's Tragedy" once more, and though there were not a few points which still struck me as successful in design and execution, yet on the whole I came to a decided opinion, that it will be better to postpone the publication of it for the present. It is not a good ending, an auspicious wind-up of this series; subject-matter and style are alike unpopular even for the literary *grex* . . .[19]

One suspects that among the "points" in "design and execution" that Browning felt would in no way hinder the work's reception were the small, brilliant bit of stage action at the end of Part I (where Chiappino changes clothes with Luitolfo and faces what he thinks to be a murderous Faenzan crowd) and the rather Falstaffian prose of Ogniben in Part II. The melodrama of the one and the rich humor of the other are immediately impressive. But Browning's reservations about the "subject-matter and style" of the whole are not without a certain justice and significance. In these matters *A Soul's Tragedy* differs rather surprisingly from any of the dramas or dramatic poems written before it and suggests a new step—beyond *Pippa* and toward the dramatic monologues in Browning's treatment of character.

The "subject-matter" of the work is essentially the character of Chiappino and the artistic aim behind it is clearly that which was behind *Paracelsus*, the dramatic work which in form it most nearly resembles. Browning is still interested in avoiding the external machinery of incidents of the ordinary drama, and in portraying the "mood" of a single character in its apparent "progress." [20] If *Paracelsus'* chief failure is that the mood-glimpses the reader has of the hero are too far removed from each other in time and event to produce a coherent impression of character and so widely spaced that details of background—the few that Browning

18. Ibid., p. 470; RB to EBB, February 11, 1846.
19. Ibid., p. 474; RB to EBB, February 13, 1846.
20. See the preface to *Paracelsus* (1835).

includes—are not sufficient to clarify each "scene," *A Soul's Trag-edy* remedies the fault by being more selective in its scope. Chiap-pino's "mood" is shown at two intervals in his life instead of five.[21] Moreover, the two intervals are separated by only one month, and the situation in the second interval is a direct outcome of the situation in the first. In this, the form of *A Soul's Tragedy* is a development from the forms of *Paracelsus,* the stage plays, and *Pippa*—taking something from each. *Paracelsus* had set the prec-edent of showing character at separate, near-crisis intervals; the stage plays had demonstrated the value of having some dramatic connection between the intervals; and *Pippa* had suggested the value of a structure which did not require a protracted presenta-tion of character through a succession of scenes. *Pippa's* contribu-tion to the new form is the least obvious, perhaps, because Chiap-pino does appear in two separate scenes—so that the only true synthesis of the *Pippa,* stage-play, and *Paracelsus* forms might seem to be the dramatic monologue form itself. But this is not quite so. *A Soul's Tragedy* presents, in effect, very nearly two com-plete Chiappinos. To a remarkable extent the portraits of Parts I and II have an independent existence; they have the effect of two fully wrought dramatic monologues about the same person, an effect most nearly paralleled in the two monologues of Guido in *The Ring and the Book.* Part I reveals Chiappino at the nadir of his life, when he has no hope for the future and nothing to lose, and Part II represents him in just the opposite condition, successful, powerful, having risen to the peak of fortune—and the second portrait is an incisively ironical commentary upon the first. Yet each part of *A Soul's Tragedy* involves a full exploitation of the moment at hand to reveal the very springs of character. The vital difference between this dramatic poem and all of the dramatic monologues, save Guido's two, is not that other char-acters (Eulalia, Luitolfo, Ogniben, and some of the Faenzan populace) speak to Chiappino, for their speeches are not of funda-mental importance in revealing his character, but that Chiappino

21. They are explained and introduced with the words, "PART FIRST, BEING WHAT WAS CALLED THE POETRY OF CHIAPPINO'S LIFE: AND PART SECOND, ITS PROSE." See *A Soul's Tragedy,* p. 23. My citations from *A Soul's Tragedy* and *Luria* are to the unnumbered texts in Robert Browning, *Bells and Pomegranates. No. VIII. And Last. Luria; and A Soul's Tragedy,* London, 1846.

is only entirely revealed through the presentation of two dissimilar situations. The dramatic monologues represent a final perfection of character-revealing form, made possible by the perfection of character-revealing techniques, in the condensation and complexity of situation, where, in each case, a single setting is so carefully selected and expertly rendered that it is sufficient to help reveal all one needs to know about a character. Having read *Fra Lippo Lippi* one might predict with some accuracy how Lippo would act in almost any given set of circumstances; a second monologue of the Florentine monk would contain no fundamental surprises about his character.

In subject matter and form, then, *A Soul's Tragedy* is at once a continuation and a synthesis of Browning's earlier dramatic experiments, and a single, small step away from his personal discovery of and concentration upon the form of the dramatic monologue itself.

The subject matter of *A Soul's Tragedy* would seem to have dictated its form, and its form would seem to have dictated its style. Its style represents some progress in Browning's perfection of character-revealing techniques and particularly justifies the poet's fear that the work would not be well-received even by the "literary *grex*" of his time—insofar as that fear was based upon the presence of certain innovations.

The poetry of Chiappino's life often seems to reveal its speaker's mind at the expense of easy comprehension for the reader; in the rapidity of its associations and in its reflection of mental operations it seems, at certain points, to anticipate Joyce's stream-of-consciousness technique.[22] "I've spoke," Chiappino tells Eulalia in Part I, for example,

> my mind too fully out, for once,
> This morning to our Provost; so ere night
> I leave the city on pain of death—and now
> On my account there's gallant intercession
> Goes forward—that's so graceful!—and anon

22. Cf., e.g., the excerpt above with Marian Bloom's unpunctuated reverie at the end of *Ulysses*—a passage in Joyce often cited as an illustration of the stream-of-consciousness method; the resemblance is particularly striking in those places where Joyce employs a series of short clauses linked by simple coordinating conjunctions.

He'll noisily come back: the intercession
Was made and fails—all's over for us both—
'Tis vain contending—I had better go:
And I do go—and so to you he turns
Light of a load, and ease of that permits
His visage to repair its natural bland
Œconomy, sore broken late to suit
My discontent: so all are pleased—you, with him,
He with himself, and all of you with me
—Who, say the citizens, had done far better
In letting people sleep upon their woes,
If not possessed with talent to relieve them
When once they woke;—but then I had, they'll say,
Doubtless some unknown compensating pride
In what I did—and as I seem content
With ruining myself, why so should they be,
And so they are, and so be with his prize
The devil when he gets them speedily! [23]

The passage is clear, if taken slowly, despite the quickness of its associations and the very length of it as a single period. It is composed of short phrases and, for the most part, independent clauses, joined by dashes and monosyllabic conjunctives (*and, but, so,* and in one case a relative, *who*), which speed the movement, so that the utterance seems to be a quickly moving mosaic of more or less independent parts. With considerable economy the lines sketch in dramatic background and outline what Chiappino is thinking. But they also reveal Chiappino's attitude toward what he is thinking and through this the condition of his mind. Chiappino, after being fined and reprimanded on several occasions for casual political agitation, has overstepped himself this morning in taunting the Provost and so has been banished from Faenza; his friend Luitolfo has gone to the Provost to intercede. In recounting the incident Chiappino reveals at once his conviction of its outcome, his attitude toward the principal figures involved, his outlook on life, and his psychological condition. For, unavoidably (he thinks) Luitolfo will come back feigning despair over

23. *A Soul's Tragedy,* I, 207–29.

the failure of his mission but really delighted to be rid of Chiappino now and free to enjoy his happiness with Eulalia; Eulalia will in turn be pleased with Luitolfo's honorable handling of the situation, which will in turn cause Luitolfo to be pleased with himself; the lovers will be happy for Chiappino as well, because he will then enjoy a fate deliberately courted to gratify his own pride; and the Faenzan populace will be content with the whole situation because it will seem to them that Chiappino has achieved happiness in ruining himself—similar to their own achievement of happiness under the humiliation of a dictatorial Provost; and the devil will be happy, too, when he gets them all—as he will —for the whole town has sold its soul. The thought is one thought, for Chiappino. It is expressed in one chain-like sentence, made up of short vivid clauses and phrases that follow one another, as it were, in links, inexorably. The consequences of his own heroic act are immediately clear—for Chiappino views his best friend, the woman he loves, and the world at large in the same way, with lightly detached cynicism. There is no real complexity in this world; no one entity is subordinate to another; all of its citizens are easily predictable, and as they are, events are predictable, too. The easy and rapid enumeration of supposed consequences that are, in fact, complex in themselves and universal in their implications, suggests here the light-hearted cynic; the lack of special grammatical emphasis in their enumeration reveals the man who looks on all things as one—who is uninvolved with life, either above or below the level of worldly hope or caring.

The speech is unique among those that have been examined so far because its first concern is with the revelation of the speaker's character. It contains information necessary to the reader in understanding the dramatic situation of *A Soul's Tragedy;* but its situation-informing function is less important than its character-revealing one, which necessitated the presentation of diverse details of background and event in a form which in no way emphasizes those details. The details instead help to reveal character in the special way that they are introduced. In the great dramatic monologues, details that establish situation do not give the *effect* of being subordinated to character portrayal; and a comparison of those monologues with *A Soul's Tragedy* indicates the weakness of the present work—and incidentally suggests one reason why it has never been among Browning's most popular. One must read far into Part I before one comes across those details of background that make Eulalia's and Chiappino's speeches intelligible and meaningful, and one must read closely even so, for necessary details tend to be imbedded in speeches which do not adequately emphasize them. The contrary may be seen in a monologue such as *The Bishop at St. Praxed,* where the situation seems to be fully established in the title and the first few opening lines of the poem.[24]

The "Prose" of Chiappino's life introduces the formidable comic figure of Ogniben, who may be said to represent an aspect of Chiappino's own character—to be, in one sense, the supremely worldly, practical, cynically wise worshiper of power that Chiappino may one day fully become; his presence is instrumental in completing the dramatic action; but Ogniben is not essential to an understanding of Chiappino's character as it appears in the "Prose" for in his own speeches Chiappino completes his self-revelation, as when he confesses to Eulalia:

> I had despaired of what you may call the material instrumentality of Life; of ever being able to rightly operate on mankind thro' such a deranged machinery as the existing modes of government—but now, if I suddenly discover how to inform these perverted institutions with fresh purpose, bring the functionary limbs once more into immediate communication with, and subjection to the soul I am about to bestow on them . . . do you see? [25]

Chiappino's previous opinion of government had been dictated by his vague but purely cynical outlook upon life in general: all modes of government were "deranged machinery." Now, all but formally installed as Provost himself, he attempts to remold his old notions into a formula that will justify his assuming an absolute power he had once decried. He begins by rhetorically linking the idea of mechanization with the world itself, "the material instrumentality of Life," from which point he ascribes to the "machinery" of government "functionary limbs" and an all-powerful "soul," which he himself will install to govern the whole

24. See below, p. 129.
25. *A Soul's Tragedy,* II, 228–37.

apparatus. The union produces a false image, that of a machine
with human limbs and a soul, which not only suggests the im-
possibility of the reforms he envisages but reveals the deteriora-
tion of his own character—he, too, has become perverted through
a compromise which has sacrificed the truth. He has lacked mettle
all along, in fact; his heroism in Part I was inspired by boredom,
not vision; he is the lazy opportunist, not the principled revolu-
tionary. And after Ogniben's entry several speeches later, Chiappino, now aware of his own motivations, is able to cast off the role
of political reformer—a role he had half believed in himself—and
scheme, as far as he is permitted, for the power that he hopes to
win through Ogniben's sanction. Browning's use of false imagery
is more fully developed in monologues such as *Mr. Sludge, Prince
Hohenstiel-Schwangau,* and the Guido and Bottini sections of
The Ring and the Book; but in Chiappino's prose may be seen
its early examples. Chiappino's diction in Part II is formal and
pretentious in contrast to his diction in Part I; the short, simple
substantives and adjectives of the verse passage quoted are ironically paralleled in the almost equal frequency of trisyllabic and
polysyllabic nouns and qualifiers in the prose above: *material instrumentality, machinery, government, perverted institutions,
functionary, immediate communication,* and *subjection*—a contrast all the more revealing of duplicity as these words are addressed to the same audience of Eulalia alone.

   In the two settings in which he is presented Chiappino comes
to life as no previous figure of Browning's had outside *Pippa Passes,*
and he is probably at least as fully revealed as Pippa herself, Ottima,
Sebald, and the Monsignor. It remained for the poet to concentrate upon a blank-verse form that would exploit his already well-
developed techniques of character delineation to the utmost by
providing a framework that would demand an even greater degree of intensity in their application.

Luria

   "Domizia is all wrong; I told you I knew that her special colour
had faded . . . I will try and remember what my whole character
did mean—it was, in two words, understood at the time by 'pan-
ther's-beauty'—on which hint I ought to have spoken! But the

work grew cold, and you came between, and the sun put out the fire on the hearth *nec vult panthera domari!"*

Thus Browning wrote to Elizabeth Barrett on February 11, 1846 [26] of the character of Domizia and *Luria*—a tragedy largely composed between October 27, 1845 and January 22, 1846.[27] During this three-month interval the twenty-four page pamphlet *Dramatic Romances and Lyrics,* seventh of the *Bells and Pomegranates* series, was published, and among the twenty-one poems that it contained was a blank-verse dramatic monologue entitled *The Tomb at St. Praxed's.*[28] *Luria* was written after the poet's perfection of the character-revealing dramatic monologue—after the writing of one of its finest examples—but the tragedy is of some interest in the present study for its illumination of Browning's dramatic strengths and weaknesses, and it may be considered briefly before a survey of character technique in the monologues themselves.

The character of Domizia seemed "all wrong" to Browning in February and, despite probable alterations made during the two months before *Luria's* publication in April 1846,[29] Domizia emerges in the tragedy as one of the most shadowy, unconvincing portraits in all of the poet's dramatic work. Fairly typified by the following extract from her sixty-line address to Luria in Act IV,

> —Inconsciously to the augustest end
> Thou hast arisen: second not to him
> In rank so much as time, who first ordained
> That Florence thou art to destroy, should be—
> Yet him a star, too, guided, who broke first
> The pride of lonely power, the life apart,
> And made the eminences, each to each,
> Lean o'er the level world and let it lie
> Safe from the thunder henceforth 'neath their arms—
> So the few famous men of old combined,

26. *Letters of R.B. and E.B.B., 1,* 470.

27. DeVane, *Handbook,* pp. 185–87.

28. The pamphlet appeared on November 6, 1845; the title of the monologue mentioned was changed to *The Bishop Orders his Tomb at St. Praxed's Church* for the collected edition of 1849. DeVane, *Handbook,* pp. 150, 166–67.

29. Ibid., p. 184.

And let the multitude rise underneath,
And reach them and unite . . . ,[30]

Domizia's speeches lack dramatic immediacy and display uses of diction, syntax and imagery that in no sense serve to distinguish her character.[31] Her portrait seems rivaled in ineptitude only by those of several other figures in the tragedy, Braccio and Husain, in particular. Braccio speaks in passages of up to eighty-one lines in length, which, while lucid, are remarkable in their almost un-exampled prosiness and lack of human interest. Husain, the Moor-ish friend of Luria, seems to hover through the drama like a ghost: he has no stated occupation, office, duty or function in Luria's army, no place of residence, no past and apparently no future. He seems to be merely a faintly embodied essence of Luria: "Oh, friend, oh, lord—for me, / What am I?—I was silent at thy side / That am a part of thee . . ." (IV, 155–57). And yet one does not feel that Husain, Braccio or Domizia represent any significant element in Luria's make-up or that, in the manner of Festus and Michal in *Paracelsus,* they stand for alternate attitudes existing in the hero's mind. Instead, the supporting characters seem to be little more than arbitrary, mechanical devices created for the sole purpose of bringing to light Luria's nobleness; their portraits are so insufficient and unconvincing in themselves that they hardly begin to suggest the presence of living people around Luria.

But the work fails because Luria himself is unconvincing. If

30. *Luria,* IV, 199–210.

31. E.g. the awkward *inconsciously* and *augustest* of the first line might seem to convey pomposity or dryness—but their momentary effect is not reinforced by that of other words in the passage, so that diction in this case does not seem to characterize the speaker but only to be awkward in itself. Syntactically, the passage is so complex that it departs from normal speech patterns. The imagery is con-fused, and the confusion *itself* is not sufficiently clear or striking to help char-acterize the speaker in the way that "false imagery" may; see below, pp. 203–6. One of the founders of Florence, guided by a star, caused other "eminences"—strong individuals—to "lean o'er the level world" in order to protect the spot from "thunder" so that the masses below might "rise underneath" to form the city of Florence. Figuratively, a star indirectly causes tall men to lean together so that thunder will not reach a great number of tiny, rapidly growing men, who will soon reach the height of their tall leaders and thus form a city. The image is very nearly ridiculous when analyzed; but when read in context it is simply vague, complex and rather unintelligible, so that it fails to produce any impression of character.

Browning had succeeded in writing effective speeches for the Florentine general—speeches even very remotely approximating those of Othello, for example—*Luria* would certainly be an important work in a unique dramatic form. The difficulty is that in this form all is dependent upon the success of the hero's own portrait; all six of the minor characters would, in one sense, fulfill their artistic functions if Luria fulfilled his, and the result in that case would be interesting. But Luria is nothing more than a caricature of Othello at best; he seems poorly conceived and even more poorly drawn.[32] His musings are filled with abstractions that seem unrelated to the events at hand; his feelings are not highly typical of him. In their expression, his lines are unsatisfactory, for diction, imagery, rhythm, and sound are not used in them to typify him. He comes to life in his few rather short replies, as when, responding to Tiburzio's attempt to wheedle him from Florence on the grounds of his being a foreigner, he flings back:

> Sir, I am nearer Florence than her sons.[33]

But even these lines do not have the energy, pertinence, and character-revealing effect of Othello's,

> Keep up your bright swords, for the dew will rust them.[34]

And they are small relief amid many long speeches which do not bear the stamp of their speaker's individuality.

The strengths of *Luria* are in its very occasional lines that re-

---

32. It seems clear that Browning drew on *Othello*—unconsciously or not—as his chief inspiration for the portrait of a hero he had never quite taken into his own heart. See his confession of difficulty with *Luria* to Elizabeth Barrett in *Letters of R.B. and E.B.B.*, I, 26 (Feb. 26, 1845). The resemblances—as well as the differences—between *Othello* and *Luria* have been rather fully discussed by G. R. Elliott, Lounsbury, and DeVane, and incidentally remarked upon by others. See G. R. Elliott, "Shakespeare's Significance for Browning," *Anglia*, 32 (1909), 127–32; Thomas R. Lounsbury, *The Early Literary Career of Robert Browning* (London, 1912), pp. 68–71; and DeVane, *Handbook*, p. 188. DeVane cites Elliott and Lounsbury in his own summarizing discussion. See also, e.g., C. Willard Smith, *Browning's Star-Imagery* (Princeton, 1941), p. 130. These discussions make clear Browning's considerable indebtedness to the character of Othello for his own Luria—an indebtedness that is generally evident to anyone familiar with Browning's play.

33. *Luria*, II, 166.

34. *Othello*, I, ii, 59.

veal a use of detail typical of *The Bishop at St. Praxed,* for example. Significantly, these lines are not to be found in Luria's speeches but in those of Lapo and Puccio, the least important characters in the play. The details do not serve to reveal the speaker, in most of these cases, but to reveal Luria himself, as when Lapo tells Braccio how the general

> rests sometimes,—
> I see him stand and eat, sleep stretched an hour
> On the lynx-skins, yonder; hold his bared black arms
> Into the sun from the tent-opening; laugh
> When his horse drops the forage from his teeth
> And neighs to hear him hum his Moorish songs:
> That man believes in Florence as the Saint
> Tied to the wheel believes in God! [35]

Lines of this quality are rare in *Luria.* And the tragedy is certainly more interesting for its evidence of Browning's dedication to the monologue form—in its unusual dramatic emphasis upon one character, in the near-evaporation of its supporting cast, and in the fact that most of Luria's long speeches are concerned with innermost feelings and thoughts and less with a tragic action that only very slowly and incidentally unfolds in the play. Browning felt that *Luria* grew cold in the process of composition because Elizabeth Barrett "came between" and was the sun that put out the fire on the hearth. Figuratively, too, it was perhaps the perfection of a new form—a form which utilized to the full the techniques of character revelation slowly developed through many dramatic experiments—that appeared like a sun in Browning's art in the early 1840's and put out the little hearth-fire attempts of his plays.

35. *Luria,* I, 102-9.

4. The Solitary Voice

The Problem of the Dramatic Monologue

It is by no means uncommon in reading twentieth-century criticism of the dramatic monologue to encounter a certain critical apology or a complaint—often to the effect that very little of value has been written about the dramatic monologue.[1] One of the functions of the present chapter will be to examine the sources of this complaint in some detail; in fact, it may be well to cite a rather provoking remark at the outset. "All the books dealing with classifications and systems of the arts could be burned without any loss whatever. (We say this with the utmost respect to the writers who have expended their labours upon them.)" The remark is doubly provoking here: it cannot be easily ignored, for it comes from Benedetto Croce,[2] and yet unless it is either ignored or very successfully attacked it suggests that a chapter dealing with the dramatic monologues as a class will have very little to say.

There would be no problem, perhaps, if one were able to think of Browning's dramatic monologues as being fundamentally similar in effect to typical monologues of, let us say, Marlowe, Donne, Burns, or Wordsworth. For if it seems fairly clear that poems such as *The Passionate Shepherd, The Flea, Holy Willie's Prayer,* and *The Complaint of a Forsaken Indian Woman,* represent in common the poet's assumption of a voice or a character not quite his own in presenting the poem, it is also clear that no great injustice is committed in any critic's decision to treat

1. E.g. a discussion of the dramatic monologue in the latest full-length study of the form begins: "Writers on the dramatic monologue never fail to remark how little has been written on the subject—and I shall be no exception." Robert Langbaum, *The Poetry of Experience: The Dramatic Monologue in Modern Literary Tradition* (New York, 1957), p. 75. Langbaum's study itself will be discussed below.

2. See *Aesthetic as Science of Expression and General Linguistic,* trans. Douglas Ainslie (London, 1909), p. 188.

these poems as lyrics. In each case the poet has, in T. S. Eliot's words, "put on the costume and make-up" [3] of a character other than his own—to a varying degree, for we may imagine that John Donne's own personality and outlook are closer to that of the speaker in *The Flea* than Wordsworth's are to that of his Indian squaw. Nevertheless, these four poems may be thought of as lyrical; they are more expressive of the poet's own feeling than of outward incidents or events, and they do not cause the reader to suspend his awareness of the writer's own presence (as he does in reading a play) and to imagine that someone else is really speaking. Presumably Croce would not object to a literary classification so broad and so old as that of "the lyric"; even if he would, the critic might well dismiss the objection on the grounds that the lyrical classification itself in the history of literary criticism has been responsible for very few critical atrocities. That is, the labeling of poems as "lyrics" and the investigation of them as "lyrics" has in itself rarely if ever throttled discussion of them in any way or produced initial premisses so wrongheaded that the critic has been led from the start into discussions detrimental to the general understanding and appreciation of given poems. But it is not so with classifications and definitions of the dramatic monologue; the very term "dramatic monologue" does not seem to occur in criticism before the latter part of the nineteenth century,[4] and it is only recently that suggestions were first made—largely with Browning's rather than with Tennyson's or anyone else's work in mind—that it was time to consider the existence of a new poetic class similar to but distinct from that of the lyric.

Before approaching these suggestions, and the attempts to define and to classify the dramatic monologue, it may be well to consider the looming relevance of Croce's objection: that it is not worth-while to consider the arts—in this case poetry—in terms of any but the broadest and most general of classifications.

3. The metaphor occurs in a discussion of the dramatic monologue but without reference to the particular poems that I have cited. See T. S. Eliot, *On Poetry and Poets* (London, 1957), p. 95.

4. Arthur Lyttelton used the expression "dramatic monologues" in "Mr. Browning's Poems," *Church Quarterly Review*, 7 (Oct. 1878), 73. I have not been able to discover an earlier occurrence of it in the nineteenth century. If used before Lyttelton, it was certainly not used frequently.

The objection is so fundamental that it suggests a consideration of the nature of classification itself. Are *all* systems of classification to be burned, for example? Presumably Croce would
not extend his criticism to the sciences. We know that certain
values are to be gained in botany by classifying blooms: in sys-
tematically grouping or segregating them according to their relationships with one another the botanist acquires insights into
the nature of individual flowers. Few have quarreled with the
botanist. The classification of human beings, on the other hand,
brings to light difficulties which display the limits—even, to a
degree, the undesirability—of classification schemes. Due to the
enormous variety and complexity of individuals, we may say that
human beings are, ultimately, unclassifiable; many separate, often
overlapping and often totally unrelated classification systems do
exist and are useful; but no physiological or sociological or an-
thropological scheme can be expected to describe, to account for,
or to classify the whole man. More important, no one system of
human classification may take precedence over all the rest—as
being in any sense more important, more just, more comprehensive than certain others. For example, we may classify men according to race, or to the work they do, or (with difficulty) to intelligence. But if we were somehow able to proclaim forcefully that
the intelligence of a man represented his fundamental distinction
from other men and was the "correct" setting in which to begin
any discussion of humankind whatever, we would in fact limit
and discourage a good deal of valuable investigation and discussion. Similarly, Croce's objection to "classifications and systems of
the arts" will be seen to be justified insofar as any classification or
definition tends to delimit or to discourage criticism and appreciation that might otherwise be elicited by a work of art. In other
words, the attempt to segregate permanently two or more works
of art into any labeled category will defeat its own intention—that
of increasing our understanding of an individual work—if the
category tends to stress an aspect of the work that is not indis-
putably of prime importance to its being. The difficulty involved
with the defining and classifying of the dramatic monologue is that
a good deal of uncertainty has existed and still does exist as to
what the essence of the dramatic monologue may be. Anyone who

proposes a new system of classification, moreover, does so at the risk of adding an irrelevancy to Browning criticism not only useless in itself but—worse—damaging to the appreciation and understanding of the poems themselves. Fortunately, as we shall see, many attempts to define and to classify Browning's monologues have been so plainly far-fetched and arbitrary that they have influenced neither criticism nor, presumably, general appreciation. The danger is that as classification systems become more elaborate, carefully detailed, and documented with select illustrations, they have a more compelling effect on the imagination of critic and interested reader alike, and so are apt to become pernicious.

The convention of writing lyrical poems from the point of view of an assumed personality came into the nineteenth century without marked critical comment. An enormous number of works written in this convention had already appeared in English, and the convention itself had been adopted by poets as different from one another as Skelton, Lovelace, Donne, Swift, and Pope.[5] No important literary critic had seen fit to remark at length upon the convention as such, or to separate or categorize poems written within its rather unexacting limits. In the Romantic period an increased use of the convention is evident; Mrs. Felicia Hemans, for example, became probably the most prolific writer ever to use the form of the poetic monologue before Browning, and in producing many bad examples of it may be said to have adopted the form as her own.[6] Both Wordsworth and Byron had experimented significantly with the convention, and Wordsworth had, with *The Complaint of a Forsaken Indian Woman,* produced a rather elaborate

5. See, e.g., poems such as Skelton's *The Boke of Phyllyp Sparowe,* Lovelace's *A Forsaken Lady to Her False Servant,* Donne's *The Flea,* Swift's *The Humble Petition of Frances Harris,* and Pope's *Eloïsa to Abelard.*

6. Fuson found, in a survey of a very large number of poems, including one thousand "monologic" works written by almost one hundred poets during 1790–1840, that Mrs. Hemans wrote more "objective monologs" than any other pre-Victorian poet, and that among these poems were "some of the worst specimens extant." Benjamin Willis Fuson, *Browning and His English Predecessors in the Dramatic Monolog* (Iowa City, 1948), pp. 9–10, 82. That Mrs. Hemans produced many bad poems in the monologue convention may be seen from the examination of works such as her *The Soldier's Deathbed, The Dying Bard's Prophecy, Ivan the Czar,* and others, which lack concentration of effect and are in texture almost indistinguishable from one another—and this, despite the fact that they are composed in different meters.

explanation of his poem's setting and background in the form of a prefatory note to it.[7] Tennyson seems to have been the first Victorian poet to call critical attention to the convention itself through the use of certain titles that specially emphasized the nature of it: *Will Waterproof's Lyrical Monologue,* and *Maud; A Monodrama;* and as Browning, at about the same time, was publishing collections entitled *Dramatic Lyrics, Dramatic Romances and Lyrics,* and *Dramatis Personae,* it would seem likely that the terms "dramatic" and "monologue" were first combined from hints in these and Tennyson's titles.[8] The epithet "dramatic monologue" did not come into very common use until the twentieth century and never seems to have been used by Browning himself. Nevertheless, beginning in the late 1840's—after the publication of the final number of *Bells and Pomegranates*—Browning criticism displays signs of an awareness that not all of Browning's poetry is to be discussed effectively in the traditional, well-established terms of poetic criticism; an attempt begins to describe, to define and—a little later— to classify the dramatic monologue.[9]

7. See, e.g., Byron's *The Prisoner of Chillon, The Lament of Tasso,* and *Jephtha's Daughter.* Wordsworth's *The Complaint of a Forsaken Indian Woman* represents a departure from most of his lyric verse, as Wordsworth seems to have written few monologues in which the sole "speaker" is very clearly not intended to be taken as being the poet himself.

8. There is evidence that Browning's early critics sometimes used Browning's titles to describe his poems, for example. "The dramatic lyrics are very clear in parts . . ." occurs in a review of the first four parts of *Bells and Pomegranates* in 1843; see *The Gentleman's Magazine,* new ser. 20 (Aug. 1843), 169. And E. P. Hood, in "The Poetry of Robert Browning," *Eclectic Review,* 6th ser. *4* (May 1863), 438, wrote in part: "[Browning] is a dramatist in all that we usually imply by that word, entering into the innermost arena of the being. His poems are, to quote the title of one of his dramas, 'Soul Tragedies.'" There is also at least a possibility that the term "dramatic monologue" was suggested by the word "monodrama" alone. F. J. Furnivall in the *Browning Society's Papers* (London, 1881–91), *1,* 114, notes that "monodrama" was used by Lamb in 1823, by Carlyle in 1831, and that it was applied to Browning's monologues as early as 1849 in *Eclectic Review,* 4th ser. *26* (Aug. 1849), p. 211. Tennyson probably brought the word to the more general attention of Victorian critics with *Maud; A Monodrama* in 1855.

9. In *Eclectic Review,* 4th ser. *26* (Aug. 1849), 212, the reviewer cited by Furnivall (see note 8 above) for relating the expression "*mono*drama" to Browning's poetry, also felt obliged to employ a special epithet of his own: "In Browning's *un*formal drama we find the highest success of poetic and creative power achieved . . ." Thus at an early point in Browning criticism two rather special expressions not ordinarily applied to lyric or dramatic poetry, "*mono*drama" and "*un*formal drama" were used to describe some of the dramatic monologues.

Not surprisingly, most descriptions or brief definitions of the form that have been offered in the last one hundred and ten years have emphasized its relationship to traditional drama, or have attempted to treat the form in terms relevant to the drama. A fair sampling [10] of such dramatically-slanted descriptions of the dramatic monologue might include:

soliloquy [11]

soliloquies of the spirit [12]

pseudodialogs [13]

a dialogue of which we hear only the chief speaker's part [14]

a dramatic scene in the history of a soul [15]

monodrama [16]

a drama of the interior [17]

subjective dramas [18]

10. The descriptions of the dramatic monologue in the two following lists have been taken from various contexts, but unless otherwise indicated the context in each case has been one which implied that at least a group of Browning's dramatic monologues—if not all dramatic monologues or the dramatic monologue form itself— was being referred to by the writer. These descriptions, of course, do not necessarily summarize all of the thought of any one writer about dramatic monologues. The items in the lists are not in chronological order, nor do the lists give equal attention to chronological periods. My object is simply to indicate some of the leading ways in which dramatic monologues as a group have been described.

11. George Santayana, *Interpretations of Poetry and Religion* (London, 1900), p. 212.

12. Algernon Charles Swinburne, "Essay on the Poetical and Dramatic Works of George Chapman," *The Works of George Chapman: Poems and Minor Translations* (London, 1875), p. xviii.

13. Fuson, *Browning and His English Predecessors in the Dramatic Monolog*, p. 21. The writer states that he "is tempted to classify" some of Browning's monologues under this heading.

14. Bliss Perry, *A Study of Poetry* (London, 1920), p. 268.

15. Edward Dowden, *Robert Browning* (London, 1904), p. 162. In this case the description was offered for the poem, *Mr. Sludge, "The Medium,"* but has been included here because of an implication in Dowden's treatment of Browning that it might be used for other dramatic monologues as well.

16. A term frequently employed in the Victorian period to describe Browning's monologues; see notes 8 and 9 above. It still occurs in Browning criticism. See, e.g., Arthur E. DuBois' use of it in "Robert Browning, Dramatist," *Studies in Philology*, 33 (1936), 626.

17. Arthur Symons, "Is Browning Dramatic?" *Browning Society's Papers*, 2, 4.

18. Claud Howard, *The Dramatic Monologue: its Origin and Development* (Chapel Hill, 1910), p. 70.

introspective and retrospective drama [19]

little dramas in which only one of the actors speaks [20]

veritable dramas, involving several persons, to only one of
whom do we attend [21]

a tabloid play [22]

Collectively, these descriptions employ the terms "soliloquy,"
"dialogue," "scene," "drama," "actors," and "play," and in thus
relating the form to traditional stage drama suggest the possibility
that the Browning monologue is not to be considered as a poem
at all, but as a special type of play. But in so doing such descriptions accomplish very little: it is of small help to reader or critic
to know that he is reading "little dramas in which only one of the
actors speaks," for such dramas are clearly not ordinary dramas
and, as they are not, demand a type of interpretation different
from that called for by the stage play; such descriptions of the
dramatic monologue do not suggest the special nature of the form
or a useful basis upon which it may be critically discussed. Other
descriptions have treated the dramatic monologue in terms borrowed from a variety of arts and disciplines:

head and bust portraits [23]

limited portraiture [24]

analytical portraits, or . . . dissertations [25]

one end of a conversation [26]

19. Symons, p. 5. See also Symons' reference to the dramatic monologues simply
as "introspective drama" in *An Introduction to the Study of Browning*, p. 7.

20. Harlan Henthorne Hatcher, *The Versification of Robert Browning* (Columbus,
1928), p. 38.

21. George Herbert Palmer, "The Monologue of Browning," *Harvard Theological
Review, 11* (1918), 131.

22. Homer A. Watt and William W. Watt, *A Dictionary of English Literature*
(New York, 1945), p. 353.

23. C. N. Wenger, "The Masquerade in Browning's Dramatic Monologues,"
College English, 3 (1941), 235.

24. Ibid.

25. Louis Cazamian, "Modern Times (1660–1937)," trans. W. D. MacInnes and the
author, in Louis Cazamian and Emile Legouis, *A History of English Literature*
(rev. ed. London, 1940), p. 1196.

26. S. S. Curry, *Browning and the Dramatic Monologue: Nature and Interpretation of an Overlooked Form of Literature* (Boston, 1908), p. 7.

a monopolized conversation [27]

a combination of discourse, conversation, argument, soliloquy, reminiscence [28]

a psychological vehicle [29]

[a work] drawn out . . . for the purpose of psychological anatomy [30]

psychological stories [31]

case-histories [32]

a self-disclosure in which we have the collaboration of an analyst at work [33]

a few leading ideas in a vast series of incarnations [34]

a type of narrative poetry in which a single character is represented as speaking [35]

It would be wrong to say that these descriptions are inaccurate or "untrue"—perhaps not one of them is really invalid—and it would be uncharitable not to say that several are ingenious. But in relating the dramatic monologue to sculpture, fictional conversation, rhetorical argument, reminiscence, psychology, psychiatry, anatomy, the notion of incarnate ideas, or narrative poetry, one does not provide a working description of the form—that is, a description of much use to anyone attempting to understand and to criticize the blank-verse poem *Fra Lippo Lippi*, for example—one merely provides a more or less figurative alternate or an analogue for the term "dramatic monologue."

Attempts to classify Browning's poems began during the poet's

27. Claud Howard, p. 39.
28. Arthur Symons, *An Introduction to the Study of Browning* (London, 1906), p. 105.
29. A. Allen Brockington, *Browning and the Twentieth Century: A Study of Robert Browning's Influence and Reputation* (London, 1932), p. 134.
30. M. W. MacCallum, "The Dramatic Monologue in the Victorian Period," *Proceedings of the British Academy, 11* (1924–25), 280.
31. Samuel C. Chew, "The Nineteenth Century and After (1789–1939)," *A Literary History of England,* ed. Albert C. Baugh (London, 1950), p. 1402.
32. Ibid.
33. Cazamian, p. 1195.
34. Phelps, *Robert Browning*, p. 115.
35. Watt, *A Dictionary of English Literature*, p. 353.

lifetime, although it is only in the twentieth century that classifications of the poems have been accompanied by elaborate and systematic attempts to define the form of the dramatic monologue
itself. One of the earliest—and simplest—classifications, occurring
in an unsigned article in *The Contemporary Review* of January
1867, rather clearly illustrates the difficulties and weaknesses of
subsequent classifications involving dramatic monologues. Browning's work was divided into three classes:

I. Poems dramatic in their structure. [*Paracelsus, Pippa
Passes, In a Balcony,* and "the Plays"]

II. Lyrics and Romances, dramatic in character though not
in structure, and dealing chiefly with passions which
have man, as such, for their object. [*By the Fireside, My
Last Duchess, Andrea del Sarto, Cavalier Tunes,* and sixteen other poems]

III. Poems representing forms, true or false, healthy or morbid, of religious life. [*Johannes Agricola, Bishop Blougram, Mr. Sludge,* and ten other poems] [36]

If this scheme appears weak at first glance, it is still not quite in-
defensible. One might draw up a fairly logical case for it by first
carefully defining the terms "dramatic" and "passions" and the
expression "man, as such" as they appear to be used in context,
and then offering evidence to show that "forms" of "religious
life" are indeed represented in the subject matter of *Johannes
Agricola, Bishop Blougram* and *Mr. Sludge.* Yet no matter how
logical and forceful the argument on its behalf the classification
would seem arbitrary, for all of the poems in Group III could be
placed in Group II, and a dozen equally valid classifications involving various rearrangements of the cited works could be produced. The classification might still justify itself if it suggested to
its author—or to anyone else—important and previously unno-
ticed thematic or technical resemblances between any two or more

36. See "Robert Browning," *Contemporary Review, 4* (1867), 11–15, 133–48. The
classification has been commented upon by F. J. Furnivall, who wrote that he was
"not satisfied" with it, although he did not "know the Poems well enough to propose a better scheme" in 1881. See *Browning Society's Papers, 1,* 26, n. 1. I am indebted to Furnivall's note for drawing my attention to this scheme.

of Browning's works; that is, if it demonstrated its usefulness to criticism or to scholarship by serving as a temporary aid in any discussion or investigation of the poems, then one would not be inclined to quarrel with it. Any classification justifies itself at least temporarily if it helps to increase one's understanding of the items classified. But the classification of 1867 appears to have produced no favorable results at all; taken seriously, such a scheme only serves to delimit criticism and to discourage understanding of the works that it classifies—in this case, to mention one effect, by implying that *Bishop Blougram* is a poem that does not have "man, as such" for its "object" whereas *By the Fireside* does.

The classification of 1867 is among the more naive that have been proposed for Browning's poems. Yet its weaknesses may be seen in the systems of J. T. Nettleship (1881), who suggested separate categories for Browning's poems dealing with the "spiritual element in man, and the attributes of his soul" and with "some play of human emotion," for example,[37] or in the derivative classifications of Mrs. Orr (1881 and 1885),[38] and even in the schemes of the twentieth century. Fletcher's classification (1908) attempted, in a detailed and scholarly fashion, to take some account of the structural and thematic nature of all Browning's known works. But its weakness was partly acknowledged by its author and may be seen, for example, in its placing poems such as *At the Mermaid, Easter-Day* and *Fra Lippo Lippi* in one category, *Cleon* in another, and *Caliban* in still another.[39] Karl Bleier (1910) took a selection of Browning's poems and developed three categories: "Charakteroffenbarungsmonologe," "Apologien," and "Reflektionsmonologe." While the failure of such a scheme is at once apparent in *Fra Lippo Lippi's* appearance in the first category, *Mr. Sludge's* in the second, and *Cleon's* in the third (with

37. Altogether, ten categories were developed, of which these represent the central principles of only two. See "Mr. Nettleship's Classification of Browning's Works," *Browning Society's Papers, 1,* 231–34.

38. See [Mrs. Sutherland Orr,] "Mrs. Orr's Classification of Browning's Poems," *Browning Society's Papers, 1,* 235–38, and the preface and table of contents in *A Handbook to the Works of Robert Browning,* London, 1885.

39. See R. H. Fletcher, "Browning's Dramatic Monologs," *Modern Language Notes, 23* (1908), 108–11. Fletcher declared his scheme to be "defensible, though like all such attempts it is open to various objections, general and particular" (p. 109).

equal justice one might place all three poems in any one of the categories), Bleier was the first to segregate some of Browning's poems on the basis of their common function as revelations of character (Charakteroffenbarungsmonologe).[40] The publication of DeVane's descriptive *Handbook* in 1935 was almost certainly a stimulus to the close study of Browning's poetry, and in the next decade two works were produced which still offer the most detailed and carefully supported definitions and classifications of the dramatic monologue that we have. Ina Beth Sessions (1947) suggested the concept of the "Perfect dramatic monologue," or,

> that literary form which has the definite characteristics of speaker, audience, occasion, revelation of character, interplay between speaker and audience, dramatic action, and action which takes place in the present.[41]

Poetic monologues lacking in one or more of these elements, or displaying a "shifting" of interest from the speaker or a "fading into indefiniteness" of one of the other six elements, were to be classified as "Approximations" of the dramatic monologue, and "Approximations" were to be subdivided in a descending order from the "Perfect" type, into "Imperfect," "Formal," and "Approximate" types.[42] Examples of Browning's poems in the "Perfect" category were *My Last Duchess* and *The Laboratory,* in the "Imperfect" *Count Gismond* and *Soliloquy of the Spanish Cloister,* in the "Formal" *A Woman's Last Word,* and in the "Approximate" *Evelyn Hope.*[43] In 1957 Robert Langbaum vigorously criticized this scheme in two respects. He pointed out that the most ideal dramatic monologues in the Sessions scheme—the "Perfect" ones—are not necessarily the best ones, and some of the best and most famous dramatic monologues become mere approximations; secondly, for Langbaum, the system "suggests a decline of the dramatic monologue since Browning's time. It blinds us . . . to the importance of dramatic monologues in the work of such twentieth-century poets as Yeats, Eliot, Pound, Frost, Masters, Robin-

40. See *Die Technik Robert Brownings in seinen "dramatischen Monologen"* (diss., Marburg, 1910), pp. 13, 15, 50, 66.
41. "The Dramatic Monologue," *PMLA, 62* (1947), 508.
42. Ibid.
43. Ibid., pp. 512–14.

son and both Lowells, Amy and Robert . . ." [44]—poets who, in different ways and for different purposes, have used and developed the form. To Langbaum's objections might be added several others. The Sessions scheme is unfair to Browning's short lyrical monologues, such as *Evelyn Hope* and *A Woman's Last Word,* which may be complete and "perfect" enough in their own right; a classification which ranks them as structurally "imperfect" or "approximate" is one that really does not deal with them at all. A more basic objection is that the Sessions scheme is in fact a very arbitrary one. It does not take into account, any more than the 1867 *Contemporary Review* scheme does, the chief effect of any particular monologue, and it does not make clear in what way the effects of any group of monologues may differ from those of other poems. Like all classifications of Browning's poetry that we now have, it represents a kind of mathematical, least-common-denominator approach; in its attempt to express what all dramatic monologues may have in common, it omits or minimizes characteristics that any one monologue may have in particular—and regardless of whether those characteristics are of vital importance in an individual case. Certainly, no classification system which attempts to isolate common factors in many dramatic monologues at the expense of omitting or even minimizing characteristics that account for the chief effect of any one of them can claim to be a permanent or useful classification.

In 1948 Benjamin Willis Fuson, citing Ransom's argument that all poems written in the first person—all lyrics—might be considered "dramatic," attempted to modify the term "dramatic monologue" in order to deal specifically with certain poems in the monologue tradition.[45] A "broad working definition" of the "objective monolog" was offered first: "An objective monolog is an isolated poem intended to simulate the utterance not of the poet

44. *The Poetry of Experience: The Dramatic Monologue in Modern Literary Tradition* (Random House, Inc.: New York, 1957), p. 76.

45. See *Browning and His English Predecessors in the Dramatic Monolog,* pp. 13–14, esp. p. 14, n. 16, and passim. Also see John Crowe Ransom, *The World's Body* (New York, 1938), pp. 254–60, as cited in Fuson. A milder view than Ransom's, but one with similar implications, may be seen in Cleanth Brooks, *The Well Wrought Urn* (London, 1949), pp. 186–87, 229. It seems possible that rather recent suggestions to the effect that all poetry may be viewed as being "dramatic" have given fresh impetus to attempts to classify and to define the dramatic monologues rather rigidly.

but of another individualized speaker whose words reveal his in-
volvement in a localized dramatic situation." [46] From the "objective" the "psychodramatic monolog" was developed by certain of
Browning's predecessors and fully exploited by Browning himself,
according to Fuson. This type was defined as follows:

> A psychodramatic monolog is an isolated and satisfactorily
> self-contained poem successfully simulating a spoken utter-
> ance by a specific and subtly delineated individual clearly
> not the poet, uttered on a specified occasion and involving a
> particular localized dramatic situation of perceptible tensity,
> usually directed toward an individualized and responsive
> auditor, and affording the reader rich opportunities for in-
> sight into the speaker's personality.[47]

Appearing a century after one of the earliest attempts to describe Browning's monologues (as "*un*formal drama" and "*mono*-
drama" in the *Eclectic Review* for August 1849), this definition is
probably the most detailed that has been offered for a group of
monologues; its thoroughness must appeal to anyone insisting
upon scientifically defined categories in literature. However, it
does not account for very many poems. It describes none of the
monologues that constitute *The Ring and the Book*—presumably
none of these are "psychodramatic." And, if it describes *Andrea
del Sarto* and *Mr. Sludge,* for example, it does not quite describe
the epistolary *Karshish,* or the soliloquy of *Caliban,* or *Fra Lippo
Lippi* (which has more than one auditor), or *Bishop Blougram*
(at the end of which we hear Browning's own voice). Perhaps it is
fair to ask whether a sixty-word definition is worth while that suggests that *Andrea del Sarto* has slightly more in common with *Mr.
Sludge* than with *Fra Lippo Lippi.* Is *Karshish* less "psychodramatic" than *Prince Hohenstiel-Schwangau?* The sub-classification
of the "psychodramatic monolog," for all the careful elaboration
of its definition, would seem to be no less arbitrary than many
earlier attempts to subdivide Browning's poems. Moreover, is such
a lengthy definition of more use to any discussion of the dramatic
monologue than the simple descriptive expressions of the 1849

46. Fuson, pp. 10–11.
47. Ibid., p. 22.

reviewer: *un*formal drama and *mono*drama? The latter are less
unwieldy and also less malicious, for they imply a distinction between ordinary drama and the dramatic monologue that is certainly not an arbitrary one, rather than distinctions and relationships that are, demonstrably, quite arbitrary.

The difficulties that attend any discussion of the dramatic monologues as a class have been dealt with by two very recent writers.
In 1957 Roma A. King, Jr., published a study of only five poems
of Browning, *Andrea del Sarto, Fra Lippo Lippi, The Bishop at
St. Praxed, Bishop Blougram,* and *Saul.*[48] One of King's aims was
"to suggest the kind and range of aesthetic response which Browning's shorter dramatic poems are likely to produce," [49] although
his chief aim was to describe and evaluate the poems individually
through examining them for matter, structure and meaning. He
explained his own use of these terms:

> By *matter* I mean all the materials out of which the poem is
> made (sensuous, emotional, and intellectual), and by *structure*
> all the devices used to arrange and hold matter in artistic
> form (diction, sentence structure, rhythm, sound repetition,
> imagery, paradox, irony). . . . Meaning is that end produced
> by the union of matter and structure; it is . . . an incarna-
> tion in structure.[50]

In five central chapters, one devoted to each monologue, King
produced five detailed and analytical descriptions of the chosen
poems. Some points in the analyses, inevitably, are open to question; but it cannot be denied that they are cogent and valuable in
the main. In his final chapter King attempted to summarize and
coordinate his findings—and the result is, in some respects, disappointing to anyone attempting to discuss, define or classify Browning's dramatic monologues as a whole. "As a rule, it is safer to
generalize about Lippo's, Andrea's, or Bishop Blougram's diction
than about Browning's." [51] So, as a rule, would it seem safer to
generalize about any one dramatic monologue than about all of

48. *The Bow and the Lyre: The Art of Robert Browning* (The University of
Michigan Press: Ann Arbor).
49. Ibid., p. 9.
50. Ibid.
51. Ibid., p. 141.

them. But King found that certain qualities were common to at least four of the poems: they demonstrated "intellectual and psychological consistency" [52] and had "depth, intensity, irony, paradox, wit, whimsy, and humor," [53] for example. They were found to be

> dramatic, presenting a fully developed speaker compelled to communicate to a listener (more adequately developed in some cases than in others); the tone, structure, and cadence are colloquial; the unity is a tension produced by the interplay of opposing intellectual and emotional forces.[54]

If such a description contains little that is strikingly new, it contains little that is arbitrary; it does not open the way to misinterpretation or a mistaken classification of the few poems that it treats. King found that many elements of the several poems "have their origin in character," [55] and concluded in part—perhaps too generally, in view of the self-imposed limits of his study—that "the first criterion by which to judge a Browning monologue is the effectiveness of its characterization." [56]

To the extent that King's summary is derived from findings in a series of careful examinations of dramatic monologues, his work demonstrates the possibility that, through a close study of other dramatic monologues from different points of view (e.g. King's "matter, structure and meaning"), one may eventually derive classifications involving limited groups of monologues that will not be merely arbitrary. On the other hand, it would seem that such small-group classifications would have to remain, to a degree, independent from one another: that is, monologues found to be different from one another in "meaning," such as *Fra Lippo Lippi* and *Saul,* could not be placed in a single classification system, en-

52. Ibid., p. 131.
53. Ibid., p. 136.
54. Ibid., pp. 139–40.
55. Ibid., p. 144.
56. Ibid., p. 145. See the discussion below, pp. 125–28. The statement would seem to be manifestly unfair to monologues such as *Rabbi Ben Ezra* and *Abt Vogler,* where "characterization" is less important than in *Cleon* or *Bishop Blougram,* e.g., but which are certainly not inferior poems for this.

couraging the discussion of one poem by standards implied for the other.

Robert Langbaum in 1957 dealt with the problems inherent in discussing the dramatic monologue as a class in a different way. He attacked the Sessions scheme, denying the value of sub-classification, and proposed that we abandon "exclusive concern with objective criteria." [57] Citing a remark of M. W. MacCallum's in 1925, that "the object" of the dramatic monologue "is to give the facts from within" and that the essential condition and cause of the form lies in its eliciting "a certain dramatic understanding" and "sympathy" for the monologue speaker, Langbaum proposed that all dramatic monologues have one purpose in common:

> Although the fact that a poem is a monologue helps to determine our sympathy for the speaker, since we must adopt his viewpoint as our entry into the poem, the monologue quality remains nevertheless a means, and not the only means, to the end—the end being to establish the reader's sympathetic relation to the poem, to give him "facts from within." [58]

Thus the dramatic monologue could best be considered "as a poetry of sympathy." [59] *My Last Duchess,* for example, "carries to the limit an effect peculiarly the genius of the dramatic monologue—I mean the effect created by the tension between sympathy and moral judgment." [60]

That Langbaum's thesis is useful is clearly demonstrated in his book: a consideration of "the effect created by the tension between sympathy and moral judgment" led to a detailed and perceptive study of *My Last Duchess.* But this effect hardly isolates or specially typifies the dramatic monologue. Langbaum decried the fact that once

> we treat the dramatic monologue as a traditional genre, then every lyric in which the speaker seems to be someone other

57. *The Poetry of Experience,* p. 77.
58. Ibid., p. 78.
59. Ibid., p. 79.
60. Ibid., p. 85.

than the poet, almost all love-songs and laments in fact . . .
become dramatic monologues; as do all imaginary epistles
and orations and all kinds of excerpts from plays and narratives—e.g. all long speeches and soliloquies . . .[61]

But similarly, once we speak of a "poetry of sympathy" or even
of an "effect created by the tension between sympathy and moral
judgment," do we not equally well describe many lyrics, love-
songs, laments, imaginary epistles, orations, long speeches and
soliloquies in plays? Can it be said, for example, that Macbeth's
soliloquies depend any less for their effect than *My Last Duchess*
upon a "tension between sympathy and moral judgment"? One
might argue that any successful lyric poem may be considered
under the heading of "a poetry of sympathy," inasmuch as every
successful lyric involves the expression of a particular emotion or
feeling which is not, presumably, the reader's own at the moment
he begins to read, but which, as he reads, he is led to sympathize
with. Moreover, the reader's being made to feel sympathy for some
experience is not *incidental* to the effect of most poetry. For unless
we are led to sympathize in reading a poem we feel nothing, and
if we feel nothing then the poem has failed to create any effect at
all. There is of course no harm in discussing one dramatic monologue—or even a group of them—from the point of view of any
conceivable thesis at all if the resulting discussion reveals pertinent new insights. Langbaum's thesis does produce new insights
and his discussion is of value. But his thesis itself does not suggest
the uniqueness of the dramatic monologue or reveal "an effect
peculiarly the genius" of the form.

Still, the studies of Langbaum and King would seem to demonstrate two different and legitimate ways in which one may discuss
groups of dramatic monologues. In the manner of King one may
examine a few examples very closely, preferably from several
points of view, and then deduce salient characteristics that two or
more of the monologues seem to have in common. If these characteristics are to become the basis of a classification scheme (which
King does not propose), then one runs the risk of producing arbitrary classifications which may omit or minimize characteristics

61. Ibid., p. 75.

particularly vital in the case of one dramatic monologue. One runs a risk, common to the problem of all literary classification systems, of developing a scheme which implies a relationship between several works that is not a fundamental relationship and which therefore may discourage proper criticism of one or more of the works. The Sessions scheme illustrates this risk. In the manner of Langbaum, on the other hand, one may abandon "exclusive concern with objective criteria" and so in effect abandon the attempt to classify or to define the dramatic monologue. One may select a quality or an artistic effect that many dramatic monologues seem to have in common and, in examining this quality or effect in several cases, establish a connection between two or more poems. Such an analysis will not suffer if the isolated effect is one which is also common to poetry not in the dramatic monologue form. A rather broad critical approach to the dramatic monologue may suggest insights of considerable value. But such an analysis may not be expected to distinguish the Browning dramatic monologue as such from other dramatic and lyric forms.

A DEFINITION OF THE POETIC FORM

There can be no doubt that some elementary definitions and classifications in literature are not only desirable, but inescapable. One does not define the literary class "poetry" every time one speaks of a poem, for example, but in the act of speaking about a poem one subscribes to the classification "poetry"—broad and indefinite as it may be. One may have a definite notion as to what "poetry" ought to include or exclude; but at the same time one realizes that there is a common notion—perhaps only a very vague notion—in the minds of poetry readers as to what the term signifies.

Does the term "dramatic monologue" signify anything in common—however vague and general—to many readers of English poetry? Or, to state the problem in another way, may one say that "dramatic monologue" signifies anything at all that most readers and students of poetry would agree upon?

Probably few would be inclined to take issue with a definition of the term "monologue" itself which adhered to one set of meanings for the Greek roots: *monos,* that is, "single" (rather than "alone," which might be troublesome) and *logos,* in this case, "discourse." "A single discourse" would seem to be one unobjectionable definition for the term "monologue" in its poetic sense.[62] Many definitions are possible for the term "dramatic." Browning, in writing to Wilfred Meynell, suggested what he meant by the word in using it in the title, *Dramatic Idyls:*

> An idyl, as you know, is a succinct little story complete in itself; not necessarily concerning pastoral matters, by any means, though from the prevalency of such topics in the idyls of Theocritus, such is the general notion. These of mine are called "Dramatic" because the story is told by some actor in it, not by the poet himself.[63]

Without implying that other meanings are not equally or even more common, we may say that one meaning of the word "dramatic" is indicated by that which Browning assigned to it in the case of his *Idyls:* applied to poetry, "dramatic" may mean, "pertaining to that which is told by one whose presence is indicated by the poet but who is not the poet himself."

Will these meanings yield an acceptable definition for the combined term?

The rather simple definition for "dramatic monologue" that seems to result is, "A single discourse by one whose presence is indicated by the poet but who is not the poet himself." If this were to be taken as a definition of "dramatic monologue" it would at least have the effect of *including* many other more specific definitions that have been proposed. Also, it is a definition that seems to be sanctioned not only by much of the poetic practice of Browning, but in part by a statement of Browning's own. In addition, it would seem to describe as closely, probably, as one can hope, what has in fact generally been meant by those who have employed the

62. Cf. *OED* definition 2c for *monologue, sb.:* "A poem, or other non-dramatic composition, in the form of a soliloquy." And for *soliloquy:* "1. An instance of talking to or conversing with oneself, or of uttering one's thoughts aloud without addressing any person . . . b. A literary production representing or imitating a discourse of this nature."

63. Letter published in the *Athenaeum* for January 4, 1890; quoted in DeVane, *Handbook,* p. 430.

term "dramatic monologue" since 1878. Such a concept seems to represent the general basis upon which more detailed—and inevitably more arbitrary—definitions and classifications have been constructed.

And yet, it must be asked, if this definition represents a concept common to most discussions of the dramatic monologue that we now have, does it tell very much in itself? "A single discourse by one whose presence is indicated by the poet but who is not the poet himself" indicates no distinction between the monologues of Marlowe, Donne, Burns, Wordsworth, and Browning, for example. More than that, it would seem to include many lyric poems, imaginary poetic epistles, speeches in narrative poems and long speeches and soliloquies in plays—types of poetry that we have tried in various ways to exclude from the dramatic monologue classification. Does it, moreover, escape the weakness of labeling the dramatic monologue as "a poetry of sympathy"?

It is true that such a definition includes a good deal of poetry that is very different from Browning's more famous dramatic monologues. In the manner of any generally acceptable definition for "narrative poetry" or "lyric poetry," it seems to include at least a proportion of works that could also be placed in other categories, and also works varying immensely from one another in quality. But is it any the less valuable? It does not attempt, or imply an attempt, to sub-classify dramatic monologues in a rigid manner, and thus does not abet false comparisons; its generality and inclusiveness, at least, are evident at once. It does indicate a certain fundamental difference in form between the dramatic monologue on the one hand, and the common lyric, the third-person narrative, the ordinary dramatic poem, and the stage play, on the other. If it implies that many poems might be considered as both lyrics *and* dramatic monologues, it seems to reflect a truth. Is *Evelyn Hope* or is *Porphyria* not a dramatic monologue? Is either one not a lyric? It would seem likely that no injustice will be done to the vast number of poems which shade off between the lyric and the type of poem represented by *Fra Lippo Lippi*, by a definition of the dramatic monologue which "overlaps" the lyric one. It avoids the weakness inherent in thinking of the dramatic monologue primarily as "a poetry of sympathy," for such an

expression implies virtually no distinction between poetic forms—
sympathy being a condition of all lyrics as well as all dramatic
monologues. Moreover, the definition does not blind one to the
presence or the adaptation of the dramatic monologue in the work
of poets who have come after Browning.

A serious objection still remains. If we are to call the poetic
form of the dramatic monologue merely, "A single discourse by
one whose presence is indicated by the poet but who is not the
poet himself," will we suggest anything very helpful to the criticism of any specific poem? Does the definition tell anything pertinent about *Fra Lippo Lippi?* It is true that such an elementary
definition does not treat the dramatic monologue in terms common
to the theater, to sculpture, psychology, or other disciplines; it
seems to avoid the implication of relationships that are not absolutely fundamental and inevitable ones. Yet it emphasizes no feature that suggests a leading basis for critical investigation. However, need we demand this of any definition of a literary class?
In fact, if we do demand it, and attempt to suggest within the
confines of a definition of the dramatic monologue a basis for
criticizing several specific works, do we not in effect introduce an
arbitrary element—arbitrary in suggesting that one particular
critical basis must be of more value in discussing a poem than
others? This is not to say that a literary definition should not be
supplemented by hypothetical and temporary groupings from time
to time for the better understanding of several works. These
groupings themselves will inevitably be "arbitrary"—the understanding of Browning's work certainly will profit if very different
selections of dramatic monologues are considered for one or several
aspects that the poems seem to have in common. But the arbi-
trariness of temporary groupings is not a dangerous thing in itself;
the discussion of a similarity in theme, in structure, in the poet's
artistic intention as it seems to reveal itself in several works, need
not imply that the works themselves are related in all significant
respects, or in any respect that is not specifically discussed, or that
these works must inevitably be discussed together and not in very
different collocations.

It does not seem to be necessary to abandon "exclusive concern
with objective criteria" in a given study of Browning's poems. A

great deal may still be learned about poetry by taking up a few
select "objective criteria" and exploring a group of poems for
what they tell when examined solely in the light of these criteria. Roma King's recent study of five dramatic monologues in
part illustrates the value of a rather objective approach with a few
specially formulated criteria in mind. For certainly any way of
examining a poem or a group of poems is worth while, and not
misleading, if that way seems to bring to light something new and
interesting without implying that its way is the *only* way, or that
it is the most proper way, or that it is a way which suggests a permanent system of classification. Is there not one idea that needs to be
abandoned—the idea that great poems may be "summed up" by
any writer, classed and thus critically disposed of?

CHARACTER IN TWENTY POEMS

In the three foregoing chapters we have seen that Browning's
interest in portraying character dramatically informed a majority
of his youthful productions. Moreover, this interest to some extent accounted for Browning's early artistic failures in that it
taxed his techniques and chosen literary forms from time to time
with tasks beyond their effective compass. Almost every new play
or long poem produced before 1845, while instancing some further
progress in the direction of an effective means of character portrayal, was at the same time less than satisfactory as a work in itself. The blank-verse dramatic monologue as exemplified in *The
Tomb at St. Praxed's* (which Browning sent to F. A. Ward, sub-
editor of *Hood's Magazine,* in February 1845) provided an end to
Browning's search; [64] its form emphasized to the greatest degree
possible the effect of the special character-revealing techniques
that had been evolving. For by writing a single poetic discourse

64. After 1846 (the year *Luria* and *A Soul's Tragedy* were published) Browning
continued to write lyric poetry, some of it in the form of the dramatic monologue,
and beginning with *Balaustion's Adventure* (1871), a series of translations, narratives,
and dramatic poems of many types appeared. But few of the lyric, narrative, or
dramatic poems written after 1846—other than those dramatic monologues, including
the ten contained in *The Ring and the Book,* that seem to be specially concerned
with the nature of their speakers—are particularly noteworthy for their treatment
of character. Browning's interest in portraying character thus seems to have reached
its fulfillment in the character-revealing dramatic monologue.

for one character the poet who is skillful enough may exploit a rather large number of dramatic, prosodic and verbal elements in such a way that they all have the chief effect of realizing character. A scene—or situation—may be selected and suggested in the title and verse of a dramatic monologue with the utmost economy and with the smallest amount of emphasis upon *scene* for its own value: that is, with the maximum emphasis upon its usefulness in helping to establish and to reveal a personality. A second character, or many other characters, may be suggested, but with the minimal emphasis upon such an "audience" in its own right—for its presence is to be indicated solely through the words of the speaker; skillfully handled, such an audience may be used strictly for its function in helping to reveal the speaker's character and deprived, as it were, of any extra effect, any superfluous artistic importance of its own. To the degree that thought and feeling are part of the content of any poem, these elements too may be used with the highest degree of relevance to character; thoughts and feelings expressed in a dramatic monologue are by implication the character's own and they may be selected and expressed in such a way that they help to reveal the springs of his nature. Diction, imagery, rhythm, syntax—all may become characteristic of the speaker portrayed and, if employed with exceptional skill, may be used so that they help to reveal him. Other less obvious architectonic elements—the phonetic quality of vowels and consonants, even punctuation—may take on a special unity and purpose in helping to expose character; the dramatic monologue used as a character-revealing vehicle is able to heighten the effects of these minutiae in the manner of the lyric, while presenting character dramatically in the manner of the play, thus affording the poet an opportunity to relate the minutiae of verse technique to the portrayal of character—an opportunity which neither the stage play nor the ordinary lyric poem can possibly afford. The dramatic monologue used as a means of character presentation may dispense with or modify certain dramatic elements; speaker and audience may be one, or the speaker may in effect conjure up his own auditors imaginatively, or may become a letter-writer or a poet himself and write to a distant, but nevertheless felt (and functional) audience. If *The Bishop at St. Praxed* is a dramatic monologue that uses almost every analyzable element in its make-up to reveal the character of its speaker, there also appear to be, in Browning's poetry, at least nineteen other monologues that are similar in this respect. If so, then their nature as delineations of character suggests that each one of these poems possesses a special artistic unity, and if we are aware of some unifying center in a poem we also know one viewpoint which we may adopt in order to criticize it thoroughly and pertinently.

Before any of these poems may be discussed with profit as a portrait of character, however, a rather formidable and many-faceted task faces the critic: that is, he must understand the ways in which Browning's technique operates in the character-revealing dramatic monologue, and quite possibly before he can be sure of what is happening in any one poem he must be familiar with many others, even with those productions, not in the monologue form, in which the techniques were developed. For this reason some care has been devoted in the previous chapters to an analysis of the early poetry for what it tells about Browning's treatment of character. What is now proposed is that twenty character-revealing monologues be taken up collectively, and that some of the various elements of which they are composed be examined in special chapters. No attempt will be made to discuss all of the poems for all that they seem to show of Browning's character-revealing techniques; rather, what will be attempted will be a kind of preliminary and suggestive but by no means exhaustive survey of the ways in which Browning uses certain dramatic elements (Chapter 5), imagery (Chapter 6), diction (Chapter 7), and rhythm, alliteration, phonetic quality, syntax, and punctuation (Chapter 8) to reveal—or to help reveal—the character of the central figure in each of these poems. The twenty included will be: *The Bishop at St. Praxed, Fra Lippo Lippi, An Epistle of Karshish, Bishop Blougram's Apology, Andrea del Sarto, Cleon, A Death in the Desert, Caliban upon Setebos, Mr. Sludge, "The Medium," Prince Hohenstiel-Schwangau,* as well as ten dramatic monologues from *The Ring and the Book: Half-Rome, The Other Half-Rome, Tertium Quid, Count Guido Franceschini, Giuseppi Caponsacchi, Pompilia, Dominus*

Hyacinthus de Archangelis, Juris Doctor Johannes-Baptista Bottinius, The Pope, and *Guido.*[65] It is not suggested that any one of these poems is a character study alone, or that all twenty of them constitute a special sub-class among other dramatic monologues—that they must necessarily be thought of together. The ten monologues from *The Ring and the Book* are of course related thematically and in other ways and have functions other than that implied in their being delineations of character. *Bishop Blougram, A Death in the Desert,* and *Caliban* seem to have thematic interests that have nothing to do with their being portraits. Nevertheless each of these poems has a special and profound unity as a character delineation, for on many different technical levels each is concerned with the revelation of its speaker. While a study of this kind cannot attempt to prove—even if that were desirable at present—that all of these poems are *most* important or effective as character delineations, it should indicate that all of them may be considered with particular profit as human portraits. It will be seen that typical passages from two of them do possess a unique, analyzable unity when considered in this light (Chapter 9).

Finally, the following chapters are intended to be descriptive rather than evaluative—although, to be sure, the act of description presumes some evaluation, if only in the selection of the details that are to be described. And we shall indulge in forthright evaluation occasionally when that seems to be of some help to the descriptive analysis. "Well!" Berthold says of Melchior in *Colombe's Birthday,* at one point, "he o'er-refines—the scholar's fault!" [66] We shall attempt to keep this warning in mind in analyzing Browning's character-revealing techniques in twenty of the great dramatic monologues, but we shall not let it inhibit us in seeking, even in the most minute details of diction, rhythm, sound quality, or syntax, the very elements of his mature artistry.

65. A few of the actual titles are abbreviated here for convenience; for the full titles of all twenty monologues see pp. x–xi above. Abbreviated titles will be used for some of the monologues in the chapters that follow.
66. III, 76.

5. The Speaker's Situation

THE HISTORICAL CRISIS

THE twenty dramatic monologues of Browning now grouped together have one very obvious element in common: each depicts a
"speaker" in a type of situation or setting that is highly particu-
larized.[1] In some cases the time and place of the speech is indicated—or at least hinted—in the title of the poem. The title *Fra
Lippo Lippi* itself suggests a discourse set in fifteenth century Florence, the historical context of the real Fra Filippo Lippi. And
Lippo's particular predicament is clarified and emphasized in the
six opening lines of the poem. Even when relatively little is sig-
nified by the title, as in *Cleon,* where the speaker has no historical counterpart and where we have no previous information about
him, his situation—the time, location, audience and special predicament involved in his utterance—is presented in detail at an early
point.

May one risk other generalizations about Browning's use of
situation in these twenty poems? One other critical generalization
—usually worded to include all or almost all of the dramatic monologues in this group—should be examined first.

1. For convenience the term "speaker" will be used to describe the central characters of all twenty monologues, although the terms "soliloquist" and "letter-writer"
will be used on occasion, too, in reference to particular monologues in which Browning supposes no auditor to be physically present—e.g. the "soliloquies" of *Caliban,
Archangelis* and *The Pope,* and the "epistles" of *Karshish* and *Cleon.* It would be
misleading to classify Browning's monologuists rigidly as "soliloquists," "letter-
writers," or "speakers" because some monologuists, as we shall see, speak to imagined
auditors when no one is present or soliloquize even when auditors are present.
Arcangeli, for example, writes for future auditors, soliloquizes, and addresses
imagined auditors, all in the same monologue. Even in a monologue such as *Fra
Lippo Lippi,* where auditors are present from start to finish, the psychological
border-line between speech delivered for the benefit of specific auditors and speech
delivered as soliloquy, seems to be crossed repeatedly.

"If we would know what a man is, we have only to throw a flash-light on him at a crisis-moment and watch his reaction. That is Browning's new method . . ."[2] The idea that characters are shown at a "crisis-moment" or at a moment of "great intensity"[3] or "at climactic moments"[4] in Browning's more famous dramatic monologues has been stated frequently. To what extent is this valid? Surely it would be hard to imagine anyone involved in less of an immediate personal "climax" or "crisis" than Cleon is as he sits down to write his epistle to Protos. An aged and widely-honored Grecian poet, profoundly certain of the stoic wisdom of his own world-view, flattered by the receipt of a letter and a galley full of gifts from a monarch anxious to partake of his wisdom, Cleon writes his own letter on a calm evening in the comfort of his isolated island residence. Before his eyes Protos' galley slaves pile gifts along his portico. He rejoices in the scene. Nothing that he writes, nothing that he thinks of as he writes, despite his deep spiritual anguish, causes him truly to swerve a hair's breadth; Protos' queries and proposals are easily answered, for they are ostensibly those of a philosophic amateur;[5] at the end of his monologue Cleon is at least as self-confident, certain of his own wisdom, fame, and the quality of his accomplishments, as he was at the beginning. Some of the speeches in *The Ring and the Book* —*Half-Rome* and *Tertium Quid,* for example, even the monologues of the two lawyers—involve their subjects in no greater crises. It might even be argued that though Fra Lippo Lippi is shown in a jam—it is still not a very bad jam, at least not an unusual one for Lippo to be involved in, considering his nightly habits; his apprehension by the Prior of the Carmelites might have resulted in a genuine "climactic" moment; the Florentine police chief, luckily for Lippo, is not capable of great moral indignation.

2. George Herbert Palmer, "The Monologue of Browning," *Harvard Theological Review, 11* (1918), 132.

3. Claud Howard, *The Dramatic Monologue: Its Origin and Development* (Chapel Hill, 1910), p. 77.

4. King, *The Bow and the Lyre,* p. 144. It is possible that King's statement is intended to apply only to four monologists of his study; even so, it may fairly be called into question.

5. Protos is an amateur in this sense in the eyes of Cleon, who remarks that the Tyrannt is simply not reasonable (*C,* 221) and that he trips over mere words (*C,* 302), e.g.

Benjamin Willis Fuson has pointed out that even the Bishop at St. Praxed is not gasping his last breath—he is only ordering his tomb; Fuson has suggested that the crises of the dramatic monologues ought to be called "minor" ones, and not "major." [6]

Certainly it would be misleading to say that Browning throws "a flash-light" on a speaker "at a crisis-moment" in each of the monologues under discussion without severely qualifying the statement. But there is another sense in which the concept of "crisis-moment" does in fact apply, and it is quite important. Each of the twenty speeches at hand is involved in some situation that is itself part of what may be called a significant historical crisis; and Browning uses this type of crisis primarily, in each case, to reveal the character of the speaker he is attempting to portray.

Although Cleon is scarcely aware of it, his correspondent Protos has been touched, if not shaken, by one of the more momentous historical crises the West has endured in the last two millennia: that resulting from the impact of Christianity upon paganism in the European and Middle Eastern community. An Epistle of Karshish and A Death in the Desert are also involved with this event. A kind of crisis which is, perhaps, second in historical importance only to this one, infects the situation of three other dramatic monologues in the group. The Renaissance informs The Bishop at St. Praxed, Fra Lippo Lippi, and Andrea del Sarto. The ten dramatic monologues of The Ring and the Book are related to a much more localized and transitory historical happening; but the murder of Pompilia and her foster-parents is presented in The Ring and the Book as being a kind of moral crisis that, in late 1697 and early 1698, indirectly involved all the citizenry of Rome, dividing it into two camps of conflicting belief.[7] Even the four remaining character-revealing monologues are involved with actual problems that may—from the point of view of the nineteenth century—be considered historically critical ones. Bishop Blougram, Mr. Sludge and Prince Hohenstiel-Schwangau are monologues set in the time of the Victorian present. So in fact is Caliban upon Setebos; or, Natural Theology in the Island, for

6. Page 90.

7. See The Ring and the Book, I, 839–942, also the excerpt from the sermon at San Lorenzo quoted by Bottini in Book XII (459–642).

despite the fact that its setting and characters are derived from *The Tempest*—so that in one sense it may be said to be mythical and timeless—it is, as its full title implies, intimately involved with the mid-century theological crisis centered on the concept of anthropomorphic theology that took shape after the publication of Darwin's *Origin of Species*.[8]

These larger, background crises that infect all twenty of Browning's situations tend to expose the characters of his monologue speakers in one of two basic ways. A speaker may react to an historical crisis in a manner that is in certain respects different from what the reader might normally expect; and the very difference, or unexpectedness, of the speaker's reaction may then suggest his particular individuality. Thus the speaker in *Tertium Quid* reacts with a certain callousness and fashionable indifference to the appalling murder that forms the subject of his discourse and informs the situation of his monologue; he uses the situation—the historical crisis at hand—to further his own ends; in his casual exploitation of the murder he reveals himself for what he is: a shrewdly grasping, unprincipled social climber, willing enough to use every means at his disposal to further his own cause in the upper echelons of Roman society. In this case a kind of tension is established between what the reader would normally expect of any character in Tertium Quid's place (a reaction commensurate with feelings that the human tragedy of murder normally elicit) and what the reader does in fact witness (a reaction epitomized by the speaker's unfeeling exploitation of the murder for his own purposes).

On the other hand, the historical crisis may be one which has the effect, as it were, of splitting the speaker's own personality into two or more opposing elements; and the conflict of these elements may be such that the speaker in effect illumines himself—without the necessity of the reader's coming to the poem with a special attitude toward the crisis in mind. Thus Fra Lippo Lippi, child

---

8. See, e.g., J. Cotter Morison, " 'Caliban upon Setebos,' with Some Notes on Browning's Subtlety and Humour," *Browning Society's Papers*, *1*, 494–98, and DeVane's summary of the poem's connection with anthropomorphic theology, in *Handbook*, pp. 299–301.

of the Renaissance that he is, is both man of God and frank sensualist:

> I always see the garden and God there (*FLL*, 266)
> A-making man's wife: and, my lesson learned,
> The value and significance of flesh,
> I can't unlearn ten minutes afterwards.

Lippo's religious nature provides a revealing backdrop against which his sensuality becomes vivid; in the same way, his sensuality is a characteristic against which his religion is contrastingly seen; his two diametrically opposed character traits light up each other. In this case a tension is created within the speaker, and we tend to judge him and to see him as he sees and judges himself. The ironical situation in Browning's monologues operates as a compact means of character illumination.

It is probably possible to think of any one of the twenty monologues at hand as using the element of historical crisis in one or the other of these basic ways to establish character. All of the monologues of *The Ring and the Book* depend for their character-revealing effects upon the reader's own attitude toward the Roman crisis—the murder. We see each speaker against the backdrop of our own emotional expectations: and it is partly for this reason that the villainous Guido is a more vivid and successful portrayal than is the heroic Caponsacchi, for Caponsacchi's reaction to the historical event much more nearly parallels our own emotional attitude as it has been conditioned by Browning's narrative in the very first section [9] and, to some extent, by the preceding monologues. *Cleon* is a monologue whose situation places it in this category; Cleon is not touched by the message "a mere barbarian Jew" called "Paulus" has been delivering to the lilied isles, nor can he imagine why Protos wishes to reach the man who talks of Christ; Cleon is oblivious to the historical crisis that informs his situation. But it is just in this way that the situation most effec-

9. For all his sprightliness of tone and superficial detachment in Book I, Browning leaves no doubt in the reader's mind as to who is right and who is wrong in the books to come, and Caponsacchi appears rather clearly as the hero with whom the reader is to identify himself. See, e.g., *The Ring and the Book*, I, 1016–75, and the discussion in Chap. 9, below.

tively lights up his character—for his vanity, his blinding pride, his self-centered smugness and limited intellectuality are all illustrated in his reaction to an event drastically different from our own reaction to it. Fundamentally *Cleon* is a monologue that does not even depend for its effect upon being read from the Christian viewpoint, for the purely historical significance of Paul's proselyting is factual and enormous, Cleon's blindness to the importance of Paul and his message serving to reveal the characteristic limitations of his make-up. *A Death in the Desert* operates in a similar manner. But in this case the speaker's reaction to the historical event—one, indeed, that the speaker himself is intimately connected with—is a reaction very much more nearly akin to our own. Thus while the monologue exploits a profoundly moving and dramatic subject, the death of Saint John in the desert—John, hunted, in pain, almost alone, ostracized from an unbelieving world—the historical crisis in the background does not light up John's character as effectively as the same crisis lights up Cleon's, for John thinks approximately what all Christianity thinks; he says very little that we do not expect a good Christian to say; our own expectations are rather too precisely fulfilled, and the historical crisis creates comparatively little tension between the speaker's response to it and our own.

The Bishop at St. Praxed and *Andrea del Sarto* exploit an historical crisis to reveal the characters of their speakers in the second way—the way of *Fra Lippo Lippi*. The superbness of the Bishop's portrait is partly due to the fact that Browning is able, in a mere one hundred and twenty-five lines, to use three aspects of the Renaissance—its sensuality, art, and religion—to create a kind of multiple character-revealing tension within the Bishop. Each of these Renaissance qualities is present in the Bishop's make-up, and his love of art becomes clear against the background of his love of God and his love of things sensuous, just as his religion and voluptuousness are each brought to light by the presence of the other two qualities. If the line,

> Blue as a vein o'er the Madonna's breast, (*BSP*, 44)

is one of the more celebrated in Browning, it has some justification for being so, as, in a single verse, the poet is able to make use of an historical crisis in three different, mutually illuminating ways to reveal the speaking character.

The four dramatic monologues of the Victorian present, *Bishop Blougram, Caliban, Mr. Sludge* and *Prince Hohenstiel-Schwangau* are unique for their rather special uses of historical situation to reveal their speakers. In one sense, the effect of a background "crisis" operates in each case in the first manner outlined—the *Tertium Quid* manner. That is, we see Mr. Sludge, for example, against the contrast of our own expectations. In a general way the subject of *Mr. Sludge* is religion. Mr. Sludge is a spiritual imposter; he has fooled Hiram H. Horsefall (as he will presumably go on fooling the Horsefalls of the world) into thinking that he, Mr. Sludge, has a special and privileged connection with the supernatural world—indeed, a priestly connection. On one level Mr. Sludge is lit up against the contrast of our own normal expectations for what a mediator between the supernatural world and the natural world should be: the priest, the theologian, is a man of particularly high honesty and integrity in society, and Sludge is a man of no honesty and integrity at all; his special characteristics come to light against our own sense of what is normally characteristic of a man of religion. However, there is another element in the Medium's portrait. Mr. Sludge has not always been an imposter. He even might not have become one but for society itself:

>   . . . suppose   (*MSM,* 97)
> A poor lad, say a help's son in your house
> Listening at keyholes, hears the company
> Talk grand of dollars, V-notes, and so forth,
>
> .   .   .   .
>
>   . . . if, suddenly, in pops he—(*MSM,* 102)
> "*I*'ve got a V-note!"—what do you say to him?
>
> .   .   .   .
>
> Would not you, prompt, investigate the case (*MSM,* 116)
> With cow-hide? . . .
>
> .   .   .   .
>
> But let the same lad hear you talk as grand (*MSM,* 130)
> At the same keyhole, you and company,

> Of signs and wonders, the invisible world;
> How wisdom scouts our vulgar unbelief
> More than our vulgarest credulity;
> How good men have desired to see a ghost,
> What Johnson used to say, what Wesley did,
> Mother Goose thought, and fiddle-diddle-dee:—
> If he break in with, "Sir, *I* saw a ghost!"
> Ah, the ways change! He finds you perched and prim;
> It's a conceit of yours that ghosts may be: . . .

It is a conceit of society that the Medium may be. And there is a hint in this passage, which itself must be taken as truthful of the speaker's own background, that the historical situation of nineteenth-century America forced young Sludge into a calling that he might not otherwise have adopted. Thus there is a special and evident tension within *Mr. Sludge.* Mr. Sludge is a complete imposter, but he is an imposter not wholly because he wanted to become one: society has forced him into his role, and he is partly revealed in the way that Fra Lippo Lippi, the Bishop at St. Praxed, and Andrea del Sarto are revealed—through an illuminating contrast between two very different elements in his make-up. He is different from Lippo, the dying Bishop, and Andrea, in that one of these conflicting elements has been virtually smothered: Sludge's boyhood innocence has been ironed out. But we are apprised of it; and we are significantly aware of duality in his whole portrait.

There is a similar, special duality in *Bishop Blougram, Caliban* and *Prince Hohenstiel-Schwangau.* Like Mr. Sludge, the speakers of these monologues are all peculiarly forced to be what they are, partly against some natural tendency in their characters, by the operation of their historical situations. Bishop Blougram is a man of God at a time and in a region of unbelievers. Belief for Blougram is salvation; he does not freely embrace doubt; but his historical setting has forced doubt upon him, certainly against his will, and he has now developed a rationale which places some value upon doubt as such:

> The more of doubt, the stronger faith, I say, (*BBA*, 603)
> If faith o'ercomes doubt.

But history has pushed Blougram, as it has pushed Sludge, into a role that he does not entirely welcome; in the manner of Sludge he has rationalized the present so that he seems to live in it harmoniously; but he is living in a world not of his making—not the type of world from which Lippo or the dying Bishop speaks, that is, a conflicting world but a world whose conflicting elements are all passionately welcomed by the speaker.

Similarly, Caliban and Prince Hohenstiel-Schwangau have been ill-treated by their respective historical situations. Caliban is probably not a human being; he seems to be an anthropoid animal, capable of speech—his mother was a "dam" and we see him in an animal-like position, "Flat on his belly in the pit's much mire," feeling "small eft-things course" over his spine (*CUS*, 16, 2, 5). Setebos represents a kind of deific amplification of the subhuman nature of Caliban himself, but Caliban the anthropoid hardly welcomes the opportunity to worship Setebos, and his own character would be different—for example, he would not cringe and pretend to adore another being; he would not have developed into the cheat and the sycophant that he is; he would be sheerly arrogant—if it were not for the fact that a tyrannical deity (a god fashioned in his own image, in the pattern of Browning's view of nineteenth-century Natural Theology) had been foisted upon him. Prince Hohenstiel-Schwangau, like Mr. Sludge and Blougram, is apparently satisfied with his own condition, but we are also aware that the Prince before coming to power was a different man:

> And once upon a time, when I (*PH-S*, 819)
> Was like all you, mere voice and nothing more,
> Myself took wings, soared sunward, and thence sang,
> "Look where I live i' the loft, come up to me,
> Groundlings, nor grovel longer! gain this height,
> And prove you breathe here better than below!
> Why, what emancipation far and wide
> Will follow in a trice!["] . . .

From being one who felt it his idealistic mission to elevate humanity, the Prince has been altered by the historical crisis that gave him political power and taxed him with practical responsibilities, into being one whose only purpose is to "save" and preserve the whole structure of society in exactly the condition he found it.

The characters of Mr. Sludge, Blougram, Caliban, and the Prince—Browning's nineteenth-century figures—have all been forcibly altered in some way by an historical situation. In each case, the personality which the speaker has been compelled to adopt is very different from the personality that he once had, or that he would have but for his historical context; in each case there is a special contrast between these two personalities: each speaker is partly revealed through our awareness of what he might ordinarily be but for history. Thus all four are revealed through the presentation of an inner contrast that is similar to the inner contrast in the monologues of the Renaissance. Yet each of the four nineteenth-century characters, unlike the Renaissance ones, has passed into a *present* condition which has eliminated one of the earlier contrasting elements in his character, and thus each is partly revealed through a contrast produced between our expectations for a character in his position and our apprehension of what his own present thoughts, feelings and actions really are.

The historical crisis involved in *The Epistle of Karshish* helps to reveal Karshish in two basic ways also—that is, in the way exemplified by *Tertium Quid* or *Cleon* as well as in the way exemplified by *Fra Lippo Lippi*. Like Cleon, Karshish is involved in the historical crisis produced by the early impact of Christianity upon paganism. Karshish's reaction to Christianity is similar in effect to Cleon's in that Karshish does not respond to the significance of the historical event in quite the way that the reader does. Both Cleon and Karshish are revealed against what is, we may say, our own "modern" orientation. As Cleon's smugness, vanity and intellectual pride are revealed in his ignoring the message of Paul, so Karshish's profound religious nature comes to light in his fervid seizing up of the message of Lazarus: "The very God! think, Abib; dost thou think?" (*EK*, 304). Nevertheless this fervidness alone is not sufficiently distinguishing, inasmuch as the reader himself has been conditioned after eighteen centuries of Christian history to accept a degree of ecstasy as a rather natural concomitant to some Christian experience, particularly to Chris-

tian conversion. It is true that Karshish's fervor is the fervor of
a man who experiences a miracle first-hand and Christianity for
the first time; but his reaction is less revealing than Cleon's reaction—which contrasts not only with our feelings about Paul and
Christ but with our awareness of the enormous historical significance of Paul's proselyting. Thus, for his vividness, Karshish must
also be revealed through the operation of an inner tension or contrast conditioned by the historical setting that informs his situation. He is not only the "not-incurious in God's handiwork"—
the man of religious susceptibilities, but "the picker-up of learning's crumbs"—the factual scientist. His two characteristics illu-
minate each other by way of tension and contrast: his religious
nature is seen most sharply against the background of his medical
interests and training, and the scientific element in his character
comes to light against the contrasting screen of his religion.

In the case of all twenty monologues, to conclude, we may say
that a kind of historical crisis informs the speaker's situation and
in so doing serves to distinguish his character. The crisis may be
one which the speaker simply reacts to in a manner that contrasts
with what we expect; in this case we are always fully aware of
the nature of the crisis: Browning may rely on a very well-known
one (the impact of Christianity) or in the instance of *The Ring
and the Book* monologues, apprise the reader of the significant
details of one not well-known (the Roman murder). The effect
of the historical crisis in revealing character will be greatest when
the speaker's response to it most strikingly contrasts with our own.

On the other hand, the historical crisis may be one which so
infects the speaker's personality that a kind of inner tension is
produced between two or more conflicting elements, and the revelation of the speaker is then not dependent upon our own response to the crisis. In this case one element of the speaker's character always emphasizes the other in marked contrast; two or more
traits of the speaker light up each other.

An Epistle of Karshish and the four monologues whose settings
are most clearly involved with the nineteenth century all make
use of historical crises in both ways to reveal their speakers. In
each case the speaker is revealed through a contrast between his

own attitude and the attitude that we tend to expect of a human being in similar circumstances; but he is also revealed through the presence of an illuminating inner conflict. In the case of *Karshish* the twin elements of this inner conflict are equally prominent; in the other four monologues one of the elements has been severely diminished or obliterated, so that the speaker is in part revealed against the image of the man that he might have been.

Personal Circumstance and the Moment

But the "crisis" aspect in the situation of any one of our chosen monologues—with the possible exception of Guido's two—certainly does not carry over to a discussion of situation in terms of what the speaker himself thinks or feels. Cleon is aware of no "crisis," for example, and we may presume that the speaker of *Tertium Quid* has enjoyed many more exciting evenings than the one on which he harangues his bored audience about poor Pompilia. Yet, each speaker is delineated at a specific moment, and it will now be of interest to examine the nature of that specific time in relation to the speaker's own mental and emotional condition. If the monologues are not concerned with "crises" or "climaxes" in individual lives, what is the nature of their personal circumstances? And, specifically, in what sense do personal circumstances in all twenty monologues assist in the revelation of character?

Browning, on July 10, 1886, answered "a few questions" put to him by William Rolfe and Heloise Hersey through the offices of Dr. Furnivall of the London Browning Society; one of the questions concerned *The Bishop at St. Praxed*—why does the Bishop err in attributing Christ's Sermon on the Mount to Saint Praxed in that poem? [10] Why does he hear

> . . . a certain humming in my ears, (*BSP*, 92)
> About the life before I lived this life,
> And this life too, popes, cardinals and priests,
> Saint Praxed at his sermon on the mount[?]

10. *Select Poems of Robert Browning*, ed. William J. Rolfe and Heloise E. Hersey (New York, 1887), "Addenda," p. 195.

"In *St. Praxed*," Browning replied, "the blunder as to 'the sermon' is the result of the dying man's haziness; he would not reveal himself as he does but for that." [11]

The Bishop must be shown at a moment of mental "haziness" if he is to expose his own character. More than that, it would seem, he must be shown at a moment when the "haziness" of his state is most evident: not when he is merely mumbling to himself, daydreaming, musing about his past—anyone's vocalized daydreamings might conceivably be hazy—but when he is attempting to do something quite specific and exacting. The Bishop sets out to order his tomb. The first requirement of the specific moment for a character-revealing speech in Browning is thus a simple but vital one: it must be a time when the speaker—very simply—feels that he has something to gain by speaking. The moment of the dying Bishop's address is not critical—in his own eyes; rather it is just urgent enough to cause him to gather up his strength and his wits, such as they are, for a discourse.

It has been said that the Browning monologue situation is one "in which the speaker should be able to unburden his mind with absolute freedom." [12] But even this is not quite true: the Bishop is at the mercy of his audience, which he hopes, through the use of certain calculated appeals, to bring to do his bidding, and even when "haziness" sets in and his mind wanders he is at the mercy of his own fears and promptings and the hovering specter of Gandolf. Mr. Sludge and the advocate Bottini reveal themselves not while speaking "with absolute freedom," for throughout almost the entire length of both monologues—when they are most clearly exposing themselves—these men do not forget for an instant the special audiences they are attempting to persuade. Lippo and Blougram say much that is true of themselves, but neither speaks without certain reservations in effect imposed by their auditors. Does Andrea even, alone with his wife, talk with perfect freedom? He touches the subject of Lucrezia's "Cousin" very delicately; he takes pains not to offend his audience; he holds back thoughts we may well imagine are present but which, if

11. Ibid.
12. Bernard Groom, *On the Diction of Tennyson, Browning and Arnold*, SPE Tract 53 (Oxford, 1939), 120.

uttered, would cut short his discourse. Beyond this, perhaps it is pertinent to ask whether any one of Browning's speakers at any one instant speaks quite freely.

"I found," Pompilia tells the nuns who listen to her, "that such as are untrue / Could only take the truth in through a lie." (*P*, 1196–97). Yet no one but God is wholly true, for Pompilia; man invariably lies, and thus speaks with something less than perfect freedom to all his fellow men. Speech itself is a lie, as the Pope declares, and there will be no speech at "God's judgment-bar," none of

> this vile way by the barren words (*TP*, 348)
> Which, more than any deed, characterize
> Man as made subject to a curse: no speech—
> That still bursts o'er some lie which lurks inside,
> As the split skin across the coppery snake,
> And most denotes man!

To the extent that the poet's view of human speech is expressed in *Pompilia* and *The Pope*, Browning believed that we lie even to ourselves when we speak to ourselves; thus we never unburden our minds with absolute freedom in speech; and when we address an audience we lie, we limit ourselves, even when we wish to say what we feel. In this sense none of Browning's monologuists express themselves quite freely, and some of them do not even wish to attempt to do so.[13]

Yet the speakers in all twenty monologues are shown at moments when they particularly *desire* to speak. The dying Bishop wishes to order a tomb; the dying Disciple wishes to have a message preserved. Lippo and Mr. Sludge wish to escape the consequences of an embarrassing predicament—Mr. Sludge, successful at an early point, also wishes to cozen money from his audience; Karshish wishes to communicate a profound personal discovery; Caponsacchi and the Pope wish to contribute to an act of justice, to preserve the reputation of the innocent; Arcangeli and Bottini

13. More paradoxically, in Book I of *The Ring and the Book* Browning seems to suggest that the lie—or the fiction—that must go with a certain truth to make it understood *may* become truth itself by virtue of its being the artist's means to a truthful end (see I, 698–706). If so, then the artist alone is the only man who "speaks" the truth, as it were, and then only by expertly fashioned falsehoods.

wish to impress their auditors professionally, to win cases; Blougram and Hohenstiel-Schwangau really wish to convince themselves of their own moral rightness; Tertium Quid desires personal advancement; Half-Rome and Other Half-Rome wish mainly
to assuage personal vexations; Pompilia wishes to cleanse herself
of personal concerns before the moment of her death; Andrea
wishes to hold his wife's attention so that he may enjoy her for
a few moments at the weary end of a day; Caliban wishes to cheat
his God—while he can. Each speaker has a clear personal reason
for talking, a strong enough reason to cause him to talk at some
length. It may be true that each speech is uttered partly because
its speaker desires to learn something new about himself, to grope,
as King says of Fra Lippo Lippi's reason for haranguing the Florentine police chief at such length, "his way toward a clearer
understanding of himself and his mission." [14] But one might
equally well say that Lippo understands himself and his "mission" perfectly the instant he begins to speak. Indeed, in each case
the speaker's interest in speaking is chiefly a very limited one, and
it is only Hohenstiel-Schwangau who seems to be fully aware of
Browning's special purpose—when he cries:

> Good! It shall be! Revealment of myself! (*PH-S*, 22)

This limited interest is always enough to make the speaker say,
in effect, with Bishop Blougram, "Now, we'll talk" (*BBA*, 12),
and in just this he is exposed—for anyone, real or successfully imagined, will certainly reveal the sort of person he is if he is permitted to go on talking long enough.

In the monologues we are examining, of course, the speaker
talks at a time when he tends to reveal himself quickly. Those
speakers reveal themselves most quickly who seem least conscious
that they are revealing themselves at all. The conscious self-
apologists—Blougram, Guido, Hohenstiel-Schwangau, for example—take much longer to expose themselves than do those speakers to whom the idea of self-apology is most remote: the Bishop
at St. Praxed and Caliban.[15] And this suggests the second common

14. *The Bow and the Lyre*, p. 51.
15. Of the twenty monologues at hand *Guido* is the longest and *Prince Hohenstiel-
Schwangau* and *Bishop Blougram* the longest of those not in *The Ring and the Book*:

principle that informs the speaker's personal situation: even in
the case of the conscious self-apologists, Browning selects a specific
moment in which the speaker is less wary than he would be at
other times to guard the deeper secrets of his personality.

Andrea's weariness at the end of a day's meticulous painting
renders him less alert—he talks with more abandon than he would
at another time of day. His age adds to the weariness of day's end,
and he has less of the protective pride and vanity that would have
obscured his secrets at an earlier point in his career. Of all the
monologuists the Bishop at St. Praxed is farthest removed from
his usual mental condition—much farther removed from normal-
ity than Pompilia, who is closer to death; but his inner conflicts
are also the sharpest and most powerful. If it is true that the human defense mechanism is most formidable when inner conflicts
are keenest and that the mechanism must be destroyed or temporarily removed before the nature of conflicts may be brought
to light, then his near-deliriousness represents a state of being similar to that of a man who has been subject to prolonged psychotherapeutic treatment: the defenses of a strong ego have been destroyed and the libido—the vital impulses and urges that characterize the Bishop—may be seen.

Yet this second common aspect of the specific moments in the
twenty monologues—the speaker's being caught up at a time when
he is off guard, less aware than usual of the total significance of
what he is saying—is not always achieved by Browning in showing the monologuist in a state of mental lull. Bishop Blougram,
Prince Hohenstiel, Mr. Sludge, Count Guido, Fra Lippo Lippi,
are all particularly alert—fresh from torture at the moment of
his first speech, Guido has sharper wits than usual, if anything;
Lippo's jam puts him on his toes—as does Mr. Sludge's; Blougram
and the Prince have been primed mentally by their food and drink
or cigars. But in these cases *alertness* itself paradoxically puts the
speaker off guard, for the very brilliance and intensity with which
he discourses have the psychological effect of making him less
aware of the totality of his meaning: his character portrait. In

---

their lengths, respectively, are 2,425, 2,155, and 1,014 lines. *The Bishop at St. Praxed*
and *Caliban* are only small fractions of these in length—125 and 295 lines, respectively.

each case, intent on achieving a calculated effect upon his listener, and well aware of his success—for even Guido's rhetoric momentarily holds his judges spellbound—he lets the innermost secrets of his character slip out. In a sense, part of Fra Lippo Lippi's method for getting out of his jam is to sketch—consciously and calculatedly—a character portrait for the Chief of Police; he hopes in this way to secure the sympathy and lenience from his audience that he must win in order to escape sad consequences. Sometimes the speaker's own purpose is in part the purpose of Browning. Yet when Lippo says, for example,

> . . . my whole soul revolves, the cup runs over, (*FLL*, 250)
> The world and life's too big to pass for a dream,
> And I do these wild things in sheer despite,
> And play the fooleries you catch me at,
> In pure rage!

—his intention is to convince the Chief of Police that a monk such as Lippo should be excused from doing a particular "wild" thing, even though the statement is perfectly true about him and brilliantly revealing of his character. He has been led, through concentrating on a specific object—obtaining his release from the police—into exposing inadvertently the springs of his character. The urgency of his situation and the success of his gambit cause him to drop his normal defenses. His very alertness and articulateness betray him.

Of the monologues of *The Ring and the Book*, perhaps only *Pompilia* does not make rather similar use of a specific moment of utterance; that is, *The Ring and the Book* speakers are shown at times when it is particularly of interest for each one of them to influence his audience in a special way, and, in sensing his necessity, each speaker becomes forgetful of himself—less alert to guard his own secrets.[16] Pompilia alone speaks at a moment free of rhetorical necessity; her object is not primarily to convince her auditors of her own innocence, or to help convict Guido, or even

16. The Pope, even in soliloquizing, has perhaps the most difficult audience of all to convince, and so might be considered the speaker who is least aware of the character portrait he draws. A discussion of audience in *The Pope* follows below, pp. 150–52.

to clear Caponsacchi's name: she wishes to rid herself of a burden of truth before she withdraws "from earth and man" to God (*P*, 1769). Physical death is her one antagonist—and only in the sense that it threatens to deprive her of time needed to tell all of the truth that she would:

> Is all told? There's the journey: and where's time (*P*, 1528)
> To tell you how that heart burst out in shine?

Unlike the self-revelations that surround it, her own revealment does not require the use of a specific moment of diverting urgency for Pompilia wishes to keep nothing secret; her purpose in speaking is to cast off her human character, as it were, to shed all vestiges of her privacy; like John the Disciple, in Browning's eyes, she is already, perhaps, a saint.

The specific moment of the monologues under discussion may have other character-revealing qualities or functions—and not the least of these might be called symbolic. A kind of inverse symbolism in situation, or a symbolism through direct contrast, helps to characterize Caliban. Caliban speaks at a moment when he is in the closest possible contact with nature in the wild, stretched out in the fetid mire, and

> . . . while he kicks both feet in the cool slush, (*CUS*, 4)
>
> .   .   .   .
>
> [He] talks to his own self, . . .   (*CUS*, 15)
> Touching that other, whom his dam called God.

As such, his moment is distantly paralleled in Christ's days in the wilderness, and in those traditional wilderness retreats for spiritual purification and communion made by numbers of Christian saints. Like Jesus—even like Gotama and Mohammed—Caliban is alone in the midst of nature with his God; like St. Francis he is on intimate terms with the lowliest of animals; prostrate, contemplating his maker, he might in this sense be a devout hermit. His personal situation, in other words, makes Caliban a symbol of the purest religious type: a symbol of incarnated devotion, humility, religious ardor, and intense self-discipline. Thus his real savagery comes brilliantly to light against the contrast of the symbolic role imposed by his situation. For he is of course the least saintly figure imaginable—a being at the other end of the spiritual universe from Christ. He has gone into his cave not to seek his god but to hide from him; he is at home in nature not because of his elevated spirit but because of his utter depravity; he welcomes animals not because he sympathizes with them but because he delights in giving them pain, in exercising merciless power over their helplessness. The monstrosity of his character is heightened and partly revealed through the enormous contrast between the tenor of his brutal remarks on the one hand, and on the other the symbolic meaning that his situation imparts to his portrait.

An element of situation may help to reveal character by symbolizing in itself two conflicting elements of a speaker's personality. Bishop Blougram, for example, wines and dines Gigadibs on "a Corpus Christi Day" (*BBA*, 34), the day of the festival in honor of the sacrament of the Lord's supper, or the Eucharist; and the Eucharist, consecrated elements of bread and wine, is symbolically consumed by Blougram and Gigadibs—for the Bishop has offered the journalist his food, and now offers him wine. But the Eucharist is both sensuous and spiritual: if one partakes of it one eats, as it were, for a spiritual purpose. It is thus suggestive of the Bishop's two characteristic drives: the one based upon a yearning for good food, bodily comfort, pleasant surroundings, practical power and influence—the other upon a passion for God. The day of the Eucharist symbolizes these two—and also suggests, it would seem, which drive in Bishop Blougram is indeed subordinate to the other. The Bishop, too, dines in the evening. Evening, or "sober night" (*BBA*, 448) in the poem is a symbol for religious doubt.[17] Yet the time of day is not only evening. "Now's the time:" Gigadibs is told at the beginning of his discourse, "Truth's break of day!" (*BBA*, 20–21). Evening is the factual, inevitable time, as it were, for evening (or doubt) surrounds the Bishop on all sides; historically, an age of doubt has conditioned his character. Daybreak is the time that the Bishop suggests it is, or wills it to be, for day-

17. The meaning of the symbol is indirectly reinforced by associations of "faith" or "belief" (doubt's opposite) with light or brightness, and at line 448 the Bishop definitely links "unbelief" (doubt) with "night." "In our common primal element / Of unbelief," he asks (439–40), ". . . Where do you find [Napoleon's] star?—his crazy trust[?]" (445), "Have we aught in our sober night shall point / Such ends as his were . . . [?]" (448–49).

break (or belief) represents a state of being that the Bishop himself has achieved only through an act of will that has struck out against the tendency of his era. Worldiness and a propensity toward skepticism, informing the outer layer of his personality, and a contrasting core of belief lying within, in opposition to his age, are symbolized and partly revealed by means of a special duality in time.

Two aspects of time in *Andrea del Sarto* help to suggest the condition of Andrea's being. As with *Bishop Blougram*, it is evening—a time frequently associated with death, waning, or negation in Browning. Evening is at once linked with Andrea's physical state:

> I often am much wearier than you think, (*AdS*, 11)
> This evening more than usual . . .

A little later it is linked with Lucrezia insofar as her relationship with Andrea is concerned—that is, Lucrezia is silvered by evening "at the point" of her "first pride" in Andrea, pride now dead:

> A common greyness silvers everything,—(*AdS*, 35)
> All in a twilight, you and I alike
> —You, at the point of your first pride in me
> (That's gone you know),—but I, at every point . . .

In Andrea's eyes Lucrezia's face is seen as "my moon" (*AdS*, 29), and even here, as it does throughout the poem, the symbolism of the evening reflects Andrea's perception of his own physical debility and nearness to death. He himself and the world as it immediately relates to him are one with the dying day. The strength of this time symbolism is reinforced by the time of year that it is—the dying season, when "days decrease" and "autumn grows, autumn in everything" (*AdS*, 44–45), so that both season and time of day symbolize Andrea's physical state and suggest the prevailing note of his character—that of soul-weary resignation.

More minute details of situation in all twenty monologues symbolize or reflect character traits, and one might compile a considerable list of examples. Such a list might include, for example, *Tertium Quid's*

> Her Eminence is peeping o'er the cards (*TQ*, 1485)

which in its delicate hint of corruption in Roman high society —a Cardinal of the Church is seen by the speaker as looking up from his gambling after overhearing the word "penitence" (1482) —helps to suggest the speaker's own moral character, as he attempts to associate himself with the Cardinal's milieu. Even Mr. Sludge's drink—eggnog—a rich, viscous and rather indelicate American beverage, hints at the provinciality and perhaps the vulgarity of Mr. Sludge and Mr. Sludge's host alike. The pharmaceutical and zoological details of *Karshish* not only illustrate the type of scientific collecting that Karshish is engaged in and that is instrumental in leading him to Lazarus, but indirectly reveal his own practicality, inquisitiveness and professional discipline. One of his reports is suggestive of something else:

> A black lynx snarled and pricked a tufted ear; (*EK,* 29)
> Lust of my blood inflamed his yellow balls:
> I cried and threw my staff and he was gone.

Karshish relates that he has defeated the lynx in quick combat, crying and throwing his stick; the lynx had met its equal, for its own "lust" and "yellow balls" symbolically reflect the passionate intensity of Karshish himself.

AUDIENCE

The audience element in the monologues at hand is complex, often in its constituents, and always in its character-revealing functions, and we may begin with a brief survey of the complexities involved.

In *The Bishop at St. Praxed,* Browning's earliest monologue of the group, four different audiences seem to be addressed by the speaker, although due to the Bishop's delirium in the latter part of the poem it is occasionally difficult to tell which among the four is in the forefront of his mind. The Bishop begins by talking to all of his sons, "Nephews—sons mine" (*BSP,* 2), mentioning Anselm, but not addressing him directly until line 63: "What do they whisper thee, / Child of my bowels, Anselm?" As his delirium creeps on, the Bishop's shift of address, from words directed to his first audience (his sons as a group) to those directed to his second (Anselm alone) becomes quicker and less marked:

> All *lapis,* all, sons! Else I give the Pope   (*BSP,* 102)
> My villas! Will ye ever eat my heart?
> Ever your eyes were as a lizard's quick,
> They glitter like your mother's for my soul . . .

At the height of his delirium the Bishop seems to address, in effect, a third audience consisting of himself alone:

> . . . Stone—   (*BSP,* 115)
> Gritstone, a-crumble! Clammy squares which sweat
> As if the corpse they keep were oozing through—
> And no more *lapis* to delight the world!

At this point, a fourth, imagined audience also seems to be present—the ghost of Gandolf, listening and gloating. Gandolf marks the Bishop's delirium: early in the poem Gandolf is a dead figure of the past, one who "envied" and "cozened" but is no more (*BSP,* 5, 17). A little later Gandolf appears to the Bishop to be living a ghostly existence, confined to his sepulcher:

> —Old Gandolf with his paltry onion-stone,   (*BSP,* 31)
> Put me where I may look at him! . . .
>
> .   .   .   .
>
> For Gandolf shall not choose but see and burst! (*BSP,* 50)

Then Gandolf moves up to "his tomb-top" from which he "chuckles" (*BSP,* 67). At the peak of the Bishop's delirium in lines 115–118, Gandolf at last seems to become a spectral audience, for the Bishop's mind burns with the feeling of his rival's likely triumph now, and Gandolf is more with him than ever. The four audiences and the shifts of address that the Bishop makes from one to another help to suggest the state of his mind at each point in the poem, and a single auditor, or even a more explicitly delineated set of auditors, would be less useful.

The audience element in *The Pope* is even more complex in its constituents. Although, strictly speaking, the Pope soliloquizes for the most part, he addresses in effect one auditor who is continuously present, namely God:

> O Thou,—as represented here to me (*TP*, 1307)
> In such conception as my soul allows . . .

And in the last line of his monologue he speaks to a papal mes-
senger (*TP*, 2134). But there are eight imaginary audiences as
well: the Pope's own "ancient self" Antonio Pignatelli, Guido,
Marzi-Medici (the Governor at Arezzo), the Archbishop, Pompilia,
Caponsacchi, the two Comparini, and an hypothesized tribunal of
"educated" men.[18] In addition, the Pope addresses himself, sometimes objectifying a second, prompting personality that may interrupt the main thread of his discourse to call his attention to
a particular matter, as in: "So plans he, / Always subordinating
(note the point!) / Revenge . . ." (*TP*, 597–99). There are thus
ten sets of audiences in *The Pope*, one of which, God, is actually
addressed in two different respects—that is, specially and directly,
as in the Pope's prayer (*TP*, 1307 ff.), and indirectly, as, in the
Pope's mind, overhearing all that is said. The Pope speaks to each
one of these audiences in a different manner, and each one has
the effect of bringing to light something new and different in the
Pope's character-complex. For example, his modesty and self-re-
spect are at once revealed in his words to Pignatelli, his old self:

> Wilt thou, the one whose speech I somewhat trust, (*TP*, 394)
> Question the after-me, this self now Pope,
> Hear his procedure, criticize his work?

Spiritual humility and reverence are revealed in the prayer at
line 1307; mercy and a capacity for indignation come to light before the conjured up image of Guido the murderer, whom he addresses, alternately, as "thou fool and blind" and "my son" (*TP*,
854, 858); scorn is aroused by Marzi-Medici (*TP*, 970–84); muted
anger by the Archbishop who turned a deaf ear to Pompilia (*TP*,
985–92); admiration, wonder, and even spiritual adoration by the
image of Pompilia herself (*TP*, 1002 ff.); a certain decorousness,
but also manliness, a sense of humor, and stoicism, by the image
of the truant priest, Caponsacchi (*TP*, 1094 ff.); severity and a
basically uncompromising moral absolutism by the image of the

18. See *The Pope*, 382–83, 854, 971, 985–86, 1003–4, 1095, 1215, and 1975–76, for
these identities.

two Comparini (*TP*, 1212 ff.). Browning gained a considerable artistic advantage in placing the Pope, physically, quite alone, for Innocent does not soliloquize because no auditor is needed for his self-revelation, but rather because his revelation requires a particularly heterogeneous set of them. Alone, the Pope may call auditors up at will regardless of their location, their state of being, even their physical existence; the right entity troops before him at once and is as easily dismissed. The form of the soliloquy greatly facilitates the dramatic problem of audience in this sense. And the soliloquy, in Browning, far from being unimportant for its use of the auditor element, generally makes a more specialized use of it than do those monologues whose audiences are on hand. In *Archangelis,* the speaker's two chief attributes—what one might call his domesticated sensuality on the one hand, and on the other his routine and unimaginative professionalism—are illustrated in a condition of soliloquy for the reason that his family and professional lives are, as it were, worlds apart. Strictly speaking, no one human being in Arcangeli's life would be likely to call forth both the professional and the sensual, familial aspects of his character; moreover, a faulty impression of Arcangeli would result if, for example, Bottini and the eight-year-old Giacinto were shown together, for only Arcangeli merges his own two worlds: the worlds never meet or conflict in practice as Fra Lippo Lippi's rather embarrassingly do. They do meet psychologically—within Arcangeli—and so it is just in a psychological sense that the lawyer's complete, character-revealing audience may be said to have its existence. He may freely conjure up his professional rival:

> Bottini, burn your books, you blazing ass! (*HdA,* 1804)

—and his son:

> What, to-day we're eight? (*HdA,* 2)
> Seven and one's eight, I hope, old curly-pate!

—at one sitting, one moment of utterance, the two serving to reveal the twin, separate, unconflicting sides of his nature, without unnaturally merging them, as it were, or seeing them, or causing us to see them, as representing a conflict which does not in fact exist. A soliloquy may make use of the speaker himself as an audience for his own self-revelation. The Pope's stern inner promptings, "(note the point!)" (*TP*, 598) are paralleled in Arcangeli's, "Mum, mind business, Sir!" (*HdA*, 138), for example, which, though equally intended by the speaker to draw his own attention to a matter of justice at hand, in Arcangeli's case serves to point up the one light psychological conflict the lawyer does experience, that between duty and pleasure.

But very often in the Browning monologue, even when audience constituents are fairly simple, the character-revealing effects of those constituents may be quite complex. Indeed the complexity of the auditor element is largely a matter of the varied, subtle and not always easily analyzable ways in which the hearer's presence serves to illumine the speaker's character.

For example, the audience Fra Lippo Lippi addresses in his first twenty lines is composed of a small squad of Florentine police, including their captain—we may call him the Police Chief—whom Lippo will address in private in lines 21–392. Lippo's encounter with the squad is very brief in terms of his whole utterance, and the squad is only sketchily delineated. But, before it, Lippo runs quickly through a whole gamut of emotions—both real and feigned or tactical. His first reaction is one of alarmed surprise, and his opening words express fear and instinctive self-deprecation:

> I am poor brother Lippo, by your leave! (*FLL*, 1)

This leads to a protest, motivated in part by the discomfort of having torches ablaze in front of his face but also by Lippo's desire to draw attention from himself, to see his adversaries as they see him, to begin his own counterattack.

> You need not clap your torches to my face. (*FLL*, 2)

The torches are lowered and in line three the counterattack begins:

> Zooks, what's to blame? you think you see a monk! (*FLL*, 3)
> What, 't is past midnight, and you go the rounds,
> And here you catch me at an alley's end
> Where sportive ladies leave their doors ajar?

Progressively Lippo augments the intensity of his onslaught. From the mild protest of "Zooks, what's to blame?" he moves to indignation in a three-line summary of circumstances. The apparent candidness and brevity of the account reinforce tactical indignation: there is nothing extraordinary in the whole situation, for the time is merely past midnight and the squad on its rounds has apprehended a monk in an alley where sportive ladies happen to reside. Indignation now turns to sarcasm, as Lippo seizes a rhetorical metaphor: if the police are so zealous they should indeed hunt up rats and mice where they can be found.

> The Carmine's my cloister: hunt it up, (*FLL*, 7)
> Do,—harry out, if you must show your zeal,
> Whatever rat, there, haps on his wrong hole,
> And nip each softling of a wee white mouse,
> *Weke, weke*, that's crept to keep him company!

The sarcasm is many-edged: the police "must show" their "zeal" for no policeman performing normal duties would bother to stop a monk in the street after midnight; Lippo has been arrested owing to an absurd excess in the execution of official duty. Moreover, Lippo implies, his own action is common enough for monks: in the Carmine many a sportive lady is to be found, and there is nothing outrageous about this for it is all of no more importance than rat and mouse keeping company together: the very action of the police puts them on the level of rat-hunters. In the last line of this attack sarcasm is intensified through even bolder, outright mockery—"*Weke, weke.*" The squeak of a mouse epitomizes the arrest: the police have done nothing more important for all their bustling and clapping of torches than to locate a mouse's clamor. Following this, Lippo quickly assumes a superior role (*FLL*, 12–14), only to drop his superiority in answering the Police Chief's query, the better to impress with the name of a "friend," Cosimo of the Medici. As the underlings release him, he assumes an air of aristocratic disdain, "Boh! you were best!" (*FLL*, 18) and, in the protection of the squad's leader, delivers a boldly slanderous, undisguised parting thrust at the men who have held him:

> Remember and tell me, the day you're hanged, (*FLL*, 19)
> How you affected such a gullet's-gripe!

In a very few lines Lippo's audience has drawn him out considerably. Lippo's shrewdness and quick wit are demonstrated;

his robustness, self-control under tension, his awareness of human nature, his ability to cope with society, are also plain. The humor and effervescence of his character—central to it—come immediately to light in his swift run through a gamut of attitudes. Moreover, his historical and social identity are strongly established. A characteristic episode in his career has been recounted, and we have Lippo's apparent reaction to it. His own personal philosophy and his relationship to the Church are hinted—though our awareness of Lippo's real moral stature, such as it is, is by no means clear: our opinion of him will undergo a certain change as he continues to speak. Still, we have at this point a fair notion of his sensuality—the police squad has turned up that—and we should now be prepared for some rationalization of it. In a sense, Lippo has now used his group-audience for all that it can possibly reveal of him, and beginning with line 21 he turns to a single auditor, who will in turn occasion Lippo's self-disclosure of everything else of pertinence to our understanding of him that must be told.

Bearing in mind the complexity of audience—in its possible components and in its character-delineating effects—we may now, perhaps, risk a generalization concerning the relationship between monologue speaker and audience which should be useful in considering the delineating functions of the auditor element in any one of Browning's twenty poems at hand. In every case, even in complex instances, the speaker's audience in effect objectifies or symbolizes one or more elements in the speaker's own character. In this particular sense the speaker is always larger than his audience. He includes the audience characteristics presented. This is even true of *The Pope*, for though Innocent is an infinitely smaller entity metaphysically than the God whom he addresses, Innocent's God is presented within the framework of the monologue as in fact contributory to Innocent: it is incidental that God has created everything and everyone, for God is revealed as an embodiment merely of the love and devotion to truth that are, in turn, only characteristics in a more complex sum of characteristics constituting Innocent's character. We may indeed imagine a greater existence for an auditor than the auditor has within the framework of a monologue, for not one of Browning's twenty poems presents, relatively speaking, an auditor fully defined, fully sketched in; every auditor exists only through a few, select, emphasized characteristics. And the sum of these few characteristics, or the character of each auditor as presented, is always less than the speaker's own character and always symbolically duplicated in it. Thus in each of the twenty poems the auditor element may be said to be an objectified representation of some aspect of the speaker's own being.

The hypothesis is a useful one, for it helps to explain several things. If the audience in a dramatic monologue is merely a symbolic embodiment of an aspect of the speaker's character, then the artistic unity of that dramatic monologue as a delineation of the speaker is preserved; this accounts for the fact that though Gigadibs, let us say, seems particularly vivid in his own right, he does not detract from the artistic unity that *Bishop Blougram* derives from its quality as a portrait of the Bishop. The audience's whole being, as presented, is wrapped up in the speaker's. And the entire effect of the audience, then, is one of revealing or illustrating something about the speaker to whom it attends.

Let us consider, for example, *Andrea del Sarto*. Andrea's audience is his wife Lucrezia, younger than himself, beautiful physically as Andrea is not, and almost totally unconcerned with the supreme passion of Andrea's life, his painting. Yet for all this she is a true symbol for certain characteristics of Andrea. "How could you," he exclaims at an early point,

> prick those perfect ears,   (*AdS*, 27)
> Even to put a pearl there! oh, so sweet—
> My face, my moon, my everybody's moon,
> Which everybody looks on and calls his,
> And, I suppose, is looked on by in turn,
> While she looks—no one's: very dear, no less.

One element of Andrea's own being is, as it were, perfect. He is "Called 'The Faultless Painter' ": he commands perfect artistic technique, which is to his detriment unsupported by the ability to give his paintings particular depth and meaning—his work lacks soul. But his work reflects his own being; it is part of him and speaks for him. Andrea himself lacks depth, although his character is superficially disciplined enough to enable him to create a kind of surface beauty in his art. Thus Lucrezia with her absolutely perfect physical attributes—"perfect ears" above, and later, "perfect brow, / And perfect eyes, and more than perfect mouth" (*AdS*, 122–23)—symbolizes and reveals Andrea's own limited self-discipline and superficial mastery—"perfect" discipline and mastery within their limits. Lucrezia's lack of moral fibre reflects Andrea's own lack: her waywardness is equivalent to his own spiritual deficiency. But Lucrezia is included in Andrea in an even more important sense. She is one of his paintings, come to life. And in this perhaps may be seen one of Browning's most impressive structural accomplishments, for Lucrezia operates in the poem as an embodiment of one enormous and integral part of Andrea's being that had to be suggested if Andrea were to be revealed at all, and yet which could not possibly have been suggested with proper emphasis in another way. Andrea has become identified with his own art; his paintings not only stand for him but are a part of him—the energy, talent, time and devotion of his life have been drained from him, as it were, and incorporated in his canvases. Psychologically, at the moment of his utterance, the man has been conditioned by the paintings, and no complete delineation of Andrea's character could be accomplished without, somehow, also picturing those canvases whose images exist in Andrea's mind and with which he identifies himself. Lucrezia illustrates these canvases; early in the poem, as she sits still by the window, she becomes a painting in her husband's eyes: "You smile? why, there's my picture ready made, / There's what we painters call our harmony!" (*AdS*, 33–34). She is perfect, surpassingly lovely, one whom "everybody looks on" while "she looks—no one's: very dear, no less." She is Andrea's "beauty." She remains passive, totally uncomprehending as he talks. And the horror of her is only fully seen at last, in two ways: when Lucrezia, the incarnated canvas of Andrea del Sarto, rises to go frankly out to her illicit lover, the "Cousin," thus revealing the spiritual quality of all Andrea's work and ultimately of Andrea himself; and when, in the face of this, Andrea declares that he would have her to his artistic undoing even in heaven. It is for this reason that the climax of the poem is so effective, for it marks the climax of Andrea's self-revelation—which is dependent upon Lucrezia's function as an embodiment of his art and therefore of a vital element of his psyche.

>   . . . What would one have?   (*AdS*, 259)
> In heaven, perhaps, new chances, one more chance—
> Four great walls in the New Jerusalem
> Meted on each side by the angel's reed,
> For Leonard, Rafael, Agnolo and me
> To cover—the three first without a wife,
> While I have mine! So—still they overcome
> Because there's still Lucrezia,—as I choose.

> Again the Cousin's whistle! Go, my Love.

The tragedy of Andrea's character is that the soulless facility of his work—represented in Lucrezia—has become inextricably merged in his own being.

In *Fra Lippo Lippi* the police in the first twenty lines are an embodiment of the robustness, earthiness, even the crudeness, that are essences of Lippo's own make-up. The monk is physical: the bodily handling he receives from the watch is *in* character for him—a man caught shortly after a chance engagement with "sportive ladies." The Police Chief is far more sophisticated and worldly:

> What, brother Lippo's doings, up and down, (*FLL*, 40)
> You know them and they take you? like enough!
> I saw the proper twinkle in your eye—

and the worldliness, the good-humored twinkle, even the difficulty the Police Chief experiences in reconciling Lippo's nightly recreations with his monkhood are all Lippo's own: for Lippo twinkles, knows the world, and encounters exactly the same moral dilemma in private. As dawn comes, the work Lippo promises his auditor is significant:

> And hearken how I plot to make amends. (*FLL*, 343)
> I have bethought me: I shall paint a piece

> .   .   .   .

> . . . I shall paint   (*FLL*, 347)
> God in the midst, Madonna and her babe,
> Ringed by a bowery flowery angel-brood,
> Lilies and vestments . . .

"I shall paint a piece"—a typical, Fra Lippo Lippi piece, in fact. Is not this the very atonement that Lippo promises *himself* every morning of his life?

Gigadibs is no lightweight opponent for Bishop Blougram. On the surface Blougram addresses merely a clever, thirty-year-old reviewer for *Blackwood's Magazine;* a holder of the latest, most fashionable intellectual and artistic opinions; a Free Thinker and probable admirer of Goethe, Shakespeare, Buonaparte, Strauss, and even Count D'Orsay; rather alert, well-polished socially, skeptical toward religion and cynical toward religious professionals.[19] But Gigadibs' objections—framed in Gigadibs' own monologue, as it were, before Blougram's begins [20]—might be considered the objections of the age, as Blougram repeats them:

> I hear you recommend, I might at least (*BBA*, 731)
> Eliminate, decrassify my faith
> Since I adopt it; keeping what I must
> And leaving what I can—such points as this.[21]

The Bishop constantly treats Gigadibs not as a person with peculiar predilections and prejudices of his own, that might distinguish him, however slightly, from his age, but rather as a representative of mid-nineteenth century intellectual thought—sometimes as the whole age itself:

> How you'd exult if I could put you back (*BBA*, 678)
> Six hundred years, blot out cosmogony,

19. For hints as to Gigadibs' character, see especially *BBA*, 21–44, 82–84, 104–18, 150–55, 436–40, 487–93, and 944–53.

20. At least one fair-sized discourse of Gigadibs seems to be implied in Blougram's "It's fair give and take" and "You have had your turn" (*BBA*, 46–47).

21. Whether or not Gigadibs did actually "recommend" such points is immaterial as Blougram speaks to him as though he did, in any case, thereby answering his antagonist as he might answer those mid-Victorian attacks upon the clergy conditioned by the impact of the higher criticism, among other events.

> Geology, ethnology, what not,
> (Greek endings, each the little passing-bell
> That signifies some faith's about to die) . . .

As such, Gigadibs is not quite the embodiment of his age, but he is the embodiment of the Bishop's own doubts that have been nurtured by the age; Gigadibs is a very disturbing incarnation of that element in Blougram that challenges his deeper religious promptings and conditions his way of life, filling it with certain apparent compromises. Significantly, "the great bishop" triumphs over Gigadibs, who is, ostensibly, merely an inquiring reporter for *Blackwood's*, only by rolling "him out a mind," as Browning tells us at the end of the poem (*BBA,* 978), and only, even so, by resorting to duplicity:

For Blougram, he believed, say, half he spoke.   (*BBA,* 980)

.   .   .   .

He said true things, but called them by wrong names. (*BBA,* 996)
"On the whole," he thought, "I justify myself
"On every point where cavillers like this
"Oppugn my life: he tries one kind of fence,
"I close, he's worsted, that's enough for him.
"He's on the ground: if ground should break away
"I take my stand on, there's a firmer yet
"Beneath it, both of us may sink and reach.

The Bishop has had difficulty not because a casual young man tried to "oppugn" his life—surely the Gigadibses of this world have rarely driven its bishops to such lengths—but because Blougram found himself, one Corpus Christi Day, confronted with an integral element of his own character: his own doubting intellectuality.

We shall have time to test the value of this general hypothesis, and to document it a little more thoroughly, when we explore the character-revealing functions of Browning's monologue audiences in the case of Guido's two speeches in the final chapter of the present study.

The Epistolary Situation

The two epistles among the twenty monologues that we have grouped together place the "speaker" in a rather special situation. It will be of interest now to consider quite briefly the special contributions of the epistolary situation to the revelation of character.

Both *Cleon* and *Karshish* are, in the first place, fundamentally dissimilar in their dramatic situations from monologues such as *Archangelis* and *The Pope*. In the soliloquy, as we have seen, Browning tends to gain a certain freedom in his handling of audience; Innocent or Arcangeli may conjure up and dismiss auditors at will; metaphysical auditors, auditors from the past, auditors who would not or should not be seen together, may appear in the same monologue; and in each case the soliloquist may through an act of imagination address a supposed auditor exactly as though he were present. The epistolary monologue is more rigid in this respect. The epistle-writer is in fact a soliloquist in the sense that no one else is present as he discourses. But his words will eventually be "heard," and once the auditor whom he imagines is conjured up that auditor cannot be dismissed until the discourse itself is complete.

Yet if less rigid the soliloquy has a particular disadvantage just in this. For the soliloquy auditor may with equal freedom be willed into existence and willed out again by the speaker—and so cannot compel the speaker to talk. Arcangeli, for example, may dismiss Bottini the moment Bottini becomes unpleasant.[22] But many of Browning's characters would not reveal themselves but for the unpleasantness of their situations. Mr. Sludge and Lippo wish to talk about themselves in order to escape malicious consequences; their private reveries would be rich and delightful, surely, but much less revealing. For this reason few of Browning's dramatic monologues are soliloquies despite the fact that auditors are so much more easily handled—dramatically speaking—when the speaker is permitted to will them into existence.

22. Similarly, Caliban the soliloquist may, in effect, regulate the very distance of his audience as he talks. See E. K. Brown's ingenious study of this operation in "The First Person in 'Caliban upon Setebos,'" *Modern Language Notes*, 66 (1951), 392–95.

The more ordinary dramatic monologue situation has its disadvantages, as well. Lippo, confronted by the police, cannot relax:
it is just as well in his case because we see Lippo best through his
dazzling, unrelenting, brilliantly improvising performance. But
when a speaker faces a real audience he does not have time for
reflection, and this is an insurmountable drawback if he must
reflect in order to reveal himself. Moreover he cannot keep on
talking if he says anything that would incite his auditor to talk
at length; he must hold the floor, mesmerizing his hearers into
prolonged and almost complete silence through a swift flow of
rightly chosen words. Browning in fact managed to mitigate these
difficulties to some extent in his ordinary speaker-auditor situations: Blougram takes his "turn" to speak after, presumably, an
equally long harangue by Gigadibs; Andrea speaks after an argument in which Lucrezia presumably has done most of the talking;
Lippo, Mr. Sludge, and most of the *Ring and the Book* speakers
are all momentarily interrupted—the interrupted words usually
repeated or otherwise clearly indicated in the speaker's own words.
But the fact remains that the ordinary speaker-auditor situation
rules out, by its nature, some types of verbal self-revelation, and
therefore some types of speakers.

The difficulties were overcome in the epistle, which, in situation, is a kind of hybrid cross between the soliloquy and the normal speaker-auditor relationship in Browning. In *Karshish* and
in *Cleon* the audience compels the speaker to direct everything
that he has to say at one man who will "hear" but not interrupt.
Time is unimportant; the speaker may reflect almost as long as he
likes. He may pour forth thoughts and phrases that might cause
the audience to stop him altogether if present. He may forget the
audience for moments at a time and concentrate singlemindedly
upon what he is saying; he may scratch out what he has said and
replace it with something better, reread and polish his discourse.
What is lost, of course, is immediacy. The epistle-writer is less apt
to be carried away—to let truths about himself "slip" out, to tell
self-incriminating things. Written address is more formal than
spoken address; and diction, syntax and, generally, style, in the
poetic letter will tend to be literary and restricted, and less colloquial, colorful, and spontaneous.

But the special attributes of the epistolary dramatic monologue are those to which the revelations of Karshish and Cleon are particularly suited and Browning exploited these qualities fully for purposes of delineation.

The professional character of "Karshish, the Arab Physician," as he is announced in the title of his epistle, is that of the painstaking scientist. No natural detail that his training has equipped him to observe is beneath the notice of Karshish, who finds, for example, three different matters of interest in Judaean gum-tragacanth (*EK*, 55–58). The epistolary form of his discourse enables him to note specifically these findings, and the carefully noted findings in turn reveal his thorough scientific indoctrination. More important, by means of the epistle even unscientific matters may be expressed with painstaking care and formality: his twenty-line salutation to Abib, for example, or almost any one of his sentences in their very structure reveal the extent to which professionalism has conditioned his character. In a more subtle way, Karshish is revealed through the immediate epistolary nature of his relationship with Abib in this twenty-second report, written just after the encounter with Lazarus. We should note, first of all, that the epistle holds Abib at a distance. On hand Abib certainly would not tolerate Karshish's narrative for long: either he would not listen to a "diurnal" case (*EK*, 102), or he would protest Karshish's account of it, and Karshish in any event would not be able to continue in the steady tone and cadence of his discourse leading up to what is now the impassioned and extremely revealing psychological cadenza of his postscript (*EK*, 304–11). Moreover, his religious nature would not come to light at all but for the epistolary framework, for through it Karshish is able momentarily to objectify and to transfer his inhibiting professional characteristics.

In the first third of his letter Karshish either avoids the subject of Lazarus—and instead pays homage to his teacher, recounts late adventures, itemizes observations (about choler, falling sickness, scalp disease, medicinal spiders, and the like)—or refers to the miracle and his own experience of it precisely from Abib's point of view or, one may say, from the point of view of his own professionalism:

His case has struck me far more than 't is worth. (*EK,* 70)

'T is but a case of mania—subinduced   (*EK,* 79)
By epilepsy, at the turning-point
Of trance prolonged unduly . . .

Twice Lazarus is referred to as a "case." A third of the way through his discourse Karshish puts the word—and his own professional judgment of Lazarus—literally in Abib's mouth:

"Such cases are diurnal," thou wilt cry. (*EK,* 102)

From this moment on, that is, from Karshish's surprisingly defiant, "Not so this figment!" in the very next line, until the end of the monologue, the letter-writer stoutly defends, with a few politic but ineffectual disclaimers, his religious perception of the miracle that he has seen. Thus in his opening salutation to Abib, in his scientific recountings, and in his treatment of Lazarus in the first third of the poem, Karshish has expressed and made clear to himself his own professionalism, he has objectified this element in his character, and in line 102 that professionalism is transferred to Abib; Abib now in effect has taken on one full opposing half of Karshish's own identity; and Karshish is free to see and to express fully the religious essence of his own being. The epistle itself in this case has helped to establish an extremely delicate relationship, depending for its effect upon proper distance between speaker and audience, and indispensable to the full revelation of the speaker's character.

Several advantages are gained by Browning through the epistolary aspect of situation in *Cleon.* Cleon's delineation depends not so much upon the expression of what Cleon comprehends, but upon the reader's awareness of what it is that Cleon does not comprehend—that which is beyond the horizon of his egocentricity. In the letter form Cleon may pour out the deepest and most subtle of his profundities: he has time to formulate carefully an entire philosophy, so that its omissions are not in fact accidental ones, or careless ones, as they might appear to be if Cleon were talking, but intrinsic ones, as it were, those arising from Cleon's own inadequacies and limitations and revealing of them. Replying to Protos' letter, he is free to misinterpret Protos, as well. The epistolary audience guides the epistle-writer only by means of his own past words; thus while Cleon follows Protos' letter as he writes his reply, he is able to dwell at much greater length on his own artistic and philosophic accomplishments and at less length on Protos' urgent inquiry about Paulus, for example, than he would if Protos were present. Moreover, Cleon's vanity is able to come fully to light in his physical separateness from Protos. In the security of his isolated isle, as one "lyric woman" offers him wine and other slaves flatter him by busying themselves with Protos' gifts,[23] Cleon is primed to expose his own ego. He takes Protos the Tyrannt to task—as he would hardly do in that royal figure's presence.[24] And, most important, he is able, as he is not intimidated by Protos' material presence, psychologically to identify his audience with one element of his own being. Cleon sees Protos as an equally elevated and triumphant man in the world. Cleon, whose reputation locally is that of a Plato, a Leonardo and a Goethe all in one,[25] is willing to speak to the famous Tyrannt on equal terms: "Nay, thou art worthy of hearing my whole mind" (C, 181). He sees the Tyrannt as representative of his own fame, the factor that makes Protos "worthy." Protos merely lacks Cleon's intellect. Thus Cleon is drawn out through the presence of an objectified element of his own being, his worldly success—itself a pointless and futile-seeming entity—which pleads to his intellect for a rationale, for some justification in the order of things. It is in offering this rationale as carefully, completely and with such characteristic vanity as he does, and in leaving out of it the things that he does, that Cleon reveals himself. But the very process of self-identification that occurs—Cleon's seeing one element of his own being in Protos the Tyrannt—is made possible only by the epistolary nature of the situation. On hand, Protos would destroy the illusion.

23. See *Cleon*, 5–18, in which Cleon describes the scene before him as he writes.
24. See, especially, C, 221, 301–2, 346.
25. That is, he has "effected all those things" that Protos "wonderingly" enumerates, including the creation of a long "epos", "three books on the soul, / Proving absurd all written hitherto" (C, 45–47, 57–58), and has won complete acclaim: "In brief, all arts are mine; / Thus much the people know and recognize, / Throughout our seventeen islands" (C, 61–63).

6. Imagery

IMAGERY AND CHARACTER

For the moment let us define the word "imagery" very broadly as figurative language—the word "image" we may take to mean simply an instance of it. In this sense, there seem to be at least three ways in which we may investigate an image in a verse play or a dramatic poem.

We may examine the image for what it tells about the poet or the playwright who used it, even for what it may tell about his era—the place and the historic time of his writing; we may examine the image for what it tells about the dramatic character who is made to utter it; and finally we may examine it for other aesthetic, symbolic and structural effects in the context of the work in which it appears. To some extent Miss Caroline Spurgeon's celebrated study of Shakespeare's imagery exemplifies all three approaches.[1]

It seems likely that the imagery in almost any dramatic poem or verse play might be investigated with some profit along all three separate lines. The dramatic image, we may say, seems to have three meanings: that which is extrinsic to its artistic effect and which derives from its being the creative product of a particular author, that which derives from its being uttered by a dramatic character, and that which derives from its other artistic effects

1. Caroline F. E. Spurgeon, *Shakespeare's Imagery and What It Tells Us*, Cambridge, England, 1935. Miss Spurgeon's study is largely occupied with the problem of what Shakespeare's imagery tells about Shakespeare the man; but see "Appendix VII. Notes on images as a revelation of character in the dramas," and also the interspersed comments on various other purely artistic effects of the imagery. In W. H. Clemen's *The Development of Shakespeare's Imagery* (London, 1951), the investigation of images in the plays as they relate to character delineation has been considerably advanced.

within the work. These distinctions—theoretical as they may sound—are rather important to bear in mind when we attempt to account for Browning's imagery as an instrument of character delineation in twenty dramatic monologues.

For, in practice, in the light of Miss Spurgeon's findings about Shakespeare, it is legitimate to ask whether any investigation involving Browning's image choices may not in reality be more of an investigation of Browning the man than of artistic effects. To what extent, when we investigate the imagery material of the monologues, are we merely investigating the poet's own unconscious preferences? Is there evidence that Browning was particularly aware of his own imagery, that he used it calculatedly for character portrayal, that he was not carried away at moments of "heightened feeling," as Miss Spurgeon thinks Shakespeare was,[2] into forgetting the needs of his speakers in the very *choice* of images? At least one of the few studies of Browning's imagery that have been undertaken so far, in which the "fulness, richness, and great range" of the poet's "touch imagery" was documented, comes to a conclusion that one aspect of imagery in many of the poems was strongly conditioned by Browning's own personality; the implication is that the poet himself was scarcely aware of the reason why he chose certain images at certain times.[3]

But in a poem, as Miss Spurgeon has said, "the writer is more definitely and consciously seeking the images" that will express his meaning than the playwright usually is,[4] and so there is at least less likelihood that Browning's image subjects were "unconscious"—or chosen for reasons not dictated by the nature of the subject matter and artistic needs at hand. The likelihood is strengthened by evidence that has come to light in Chapters 2 and 3 of the present study: that is, we have seen that Browning's use of imagery underwent a surprisingly steady development through

2. "The imagery he [i.e. Shakespeare] uses is thus a revelation, largely unconscious, given at a moment of heightened feeling, of the furniture of his mind, the channels of his thought, the qualities of things, the objects and incidents he observes and remembers, and perhaps most significant of all, those which he does not observe or remember" (Ibid., p. 4).

3. See John Kester Bonnell, "Touch Images in the Poetry of Robert Browning," *PMLA*, 37 (1922), 597 and passim.

4. *Shakespeare's Imagery*, pp. 5–6.

the plays, successive works instancing richer and more subtle uses of dramatic imagery as a means of character portrayal. By the time of *Pippa* and *Colombe* the imagery had reached a remarkable stage of development; by then, its character-revealing potential well-explored, it could be used expertly and varyingly to aid in delineation. In the dramatic monologues one would expect to find continued evidence of this superb control—more certain evidence of Browning's conscious artistry in imagery than ever before, if anything. And so one really does. For nowhere is Browning's own awareness of imagistic device more apparent than in these twenty monologues, where, in fact, the speakers themselves are shown as being conscious of imagery and of its effects.

"Sirs," Caponsacchi tells his judges, "that first simile serves still" (*GC*, 909); Half-Rome stops to ask himself, "Where was I with that angler-simile?" (*H-R*, 322). Tertium Quid, having pictured Guido as a bull, returns to his "bull-similitude," as he calls it, four lines later (*TQ*, 1559–62), and Guido himself is aware of the appropriateness of the "wolf" figure: "How that staunch image serves at every turn!" (*G*, 1177). Bottini knows that the Pope will relish "a sea-side simile" (*JDB*, 373), and even Mr. Sludge may explain, simply: "To use a figure" (*MSM*, 833). Blougram announces his intricate ship's-cabin image with: "A simile!"—and never seems to forget, or to let Gigadibs forget, the nature of it as a device: "Returning to our image, which I like" (*BBA*, 99, 220). The Bishop may even pick an image and then deliberately reject it for a better one:

> . . . faith means perpetual unbelief (*BBA*, 666)
> Kept quiet like the snake 'neath Michael's foot
> Who stands calm just because he feels it writhe.
> Or, if that's too ambitious,—here's my box—
> I need the excitation of a pinch
> Threatening the torpor of the inside-nose
> Nigh on the imminent sneeze that never comes.

Tertium Quid excuses the indelicacy of his "crayfish":

> . . . Had each pretence (*TQ*, 539)
> Been simultaneously discovered, stripped

> From off the body o' the transaction, just
> As when a cook . . will Excellency forgive?
> Strips away those long loose superfluous legs . . .

And Half-Rome begs his hearer's pardon when his own invention
runs out in mid-image, as it were: he sees too late that he has
picked a figure more complex than he can handle.[5]

It appears that Browning not only was conscious of his own
image choices in these monologues, but wished his speakers to
appear to some extent conscious of them, and perhaps we can best
understand what he was doing by saying that in this way he rather
anticipated Miss Spurgeon. For just in the Spurgeon sense, each
imaginary Browning monologuist is himself a little Shakespeare,
selecting and forming images as he goes along in order to make his
thought clear and to create special effects, but unwittingly revealing himself in the process, and the images are always those
that seem to have been fashioned within his own being and yet
supplied by the raw materials of his everyday life—by objects
that he sees and touches or uses, or by the books that he reads,
or by those aspects of nature that he specially perceives as vivid
and striking. Indeed, one might say that in twenty dramatic monologues Browning manages to use imagery to reveal imaginary men
in practically every way that Miss Spurgeon found Shakespeare's
dramatic imagery revelatory of Shakespeare the man.[6] In *The
Ring and the Book,* in effect, nine different "poets" are hard at
work consciously imaging each other and in that very process unconsciously revealing themselves; each speaker—each "poet," as
it were—tends to use certain key images that the other speakers
do, as well as many unique images, but to use even the key
images in a way that particularly distinguishes and exposes his
own character. The process is a remarkable one, and we shall follow it through presently in the case of Browning's animal imagery
in *The Ring and the Book.*

One other matter remains to be settled first: exactly what are we

5. See *Half-Rome,* 440–45. The speaker's intellectual limitations and pretentions
are revealed in his attitude toward imagery itself.

6. In the survey that follows, the validity of this should become generally apparent, although no attempt will be made to discuss specific parallels in Miss Spurgeon's
work, as that would be a bit extraneous to my purpose.

to mean by "imagery"? "The subject is very complex," as a recent student of poetic imagery has wisely said,[7] and we are perhaps likely to complicate an already complicated matter if we try to arrive at a thoroughly satisfying definition at this point. The present writer has made use of certain suggestions of C. Day Lewis and John Middleton Murry simply because these writers have thought of poetic imagery not so much in terms of its various possible forms—metaphor, simile, metonymy, synecdoche, for example—but in terms of its more or less constant psychological effect:

> In its simplest terms [the poetic image] is a picture made out of words. An epithet, a metaphor, a simile may create an image; or an image may be presented to us in a phrase or passage on the face of it purely descriptive, but *conveying to our imagination something more than the accurate reflection of an external reality.*[8]

Murry has mentioned what he calls "the highest function of imagery—namely, to define indefinable spiritual qualities."[9] Thus, any instance of poetic speech in the twenty poems that seems to convey to the imagination "something more than the accurate reflection of an external reality" and, too, which seems to help define the ultimately indefinable spiritual qualities of human character, has been taken as fair subject matter for a study of Browning's imagery as an implement of portrayal. This is not to say that the structure and the form of a Browning image is irrelevant to character delineation; indeed the *way* an image is expressed is often more revealing than is the simple identity of the image itself in context, and we shall pay close attention in some instances to form and structure in the image. However, a survey of imagistic effects in a number of poems cannot expect to treat the subject of imagistic structure—even as it relates to character—very exhaustively. In fact, we shall be obliged to move somewhat quickly over this enormous stretch of rich land in the monologues

7. Theodore Howard Banks, *Milton's Imagery* (New York, 1950), p. xi.
8. C. Day Lewis, *The Poetic Image* (London, 1947), p. 18; italics mine.
9. John Middleton Murry, "Metaphor," *Countries of the Mind: Essays in Literary Criticism, Second Series* (London, 1931), p. 9.

if we are to cross it at all. The following sections are intended primarily to indicate some of the leading ways in which Browning used imagery to reveal character, and—incidentally—to suggest that Browning's images when explored in this light (in the case of at least twenty character-revealing poems) provide unusual opportunities for new investigation.

THE IMAGERY OF ANIMALS

Perhaps it is not surprising that Browning's poetry as a whole seems to be packed with references to more animals than probably exist in any city zoo. We know from poems such as *Sibrandus Schafnaburgensis,* and from Browning's biography generally, that the poet was fond of "live creatures," whether "worm, slug, eft, with serious features" or more imposing ones; [10] and it may be possible to explain the phenomenal number of animal images in the twenty poems at hand biographically

There are animal images in *Pauline,* but one only senses the poet's apparent obsession with them in *Paracelsus,* where animals sometimes seem to get in each other's way:

> I have got rid of this arch-knave that dogs me
> As a gaunt crow a gasping sheep . . .[11]

Paracelsus is talking to Festus about Oporinus at this point, but the three images seem appropriate to no one, and the clashing dog, and crow and sheep references almost cancel out one another in effect. Yet is it merely Browning's obsession with the animal world that accounts for this imagery in a poem whose chief object was the portrayal of a human character? And is it a mere coincidence—or evidence of a still greater obsession—that animal imagery is even more obvious in those monologues whose artistic unity in each case seems to derive from the poem's nature as a character portrait? Man is similar to animals: no other objects in his universe are more related to him. And yet by virtue of his spirit—"the soul" Browning was attempting, from *Paracelsus* on,

---

10. See stanza VII of Browning's *Garden Fancies II.—Sibrandus Schafnaburgensis.* See also, e.g., Griffin and Minchin, *Life,* pp. 36–40.
11. *Paracelsus,* IV, 37–38.

to reveal, or the core of his character—he is most dissimilar. "The essential" in any imaging "is simply that there should be that intuitive perception of similarity between dissimilars of which Aristotle speaks." [12] If this is generally so, is it not true that animals themselves are indeed excellent imagery material for a poet whose object is to delineate human beings and whose special intention, in portraying conditions of "soul," or in emphasizing that which fundamentally distinguishes one character from another, itself emphasizes the *dissimilarity* between animals and men?

That dramatic monologue among the twenty at hand which makes the most concentrated use of animal imagery is *Caliban*, and it may be of interest to examine first Browning's portrait of a character scarcely human itself—that of the anthropoid who speaks of God.

In *Caliban* there are about sixty-three references to animals in 295 lines. [13] Some of these references are rather vague: "things o' the isle" (*CUS*, 219), *creature*, or *brute*. But many animals are cited specifically: *bee, spider, otter, leech, auk, badger, pie, worm, finch, maggots, hoopoe, grigs, crabs, jay, quails, cuttle-fish, ape, ocelot, mole, crane, orc, sloth, tortoises, snake, newt, squirrel, butterflies, beetles, flies, crickets, raven,* and *whelks*. Each of these instances— and each of the thirty-odd remaining animal references in the poem—might be examined separately for its relationship to Caliban's portrait, but their more important total effect is that of picturing Caliban's animality generically. Caliban is not vile as a worm, repulsive as a maggot, stupidly talkative as a pie, for example—he is worm, maggot and pie and all of the other animals at once: one with them: biologically and spiritually the essence of animaldom. Most of *Caliban's* animals do not occur in similes and metaphors, yet each instance has an image quality by virtue of its conveying something more than the accurate reflection of its own reality—Caliban's own being. When similes and metaphors do occur they often work in circles. Animal is imaged by animal: "Yon otter, sleek-wet, black, lithe as a leech" (*CUS*, 46). Or the

12. Murry, p. 4.

13. The sum 63 does not include repetitions of animal names, such as *jay* (*CUS*, 118, 120) or *quails* (*CUS*, 135, 136) or metaphors for animals in which the animal is not specifically named, e.g. "A crystal spike 'twixt two warm walls of wave" (*CUS*, 37).

sea is imaged by an animal, "snaky sea" (*CUS*, 30), and then an animal by the sea, "Yon auk, one fire-eye in a ball of foam" (*CUS*, 47). This circling or continuous linking effect ties together all creation and creation's maker. In one of the most vivid and sustained comparisons in the poem Setebos becomes a fresh-water fish (*CUS*, 31–43); and later Setebos is likened to Caliban and Caliban in turn to a lumpish, blinded sea-beast—the one he keeps as a pet:

> 'Saith, He [Setebos] may like, perchance, what profits Him.
>
> (CUS, 179)
>
> Ay, himself [Caliban] loves what does him good; but why?
> 'Gets good no otherwise. This blinded beast
> Loves·whoso places flesh-meat on his nose . . .

Thus the imagery characterizes Caliban by linking him to an animal world (even a kind of animalized sea) and an animal God: all illumine the animalism that is the keynote of his character. This is simple enough in its effect, perhaps. But what gives Caliban's portrait its subtlety and brilliance on the level of imagery is not so much the sheer enumeration of animals as the way in which these animals are individually rendered: his central characteristic is hammered out, as it were, in a bright, hard, glittering mosaic of animal species, including their minutely observed traits and typifying actions—the badger with its "slant white-wedge eye" or the pie "with the long tongue / That pricks deep into oakwarts for a worm" or ants that "build a wall of seeds and settled stalks," for example (*CUS*, 49–51, 54). It is through these bits of vividness that Caliban's being becomes vivid; a seeming myriad of imagistic details in effect unite in the speaker's character.

Far fewer animals occur in *Karshish*, but this monologue is related to *Caliban* in its use of natural or circumstantial animal imagery. The "black lynx" with its "yellow balls" inflamed by lust has been mentioned as an element of Karshish's situation; Karshish *encountered* the lynx, just as he encountered a mottled spider that "watches on the ledge of tombs" (*EK*, 46)—and we even feel that his old lion has been encountered in African journeyings, partly because the simile in which it occurs is particularly apt and real:

> I crossed a ridge of short sharp broken hills (*EK,* 291)
> Like an old lion's cheek teeth . . .

The lynx, the spider and the lion do not figure in rhetorical images. But other animals in the poem do: Lazarus is "obedient as a sheep" and "harmless as a lamb," a wretched "beast"—as Karshish in fact has called him to his face (*EK,* 119, 232, 221). As such there seem to be two sets of animal images in *Karshish.* The first set, the circumstantial images, characterize the speaker we first see: the lustful lynx, the watching spider, and the old lion certainly reflect Karshish's own passion, shrewd alertness, and that worldly wisdom he has acquired through experience. It would be hard to think of three animals that picture him better. The second set conflicts with these: the obedient sheep, poor beast, and harmless lamb are, as it were, the very reverse of the vicious and predatory triad, and—as the sheep and lamb tend to do elsewhere in Browning—they clearly stand for faith.[14] In depicting Lazarus not only as a meek creature but by means of animal images reflecting faith as a man of God as well, Karshish reveals his own apprehension of spiritual truth. Sheep, lamb, and poor beast reflect something surprising and conflicting in himself, the very thing that he expresses and discovers in the last two-thirds of his epistle— kinship with Lazarus the believer, or his own capacity for faith.

Not surprisingly, Bishop Blougram uses the sheep image, too, but in a more subtle way than Karshish does. Karshish discovers faith. Blougram's faith is his profession; he has been aware of faith in his own being and has dealt with faith in the world for a long time, and the biblical image ("*Pastor est tui Dominus,*" *BBA,* 877) now becomes merged in a general vision of things:

> . . . You find   (*BBA,* 877)
> In this the pleasant pasture of our life
> Much you may eat without the least offence,
> Much you don't eat because your maw objects,
> Much you would eat but that your fellow-flock
> Open great eyes at you and even butt,
>
> .   .   .   .

14. Cf. the discussion of the biblical sheep-faith imagery in *Bishop Blougram,* below.

> Though when they seem exorbitantly sheep, (*BBA*, 885)
> You weigh your pleasure with their butts and bleats
> And strike the balance . . .

But Blougram himself is not one of the butting and bleating *herd;* he sees himself as a sheep-aristocrat, ushered to the best of the meadow by those very rams who butt the flock. "I," he declares,

> Who needs must make earth mine and feed my fill (*BBA,* 893)
> Not simply unbutted at, unbickered with,
> But motioned to the velvet of the sward
> By those obsequious wethers' very selves.

And Gigadibs' limitations—the limitations of a life of petty intellectual doubting—are for the Bishop those of the sheep roped to the stake, the "velvet" forever out of reach:

> I pretty well imagine your whole range (*BBA,* 900)
> And stretch of tether twenty years to come.

So the ironic relationship between faith and material well-being that informs the Bishop's world-outlook and makes of him the sort of man that he is comes to light. A simple and moving biblical image defining man's spiritual relationship with his God now takes on a strange duality that perhaps only Blougram could give it.[15] For the spiritual sheep is now a sheep that must eat, reproduce, compete physically with its flock; faith used properly, for the Bishop, helps in the inevitable struggle for survival and success; worldliness has blended in an ironic compromise with the spirituality of his being.

In *Mr. Sludge,* another poem having to do with religion in the mid-Victorian era, animal imagery seems to reach its most repulsive level in Browning. For its sheer ability to evoke nausea (at least with regard to the reader, if not to the auditor Horsefall), Mr. Sludge's instancing of the stomach-cyst—a creature itself on

15. However, it should be noted that both Lippo and the Bishop at St. Praxed use biblical imagery distortedly; that is, they tend to use Scriptural texts to justify sheer sensuality, as Blougram uses "Pastor est tui Dominus" to justify materialism. See, e.g., *FLL,* 250–51 and *BSP,* 51–52; also the discussion of "false imagery," below, pp. 203–6.

the very threshold of animality—has a distinction. But it is surely a mistake to interpret *Mr. Sludge* merely as a bitter diatribe on spiritualism or to think of Mr. Sludge himself simply as being repulsive. Even in the animal imagery Mr. Sludge's saving traits are revealed; in fact through no other technical devices is he more clearly shown. In the earliest of these images the Medium brands himself:

> Tread on a worm, it turns, sir! If I turn, *(MSM,* 72)
> Your fault!

In his second animal image, a peacock metaphor strongly developed in nine lines *(MSM,* 86–94), twice reinforced within the next one hundred lines *(MSM,* 155–56, 160–61), and made to echo to some extent throughout the poem, Mr. Sludge characterizes the Hiram Horsefalls of Anglo-American society:

> You're prigs,—excuse me,—like to look so spry, *(MSM,* 86)
> So clever, while you cling by half a claw
> To the perch whereon you puff yourselves at roost,
>
> .   .   .   .
>
> Oh, otherwise you're sharp enough! You spy *(MSM,* 91)
> Who slips, who slides, who holds by help of wing,
> Wanting real foothold,—who can't keep upright
> On the other perch, . . .
>
> .   .   .   .
>
>   . . . pet post *(MSM,* 155)
> To strut, and spread the tail, and squawk upon! [16]

Mr. Sludge's animal imagery is not subtle. He is willing to call himself a worm. But Horsefall on the other hand must admit the aptness of being pictured as a peacock. Later, Sludge links himself with "grubs" *(MSM,* 186), with a snake *(MSM,* 272–73), with "an ant-eater's long tongue . . . / . . . crusted o'er with creatures" *(MSM,* 540–42) and, rather climactically, with the "stomach-cyst" *(MSM,* 1117–27). Horsefall in the meantime is associated rather indirectly and incidentally with a ferret *(MSM,* 178), and with

16. Note also Mr. Sludge's remark at line 221, "Now's your time to crow," e.g., and later bird images in lines 354, 641–45, 1170, and 1245. All of these have the effect of recalling or, as it were, perpetuating, the strongly established peacock image.

"black sheep" at line 220 and one who "went home shorn" at line 630, and with a beetle (*MSM*, 1250). Mr. Sludge, always conscious of the fact that he is indeed characterizing himself or his auditor with his animal references, seems to come off second-best: he is worm, grub, snake, crusted ant-eater tongue and cyst, whereas Horsefall is primarily peacock. Moreover the vileness imaged by the Sludge-animals seems to be enormously reinforced by the effect of the filth images in the poem—so numerous, varied and unique that they provide material for a considerable study in themselves. These seem to begin with the speaker's own name, *Sludge*, and include choice bits such as:

> . . . I got up from my gorge (*MSM*, 263)
> An offal in the gutter . . .

"Good fun and wholesome mud" (*MSM*, 394), "one smut has settled on your nose" (*MSM*, 502), "He's the man for muck" (*MSM*, 755), "I' the slime o' the slough" (*MSM*, 769), "I somehow vomit truth to-day" (*MSM*, 808), and so forth.

Yet if Mr. Sludge may be said to be represented by, let us say, a worm in the gutter, the wretchedness and the glory of his character shine through the imagery equally. For Mr. Sludge recognizes his lowness. Selecting these images consciously, he does not attempt to beautify or otherwise to disguise his abyssmal vulgarity, nor does he take pride in it—as we might expect him to. Vanity, of any kind, is not in his make-up. He does not fool himself. The pretense of Medium is a cloak easily put on and taken off, and underneath the cloak Mr. Sludge is quite candid. Even *as* Medium he is, in a sense, fair with a world that has wished its mediums into existence. Thus the worm-gutter imagery curiously reveals a saving self-awareness and genuineness. The dominant image for Horsefall, the peacock—self-conceited, trying to look spry and clever, puffing itself up, spreading its tail, strutting and squawking on its perch—is exactly what Sludge at heart is not. Of all Browning's characters he is the most free from self-delusion and perhaps, psychologically, the healthiest. He has no confusion about himself; rather the peacockness of Mr. Sludge—vanity, illusion, pretense, pride—all exist in his outer cloak-like role of Medium, a role whose nature he is fully aware of and which he assumes merely in

order to make his way in a society of fools. Hiram H. Horsefall is
the embodiment of pretense and therefore most appropriately the
peacock—an epitome of the pretense that is not part of the inner
Mr. Sludge, but part of Mr. Sludge's assumed make-up: the fol-
derol of his spiritualism.[17]

It is clear from Browning's use of animal imagery in *Mr. Sludge*
that the simple identity of image subject-material in the monologues does not, in itself, determine the character-revealing function of the image: "stomach-cyst" may suggest vileness and—almost the reverse of contemptibility—genuineness and self-awareness, at once. Similarly, the jelly-fish simile in *A Death in the
Desert,* an image with which John characterizes himself, illustrates
spiritual magnificence:

> "But at the last, why, I seemed left alive   (*DD*, 152)
> "Like a sea-jelly weak on Patmos strand,
> "To tell the dry sea-beach gazers how I fared
> "When there was mid-sea, and the mighty things . . .

If Christ in the speaker's mind is associated with the turmoil of
the sea, then the dying sea-jelly on Patmos strand is by virtue of
its past encounter with the sea a symbol of John's Discipleship—
or of sanctity itself. In those monologues which seem to deliver
the most intense impressions of character, however, animal imagery—when it figures importantly among the poem's devices—
seems to derive part of its delineating effect by virtue of its special
context within the poem, by virtue of the speaker's evident attitude toward the animals imaged, and by virtue of the animal identities themselves. This seems to be true of *Fra Lippo Lippi,* for
example. The general context of all Lippo's images is a highly

---

17. Indeed, one might draw up a reasonably convincing case for Mr. Sludge's
nobility of spirit were it not for his vicious soliloquy beginning at line 1500—after
Horsefall has gone up to bed. The Medium's sheer villainy at this point has troubled
perceptive students of the poem. See, e.g., Hoxie N. Fairchild, "Browning the Simple-
hearted Casuist," *University of Toronto Quarterly, 18* (1949), 234–40, for a discussion
of what Fairchild calls Browning's "give-away" of character in certain monologues.
It is at least possible that *Mr. Sludge's* troublesome and incongruous last 25 lines
were added by a poet who felt that he had come dangerously near justifying the
pranks and the character of the notorious D. D. Home; for Browning's personal
bitterness toward this popular American medium see Griffin and Minchin, *Life,*
pp. 203–6. Home was, of course, the model for Mr. Sludge.

rhetorical one. He is attempting to characterize himself in such a way that the police will sense the absurdity of his arrest, feel pity for him, and let him go. At the beginning of the poem his images include references to animals hunted or trapped and helpless:

> . . . harry out, if you must show your zeal,   (*FLL,* 8)
> Whatever rat, there, haps on his wrong hole,
> And nip each softling of a wee white mouse,

> Zooks, are we pilchards, that they sweep the streets (*FLL,* 23)
> And count fair prize what comes into their net?

> And I've been three weeks shut within my new,   (*FLL,* 47)

> You snap me of the sudden . . .   (*FLL,* 75)

> Old Aunt Lapaccia trussed me . . .   (*FLL,* 88)

Later, near the end, there are references to animals escaping: "Where's a hole, where's a corner for escape?"; "Thus I scuttle off . . ." (*FLL,* 369, 383). All of these images Lippo very clearly relates to his own person. Thus in context the images on a simple but effective level reveal cleverness, ingenuity and self-command: though caught off-guard in his alley, Lippo does indeed manage to paint a pathetic picture of himself for the police. But Lippo's attitude toward the animals imaged is also revealing: though using them for his own ends, as it were, he cannot conceal his sympathy for them: some evident feeling for rats, mice and pilchards exposes his humanity. The image for the "sportive ladies" he spies from the window—"the skipping of rabbits by moonlight,—three slim shapes" (*FLL,* 59)—though consciously intended to emphasize the innocence and harmlessness of the ladies, also emphasizes his delight in the very animals that he describes. Finally, even considered apart from their rhetorical contexts and from Lippo's own attitude, all of the animals that Lippo makes use of in the poem—rat, mouse, pilchard, rabbit, dog, mill-horse, and various snapped, trussed, or mewed up beasts—are fundamentally harmless to man, several of them providing him with some good: food, work, or companionship. Thus in various ways the animal imagery in one monologue helps to express the speaker's own cleverness, sympathy for life, and peculiar innocence.

Animal imagery is vital to character revelation in each of the ten dramatic monologues of *The Ring and the Book*, and here, partly because some of the same image subjects carry over from monologue to monologue, the imagery tends to operate in certain ways not paralleled in the independent monologues. To some extent each monologuist in the collection is revealed against the contrast of the monologues that come before his own; even Half-Rome is partly revealed against the contrast of Browning's own narrative in Book I. Similarly, an animal image used by one speaker often helps to reveal his character partly through a contrast with the ways in which the same image-subject has been used before. Moreover, as the subject-matter of each monologuist's talk in *The Ring and the Book* is approximately the same—that is, he expounds upon the same murder story and the characters involved in it, including his own, if he happens to have been one involved —he recreates the principal characters of the poem in each case, and the imagery of his monologue is often consciously employed to help delineate these figures. Thus as narrative and, sometimes, dramatic, poet, the speaker uses animal images to characterize other people, and the images tend to work in two directions. The speaker delineates other people through the use of select images. And at the same time, as the subject of his own portrait, he reveals himself through the use of these images. We shall be less concerned at the moment with the first of these operations, or with the character delineating that each speaker consciously achieves (although we shall take this into consideration in the case of Guido's two portraits, in Chapter 9 of the present study) and more concerned with what is really the chief effect of the animal imagery, resulting from Browning's use of it to expose each character as he speaks, in the sense that Miss Spurgeon "used" Shakespeare's imagery to expose the character of Shakespeare the poet.

In *Half-Rome's* 1547 lines over thirty animal images are employed by the speaker to help suggest Pietro, Violante, the general public, the Abate Paolo, Girolamo, Pompilia's mother, the Convertite nuns, and—more importantly—Pompilia, Guido and Caponsacchi. Half-Rome associates Guido indirectly with a large, prize fish (*H-R, 270–77*), more specifically with a horse ("Guido's broad back was saddled to bear all" *H-R, 391*), and later with a dog, ferret, sheep, fox, and again a fish. Pompilia becomes a snake, cat, minnow, puppy, snake again, chick, badger, lamb and fly. Neither of the two principal characters, in Half-Rome's mind, is more like one animal than another—unless the fish image for Guido and the snake for Pompilia may be said to be slightly dominant as both are repeated once. Guido and Pompilia are of little real significance in themselves for Half-Rome, as neither is focused with any intensity; he is not primarily interested in the moral implications of the murder or in the question of guilt on either side. His images are concentrated in their effect only in the case of Caponsacchi, who is labeled as a fox once, and then as a wolf no less than three times. Caponsacchi is Half-Rome's villain, as indeed it becomes very clear at the end of the monologue when we learn that

> . . . a certain what's-his-name and jackanapes (H-R, 1544)
> Somewhat too civil of eves with lute and song
> About a house here, where I keep a wife

—is the reason for Half-Rome's interest in the murder case: he sees a parallel between the actions of Caponsacchi and those of a local gallant who has threatened his own conjugal bliss. The animal imagery in the monologue underlines Half-Rome's self-centeredness and perfect indifference to goodness or guilt—even justice—insofar as they do not impinge directly on the little circle of his own affairs. The public are swine, the Convertites mere linnets, the murdered Pietro and Violante owl and cat or dog and viper; Pompilia and Guido become almost any animal at all; men and women, in general, are no more than a miscellany of beasts for a speaker whose central characteristic is that of simple self-concern.

Most of Other Half-Rome's animal images are associated with Pompilia and Guido and, unlike those in the last monologue, these images reveal strong attitudes on the speaker's part with regard to the two people pictured. Approvingly he quotes the painter Maratta's estimate of Pompilia:

> 'A lovelier face is not in Rome,' . . . (OH-R, 63)
> 'Shaped like a peacock's egg, the pure as pearl,
> 'That hatches you anon a snow-white chick.'

—and, in addition to "peacock's egg" and "chick," Pompilia becomes a finch, a lamb twice, an unspecified bird, a martin, a sheep, and a dove. Contrastingly Guido becomes one who "can hatch" crime (*OH-R*, 107–10), a cicala, lion, fox, worm, ferret, uncaged beast, wolf-in-sheepskin, scorpion, wildcat, dog, and hawk. Caponsacchi is rather quickly dispensed with as one who is "lamb-pure, lion-brave" (*OH-R*, 29), and the speaker bothers with relatively few other animal images. For Other Half-Rome, the world is thus black and white, absurdly simple. Pompilia, Guido, and Caponsacchi are seen indistinctly through an emotional curtain that simplifies all matters. His imagery reveals the speaker as a man who is at the mercy of his own prejudices, who lacks objectivity and discernment—whose discovery of guilt in Guido and innocence in Pompilia is only accidental, the lucky result of a sentimental, lazy, limited regard for truth.

The speaker in *Tertium Quid* draws the vast majority of his images from animals and from other objects and terms associated with the life of the gentleman farmer and with outdoor sport, particularly from that of hunting. The advocates in the murder case are a "leash of lawyers, two on either side— / One barks, one bites" (*TQ*, 44–45). Violante is "the load of lace" (*TQ*, 94), and Violante and Pietro together: "our brace of burgesses" (*TQ*, 313); their dead bodies are a "bale" of "cargo" (*TQ*, 29–30). Crime is merely an object encountered on the hunt: "Black hard cold / Crime like a stone you kick up with your foot / I' the middle of a field" (*TQ*, 229-31). Guido's servants at Arezzo are "house-dog-servant-things" (*TQ*, 1077), Caponsacchi is a hare, and Paolo a bird in a cage. And the casually detached nature of this imagery carries over into the animal images associated with Guido and Pompilia. Guido is a fish, a fox, swine (with his underlings), a cur, a hound, and perhaps most vividly of all, a "furious bull" (*TQ*, 1559).[18] Pompilia is a "cur-cast mongrel" (*TQ*, 611), a pet lamb, a worm on a hook (to lure Guido), a crow, a dove, and a butterfly. Thus for Tertium Quid the two chief parties in the case are at the most significant merely as litigants, equally objectionable in themselves and equally beneath serious notice. If Guido

18. The speaker is fond enough of this image to return to it—see *TQ*, 1564–65, 1579.

is a "cur," Pompilia is a "cur-cast mongrel." " 'Each of the parties,'" he imagines the Court as saying,

> whether goat or sheep (*TQ*, 1222)
> 'I' the main, has wool to show and hair to hide.

Humanity, in fact, is itself a kind of "reduction *ad absurdum*" for Tertium Quid,[19] whose use of animal imagery in particular reveals his own character as one deprived of humanity through his attempts to dissociate himself from the commonalty and mingle and identify himself with the Roman upper classes. All men are mere objects of the farm or the hunt; Tertium Quid's social striving has brutalized his own soul. Far from being, in truth, a refined and discriminating figure, he is blunt and bestial. His imagery reveals his inability to distinguish in any sense between justice and crime, virtue and depravity, Pompilia's innocence and Guido's murderous cunning.

Caponsacchi, before the "owl-eyes" of the judges who stupidly failed to appreciate Pompilia's dilemma when her first case came before them,[20] brands Guido passionately for what he is: Guido becomes a hawk, a cat, a bear, a spider, an adder, a scorpion, a viper, a beast, a mad dog, a snake, and a cockatrice. In the very verbs the priest uses to describe Guido's talk, Guido comes alive as a kind of threatening beast:

> . . . Soon triumph suppled the tongue (*GC*, 1437)
> A little, malice glued to his dry throat,
> And he part howled, part hissed . . .

And his animal images for Guido are developed ones; some are among the most vivid of all the images in *The Ring and the Book*, as that of the cockatrice (*GC*, 1938–54), or the snake:

> And thus I see him slowly and surely edged (*GC*, 1921)
> Off all the table-land whence life upsprings
> Aspiring to be immortality,
> As the snake, hatched on hill-top by mischance,

19. The meaning of line 1631, which terminates his summary of the case, is surely ambiguous: "You see the reduction *ad absurdum*, Sirs?"
20. See *GC*, 1781–1800.

> Despite his wriggling, slips, slides, slidders down
> Hill-side, lies low and prostrate on the smooth
> Level of the outer place . . .

Comparatively few other animal references exist in the monologue; the priest is not inclined to see his fellow men as beasts
—precisely because he sees them as souls. Perhaps the most notable
among the rest is a sheep image, used, as elsewhere in Browning,
to epitomize faith, but this time also to suggest stupidity. However, the faithful monk whose "nose" seemed "Smoothed to a
sheep's through no brains and much faith" (GC, 994), and whom
Caponsacchi stumbled over in his rush from church in Arezzo,
is described in terms that Caponsacchi indicates he might have
used before meeting Pompilia. Now, purified, Caponsacchi frowns
upon such a summing-up. Indeed his present humility is partly
revealed through animal figures applied to himself: he is an "over-
zealous hound" (GC, 100), a fly (twice), a bear, and a hog. His impassioned hatred of evil, his self-effacement and capacity for self-
reproof all become clear in his imagery.

In *Archangelis* animal imagery takes a surprising and comic
turn; more animals are mentioned in terms of food than in terms
which relate them to the attributes of other characters. Significantly Arcangeli dreams of eating some of the very animals used
by other speakers to characterize Pompilia—lamb, rabbit, fish, and
pigeon, for example. Not only his gluttony but his attitude toward his profession and the world in general is thus revealed; people, the law, Pompilia, are significant to the advocate only as they
are able to contribute to his own well-being and bodily satisfaction. Justice is unimportant. Truth is merely a legal fiction to be
used one way or another—so long as it helps to bring rich food
to the table, "for lambkins, we must live!" (HdA, 1805). " 'Feed
me with food convenient for me!' " he chants; "What / I' the
world should a wise man require beyond?" (HdA, 1778–79). He
sees Guido alternately as a bird, a beast, an insect, a bee, and an
elephant. The utter incongruity of these images suggests the extent to which Arcangeli appreciates the nature of evil when it
looms before his eyes. And as Guido is either bee or elephant, so
Pompilia is fox or fowl: neither is seen truly. Bottini alone, the

legal opponent who mildly disturbs Arcangeli's peace of mind, is
the only villain: he is pictured as a dog, a beast, a ferret, and (in
a moment of exultation) as an ass. Even Guido's accomplices in
murder are only fleas and hinds and in the case of one, Baldeschi,
a horse. Arcangeli sees himself as a goose and a fox, depending
upon his relative satisfaction with himself as he applies himself
to the business at hand. His animal imagery reveals an underly-
ing self-satisfaction, as well as voluptuousness, mental laziness and
a total blindness to people and to issues that lie beyond the me-
chanics of his profession on the one hand and his family circle
on the other.

A mere list of the animal images in *Pompilia* as they are directly related to character seems to indicate Pompilia's perception
of the truth. Guido's voracity is underlined: he is linked with
a lion, wolf, snake, wild beast, dog, owl, hawk, monster, and serpent, among others. Pompilia characterizes herself with images
of the lamb, young dove, cow and sheep, lure-owl, bee, fly, and
worm. Pietro is a crow; Violante an old dove; Gaetano, Pompilia's
child, a bird; Conti a stalking horse. However, the subject matter
of her images is far less revealing than the way in which the images themselves are expressed. The imagery of innocent and gentle
animals with which she pictures herself would, of course, tend
to suggest self-righteousness if Pompilia were shown as being fully
aware of its relation to her own character. Her imaging unlike
that of the other monologuists tends to reflect her utter lack of
attention to its character-revealing significance.

> —Well, I no more saw sense in what she said (*P*, 386)
> Than a lamb does in people clipping wool;
> Only lay down and let myself be clipped.

She is not aware that she is imaging Guido even when she does
it most vividly:

> I used to wonder, when I stood scarce high (*P*, 21)
> As the bed here, what the marble lion meant,
> With half his body rushing from the wall,
> Eating the figure of a prostrate man—
> (To the right, it is, of entry by the door)

An ominous sign to one baptized like me,
Married, and to be buried here, I hope.

The effect of this use of animal imagery in revealing Pompilia's
character is unique: the speaker seems to *be* true, without necessarily having an intellectual grasp of truth. Her true-seeing seems
to result from pureness of spirit alone. She brands Guido with
the same animals Caponsacchi has branded him with—snake, beast,
dog, hawk; and we feel that these animals appropriately picture
Guido's special ferocity; they are, as it were, true figures; but,
uttered in the way that they are, they do not reveal hatred or bitterness, or mental—as it is distinct from spiritual—awareness.
When Guido is directly linked with a ferocious animal the words
are not Pompilia's own but words she remembers that "friends"
cried out:

> 'Why, you Pompilia in the cavern thus, (*P*, 124)
> 'How comes that arm of yours about a wolf?
> 'And the soft length,—lies in and out your feet
> 'And laps you round the knee,—a snake it is!

Or the association is simply made through a remembered physical
resemblance: Guido had a "Hawk-nose" (*P*, 443). In one other
small but striking way her animal imagery reveals her: she is the
only speaker in *The Ring and the Book* to reverse the usual imaging process by describing an animal in terms of a human being:

> There was a foreigner had trained a goat, (*P*, 609)
> A shuddering white woman of a beast . . .

The image remains in the mind as one reads on. Pompilia alone
has compassion enough to see the "beast" and to feel for it in
the light of her own suffering.

In the penultimate dramatic monologue of *The Ring and the
Book,* the Pope summarizes with awareness the material that has
been presented from different points of view in the previous books.
Fairness, justice, mark his character. The key animal images for
Pompilia and Guido that have run like leitmotivs through the
other monologues—sometimes faintly, sometimes more clearly
heard—are now strongly reinforced. Repeatedly Guido is iden-

tified with "wolf" and Pompilia with "lamb"; the two images may even occur in the same passage, or as parts of a single wolf-lamb image. The Comparini, he says,

> . . . watched the wolf   (*TP,* 557)
> Feast on their heart, the lamb-like child his prey . . .

The Pope asks the Archbishop:

> How of this lamb that panted at thy foot   (*TP,* 989)
> While the wolf pressed on her within crook's reach?

Paolo is branded twice as the "fox" that he most resembles; Guido's accomplices are simply "swine"; the Comparini are finches; Guido's mother a "she-pard." Humankind in general for its element of guilt is likened to so many rodents, "Hurrying, each miscreant to his hole" (*TP,* 998) before the coming of God's flood—Judgment. Many animal names occur in isolation without reference to specific characters; the Pope sees men as living on exactly the level of the brute—men are, for this, no more than so many finches, flies, lions, owls, doves, fishes, elks, mudworms, and insects. However, Guido and Pompilia together occasion the greatest number of animal references. Although they are seen predominantly as wolf and lamb, Guido is also likened to a shell fish, slug, sand-fly, slush-worm, toad, and gor-crow, for example, and Pompilia to sheep, a white ermine, a fawn, a bird, a moth, a fly. These secondary animal images for the two principals echo the miscellany of animals with which they have been associated in previous monologues; but the Pope makes it clear which animal it is that most appropriately characterizes villain and heroine of the piece. Thus animal imagery reveals the speaker in several ways. The Pope's awareness is comprehensive; his mind takes in all things, all opinions. He knows what the two halves of Rome are thinking; he understands Caponsacchi's, Pompilia's and even Guido's point of view; in echoing their animal-imagery judgments, as it were, he reveals the fact that he understands and even participates in their individual thoughts and feelings. Yet the Pope is not only an understander of men: he is a judge, and the iterated lamb-wolf imagery reveals the intensity of his perception of right and wrong, innocence and guilt. The lamb as an image for innocence and the wolf as an image for guilt are, of course, simple and time-worn figures; but so is the problem of guilt and innocence, in the Pope's eyes, ultimately a simple and time-worn one. It is a measure of his moral courage and perception that, while cognizant of the many interpretations of Guido's and Pompilia's characters that exist at the time of his utterance, aware of many possible points of view, and still dedicated to truth, he is able to pronounce strong and definite judgment upon them —to see amid the confusion of circumstances and characteristics in each case the lamb and the wolf for what they really are.

COLOR, LIGHT, FOOD, PROFESSION, AND ENVIRONMENT

In the last section an attempt was made to cross a large and fertile stretch of land that is itself only one small part of a more enormous territory. Beyond Browning's animal imagery and its relation to character there lie within these twenty poems fields which we might rather arbitrarily stake out as color imagery, light-and-darkness imagery, food imagery, professional imagery, environmental-and-habit imagery, and perhaps false imagery—to suggest a prominent few, each including numerous images and imagistic effects of particular importance to character delineation. In considering any one of these "fields" with regard to a certain poem we should bear in mind two ideas that are always applicable. First, that each of Browning's portraits relies upon the interdependent effects of various kinds of imagery; if animal imagery is important in *Pompilia,* so is color imagery, light-and-darkness imagery, and particularly plant imagery,[21] and these "types" of imagery are all related and at least partly dependent on one another in helping to delineate Pompilia. Second, we must realize that any classification of imagery in these poems must itself be inadequate—Browning's images are probably no more classifiable than his monologues are. For convenience we have been consider-

---

21. " 'Why is it you are turned a sort of tree?' " Tisbe has asked her friend; Violante "plucked" Pompilia, her "wild briar-slip"; and for God Pompilia is "a bud," e.g. (*P,* 196, 302, 330). There are many other plant images. In this, Pompilia is artistically a cousin of Colombe, whom Browning imaged intricately with flowers (cf. above, pp. 75–76).

ing "animal imagery": but many animal images also involve color, lightness-and-darkness, and food; some could be considered "false" images, as well. The arbitrary marking-out of fields of imagery, however, does provide us with a means of seeing how Browning used somewhat similar imagistic subject-matter in different cases to achieve very different kinds of character-revealing effects, and no harm will be done if we bear in mind that we might well switch the field markers, or explore an image in terms of its generical relationship with other sets of images within the twenty poems or in terms of its artistic relationship with the other images in the poem in which it occurs.

Color imagery in Browning is often closely associated with animal imagery—indeed as color itself is usually seen by the monologuists as an attribute and not an entity, its imagistic effect is usually involved with that of some other kind of image—and it is not strange that in a poem such as *Caliban* we should find color images paralleling or reinforcing the effects of animal ones. Colors occur repeatedly in Caliban's animal descriptions: he imagines a brown badger with a white-wedge eye, a purple spotted crab, red crab nippers, blue feathered jays, a black otter and black beetles, and pink and purple flies, for example. And the color adjectives often receive special emphasis through syntactical and rhythmic placement:

'Say, this bruised fellow shall receive a worm, (*CUS*, 106)
And two worms he whose nippers end in red;

    . . . gives exact the scream o' the jay (*CUS*, 118)
When from her wing you twitch the feathers blue:

Or they may be emphasized through alliteration:

    . . . a certain badger brown   (*CUS*, 48)
He hath watched hunt with that slant white-wedge eye[.]

The immediate effect is to characterize vividly the animals of the poem, which in turn reflect Caliban's animality; but another effect of emphatic, contrasting colors here is to suggest the barbarian nature of Caliban directly—very much in the manner that prominent color imagery in *The Return of the Druses* had suggested the Druses' barbarism. In this sense all of the colors and

terms suggestive of color in Caliban reflect and reveal the speaker's character: *fire, icy, crystal, clay, chalk, flame, sparkles, sun,
blaze,* or specific colors applied to the sea, *green-dense,* or to the
lightning, *White flash,* for example.

A similar use of a kind of plethora of colors to suggest a dominant character trait may be seen in the earliest of the monologues
under discussion, *The Bishop at St. Praxed.* Not only are all of
the Bishop's strongest images involved with color, but it is just
color that the Bishop is most concerned with when he thinks of
his tomb. He hangs on to the notion of color, as it were, savoring
and repeating "blue" or "black" as it occurs to him with reference to the stone he wants.

> Blue as a vein o'er the Madonna's breast . . . (*BSP,* 44)
>
> .   .   .   .
>
> So, let the blue lump poise between my knees, (*BSP,* 47)
>
> Did I say basalt for my slab, sons? Black—(*BSP,* 53)
> 'T was ever antique-black I meant!

The color *peach* not only is repeated but is illustrated by the
use of *red*—so intense is the Bishop's preoccupation with it; the
passage is one of those rare ones in poetry where one named color
is successfully imaged by another:

> Peach-blossom marble all, the rare, the ripe (*BSP,* 29)
> As fresh-poured red wine of a mighty pulse.
>
> .   .   .   .
>
>   . . . True peach,   (*BSP,* 32)
> Rosy and flawless: how I earned the prize!

Yet, while dwelling upon each color momentarily, the Bishop
moves successively from color to color through the monologue,
from *peach* to *white* to *blue* to *black* to *green* to *brown,* and these
colors—all strongly emphasized either through localized repetition or through their presence in larger, arresting images, or both
—serve to point up his sensuality and love of art at one and the
same time. For his peaches, blues and blacks are themselves ob-
jets d'art for the Bishop; he treats them lovingly, almost ecstat-
ically, moving through a kind of luscious chromatic gallery of

them; so that when he is through we have the feeling that, despite
the acute anxiety and frustration that he experiences—for he
knows that he has not been able to "order" his tomb in any sense
—he has still in fact relished his discourse. Color, in being itself
exalted to the level of a prized possession, a Frascati villa, a statue
or a painting, marks the intensity of the Bishop's passion in a
way that is perhaps unequalled by the other sensuous images of
the poem.

One specific color may be used in a monologue to suggest a
character trait; the effect is most complex in certain speeches of
The Ring and the Book. At its simplest it may be seen in *Bishop
Blougram,* where Blougram's use of "my purple" (*BBA,* 942) suggests slightly more than the color of his ecclesiastical office, namely
the Bishop's consciousness of personal distinction from other men,
and pride. Purple- or dark-red-colored objects reflect Cleon's sense
of his own augustness; his portico is "Royal with sunset" (*C,* 10),
and his rhetorical illustrations include,

> The grapes which dye thy wine, are richer far, (*C,* 130)
> Through culture, than the wild wealth of the rock;
> The suave plum than the savage-tasted drupe;

and,

> The wild flower was the larger; I have dashed (*C,* 147)
> Rose-blood upon its petals, pricked its cup's
> Honey with wine . . .

Mr. Sludge's *umber, bistre,* and repeated *brown* become in effect
his characteristic colors and imagistically reflect his vulgarity and
ostensible repulsiveness.[22] His trickery—his role as Medium—is
underlined in a distorted or false color image:

> What snow may lose in white, snow gains in rose! (*MSM,* 677)

In *Andrea del Sarto,* silvery grey, the actual color of the twilight
setting, is identified with Andrea's present physical state and even,
in one sense, with his past and his art:

> A common greyness silvers everything,—   (*AdS,* 35)

22. See especially *MSM,* 755–57, 768–72.

> . . . I, at every point; (*AdS*, 38)
> My youth, my hope, my art, being all toned down
> To yonder sober pleasant Fiesole.

Andrea's art is "silver-grey / Placid and perfect" (*AdS*, 98–99), lacking in a quality that even inferior artists are able to impart because

> There burns a truer light of God in them,   (*AdS*, 79)
> In their vexed beating stuffed and stopped-up brain,
> Heart, or whate'er else, than goes on to prompt
> This low-pulsed forthright craftsman's hand of mine.

The light in other artists "burns" in their brains and hearts as it does not in his low-pulsed hand for these artists have "sudden blood" (*AdS*, 88). Burning light and blood represent the vigor and passion that Andrea has not. And yet at Fontainebleau there was a certain goldness that temporarily replaced the grey:

> I surely then could sometimes leave the ground, (*AdS*, 151)
> Put on the glory, Rafael's daily wear,
> In that humane great monarch's golden look,—
>
>   .   .   .   .
>
> The jingle of his gold chain in my ear,   (*AdS*, 157)

—except that, *too* "live the life grew, golden and not grey" (*AdS*, 168), and Andrea came home to Lucrezia with her "hair's gold" (*AdS*, 175), to see only in the mortar of a house built with money stolen from the king the remembered "fierce bright gold" of Francis' court (*AdS*, 217). His art at its best has responded to brilliance from the world without—Fontainebleau's and Lucrezia's goldness; in this sense it has absorbed some richness; but his paintings never have been fashioned with blood, burning light, passion that can come only from within the artist. A grey, soulless character has exploited gold—the rich, surface beauty of things —so that the gold has gone into his best paintings, with which he has now to an extent identified himself; but he has never possessed himself that blood-redness that grey becomes when soul is present.

As many of the same animal images recur from speech to speech so certain color images tend to do in *The Ring and the Book,* and four of its portraits are particularly significant for their uses of color—*Other Half-Rome, Caponsacchi, Pompilia,* and *The Pope.*

The speaker in *Other Half-Rome* uses six colors extensively, *black, white, red, blue, purple,* and *silver,* and the first three, which occur most frequently, are almost invariably associated with Guido, Pompilia, and Caponsacchi, respectively. In the speaker's imagination, Guido's shoe is black, his brow turns black, he has a black back, and in Rome before the murder Guido finds his way across town "by blind cuts and black turns" (*OH-R,* 1595). His blackness "broke" on Pompilia's life (*OH-R,* 15). Pompilia, on the other hand, is a "snow-white chick" (in Maratta the paint er's approvingly quoted words; *OH-R,* 65), and Other Half-Rome thinks of her "in the long white lazar house" (*OH-R,* 35), as hav- ing white lips, a wax-white complexion, as being buried in sleep by a white wave, and as a "Lily of a maiden, white with intact leaf" (*OH-R,* 365). Caponsacchi is a man of "redness and rustic- ity" (*OH-R,* 850), of "scarlet fiery innocence" (*OH-R,* 895); the priest is seen standing in "the red o' the morn" (*OH-R,* 1198), and red daybreak is in the sky when he reaches Castelnuovo with his charge. The room in which Pompilia wakes up to see Ca- ponsacchi a prisoner before her is "Ruddy with flame" (*OH-R,* 1152). When Pompilia and Caponsacchi are thought of together, Other Half-Rome links them in a blended color image:

> She makes confusion of the reddening white (*OH-R,* 1189)
> Which was the sunset when her strength gave way,
> And the next sunrise and its whitening red
> Which she revived in . . .

The color *silver* is associated with heaven, and once, rather for its nearness to white, with Pompilia ("she all silverly"; *OH-R,* 1305). The Church and its priests are associated with *purple; blue* is linked with heaven, as well, and once—in a connection with "sulphur-blaze" (*OH-R,* 1570)—with Guido. (Interestingly, Guido is not seen against the background of red flame, but blue, a color closer to Guido's characteristic one, black.) Other Half-Rome uses

black and *white* in another connection, in which, in effect, he
discusses his own color imagery—and in these lines may be found
the very key to his character:

> When we get weakness, and no guilt beside, (*OH-R,* 831)
> We have no such great ill-fortune: finding grey,
> We gladly call that white which might be black,
> Too used to the double-dye. So, if the priest
> Moved by Pompilia's youth and beauty, gave
> Way to the natural weakness. . . . Anyhow
> Here be facts, charactery; what they spell
> Determine, and thence pick what sense you may!

Even if Caponsacchi seduced Pompilia it is unimportant, we are
told, for that would indicate weakness merely, and not guilt, and
besides, if one is to find any moral significance in the facts at all,
one must reduce them to simplicities. Thus Caponsacchi is the
soul of courage: red alone. Guido is villainy incarnate: black.
Pompilia is purity itself: white. Ironically, Other Half-Rome's
color imagery is particularly appropriate for the central characters
he pictures, and Browning exploits the speaker's traits of emotionalism and superficiality—themselves revealed through Other Half-
Rome's unreflecting use of the three psychological primary colors,
black, white, and red, to characterize the three principals—in order to establish at an early point in *The Ring and the Book* certain colors that will truly suggest the moral characteristics of
Guido, Pompilia, and Caponsacchi. Other Half-Rome has stumbled
upon the truth accidentally by oversimplifying and even consciously distorting the facts as he perceives them: he insists that
Caponsacchi and Pompilia are absolutely "red" and "white" even
while admitting that the valiant priest may have compromised
the spotless girl. In effect he arrives at the truth in the wrong
way, and so exposes himself.

Black and white in *Caponsacchi* are also associated with villain
and heroine; *black* is used twelve times with reference to Guido
or Guido's presence, and *white* ten times for Pompilia. But here
the absoluteness of color imagery reveals something else about the
speaker who employs it. Caponsacchi has two strong feelings with
regard to the two principals: he hates one and loves the other. His

black-white imagery reveals his salient characteristic, passionate intensity, and it is passion rather than mere emotionalism that leads Caponsacchi to express the truth. His color images are for the most part uttered in the course of his narrative of the rescue. For example, he reports that he saw Pompilia framed in the "black square length" of Guido's window in Arezzo (*GC*, 703); Guido's false letters seemed a "black teasing lie" (*GC*, 678), and when the escape was finally arranged and the priest stood at the rendezvous near the San Spirito gate, he perceived "a whiteness in the distance" which waxed

> Whiter and whiter, near grew and more near, (*GC*, 1140)
> Till it was she: there did Pompilia come:
> The white I saw shine through her was her soul's,
> Certainly, for the body was one black,
> Black from head down to foot.

For the first hour "Blackness engulphed" him until he became aware of the "white face and hands" in the carriage (*GC*, 1179 80). Only after a day and a night's ride from Arezzo did the world itself begin to seem white: there was a "post-house, white and pleasant in the sun" (*GC*, 1322), and still later "the little white-walled clump" of Castelnuovo's buildings (*GC*, 1398). Gradually the black influence of Guido gave way to the whiteness of Pompilia, and only next morning in the courtyard of the inn—salvation almost at hand—did the whiteness revert suddenly to black. Guido caught up,

> . . . took the field, encamped his rights, (*GC*, 1435)
> Challenged the world: there leered new triumph, there
> Scowled the old malice in the visage bad
> And black o' the scamp.

"He the black figure, the opprobrious blur" leered over the prize —"Dead-white and disarmed," as she lay (*GC*, 1526, 1549). Caponsacchi's color imagery reflects honestly-felt and convincing passion, for it has arisen out of his own remembered psychological experience.

Color imagery is less striking in *Pompilia*—and it would seem for an excellent reason. Colors are peculiarly vibrant as poetic images and tend to convey intense feeling, passionate conviction, even primitivism or barbarism, when used in concentration. The Druses, Caliban, the Bishop at St. Praxed, Other Half-Rome, Caponsacchi, and even Andrea (who is acutely conscious of the fact that his life is colorless, all of a grey) have something in common for this: feeling itself is a particularly important factor in each of their character-complexes (its lack in Andrea's and Andrea's awareness of the lack, is involved in Andrea's personal tragedy), and color is used revealingly in each of their portraits. Pompilia on the other hand is half-saint at the time of her discourse; as she talks she withdraws from the world—she is "most upon the move" (*P*, 1775), and already purged of feelings that were once her own, all strictly human emotions, as it were. Her love and hate are the saint's own: love for goodness and hatred for evil as these concepts are entities in themselves. When she uses the black-white imagery of the other monologuists it is not to characterize Guido or herself but to suggest a special perception of good and evil in the world. Once, she relates, when she was ill, a doctor came with "Black jerkin and black buckles and black sword" (*P*, 415), a sour-faced, austere, ugly man, who gave her drops of "black" medicine; magically she was cured; then—

What mattered the fierce beard or the grim face? (*P*, 421)
It was the physic beautified the man.

The incident later led her to appraise Guido incorrectly, to dismiss the ugliness of his appearance and the ominous impression his personality created as immaterial to the true nature of his being; with Guido she was deceived. But the doctor nevertheless demonstrated to her a truth: that man, being in part evil, may indeed become beautified, atoning for that evil, by realizing the good. This is always man's possibility: ugly, evil, (black) as he seems, he may still become worthy of God. Pompilia is thus an advocate in man's behalf—on earth—as she is soon to become in heaven.[23]

23. Ironically, Pompilia is made to say, "Being right now, I am happy and *colour* things. / Yes, every body that leaves life sees all / Softened and bettered" (*P*, 354-56; my italic), although in fact she colors almost nothing—in any sense. In her own mind, she is now being subjective with respect to the old reality of her life with Guido; but in effect she becomes perfectly objective, for happiness functions as a purgative of her past feelings.

In *The Pope* there is a much harsher judgment of the human race, as it is represented in two of its very average members, the Comparini. "Go!" Innocent tells these two when he has conjured them up:

> Never again elude the choice of tints! (*TP*, 1234)
> White shall not neutralize the black, nor good
> Compensate bad in man, absolve him so . . .

The Pope's use of color illustrates his function as ultimate temporal arbiter and reveals not only his moral absolutism but his preoccupation with moral entities, the qualities of evil, goodness and courage in themselves. Rather than seeing primarily Guido as black, Pompilia as white, and Caponsacchi as red, he sees these colors first as representing universals with which men, in different cases, and to different extents, may be matched. Caponsacchi reminds him of olden knights who were

> White-cinct, because in white walks sanctity, (*TP*, 1162)
> Red-socked, how else proclaim fine scorn of flesh,
> Unchariness of blood when blood faith begs?

Pompilia is "Perfect in whiteness" (*TP*, 1005), and so fully partakes of white. Guido is not quite perfect in blackness because he partakes of another color-entity: the blue of lust, "hell's own blue tint / That gives a character and marks the man" (*TP*, 906–7). But blue approaches black. Yellow is identified with hypocrisy, "yellow that would pass for white" (*TP*, 882), a quality that Guido's brother Paolo shares. Caponsacchi's color is the most difficult to determine, as it were, for the priest's escapade has left much to be desired:

> . . . Do I smile?   (*TP*, 1126)
> Nay, Caponsacchi, much I find amiss,
> Blameworthy, punishable in this freak
> Of thine, this youth prolonged though age was ripe,
> This masquerade in sober day, with change
> Of motley too,—now hypocrite's-disguise,
> Now fool's-costume . . .

And Caponsacchi remains "good rose in its degree" (*TP*, 1098); for his "championship / Of God at first blush," reminiscent of the white-cinct red-socked knights, if not in every respect one of them; he stands against the red background of courage. In every case the Pope's central devotion to moral truth causes him to view the characters he must judge against a series of fundamental moral perceptions, identified with colors, so that it is in using colors with the discrimination that he does—in his matching of character to color—that his fairness and justness are reflected through the imagery.

Light-and-darkness imagery seems to play an incidental part in character delineation in many of the monologues at hand, but its role is more important in those involved with religious themes, particularly in *Bishop Blougram,* with its day-night and brightness-darkness opposites, and in *A Death in the Desert.* In the latter, light images combine in effect with those involving fire, and seeing (and its obverse, blindness), to reveal the spiritual nature of John. Pamphylax initiates the light imagery in his introductory verses: John, he writes, talked in the midmost grotto of his desert cave, where "noon's light" reached him a "little," and, when he was laid "in the light where we might see," this caused him to smile and to speak (*DD,* 26–27, 32). And John's homily begins with a fire image that not only explains its own character-revealing function, but suggests the purpose of most of the poem's images to come: "A stick," he declares,

> once fire from end to end: (*DD,* 105)
> "Now, ashes save the tip that holds a spark!
> "Yet, blow the spark, it runs back, spreads itself
> "A little where the fire was: thus I urge
> "The soul that served me, till it task once more
> "What ashes of my brain have kept their shape,
> "And these make effort on the last o' the flesh,
> "Trying to taste again the truth of things—"

When Christ Himself was alive, and during the vigorous period of his own discipleship, not only was John's soul aflame, but John burned bodily with the truth: every limb seemed alive with the purpose that animated him. The "tip" of the stick, with its spark— the soul with its perception of truth—now spreads through the ashes of the brain so that John may use his body one last time in order to give expression to that truth. And through the discourse fire and light images are constantly associated with that truth, or with its source (Christ), or with some of its effects. Thus Christ's eyes are "flame" (*DD*, 122); Christ Himself is "light" or—in man's eyes—the "indubitable bliss of fire" (*DD*, 298); miracles are "fire," and God's truth an "absolute blaze" (*DD*, 320). Terms associated with *light* and *fire* run throughout the poem, some of them often repeated—*ashes, spark, flame, fiery, torchlight, burning, blaze, sun, glimmer, glow, gleams, lamp, oil,* and *sight* (as opposed to blindness, or obtuseness to faith), for example. In the very plainness, directness, and relative abundance of these images, John's single characteristic, as it were, is strongly shown: he is entirely the man of God, the saint, the incarnation of fire and light. His portrait is, perhaps, unavoidably a monotone one; he is not permitted a human character-complex; and in reading the poem one's interest almost inevitably shifts away from John and to John's (and Browning's) argument—itself of little significance or interest to many readers now. Nevertheless, for its perfectly clear and self-evident use of imagery *A Death in the Desert* is a convincing example of Browning's practice of using imagery to reflect character traits; if the speech fails as a portrait because John's character itself lacks complexity—because John is, as it were, truth incarnate, and nothing else—the imagery at least fulfills its limited mission with effect.

Food images are common in the poems at hand, particularly in the monologues of *Mr. Sludge, Prince Hohenstiel-Schwangau,* and those of the two lawyers in *The Ring and the Book;* in the case of *Archangelis,* food, cooking, and eating are, in one way or another, connected with most of the poem's images, and we might for this reason consider in some detail the character-revealing effects of these. In *Archangelis* there is a kind of imagistic background of food references reminiscent of *Caliban's* numerous animals. Arcangeli mentions *acorn, barley loaf, cheese, cock's-comb, cucumber, egg, fennel, fish, fruit, goose, herb, lamb, liver, manna, melon, milk, mushroom, nut, Orvieto, pancake, parsley, pine-pip, porcupine, pork, rosolio, sauce,* and *soup,* as well as many other terms associated with eating or cooking: *supper-time, feast, cookery, crush cup, family board, dainties, jug, stew, roast, feed,* and *bite,* for example. In addition, most of the people and the subjects that enter Arcangeli's mind are, sooner or later, related to food images, so that Arcangeli seems to think in terms of food consistently—regardless of whatever else it is that he may be concentrating upon. Law itself

> . . . is the pork substratum of the fry, (*HDA,* 152)
> 'Goose-foot and cock's-comb are Latinity,'—
>
> .   .   .   .
>
> We'll garnish law with idiom, never fear!   (*HDA,* 155)

His adored son "chews Corderius with his morning crust" (*HDA,* 8), and soon will be

> —Trying his milk-teeth on some crusty case (*HDA,* 12)
> Like this, papa shall triturate full soon
> To smooth Papinianian pulp!

Even "Guido must be all goose-flesh" (*HDA,* 282), he reflects, and at length wearies of working on Guido's case, for

> I cannot stay much longer stewing here)   (*HDA,* 1385)
> Our stomach . . I mean, our soul—is stirred within . . .

The murderers "could masticate" their motives (*HDA,* 1619); he thinks of the *fruit* of force, of his *fattish* wife, of honor that *pours* and *sucks,* of casting his son as "bread upon the waters" (*HDA,* 1463).

Thus on two levels Arcangeli's characteristic gluttony is revealed: food, cooking and eating references through their sheer numerousness seem to form a continuous background through the monologue so that the lawyer never seems to *stop* thinking about food: part of his mind is, as it were, always at table. But at various points this steady obsession also intrudes upon specific and ostensibly unrelated matters at hand: the law, Guido, Giacinto, the accomplices in the murder, abstract concepts, are all imaged in terms of the table, and the effect of this is to show Arcangeli as a creature whose gluttony informs and to some extent dictates the nature of all his thoughts and actions. The world feeds and sustains the lawyer's own being: to the extent that it does—even Giacinto feeds his pride—it is good, and gains his support; to the extent that the world does not it is inconsequential. Truth itself is thus an irrelevant matter for Arcangeli, who is indeed blind to the very possibility of Pompilia's innocence. An individual food image may serve to point up implications of what we might call the gluttonous orientation:

> I spare that bone [a small point in the case]
> to Spreti and reserve   (*HDA,* 1575)
> Myself the juicier breast of argument—
> Flinging the breast-blade i' the face o' the Fisc,
> Who furnished me the tid-bit . . .

The food image is a particularly vivid one in this case for the action that it images: Arcangeli is selfish with his immediate colleagues (Spreti will be handed a mere bone) and vicious with legal opponents (Bottini will be struck in the face with a breast-blade); viciousness and selfishness, two of his salient traits, proceed from the still more fundamental sensuality of his character, and their relationships become clear through the character-revealing image.

A wide variety of images within the twenty monologues at hand might be considered under the heading of professional imagery. Thus Karshish's reports are professional images in the sense that they make use of professional observations to reflect certain elements of Karshish's character: his scientific orientation, his perceptiveness, and (symbolically, as in the animals that he mentions), his passion and perhaps his worldly wisdom. Fra Lippo Lippi images the world in terms of his profession:

> . . . This world's no blot for us, (*FLL,* 313)
> Nor blank; it means intensely, and means good . . .

For Lippo the artist a canvas or a fresco is either a "blot" or a "blank" on the one hand or, on the other, a work of art intense with some "good" meaning. There is no such thing as mere technical facility or superficial excellence in his art—as there is in the flawless painting of Andrea, for example; art is intense and meaningful or it is nothing, a mistake, or a blot. And the art image reflects Lippo's central characteristic: he too has passion and intensity. The world is imaged in terms of his profession, and the professional image that results underlines Lippo's nature. Cleon's professional images tend to be self-conscious and elaborate:

Suppose the artist made a perfect rhomb,   (C, 83)
And next a lozenge, then a trapezoid—
He did not overlay them, superimpose
The new upon the old and blot it out,
But laid them on a level in his work,
Making at last a picture . . .

.   .   .   .

[So] The portions of mankind [were made.] (C, 90)

Cleon, in this apology for the fact that he and his contemporaries
seem "not so great" (C, 66) when compared with their great Greek
forerunners, images men in the geometer-artist's terms: the men
of old were rhombs, lozenges and trapezoids, whereas the men of
the present are more complex geometrical figures—rhomb, lozenge
and trapezoid, as it were, superimposed. The image has been suggested to him by "the chequered pavement opposite" (C, 82), but
Cleon speaks as the professional artist and philosopher that he is,
or from a professional view-point, seeing men as so many geometrical figures and combinations of those figures. He reveals his
ingenuity in the image as well as what it is that he lacks: true
understanding of man's spirit. He oversimplifies humanity in
his cleverness, exposing his own self-complacent, vain, and un-
perceiving mind as he speaks. Many of Prince Hohenstiel-
Schwangau's images are drawn from the Prince's professional role
as national overseer of trade and industry. The Prince refers to
optics, mining, chemistry, agriculture, surveying, smelting, phar-
macy, minting, taxation, and various types of machinery and industrial processes, and suggests that an ideal "me" might well be a
manufactured one:

But grant me time, give me the management (PH-S, 1000)
And manufacture of a model me,
Me fifty-fold, a prince without a flaw . . .

His numerous industrial details imagistically reflect the mechanization of his character; whatever his virtues and vices as society's director, he has become dehumanized by the mechanical
leviathan over which he presides; the Prince is now part of it, its
machine-like "head." Thus professional imagery in Hohenstiel-
Schwangau helps to underline another kind of obtuseness in char-

acter—that resulting from the dehumanizing effect of a profession itself: the Prince has become the perfect materialist.

Images deriving from the environment and the personal habits of a speaker are almost omnipresent in the character-revealing monologues, and perhaps *Bishop Blougram* succinctly illustrates the possible range of these. His images are drawn from card-playing ("The hand's mine now, and here you follow suit"—*BBA*, 48), from chess ("We called the chess-board white,—we call it black"—*BBA*, 212), from clothes ("The naked life is gross till clothed upon"—*BBA*, 329), from the opera (of Verdi and Rossini —*BBA*, 381–86), from wealth or precious stones (*BBA*, 405–6), from French books (*BBA*, 398), sport (*BBA*, 544–49), incense (*BBA*, 552), his snuff-box (*BBA*, 669–72) or wine decanter (*BBA*, 690), and most impressively from travel. These images do not expose the Bishop's mind or heart with the same quick brilliance that some of his other images do—his animal or light-and-darkness ones—but in suggesting the things that he particularly likes or that he is familiar with they help to reveal the whole man. In effect, they circumscribe him. They illustrate or confirm those profounder insights into his make-up that come to us in other ways. Images drawn from the habits and surroundings of the other monologuists tend to have similar effects; in rare cases they may penetrate deeply, as it were, and expose something fundamental about the speaker; [24] but for the most part, in reflecting his habits, his background, and his incidental daily experiences, they help to particularize him and to lend credibility to the effects of more revealing images.

FALSE IMAGERY

The category of "false imagery" presents a special problem in the relationship between character and imagery in Browning. In

---

24. See, e.g., *TQ*, 258–67, where Tertium Quid's cruelty, scorn for the lower classes, and fawning respect for wealth are all reflected in his use of a rhetorical image inspired by the gem that His Excellency almost mistook for a stone to pelt birds with, but instead pocketed before the "five clowns o' the family / O' the vinedresser" could use for "flint's-service." The imagery material here is derived entirely from an object that the speaker's auditor happens to be wearing and from the local surroundings.

what sense are some of the monologue images "false"? When Mr. Sludge, in describing the nature of his own impulses, says,

> Beer flows thus, (*MSM*, 1303)

we feel that the image, although perhaps even comically inappropriate as a picture of normal human emotional processes, is still a fitting one in Mr. Sludge's case. But when he says two lines later:

> Don't let truth's lump rot stagnant for the lack (*MSM*, 1305)
> Of a timely helpful lie to leaven it!

—we react in a slightly different way. Mr. Sludge may liken himself to *beer;* that much of his rhetoric has comic validity in his own case; but the words "truth's lump" at the beginning of the next image introduce a figurative relationship that we feel is false and unallowable in itself; the identity only exists in Mr. Sludge's mind; we cannot share or sympathize with the same distorted perception.

But the problem of false imagery is complicated by something else. We do in fact tend to sympathize with Fra Lippo Lippi's likening of angels' wings to the "kirtles" of adulterous ladies,[25] even though the image is not only blasphemous but as far from what we feel to be true as any of Mr. Sludge's images. Whether we believe in the reality of angels or not, the concept of angels exists, and, objectively, angels have nothing whatever to do with women who play "hot cockles." We sympathize with Fra Lippo Lippi because we feel that his view of all God's creation is profoundly religious and sensual at the same time; for the moment we have been led to share this view, to look with Lippo's eyes, to see angels as he does. Thus whether an image is false in its effect would seem in general to depend upon the whole context of the monologue in which it occurs. In isolation Lippo's angels are as false as Sludge's lumpish truth.

At this point two questions arise: Is it merely an artistic deficiency in Browning that we are led to feel certain images are false even in the whole context of a monologue? And, when we are led to feel so, what is the effect of the image with relation to the character of the speaker who is being delineated?

25. See *FLL*, 347–83, especially 378–83.

Certainly it is true that some monologues among those at hand lead us to sympathize more fully with the speaker than others, and the false-image effect seems to occur most often in the speeches of monologuists for whom we feel comparatively less sympathy. Half-Rome refers to murder as a "farce" (*H-R*, 622); Hohenstiel-Schwangau speaks of great national and even metaphysical matters in terms of a *sugar-drop, tobacco-smoke,* and the "thin / White paring of your thumb-nail" (*PH-S*, 306–7). Bottini's imagery is false in its effect literally from beginning to end. Blougram jars us with images that seem, if not quite false to reality, then inappropriate, as in the reference to his church as a "lime-kiln" (*BBA*, 9). On the whole we feel less sympathy for Half-Rome, Hohenstiel-Schwangau, Bottini, and even Blougram, than we do, let us say, for Lippo, Andrea, Karshish, and Caponsacchi, whose speeches contain no images that in context impress us as being false to reality. The false-image effect might be said to be a sign of the poet's failure (intentional or otherwise) in this sense: for its occurrence—the fact that we are even aware of an image's striking us in a way that seems to jar our notion of what is true—invariably means the monologuist has failed to win our full sympathy at that point. Does this mean then that monologues full of false imagery—*Mr. Sludge, Bottinius* and *Guido,* for example—are failures as character portraits? If we accept Robert Langbaum's labeling of the dramatic monologue itself as "a poetry of sympathy" [26] then these poems are at least weak dramatic monologues; they fail, it would seem, as poems, to exploit one of the chief properties or advantages of the form. Yet we have an extremely definite impression of Mr. Sludge and of Bottini and of Guido as characters. Their portraits do not fail; but their characters appear to be prejudged by Browning. They are static in the sense that Uriah Heep is static; although some evidence is presented on their behalf the evidence is slanted, and in the end we feel disposed to condemn them as people rather than to feel compassion for them. Even Mr. Sludge, for all his peculiar glory, is in the last analysis a reprehensible man. Bottini is a comic villain, and Guido, as we shall see in detail, an arch, horrendously convincing, pure-black monster. When Bottini refers to Pompilia as a "cup" of oily nectar that lay

26. See *The Poetry of Experience*, p. 79 ff., and the discussion above, pp. 119–20.

> . . . with olent breast (*JDB,* 313)
> Open to gnat, midge, bee and moth as well . . .

we fail to sympathize with Bottini himself; we fail to accept his metaphor. And the chief effect here, as in the case of every false-image effect in the twenty monologues at hand, is to characterize the speaker as being below the level of compassionate sympathy: evil or contemptible, ultimately unpardonable.[27]

27. Although the false-image effect alienates us from the character who uses the false image, and we find him at that moment despicable and apparently unpardonable, he may win back our sympathy as we learn more about him. This seems to be the case in *Bishop Blougram,* for example, where we sense later that the church-lime-kiln comparison of line 9 has been delivered largely for Gigadibs' benefit—as a strategic move—and not because Blougram personally feels the image is a valid one. Mr. Sludge wins and loses our sympathy almost in the same breath, the frequent false-image effect functioning in this poem, it seems to me, as Browning's check on the reader's tendency to sympathize too greatly with a speaker who is honest with himself, candid beneath the cloak of spiritualism, and, above all, cheerful and courageous.

7. Diction

"In the language of Dante," said W. P. Ker, "there is no fixed rule. He can use the most artificial-seeming periphrases, he can draw where he pleases from the stores of Latin poetry and mythology, and at the same time he keeps command of the colloquial language and is not ashamed to use it." [1]

F EW critics have mentioned Dante in connection with Browning's diction—when they have, Browning has not come off very well [2]—but it is interesting that Professor Ker's remarks about *The Divine Comedy* seem to fit particularly well in the case of the twenty monologues at hand. In them, Browning certainly uses "artificial-seeming periphrases," draws in several ways from the stores of classical languages, makes the greatest and most unashamed use of colloquialisms, and demonstrates enormous variety in diction. And yet Browning's diction has a very much sorrier reputation than Dante's; apart from a few rather generalized defenses of it, and a sometimes grudging admission that Browning was a great Victorian innovator and a "forerunner" of present-day poetic diction, his use of language in the monologues is almost never singled out for particular praise. [3]

1. *Form and Style in Poetry, Lectures and Notes by W. P. Ker,* ed. R. W. Chambers (London, 1928), p. 169.
2. See, e.g., Henry Charles Duffin, *Amphibian: A Reconsideration of Browning* (London, 1956), p. 272.
3. In "Robert Browning," *The Victorian Poets . . . ,*" ed. Frederic E. Faverty (Cambridge, Mass., 1956), p. 58, William DeVane has stated that "Browning is clearly the forerunner of the modern poet in the matter of diction, as Sir Herbert Read recognized many years ago." But this judgment, however valid, has not received wide recognition among Browning's critics nor has it been clearly substantiated in any work that I have seen. Read's own statements about Browning's diction have usually been qualified. E.g. "As for Browning, he was neither mystical nor metaphysical, and I am not sure that it would not be legitimate to say that he was just wordy" ("The Nature of Metaphysical Poetry"); "Browning had no particular theory

Adverse criticisms have been numerous and they might be summarized as follows.

1. All Browning's monologuists talk alike—all, in fact, like Browning.[4]

2. Browning was unconcerned with words; he is verbose, capricious, and insensitive to the finer qualities of language.[5]

3. Browning was perversely concerned with words; he twists language for exhibitionary purposes and adopts preposterous coinages.[6]

4. Browning disdained simplicity; he uses technical terms that are not poetic, or that do not turn into poetry in his hands.[7]

Not many examples are usually cited to substantiate these claims; only Bernard Groom has attempted to document his findings appreciably—but the nature of Groom's broad survey of Arnold's, Tennyson's and Browning's diction precluded a discussion of Browning's words in context. Perhaps the most devastating

---

of diction: he wanted his verse to be expressive, and expressive it was—of his personality. But what he did do was considerably to enlarge the scope of poetry by adding certain categories of content to it . . ." ("Poetic Diction"); in Herbert Read, *Collected Essays in Literary Criticism* (London, 1938), pp. 84, 48. E. K. Brown has strongly defended Browning in his "Diction," *Victorian Poetry* (New York, 1942), pp. xxi-xxiii, a remarkable but unfortunately very brief essay.

4. This was a standard late-Victorian argument, and it is still echoed occasionally, as in the recent study of Duffin, p. 272. It is typified by: "It [i.e. *The Ring and the Book*] is marred by inordinate verbosity. The child-wife Pompilia tells her story in much the same language as her elderly and wicked husband, Count Guido, and the young Canon Caponsacchi; and all talk a good deal more like Robert Browning than any other human creature before or since." *Selections from Browning,* ed. Frederick Ryland (London, 1898), p. xvii.

5. See, e.g., Stopford A. Brooke, *The Poetry of Robert Browning* (London, 1905), *I,* 61; H. Read, *Collected Essays,* p. 84. For his insensitivity see Bernard Groom, *On the Diction of Tennyson, Browning and Arnold,* SPE Tract 53 (Oxford, 1939), p. 119: "He shows no more respect to one word than to another; he appears impatient of the finer tones of diction."

6. See, e.g., F. L. Lucas, *Ten Victorian Poets* (Cambridge, England, 1940), p. 34, and George Santayana, "The Poetry of Barbarism," *Interpretations of Poetry and Religion* (London, 1900), passim on Browning. For perversity in Browning's coining of words see Groom, pp. 127–28.

7. E.g. "[Browning's technical terms] do not in his hands immediately turn into poetry, like the technical terms of Milton in the line: / Cornice, or frieze with bossy sculptures graven. . . . No poetry is safe in ignoring altogether the ideal of simplicity. It is characteristic of Browning that he so seldom approaches the plain dignity of Biblical English. His diction is centrifugal: his restless activity impels him to avoid the norm . . ." Groom, pp. 126–27.

criticism of diction in the monologues to date has been that embodied in Calverley's parody of the ten in *The Ring and the Book:*

> I shoved the timber ope wi' my omoplat;
> And *in vestibulo,* i' the lobby to-wit,
> (Iacobi Facciolati's rendering, sir,)
> Donn'd galligaskins, antigropeloes,
> And so forth . . .
>
> . . . .
>
> . . *Ut,*
> Instance: *Sol ruit,* down flops sun, *et* and,
> *Montes umbrantur,* out flounce mountains. Pah!
> Excuse me, sir, I think I'm going mad.[8]

And indeed a speech from *The Ring and the Book—Pompilia—* is still the most frequently cited as illustrative of Browning's various failures in diction.[9]

Recently, in the revival of interest in the dramatic monologue, marked by King's and Langbaum's full-length studies in 1957, Browning's use of language in at least a handful of poems has been defended;[10] but most of the charges leveled against the language of the finest monologues have remained unanswered. One of the reasons for this would seem to be that Browning's diction has not been investigated at any length for its relationship to character portrayal. In the present chapter we shall examine ways and instances in which the monologue speaker is delineated through the words he uses. Conclusions from such a survey will pertain only

8. "The Cock and the Bull," *The Complete Works of C. S. Calverley* (London, 1901), pp. 110–14, lines 35–39, 120–23. The brillance of this parody is surely due in large part to Calverley's approximating Browning's diction—a feat that other Browning parodists have been unable to master. Cf., e.g., "Angelo Orders His Dinner," and other parodies of Browning in *A Century of Parody and Imitation,* ed. Walter Jerrold and R. M. Leonard, London, 1913.

9. See, e.g., Elmer Edgar Stoll, *From Shakespeare to Joyce* (New York, 1944), pp. 202–3; Frances Theresa Russell, *One Word More on Browning* (Stanford, 1927), p. 121; and Hugh Walker, *The Age of Tennyson* (London, 1897), p. 230. A. K. Cook's defense of *Pompilia* is important but not, in the end, convincing, as he does not account for the complex or unusual words in Pompilia's vocabulary that critics from the late-Victorians to E. E. Stoll have objected to. See *A Commentary upon Browning's The Ring and the Book* (London, 1920), pp. 139–45.

10. See Robert Langbaum, *The Poetry of Experience;* and especially Roma A. King, Jr., *The Bow and the Lyre.*

to the poems discussed, and yet these conclusions should carry a broader implication: that Browning was indeed sensitive to the finer qualities of words, and that his diction, when investigated in the light of character requirements in the character-revealing dramatic monologues, certainly seems to justify itself.

Before investigating the diction of the monologues in this light we must ask: in what sense *can* a word—in poetry or in prose—suggest something about the character of the person who uses it? "There is," as I. A. Richards has said,

> no such thing as *the* effect of a word or a sound. There is no one effect that belongs to it. Words have no intrinsic literary characters. None are either ugly or beautiful, intrinsically displeasing or delightful. Every word has instead a range of possible effects, varying with the conditions into which it is received.[11]

If we accept Richards' view, we must not take it to mean that there is no difference between, let us say, the effects of *ouf* and *antiphonary* (two words which occur in *Fra Lippo Lippi*). Yet in isolation neither the expletive nor the technical noun would be capable of suggesting unmistakably the character of the person who might utter it. Neither word has an intrinsic personality of its own. Both words have special ranges of possible effect conditioned by their natures as parts of speech, their kinds of meanings, their sounds, and perhaps even their lengths. And these possible effects are of course narrowed when the word occurs in context: then its sound, its syntactical position, and its meaning (including possible imagistic or symbolic meanings), and its other relationships to words that precede or follow it, become specific—and it is at this point that the word may convey something about the speaker who uses it.

The first basic way in which a word may convey character, then,

11. *Principles of Literary Criticism* (New York, Harcourt Brace, 1925), p. 136. See also Richards' "The Interinanimation of Words," in *The Philosophy of Rhetoric* (New York, 1936), p. 51: "I have been leading . . . to an extremely simple and obvious but fundamental remark: that no word can be judged as to whether it is good or bad, correct or incorrect . . . or anything else that matters to a writer, in isolation."

is simply through its position in a grammatical context, through its relationship with certain other words. Words often reveal their speakers in one other way as well, and in this sense the effect is less dependent upon the presence of other specific words for its operation. "In all discussions," the authors of *The Meaning of Meaning* have suggested, "we shall find that what is said is only in part determined by the things to which the speaker is referring. Often without a clear consciousness of the fact, people have pre-occupations which determine their use of words." [12] A word may tell something about its speaker through what we might call its revealing superfluousness; more may be conveyed through the speaker's *choice* of a particular word than what the speaker consciously intends. Words often carry something in addition to their denotative and even connotative meanings; and in spoken language the "addition" may tend to reflect the speaker's state of mind. In the monologues this seems to be most obvious when the word has an imagistic effect. When Lippo refers to his Florentine apprehenders as *hangdogs* (*FLL,* 27)—instead of as men, "guards," "subalterns," or the like—he does more than simply name the police underlings. His intention in using the word is complex in itself. He wishes: 1. to specify a group of men; 2. to show his disdain for them; 3. to establish the impression of his own aristocratic superiority over them and social affinity with the Police Chief; and 4. (perhaps unconsciously) to carry on his rhetorical image of the police as being hunters of animals rather than men: he associates them indirectly with "-dogs." [13] But Lippo's character is revealed in the choice as well; his cleverness and boldness come to light in its rhetorical aptness; worldliness is hinted in his use of a term certainly more common to the speech of townspeople than cloistered monks; and his own animal quality—his sensuality—is reflected, in the light of his particular situation, in his now indirectly associating dogs with men. Even when a word or a term is less vividly imagistic it may convey an impression of character in this way. For example Lippo's use of *ladies* (for the

12. C. K. Ogden and I. A. Richards. (6th ed.; London, 1944), p. 126.
13. Cf. OED, *hang-dog*, A. *sb.*, "A despicable or degraded fellow fit only to hang a dog, or to be hanged like a dog."

prostitutes of Florence) reveals Lippo's diplomacy, alertness, and even to a degree his sense of personal dignity and feeling of respect for his fellow creatures.

And yet in both basic ways the character-revealing effect of an individual word is dependent upon a larger framework: either the framework of other specific words, or the framework of a dramatic situation.[14] Words in Browning's monologues perhaps do not reveal character in any other "ways"—although within the very wide boundaries of these two basic ones a good deal is accomplished.

REPETITION AND KEY WORDS

Repetition itself is an obvious feature in almost all of Browning's poetry. We have noted its rhythmic and rhetorical uses in *Paracelsus;* and, as we shall see, it is an important element in Browning's use of sound to help depict character. In the monologues at hand marked repetition of words almost always has something to do with the speaker's revelation. Probably the most extensive use of it is made in *Andrea del Sarto.* Andrea may repeat words or phrases successively: *Quietly, quietly; Out of me, out of me; this, this, this; there, there;*—or a word in the same line,

> My face, my moon, my everybody's moon, (*AdS,* 29)

or in successive lines,

> His hue mistaken; what of that? or else, (*AdS,* 94)
> Rightly traced and well ordered; what of that?

Or adjectives may be repeated in a series—there are only two cases of this and only here does Andrea seem to be aware of his own rhetoric, as the terms receive special stress:

> But had you—oh, with the same perfect brow,   (*AdS,* 122)
> And perfect eyes, and more than perfect mouth . . .

14. In the dramatic monologue, of course, the situation itself is developed verbally, but Lippo's use of *hangdogs,* for example, tells something about Lippo even without reference to other specific words—that is, with reference only to his dramatic situation. Thus one might imagine a cinema production of *Fra Lippo Lippi* in which the monk's first 26 lines were replaced by silent dramatic action: if Lippo in his monk's garb then cried out the single word "Hangdogs!" the word would still tell us something about him—less, admittedly, than it does in the context of the poem.

They were born poor, lived poor, and poor they died (*AdS*, 253)

Apart from the more common particles, some four dozen different words occur at least twice within the two lines of one another in the monologue.[15] And yet this dense repetition is not obtrusive. In the lines,

> I can do with my pencil what I know, (*AdS*, 60)
> What I see, what at bottom of my heart
> I wish for, if I ever wish so deep—
> Do easily, too—when I say, perfectly,
> I do not boast, perhaps:

—the subject pronoun occurs seven times, *do* and *what* three times each, and *wish* twice, and there is syllable repetition, assonance and alliteration, all of which quietly reinforce the effect of the passage. Andrea's repetition suggests spiritual as well as physical debility; the relatively simple words repeated deprive his speech of an intellectual air and reflect the dominance of Andrea's mood over his whole being; even his thoughts come and go slowly; quickness, vigor, the passion of intellect are not his. Andrea is of course revealed at a particularly weary moment for him; but he reviews his life at this moment, so that the lassitude and moodiness partly conveyed through word repetition have the effect of seeming to be lifelong and inherent characteristics; it is difficult to imagine him otherwise.

His counterpart, Fra Lippo Lippi, repeats words far less often in successive lines, but when he does, he does it calculatingly, to heighten rhetoric:

> And I've been three weeks shut within my mew, (*FLL*, 47)
> A-painting for the great man, saints and saints
> And saints again.

It is a point in Lippo's favor, Lippo knows, that he began life as an orphan:

---

15. These include *autumn, blame, boils, brick, chance, come, do, does, dream, everybody, eyes, fetter, friend, gold, hour, less, look, moon, more, much, must, myself, not, one, out, own, perfect, please, point, poor, quietly, rich, rounds, should, side, smile, so, somewhat, speak, still, strive, there, this, triumph, understand, what, what's,* and *wish*.

> I was a baby when my mother died (*FLL,* 81)
> And father died and left me in the street.

The sympathy-gaining verb *died* is repeated. Lippo's very use of
repetition as a rhetorical device reflects alertness and shrewdness.
Blougram's word repetition exposes the even more consummate
master of rhetoric. The Bishop involves Gigadibs in a kind of
philosophic chess game in order to establish that there are only
two basic alternatives in life: the opposing sides of doubt and faith.
Repetition of words reinforces the rhetorical image of the game.
For example, he seems to let Gigadibs win an early move:

> I am much, you are nothing; you would be all, (*BBA,* 84)
> I would be merely much: you beat me there.

The repeated words emphasize Blougram's purpose: there are only
a limited number of pieces on either side, and a limited number of
spaces in which to move. Later the two opposing "sides" are called
for what they are, and the chess game between *faith* and *doubt*
becomes feverish. In effect Blougram takes over the whole board
and shows how the side that he favors must inevitably win:

> Once own the use of faith, I'll find you faith. (*BBA,* 600)
>   . . . You call for faith:
> I show you doubt, to prove that faith exists.
> The more of doubt, the stronger faith, I say,
> If faith o'ercomes doubt . . .
>
> .   .   .   .
>
> What matter though I doubt at every pore, (*BBA,* 610)
> Head-doubts, heart-doubts, doubts at my fingers' ends,
> Doubts in the trivial work of every day,
> Doubts at the very bases of my soul
>
> .   .   .   .
>
>   . . . shows it faith or doubt? (*BBA,* 619)
> All's doubt in me; where's break of faith in this?

Although *faith* and *doubt* (*doubts, -doubts*) occur 8 and 11 times
in these twenty lines, the words, or forms of the words, are actually used no less than 37 and 24 times respectively in *Bishop
Blougram* as a whole, and such frequent use seems to establish

them as keys. We might for present purposes call that word a
"key word" which is repeated so often or with such emphasis in
any one of the monologues at hand that the word in some way
becomes specially identified with the speaker and in so doing helps
to tell something about him, as Blougram's *doubt* and *faith* epitomize the central conflict in his own character. In almost every
monologue of the twenty Browning makes use of one or more
key words. In *Cleon,* for example, there is *joy.* The word occurs
14 times by itself, but also in such forms as *enjoy(ed), joy-giving,*
and *joy-hunger,* and its effect is reinforced through a series of
words similar in meaning and key effect: *glad, happy* (3 times),
happier, hope, and *cheer.* "Joy-hunger" is precisely what Cleon
most feels as he writes his pessimistic epistle to Protos: he yearns
for a meaningful rationale for life, an antidote to pessimism and a
source of joy, specifically, faith in some "future state" (*C,* 325),

> Unlimited in capability   (*C,* 326)
> For joy, as this [state] is in desire for joy,
> —To seek which, the joy-hunger forces us[.]

He is, as it were, a Christian without Christ, curtly dismissing the
possibility of significance in Paulus and Christus, but aware that
the fame, fortune, physical health, and enormous talents that he
now has are illusory if death is to obliterate them all. The word
joy is thus the key to his being. He is vain, arrogant, egocentric,
desperately stoic and unhappy because he lacks the very thing
that he keeps repeating.

Apart from incidental particles of speech the most frequently
repeated words in *Mr. Sludge* are *Sludge, cheat* (including other
forms of the verb, *Cheat's* [n.], and *cheatery*), and *sir.* All three are
keys to the Medium's character. The speaker's name is synonymic
for mud and slush (Browning links the word significantly in two
other poems: "sludge and slime" and "sludge and ugliness" [16]);
and the 56 instances of *Sludge* here have the function of infecting
even the most compelling arguments of Mr. Sludge with a certain
characteristic lowness and depravity. "Cheat's my name," Mr.
Sludge also says at one point (*MSM,* 430), and *cheat,* repeated in
one form or another 33 times, suggests his characteristic action and

16. See *Bottinius'* 370, and *Aristophanes' Apology,* 1708.

relationship to the world at large. The vocative *sir* appears 84 times, and yet, despite such frequency, its effect is perhaps less noticeable than that of *cheat* or *Sludge,* largely because its excessive use seems perfectly natural for the Medium:

Please, sir! your thumbs are through my windpipe, sir! (*MSM,* 17)

Nevertheless, the effect of this rather quietly omnipresent word is felt, for it constantly underlines the obsequiousness of Mr. Sludge in his role as spiritualist; in itself it is one of his little tricks—forever sirring, he is able to draw critical attention from his audacities by constantly and yet not over obviously acknowledging his hosts' superiority: he flatters away his opposition, as he must in order to survive, so that the word itself helps to characterize him as a professional, to suggest the nature of the cloak that he wears.

Pompilia has five favorite adjectives. All but one of them occur more frequently in her monologue than in any other in *The Ring and the Book,* and yet all five are among the more common in English—*good, poor, little, happy, kind.*[17] For the most part they are associated with Pietro and Violante, with God, the Virgin, or with time or event, and only rarely in a direct manner with Pompilia herself:

. . . the poor Virgin that I used to know   (*P,* 77)

.   .   .   .

Not even poor old Pietro's name, nor hers,   (*P,* 97)
Poor kind unwise Violante . . .

.   .   .   .

Good Pietro, kind Violante, gave me birth? (*P,* 135)

.   .   .   .

She could make happy, be made happy with, (*P,* 299)
This poor Violante . . .

.   .   .   .

17. She uses *good* 40 times, *poor* 19, *little* 12, *happy* 8, and *kind* (as an adjective) 5; only *little* is used more frequently in other monologues. The words receive special emphasis in being used either occasionally in series or, more often, with one another in recurring combinations. Although a few other words are used more often they do not receive such emphasis.

> . . . good at heart,   (*P*, 307)
> Good for my mother, good for me, and good
> For Pietro. . . .

But these adjectives, with the frequently occurring *love* (used as noun and verb) become identified with the speaker through her repetition and emphasis of them; the world, revealed through Pompilia's eyes, seems in turn to reveal her own image; *good, poor, little, happy, kind,* and *love,* in effect, apply to her own being primarily.

A word need not be repeated many times to have the function of a key word. Karshish for example uses *prodigious* thrice, but in each case with special reference to Lazarus.

> Discourse to him of prodigious armaments (*EK*, 146)
> Assembled to besiege his city now,
> And of the passing of a mule with gourds—
> 'T is one!

Lazarus looks at times as though

> He caught prodigious import, whole results; (*EK*, 153)

and the dead Nazarene's system of belief, which Lazarus subscribes to, is

> . . . a creed prodigious as described to me. (*EK*, 251)

The word is long and Latin, phonetically rather difficult, so that it slows slightly the rhythm of each verse in which it occurs; in sound it is reminiscent of certain others in the poem: *Karshish, all-sagacious, subinduced, exorcisation, physician,* for example, all of which, like *prodigious,* have at least two of the retarding dental continuants, (s), (ʃ), (z), or (ʒ). It seems typical of the speaker's vocabulary, and yet, unlike his other similarly sounding words, this one is reserved for Lazarus—the abnormal, extraordinary, marvelous case that Karshish reports—and unlike the other words *prodigious* is repeated. Its effect is to reveal Karshish's awe, not alone through its meaning but through its very repetition, for Karshish can think of no other word qualified to replace it; it is a key word in that it exposes through the emphasis that it receives that quality in Karshish that makes him particularly responsive to Lazarus—the scientist's capacity for and susceptibility to religious experience.

We might examine a final instance of the character-revealing effects of a key word in the case of *God* in *The Bishop at St. Praxed.*

The word occurs in the dying Bishop's monologue only seven times—although that is quite a lot considering his short 125-line speech; in a monologue as long as *Mr. Sludge* the equivalent statistical frequency would be seventy or eighty occurrences for the word. Each time the Bishop uses *God* the word has a somewhat different meaning. "Draw round my bed," he begins, inquiring of Anselm.

> Nephews—sons mine . . . ah God, I know not! (*BSP*, 3)

God here seems to represent not precisely the supernatural being whom the Bishop believes in, as the Bishop uses it, nor is it quite expletory—as the word *well* would be if the Bishop had said ". . . ah well, I know not!" Rather it is a special kind of interjection, not meaningless, for it reflects the Bishop's awareness of incongruity between his ecclesiastical office and commitments on the one hand, and on the other his own past behavior which has produced "sons." A little later, thinking of Gandolf's shrewd "snatch from out the corner South" with which Gandolf graced his bodily remains, the Bishop mutters:

> . . . God curse the same! (*BSP*, 19)

God becomes simply a convenient supernatural medium through which he may strike a last blow at his rival. The next three instances of the word come close together:

> Drop water gently till the surface sink,   (*BSP*, 38)
> And if ye find . . . Ah, God, I know not, I! . . .
> Bedded in store of rotten fig-leaves soft,
> And corded up in a tight olive-frail,
> Some lump, ah God, of *lapis lazuli,*
>
> .   .   .   .
>
> So, let the blue lump poise between my knees (*BSP*, 47)
> Like God the Father's globe on both his hands. . . .

"Ah, God, I know not, I!" in line 39 repeats the words of line 3, but the disclaimer is now slightly more emphatic, this *God* reflecting the Bishop's awareness of incongruity between his role as Bishop and, indeed, an act of the *present*. His "sons" are a sin of the past; his words now involve him in a new, venial sin, even as he speaks. In the next instance above *God* is merely an expression of his ardor with respect to the *lapis*. In line 48, *God* is the Almighty Maker of the world and Father of all mankind. Still later *God* becomes the Christ of transubstantiation: "And see God made and eaten all day long" (*BSP*, 82). And finally, *God* becomes equivalent merely to an expression of degree, a way saying that he knows his sons' wish for his death is a particularly intense one—

> For ye have stabbed me with ingratitude (*BSP*, 114)
> To death—ye wish it—God, ye wish it!

The key word itself thus has many uses for the Bishop. *God* is not only the Maker of the world and Father of man, as well as Christ, but a convenient weapon against a rival, a means of mitigating if not avoiding altogether the implications of past and present sin, a justification of sensual ardor, and a handy implement of rhetoric. It is a mark of the Bishop's ironic complexity: unlike Blougram, who is aware of the conflicting elements within himself and who must, self-consciously, seek to justify his character in his own eyes, the Bishop at St. Praxed has reached a state of being in which conflicting tendencies have produced their own rationale, in which religion and sensuality have become intertwined and inseparable.

DICTION AND DRAMATIC SITUATION: SIX CLASSES

In Browning's diction in the twenty monologues at hand there seem to be certain words that tell something about their speakers by virtue of their simply appearing at all; that is, these words are not entirely (and, sometimes, not even primarily) dependent upon a specific verbal context for their character-delineating effects, but upon a whole dramatic situation. To take a very elementary example, when Lippo, quoting his Carmelite prior, says,

> "We Carmelites, like those Camaldolese (*FLL*, 139)

—he tells something about himself simply by mentioning the name of his own great religious order as well as that of a lesser one, of the Camaldolese, who also had a monastery in Florence. The proper nouns help to identify Lippo the Florentine monk. In the monologues words which operate in this manner—often, to be sure, to a more subtle effect—seem to fall into a number of classes, and among these we might consider proper nouns, foreign expressions, compound epithets and compound nouns, archaic words, expletives, and colloquialisms. In many cases a word belonging to one of these classes may tell a good deal about a speaker by virtue of its place in a verbal context; but it will be of more interest for the moment to consider such words at least principally for what they reveal in the context of a monologue's whole effect.

1. PROPER NOUNS

Browning uses proper nouns extensively. Probably the widest collection of them all exists in *Prince Hohenstiel-Schwangau,* where the Prince's preoccupation with the social face of Europe— nations, cities, streets, historic landmarks, geographical areas— and, more importantly, his dilettantish concern for culture in almost all of its forms, are revealed just in the enormous variety of such terms that he is able to mention in a single utterance: *Leicester Square, Sphinx, Euclid, Europe, Residenz, Pradier Magdalen, London-town, Fourier, Comte, Bond Street, England, Hercules, Atlas, Œta, Proudhon, Rome, Rafael, Peter's Dome, Cayenne, Xerxes, Kant, The Critique of Pure Reason, Terni, Laocoön, Socialist Republic, Brennus, Austria, Adriatic, Alps, Savoy, Nice, Metternich, Homer,* and *Clitumnus,* for example.

Mr. Sludge's proper nouns are less eclectic; his provinciality is revealed in his citing popular American political and cultural heroes and American place-names and events, but comparatively few other proper nouns: *Catawba, Franklin, Tom Paine, Greeley, Boston, The President, Captain Sparks, Mexican War, Pennsylvanian, Horseshoe, Barnum, Shakers, Stars and Stripes, Broadway, Mars' Hill, Santa Claus, Indians, California, Jenny Lind, Emerson, the Benicia Boy, Beacon Street, Lowell, Longfellow,* and *Hawthorne.* Sludge's other proper nouns—e.g. *Bacon, Shakespeare, Solomon, Saint Paul, Mother Goose*—are neither so numerous nor uncommon as to distort the impression created by his many topical American ones.

Andrea del Sarto's proper nouns are few, but *Lucrezia, Rafael, Agnolo,* and *Cousin* all receive considerable emphasis through repetition. Andrea is not concerned with the world at large or with its places—he mentions only *France, Paris, Fontainebleau, Rome* (of his past), *Fiesole* (of the present), and the *New Jerusalem* (of an imagined future in heaven). Instead he focuses upon the few people who, in one way or another, ironically reflect his own deficiencies so that his use of proper nouns reveals a tendency toward introspection and self-criticism almost to the point of masochism; in repeating the names of the people who hurt him in their very triumph over him—*Agnolo, Rafael,* the *Cousin* and even *Lucrezia*—more often than he must in order to make his meaning clear, he does, in effect, squeeze a kind of exquisite pleasure from the horror of his own tragic predicament.

2. FOREIGN EXPRESSIONS

Foreign expressions occur in almost all of the monologues at hand although they are rarely so obtrusive as they appear to be in several monologues of *The Ring and the Book.* Incidentally their presence may serve to point up a speaker's worldly sophistication—*"Che che,"* Blougram may remonstrate to Gigadibs, for example (*BBA*, 45) [18]—or they may indicate the professional side of his character:

"We come to brother Lippo for all that, (*FLL*, 376)
"*Iste perfecit opus!*" [19]

—or even, as is partly the case with some of Arcangeli's Latin, the speaker's aesthetic sense or lack of it. Cleon does not quite depart from the English language, but many of his proper nouns are Greek—e.g. *Zeus, Poecile, Phidias, Naiad, Aeschylus*—and his vocabulary is filled with terms that have been taken over directly or

18. The effect in this case is actually emphasized in context through Blougram's calling attention to the Italian.

19. In context, *"Iste perfecit opus"* is put in the mouth of a pretty angel who is pleading to the "celestial presence" on Lippo's behalf. The only other Latin that Lippo offers is in his song—"Flower o' the clove, / All the Latin I construe is, 'amo' I love!" (*FLL*, 110–111). Lippo's avoiding Latin, or merrily denying that he knows any more than "amo," helps to suggest his own attitude toward the ceremonial and doctrinal aspects of the Church.

derived from Greek and which help not only to establish the
Greek-ness of Cleon, as it were, but to reflect his intellectual in-
sularity: *epos, phare, rhomb, trapezoid, sphere, sceptered, synthesis, spasms,* and *architect,* for example, among many others. A
number of Mr. Sludge's words are Americanisms—employed nowhere else in Browning—which reinforce the effect of the speaker's topical American proper nouns; he uses *cow-hide, egg-nogg,
hay-racks, corn-bag, prairie-dog, cock-tail, 'tisn't, V-note,* and *bran-
new,* as well as several rather magnificent pseudo-American expletives.

Approximately one verse in five of *Archangelis* contains some
Latin, 61 verses are entirely in Latin, and it is here that Browning
makes the most extensive use of foreign expressions in the monologues, even to the extent of employing a kind of auxiliary language in the lawyer's speech; thus Arcangeli may imagine Bottini's brief:

> 'Quod Guido designaverit elementa (*HDA,* 168)
> 'Dictæ epistolæ, quæ fuerint . . .

or plod haltingly through his own:

> *Enixe supplico,* I strive in prayer, (*HDA,* 1629)
> *Ut dominis meis,* that unto the Court,
> *Benigna fronte,* with a gracious brow,
> *Et oculis serenis,* and mild eyes . . .

yet if the chief effects of the Latin were merely to make the monologue seem more realistic and, perhaps, to realize new rhythmic
variations within *The Ring and the Book's* framework of 21,000
lines of blank verse, the device would probably be, as some critics
have thought it to be, a rather trying one for the reader. Arcangeli's abundant Latin, however, certainly has another purpose,
and to this effect it is ingeniously and even economically employed. Arcangeli's legal language represents the outward-facing,
professional side of his make-up; this is the part of Arcangeli that
the world sees and that directly influenced, or, in the end, lament-
ably for Guido, failed to influence, Guido's fate. But one of Browning's chief objects is to reveal the human being behind the formal
front: to show Arcangeli in relation to his worldly pose. Thus the

lawyer's attitude toward his own professional nature—the world-facing side of his make-up—is indicated in the first Latin to occur in the poem, which we may consider in context for a moment. Giacinto, Arcangeli imagines,

> —Branches me out his verb-tree on the slate, (*HdA*, 4)
> *Amo—as—avi—atum—are—ans,*
> Up to—*aturus,* person, tense, and mood,
> *Quies me cum subjunctivo* (I could cry). . . .

The gay burst of the *amare* conjugation, the strung-out snippets, the mixing of Latin and English so intimately that they combine to form the nonce word, "*quies,*" all reveal not only Arcangeli's easy familiarity with his professional role, but his lighthearted, casually detached, even partly comic view of it. Some time passes before Arcangeli gets down to work or before we hear more Latin; he is not enthusiastic about a profession which, ultimately, is for him an ordinary means of livelihood rather than a calling of particular significance. He begins his brief at line 128:

> *P-r-o pro Guidone et Sociis.*

The four words are laboriously written, the first one painstakingly spelled out; even this much deserves a self-congratulatory pat, "There!" encouraging him to continue:

> Count Guido married—or, in Latin due, (*HdA*, 129)
> What? *Duxit in uxorem?*—commonplace!
> *Tædas jugales iniit, subiit,*—ha!
> He underwent the matrimonial torch?
> *Connubio stabili sibi junxit,*—hum!
> In stable bond of marriage bound his own?
> That's clear of any modern taint: and yet . . .
>
> .   .   .   .
>
> He wedded,—ah, with owls for augury!   (*HdA*, 141)
> *Nupserat, heu sinistris avibus,*
> One of the blood Arezzo boasts her best,
> *Dominus Guido, nobili genere ortus,*
> *Pompiliæ* . . .

Slowly the case plods on. But as it does, so does the portrait of Arcangeli's mind become clear, bit by bit, and in intricate detail: despite his experience with the language it does not flow, for he is striving to build a careful image of himself as he goes along. What we are led to see in the Latin, as well as in the gaps between the Latin, in context, is the actual process of a character's constructing a social face for itself; simplicities are rejected, fantastic figures of speech are seized up, politically dangerous allusions are suppressed, human beings—Pompilia and Guido—are jammed into stock roles, flattering references to his auditors are incorporated in order to compensate for lack of logic (*"Sapientissimorum judicum"*—*HdA*, 930); Arcangeli becomes larger and more complete as his monologue continues. His Latin represents the final, pieced-together, polished, comically grandiloquent Arcangeli that the world is to see.

3. COMPOUND EPITHETS AND COMPOUND NOUNS

Over 3,000 compound epithets have been counted in Browning —more than twice the number in Shelley and Keats combined [20] —and the figure is not surprising for anyone familiar with the hyphen sprinkled *Aristophanes' Apology*, for example. It is evident that Browning was attracted (although not, perhaps, addicted) to compounding and that he used more and more compounds as he wrote; Massey found an average of one in 51.9 lines in the early verse, from *Pauline* to *The Return of the Druses;* one in 35 lines in *The Ring and the Book;* and one in 21.2 lines in the *Inn Album* to *Asolando* poems collectively.[21] The statistics are interesting, but they tend to be misleading in the implication that Browning borrowed and invented compounds without due regard for subject matter—which is, in fact, rarely the case in the poems at hand. In them, Browning uses many different types of compounds and these have very different effects and degrees of effect. For example, when Pompilia says *marriage-bond* or *bird-like* the combinations are so common that their effects *as*

20. B. W. A. Massey, *Browning's Vocabulary: Compound Epithets* (Poznan, 1931), p. 13, 38. Massey counted 3,030 compound epithets in Browning's 101,291 verses.

21. Ibid., p. 256. The over-all average for Browning's work was found to be one in 33.5 lines, and there seem to be fewest in the dramas (e.g. only 9 each in *In a Balcony* and *Strafford*).

compounds are negligible; unless used excessively, and Pompilia uses few, such compounds have no more significance than "bond of marriage" or "like a bird" would have. But when Karshish says *man's-flesh* or *not-incurious* something else happens: not only are these compounds unusual, but they are of an unusual type in English; the combining of *not* with an adjective seems to violate the genius of the language, which has been able to form negations through the assimilation of Latin prefixes. We should expect *not-incurious* to tell something in particular about the sort of speaker who would use it. In general we might say, then, that the effect of a compound in a monologue would seem to be involved with two factors always: the unusualness of the type of compounding that it involves, and the frequency of other compounds in its proximity. Tertium Quid, for example, may use many compounds within a few verses—as when he describes Guido as

> A husband poor, care-bitten, sorrow-sunk, (*TQ,* 717)
> Little, long-nosed, bush-bearded, lantern-jawed,
> Forty-six-years full . . .

And he may even coin a few: *house-dog-servant-things,* or *Wager-by-battle-of-cheating.* There is nothing unusual about *long-nosed* or *Forty-six-years,* but the presence of no less than six such compounds together is unusual enough to create a special effect: Tertium Quid's straining to be wittily descriptive, his attempt to seem engagingly sophisticated before his audience is hinted; the compounds in series reflect insecurity—one of Tertium Quid's prime characteristics. In another way his extravagant multiple compounds reinforce the effect. They are so elaborate, so plainly contrived, that they seem the result of a self-conscious act. The speaker struggles to display a quality of wit which he does not truly possess. Karshish's compounds on the other hand are not elaborate—he never links more than two words—but they tend to occur in significant clusters:

> Karshish, the picker-up of learning's crumbs, (*EK,* 1)
> The not-incurious in God's handiwork
> (This man's-flesh he hath admirably made,

> . . . fancy-scrawls (*EK*, 93)
> The just-returned and new-established soul
> So, the All-Great, were the All-Loving too—(*EK*, 305)

Most of these are uncommon or unique compound epithets; and most involve kinds of combinations that are rare in English; in the context of his monologue Karshish's compounds tend to reflect the orientalism of his mind (as the Druses' similarly do), the difference in his thought processes from the ordinary ones of the West, and in particular his scientific nature—for he treats words very much as he does scientific facts, approaching them with exacting care, employing them in new combinations to achieve new meanings. Caliban's, too, are not numerous; but some of the compounding that he does do is striking enough to tell something special about Caliban, as when he says,

> (Green-dense and dim-delicious, bred o' the sun) (*CUS*, 40)

or,

> Yon otter, sleek-wet, black, lithe as a leech: (*CUS*, 46)
> Yon auk, one fire-eye in a ball of foam . . .

Green-dense, dim-delicious, sleek-wet, fire-eye, and even *rock-stream, white-wedge, gourd-fruit,* and *flesh-meat,* have the effect of vivid sensuous images in themselves, so that Caliban's compounding seems in the context of his whole portrait to be a product of his animal-like vision and revealing of it.

4. ARCHAIC WORDS

Browning uses archaic diction frequently in the monologues at hand—particularly in *Cleon, Karshish, A Death in the Desert, The Bishop at St. Praxed, Caliban, Bottinius,* and *The Pope.* Archaic words and forms seem to have one of two different general functions in these monologues: either to indicate the distance of the speaker from the present in time, or to indicate something about his official role, or office. Cleon, Karshish, and St. John speak at the beginning of the Christian era; Caliban speaks from, ostensibly, a timeless past; [22] the dying Bishop, Bottini, and

22. Caliban's archaisms are reminiscent of those in *The Tempest.* Actually, many of Caliban's words are among those that Shakespeare's Caliban uses, e.g. *raven,*

the Pope, each speak, in a certain sense, *ex officio*. But there is a good deal of differentiation between the kinds of archaic forms that these speakers employ and the character-revealing effects of them. The Bishop at St. Praxed uses very few archaisms other than the informal pronoun form, *ye*, which he repeats more than a score of times. He uses *thee* only once—and then to coax an answer from Anselm; it is a mark of the Bishop's wiliness:

Ye mark me not! What do they whisper thee, (*BSP*, 63)
Child of my bowels, Anselm?

Apart from a few unobtrusive words such as *ay, nay, yon*, and *wot*, the Bishop's other archaic forms all occur in connection with biblical quotations or allusions ("Vanity, saith the preacher," "Man goeth to the grave," "Evil and brief hath been my pilgrimage"—*BSP*, 1, 52, 101), so that the archaic language here becomes identified with the Bishop's calling: it is the language of the Bishop as bishop in the monologue. Yet, in quietly infecting, as it were, a very large number of the Bishop's sentences through the omnipresent *ye* and the other small, unobtrusive archaisms that occur, this language has the effect of indicating that merging in the Bishop's character of worldly and spiritual elements—a merging of which the Bishop himself is scarcely aware; his ecclesiastical role and his sensuality are involved with each other, passion for God and passion for art, for the flesh, for stone, for color itself, sensuous objects and entities, are inextricably mixed within his being. Bottini uses archaic verb forms in order to impress his future auditors with the dignity of his conception of office and his own proper veneration of antiquity; the painter, in his first figure of speech (*JDB*, 17–50) "sedulously practiseth," "limneth," and "loseth" no feature of the subject that "poseth" for him. In addition he sprinkles his speech with archaic terms that reflect his literary grasp of reality rather than any true apprehension of life. He seems to have fed on the romantic literature of his day:

---

feather, isle, beetles, dam, god, fish, crabs, jay, nest (I, ii); *curse, pinch, urchin, mire, ape, bite, prick, hiss, brave, kiss, mock, lord, cheat, lie, beseech, quick, brain, books, skull, merry, catch* (II, ii); and *foot, quiet, mouth, fool*, and *toe* (IV, i). It is an interesting mark of Browning's concern for diction that he took the trouble to incorporate many of the older Caliban's words in creating his own version of Shakespeare's figure.

glebe, perdue, hist, mayhap, damsel, shoon, methinks, faulchion, scurril, and *quoth,* for example. The effect of these is reinforced through the presence of others that were rare by the nineteenth century or that represent peculiar usages (*eximious, uberous*), and by odd comparatives and superlatives: *wiselier, brisklier, clearliest, pitifullest, deliciousest.* Browning's fondness for the latter, of course, as well as for archaic and rare words, dates back to *Paracelsus;* but in *Bottinius*—as well as in the other monologues of *The Ring and the Book*—they are marshaled to serve the purposes of delineation; when they occur frequently they have an unmistakable effect. What is "beauty's sure concomitant," Bottini will ask the Court,

> Nay, intimate essential character, (*JDB,* 230)
> But melting wiles, deliciousest deceits,
> The whole redoubted armoury of love?
> Therefore of vernal pranks, dishevellings
> O' the hair of youth that dances April in,
> And easily-imagined Hebe-slips
> O'er sward which May makes over-smooth for foot—
> These shall we pry into?—or wiselier wink
> Though numerous and dear they may have been?

Bottini's diction is artificial and forced; just as his absurd figures reveal his pomposity and superficiality, so do his various types of archaisms and *-ier* and *-est* words.

There is an inconsistency in Browning's use of archaic forms in several monologues and the key to this lies in his treatment of character. In both *Karshish* and *Cleon,* for example, certain verbs appear in their modern or less inflected forms and others in their archaic. Karshish uses *writteth, blinketh, protesteth, attaineth, sufficeth, reassureth,* and *aboundeth,* but also *scales, cracks, takes, sets, puts, moves, springs* and *sinks.* At times the form of a third-person verb is clearly determined by the needs of sound or rhythm. Gum-tragacanth, Karshish writes,

> Scales off in purer flakes, shines clearer-grained, (*EK,* 56)
> Cracks 'twixt the pestle and the porphyry . . .

But here an observation is being precisely recorded; it is a mark of Karshish's fidelity to facts observed that he tries to indicate the quality of the tragacanth—its brittleness and glossiness—in the verbs he chooses: *scales* and *cracks* rather than "scaleth" or "cracketh" and *shines* instead of "shineth"; the very sounds of the archaic forms would be less exact for the purpose. Yet, turning to the larger matter at hand, he can begin by talking of his Syrian runner who *blinketh* and *protesteth*. In contrast, Cleon almost entirely avoids the archaic third person. All of his third-person verbs of more than one syllable appear in the modern form: *unlades, commends, compares, survives, refines, replies*— and he prefers the archaic only with a few very simple and short verbs, *hath, doth,* or with the second-person verbs that he uses, where the endings are slightly more mellifluous (avoiding the [εθ] sound): *sawest, followest, leavest, sayest.* Thus in *Karshish* the archaic form tends to be employed when the verb itself is longer and more complex and when the archaic ending increases the difficulty of the sound; in *Cleon* the archaic form is never employed by the speaker except to enhance rhythm, to add to the smoothness of a verse, to facilitate the easy progression of the discourse. Cleon shuns difficult forms. He is a poet, using language in a philosophic epistle to make his meaning as clear and vivid as possible. He sees clearly (as far as he sees), and wishes to make Protos see. Karshish, on the other hand, sees too much. His effort is to avoid as much as possible the direct and lucid explication of what is on his mind—even to avoid coming to it. His letter moves haltingly; he takes refuge even in diction, choosing the most difficult forms for his verbs—which at once slow down the flow of what he says and formalize the tenor of his whole report. Archaic verb forms in these two epistles are thus in large part determined by the requirements of character delineation.

5. EXPLETIVES

Browning's more ebullient monologuists tend to use the most expletives—also the most original and striking ones—and these tend to involve humor. Mr. Sludge's are certainly the most showy, his prize one constituting an extraordinary line of English blank verse:

Fol-lol-the-rido-liddle-iddle-ol! (*MSM*, 83)

Mr. Sludge chokes out two, *Aie - aie - aie* and *Ch - ch,* grumbles, *R-r-r,* sings, *illy-oh-yo,* and uses standard ones, *eh, oh, egad, ay,* and perhaps *presto.* Even words which are not used as expletives contribute to the expletory effect of much of his diction in being drawn out: *all - l - l - l, Bl - l - less, N - n - no!* The prime effect is to suggest the tenor of the speaker's normal condition: he is merry, buoyant, optimistic, overflowing with animal spirits. Touch him, and he does not quite burst into song but at least into a screech; psychologically, Sludge is a healthy extrovert. Yet the quality of his expletives suggests something else. In distorting language outrageously—grumbling, singing or shouting nonsense words and meaningless syllables—he displays little evident respect for English, specifically for the words which amount, in effect, to its most elemental convention, and in so doing Sludge reveals himself as having little evident respect for anything else. His expletives underline the immaturity and wildness that are a part of him—the eternal boy; and it is indeed just in his being a bad boy, cheating in make-believe games, shrieking, playing in the mud, that he elicits our qualified disapproval.

No other speaker quite touches Fra Lippo Lippi in his use of expletives, for even Mr. Sludge's extravagances, or Arcangeli's comic sputterings—*whew, bah, ha, hum, boh, foh, 'sbuddkins, tra-la-la*—are neither so numerous nor intense in their effect as many of Lippi's words and phrases that are best described as expletory. Lippo begins with *zooks* (used nowhere else in Browning), repeats it twice early in the monologue, and throws it out as his last word. Other expletives occur in doubles, *weke, weke,* or *well, well,* or:

> . . . Oh, oh, (*FLL*, 311)
> It makes me mad to see what men shall do
> And we in our graves!

Aha, boh, Lord, ouf, ah, ay, well, what, God wot, like enough, and *hail fellow, well met* are all used partly as expressive expletives—and many of his shorter exclamatory sentences have a similar effect: "Hang the fools!", "Bless the nuns!", "You be judge!"

(*FLL,* 335, 346, 280). Even Lippo's five famous bursts of song are expletive in the sense that they fill out Lippo's meaning emotionally without continuing his argument word for word:

> *Flower o' the quince,*   (*FLL,* 55)
> *I let Lisa go, and what good in life since?*

The effect of these lyric bursts reinforces the effect of *zooks* and the other exclamations; Lippo has more life than he can hold; indeed, the "cup runs over" and he does his "wild things" just because his mighty energy must have an outlet. His expletives reveal the intensity of his being; they express directly the superabundance of spirit that has helped to make him the magnificent painter, the God-loving monk, and the outright sensualist that he is. Unlike Arcangeli's expletory phrases, Lippo's tend to be unique, and unlike Mr. Sludge's they tend to be unique without doing violence to the language. So Lippo sees the world with independent eyes, but respects what he sees.

6. COLLOQUIALISMS

Lippo, as well as almost every other monologuist of the group, uses a diction which contains colloquial words. Lippo even resorts to special slang: *gullet's-gripe, hangdogs, stinger, hungerpinch, phiz, hot cockles.* His use of slang and colloquialisms reflects characteristic informality, unpretentiousness and modesty—traits which Lippo is anxious enough to impress his chief auditor with in order to gain sympathy, but which come to light so strongly and naturally as he speaks that we sense them to be unmistakably his own. Very often ordinary words are used in colloquial senses, as when Lippo describes his own act of painting: he "splashed" a fresco at Prato, "scrawled" men's faces on the antiphonary, and some evening soon will find him "at" his saints (*FLL,* 130, 246, 324). Mr. Sludge's colloquialisms are used in connection with almost every subject that he treats and their very frequency reflects something more than informality: the colloquial or slang mode is Mr. Sludge's normal mode of speech—behind the professional mask is the simple, robust, vulgar man, who uses *who the devil, prigs, V-notes, ma'am, rub-a-dub, puddled, cheatery, cruel* (adv.), *half-and-halfs, pothooks, tom-fool, gull, dung-heaps, fribble, wag, greenhorn, don't* (3d person sing.), *pinky, raree-show, what-d'you-call-'em, swap, blab, fiddle-fugues, stiffish, cuss,* and *throttled* ("throttled your sainted mother"), among others. Browning's use of "a-" prefixed words almost always has the effect of lending colloquialism to the context—and the presence of many of these within the whole of a monologue's diction produces a marked effect. Lippo employs such forms in order to humanize the more formal, immense, or abstract topics that he touches upon:

> . . . the slave that holds   (*FLL,* 33)
> John Baptist's head a-dangle by the hair
> . . . Giotto, with his Saint a-praising God   (*FLL,* 189)
> I always see the garden and God there   (*FLL,* 266)
> A-making man's wife . . .

Karshish uses *a-writing,* for example, to inject an air of casualness into a matter that he is anything but casual about; in context the word is a mark of his reluctance to admit to himself or to Abib the profoundly serious nature of his report:

> I half resolve to tell thee, yet I blush, (*EK,* 65)
> What set me off a-writing first of all.
> An itch I had, a sting to write, a tang!

If Browning uses colloquialisms—and types of words which have related effects, slang and a-prefix forms, e.g.—with surprising frequency, the reason is certainly not that he was obsessed by them, but that he found frequent need for them, and the need in the poems at hand is almost always involved with character requirements.

CHARACTERISTIC WORD GROUPS AND COMPLEX VOCABULARIES

But the kinds of words that we have been dealing with so far —"key" words, proper nouns, foreign expressions, archaisms, compounds, expletives, and colloquialisms—only represent a few minute categories in the monologues. There remain the great masses of the words that comprise the matrixes of the poems.

No doubt we should find it difficult to account even for a sizable proportion of all the words in any one monologue as there are over 900 even in *The Bishop at St. Praxed* (and probably 180,000 in the twenty poems at hand). Statistically-minded investigators of the future may of course take these figures in stride, but at the moment any accounting for very large numbers of Browning's words would seem to be impossible and useless, too, could it be done. In the shortest of poems there are words of no particular significance or "flavor" in themselves—these help to establish the meaning and effects of others, and are important only with regard to words that rather directly follow or precede them (or with regard to rhythm and sound effects), and in a long poem there are many. Yet we may still ask whether there are not fairly large groups of words that vary to some extent from monologue to monologue, and whether such groups are in any way characteristic of their speakers—specifically, whether they aid in delineation.

Certain words in each monologue might fall under the heading of technical or professional terms, or—when the speaker has no distinct "profession" or when, if he does have one, it is unimportant—terms which tell something about what he does, what he is like, or how he specially views the world. Browning's diction makes the most of a speaker's professional calling when the calling itself has influenced character. Thus Karshish uses a host of terms that reflect his role as physician: *blood, bone, plague-sores, ear, dead, choler, tertians, falling-sickness, cure, sublimate, ailing, eye, scalp-disease, leprosy, itch, sting, pains, ailment, mania, epilepsy, trance, drug, spell, exorcisation, out-breaking, body, life, physician, case, health, sanguine, proportioned, drug, balm, hands, brain, drunkenness, stupor, death, throb, blind, heart, feet, practitioners, disease, leech, mad, patient, sick, curer, nitrous, gum-tragacanth, cheek, teeth.*

Some of these are distinctly technical terms—*gum-tragacanth, tertians,* or *epilepsy*—and yet even words like *eye, blood, life,* or *heart* used in association with the more technical ones contribute to the effect of revealing Karshish's extremely professional mind and outlook. A relatively few specialized words condition the effect of many others.

Caliban uses many of the same physiological terms that Karshish does, but their effect is not influenced by the presence of relatively specialized ones. He sprawls:

> Flat on his belly in the pit's much mire, (*CUS*, 2)
> With elbows wide, fists clenched to prop his chin.
>   . . . kicks both feet in the cool slush,
> And feels about his spine small eft-things course,
> Run in and out each arm . . .

The terms *belly, elbows, fists, feet, spine,* and *arm* follow in close succession; later he uses *head, brow, eye, hair, beard, tongue, brain, back, mouth, leg, hand, hips, skin, toe, heart, scalp, bone, flesh, joint, skull, neck, thumb, finger,* and *tooth.*

Many of his verbs describe animal motions: *sprawl, clench, kick, creep, snap, flock, catch, crunch, scratch, scamper, cower, loll, flee, dive, run,* and *skud.* Or animal sounds: *peep, scream, snarl, chuckle, moan, groan,* and *hiss.* Or sensations: *tickle, bite, kiss, prick, pinch, sting, taste, ache, hunger, lick, ail.*

All but seven of the last sixty-four terms are monosyllables; all are common; not one is particularly arresting in itself perhaps. Yet they imbue the poem. They reflect and emphasize Caliban's physical being to the extent that even his thoughts seem to emanate from his body instead of his mind, exposing the thinking anthropoid.

Mr. Sludge has a very definite profession. But there are few terms of the spiritualist's trade in his monologue, which is somewhat surprising as the ordinary mumbo jumbo of astrologers and mediums is certainly vivid, specialized, amusing and extensive. Mr. Sludge uses *rap, tip, tilt, creak, spirit, manifestation, medium, odic lights, phosphor match, table,* and *phenomena,* all of which pertain to seances; but these suggest a very weak total of "professional" terms in 1525 lines of talk. Instead, neglecting the terms of his trade, he uses very frequently words such as *cheat, lie, gull, tricks,* or *gibberish,* and he even pokes fun at *phenomena,* stressing it so that it is italicized ("That's the bad memory . . ." his gulled gentlemen cry, "Or the unexplained *phenomena!*"—*MSM,* 151–52). However, Mr. Sludge himself is not fooled by spiritualism; his profession has little to do with his real character—it

is only his outer guise. The paucity of professional terms is a
mark of his detachment from his role; in this (as in other ways)
he is a pole apart from Karshish, whose professionalism has
molded his character—Karshish speaks constantly in the terms of
his calling. Rather, Mr. Sludge is rendered through terms which
express the very quality of his being. He is quick, loud, brash,
physically dextrous, and vulgar. These are among his typical verbs:
*scream, pops, blurt, blab, strut, squawk, ferrets, gulped, crow, rave,
foam, fling, rend, gibe, jeer, peep, hustle, spit, toss, turn, shove,
tilt, crack, twitch, snaps, scratch, cower, bully, fret, sulk, grin,
whimper, spout, spawl, spin, gull, leap, raps, hack, hew, throttle,
swap, choke, cheat, thrashed.*

A few, though not many, are the same as Caliban's. The majority are short verbs of action, and their cumulative effect through
the poem is to express vividly noise, violence, mimicking, and
vulgar movements, so that they suggest the level on which Sludge's
mind and being operate—a level which, in some respects, is not
far removed from Caliban's; they epitomize the crude agility, the
merriness and the depravity, the naughty adolescence of Mr.
Sludge.

Caponsacchi's vocabulary is composed of a few bits of Church
Latin (some of which he mimics: *"in secula / Secu-lo-o-o-o-rum"*;
GC, 448–49), *corona, angelus,* some slightly uncommon words, or
words that contrast with the prevailing tone of his others, *irre-
fragably, fulgurant, cartulary, divagation,* for example, a few of
which he puts in his judges' mouths:

Why, Sirs, what's this? Why, this is sorry and strange!—

(GC, 1955)

Futility, divagation: this from me
Bound to be rational[?]

—but the vast majority of his words are extremely common ones,
reflecting neither his profession nor his intellectuality, but his
mind's whole orientation. His nouns tend to express simple or
common abstractions—most having to do with religion or moral-
ity: *splendour, glory, beauty, soul, love, sin, hell, mirth, mystery,
peril, heaven, judgment-day, truth, courage, honour, prudence,*

wickedness, death, hate, truth, obedience, guilt, woe, joy, hope, lust, fiends, faith, doubt, grace, good, peace, devils, zeal, malice, fate, innocence, justice, virtue, grandeur.

And his modifiers are frequently adjectives of quality: *good, blameless, brave, over-zealous, wrong, best, quaint, reputable, better, worse, bad, pure, taintless, wise, honest, proper, holy, holiest, unworthy, superior, beautiful, mean, fair, hideous, wicked, false, true, perfect, divine, precious.*

People, places, concrete objects of the world, are of significance to the priest just for their being good, bad, beautiful, hideous, black, or white. The first instant that he sees Pompilia she is partly judged; finding himself "at the theatre one night / With a brother Canon," he suddenly saw:

A lady, young, tall, beautiful, strange and sad. (*GC, 399*)

She smiled a "beautiful sad strange smile" (*GC, 412* and *436*). Pompilia was the *sad strange* wife, a *great grave griefful* personality, a *wonderful white* soul. Dying, never was one "So sweet and true and pure and beautiful" (*GC, 2063*). Guido, from the first, is "the black, mean and small"—words Caponsacchi puts in Conti's mouth but which infallibly reflect his own judgment (*GC, 427*); and Caponsacchi sees himself judged through his judges' eyes alternately as "priest, coxcomb, fribble and fool" and the "very reputable priest" (*GC, 98, 117*). His vocabulary—with its high proportion of abstract nouns, many having to do with moral and religious concepts, with its adjectives frequently expressive of quality and often used in series, and with its paucity of concrete referents—reveals the morally intense, unworldly, idealistic man, and is, perhaps, as much as anything else in *Caponsacchi*, a mark of the priest's true nature.

That other man of God, the Bishop at St. Praxed, uses a notable number of technical and concrete nouns in his short discourse: *marble* (so vivid for the Bishop that it seems to live and talk— "marble's language," "great smooth marbly limbs"; *BSP, 98, 75*), *onion-stone, lapis lazuli, basalt, travertine, jasper, gritstone, tabernacle, epistle-side, mortcloth, entablature,* or *altar-ministrants,* for example. Despite haziness, he is most concrete about what he "orders":

The *bas-relief* in *bronze* ye promised me, (*BSP*, 56; italics mine)
Those *Pans* and *Nymphs* ye wot of, and perchance
Some *tripod, thyrsis,* with a *vase* or so,
The *Saviour* at his *sermon on the mount,*
Saint Praxed in a *glory,* and one *Pan*
Ready to twitch the *Nymph's* last *garment* off,
And *Moses* with the *tables* . . .

The result is that a majority of his substantives seem to represent sensuous objects; even *glory* in this context suggests something entirely different from what it would for Caponsacchi—for the Bishop, an envisioned conglomeration of haloes, harps and shimmering robes, rather than an almost unimaginable attribute of a saint. There are few enough abstract terms in his monologue so that many of the ones that he does use have the effect of seeming to be concrete. Often the abstract term is avoided for the sensuous word or phrase: for celebration of the mass, "mutter of the mass" (*BSP*, 81), or for transubstantiation—

And see God made and eaten all day long[.] (*BSP,* 82)

The Bishop's nouns and noun substitutes reveal his all-pervading, all-encompassing sensuousness, reflecting his sensuality in its ironic conflict with the aestheticism and piety of his character.

In the 2,155-line *Prince Hohenstiel-Schwangau* Browning draws from an enormous range in diction—one is tempted to say that, if the Prince does not use Mr. Sludge's wildly inventive expletives or the Greek-approximating compounds of *Aristophanes,* there is still almost no type of word within the span of Browning's own remarkable vocabulary that he does not in fact employ. The Prince's diction is in character. But the portrait is perhaps a failure—not because it fails to produce an impression of the Prince's character, or because it is filled with topical allusions and because the Prince must discuss the problems of his day at some length in order to reveal himself, but because the impression lacks intensity. Its diction is experimental in that it excludes no polysyllabic or technical term that a widely-experienced mid-Victorian Saviour of Society might not in fact employ (and *Hohenstiel-Schwangau* is in this sense a kind of imaginary literal transcript of a soliloquy that an English-speaking Louis Napoleon—perhaps a particularly resourceful Louis Napoleon—might deliver). Browning's attempt is not so much to condense his effects, to economize on diction—as he does even in the long and argumentative *Bishop Blougram*—but, to a large extent, to duplicate the real, to include all that a real talk of this kind might include.[23]

Nevertheless, the Prince reveals himself to a surprising extent through his diction—and, as it were, unwittingly. He lacks, first of all, as the very sound of his name implies, personal grace. He is essentially in Browning's eyes the mechanical chief of a large and complicated machine. He repeats his own awkward name no less than 30 times, playing upon it: *Hohenstiel-Schwangau, Hohenstielers-Schwangauese, Hohenstiel-Schwangau-fashion.* He uses every polysyllable that comes to mind, almost to the point of seeming to search for the complex Latin derivative where the shorter word might do. He loves *im-* and *in-* prefixes: *immortality, impotency, immobility, immensity, impertinence, imperative, impulsive, insincerity, incompleteness, indistinctness, insignificance, intelligency, ingredients, interlocutors, intermediate, inanimate, ineffective, intimatest, inferentially.*

Five syllables do not dismay him; he may even use words of six: *incommensurably, uncharitableness, unstridulosity, autobiography, susceptibility.*[24] And at the same time he does draw upon words from a multitude of modern affairs and a miscellany of

23. "Well, dear," Browning wrote to Miss Blagden on January 25, 1872, "I am glad you like what the Editor of the Edinburgh [Review] . . . calls my 'eulogium on the Second Empire': which it is not, any more than what another wiseacre affirms to be a 'scandalous attack on the old constant friend of England'—it is just what I imagine the man might, if he pleased, say for himself." *Dearest Isa: Robert Browning's Letters to Isabella Blagden,* ed. Edward C. McAleer (Austin, 1951), p. 372. DeVane, in quoting the last 15 words of this extract, says of it, that here "Browning gives, in little, the whole intention of his dramatic monologues . . ." *Handbook,* p. 360. But this is surely quite mistaken. Browning's monologuists, in the best instances, deliver far more intense impressions of themselves than their real-life counterparts (if we may imagine them) could possibly deliver even if they "pleased"; and Browning himself was usually aware that the disciplined and catalyzing operations of his art were needed if the raw materials of every-day life—what men might say of themselves if they "pleased," what some of them did say, in fact, in the raw materials of *The Old Yellow Book*—were to become effective character-revealing dramatic monologues. See, e.g., Browning's discussion of his own role in Book I of *The Ring and the Book,* esp. lines 698–705.

24. Even one of seven: *intercommunication.*

disciplines; a catalogue of his nouns would probably read like an index to nineteenth-century human endeavor. Among them are *amendment, bequeathment, boulevard-building, business, bureaucrat, butcher's-work, chemist, computists, conservator, convict-transport, council-chambers, custom-house, emancipation, embryo, employment, geometry, government, honorarium-fee, horticulture, husbandry, journalists, lawgiver, machine, management, manufacture, manufactory, market-place, mathematics, medicament, metropolis, ministry, mintage, mollusc, mountain-frontier, patriotism, penmanship, philanthropy, pomatum, protocols, republic, sovereignty, tenements.*

Yet if the presence of many such words reflects the Prince's connection with the mid-Victorian social machine, the connection itself is a mechanical and superficial one—for the Prince cannot talk in a simple human way about his *boulevard-building, mathematics* and *tenements.* His talk is interlarded with what is in context merely bureaucratic jargon: *whatsoever, aforesaid, stablify, nondescript, admeasurement, inferentially, unstridulosity.* The result is that he truly emerges as the bleak and bloodless governor of a social leviathan, dehumanized by his very role, his manner of expression so true to life that—from our own point of view, as readers of his long monologue—he is unforgivably tiresome. Thus the soliloquy of the Prince remains as an interesting poetic experiment lacking only in that concentration that seems to be the genius and the condition of the effective dramatic monologue (as it is, indeed, of all poetry)—whatever the special requirements of character delineation may be in the eyes of the poet. Lippo's *hangdogs* and the Prince's *horticulture* are equally appropriate for their speakers; but Lippo's word tells a half-dozen things about Lippo; it works in many ways. Beside it, the Prince's *horticulture* has the effect of a raucous clash of consonants fairly empty of meaning.

The failure in *Hohenstiel-Schwangau's* diction, however, is not due to the presence of words that are out of character for the speaker or even that completely fail to express the speaker's character, but to the presence of too many of the same kinds of words that have the effect of telling the same thing about the Prince over and over; and this is true despite the fact the Prince uses a few words, at least, of almost every kind that Browning did—very nearly sampling the range of the poet's vocabulary.[25]

The failure, too, does not seem to implicate the diction of the other monologues at hand. A failing Browning has been charged with frequently, however, and which does seem to implicate several, is that some words seem to occur from time to time that a speaker would not naturally use, and *Pompilia* is perhaps the poetic speech most often cited to support this claim.

"I am just seventeen years and five months old," (*P*, 1) Pompilia begins simply enough, but goes on to use: *unperverse, perquisite, imposthume, traditionary, suffusion, quintessence, pellucid, importunate, calumny,* and *evanishment,* among some thirty or forty words in her 1845 lines that seem too complex or rare to belong to an adolescent's vocabulary. Shakespeare's Juliet, three years Pompilia's junior, uses a number of words that seem beyond the vocabulary of a fourteen-year-old Veronese: *nimble-pinioned, wolvish-ravening, perjuries, idolatry, ill-divining, stratagem, behoveful, tributary, environed*—although her character is perhaps less dependent upon the effects of individual words in context than is Pompilia's.[26] And yet Juliet and Pompilia are both portrayed as being—in different senses—considerably beyond their years. Gaetano, Pompilia thinks, may one day ask what his mother looked like; and, she knows,

> People may answer 'Like girls of seventeen'—(*P*, 68)
>
> .   .   .   .
>
> Lucias, Marias, Sofias, who titter or blush[;] (*P*, 70)
>
> .   .   .   .
>
> Therefore I wish some one will please to say (*P*, 72)
> I looked already old though I was young;

for, despite appearances, she is no more like

> Girls who look arch or redden when boys laugh, (*P*, 76)

25. His archaisms (e.g., *rede* [as in line 11], *forsooth*) and foreign expressions are very few, and much of his diction is ironic. Slang, colloquialisms, technical terms, and various types of compounds seem especially abundant.

26. I am aware that Juliet's age and, to some extent, the nature of her vocabulary, are owing to romantic conventions within which Shakespeare was writing. Nevertheless, it is not beside the point to note that a strong precedent existed in poetic drama before the nineteenth century for assigning "adult" words to the vocabularies of young heroines.

Than the poor Virgin that I used to know
At our street-corner in a lonely niche,—
The babe, that sat upon her knees, broke off,—
Thin white glazed clay . . .

Pompilia is thus no more like a seventeen-year-old girl than she is like the Virgin Herself, who is identified with Pompilia's own color-image, white. But if she is neither one nor the other what she truly is is something of both, that is, nothing less than the girl who is the saint. Her diction reflects this duality. The vast majority of her words are so common as to be well within the ken of an English-speaking girl half her age; her typical adjectives in fact belong to a child's vocabulary: *poor, good, little, kind, happy, pretty, great, merry, strong, bad, old, young, lonely, fat, thin, gay, terrible, strange, stern, tall, wicked, greedy, friendly, cheap, right, wrong, thick, wild, ugly, fair, ill, sharp, dark, heavy, long, weak, pure, faint, quiet, blind, patient, silent, grave, round, angry, rough, true, false, blessed, cold, cruel, free, calm, dreadful, solemn, lazy, hard, small, brave, solid, magic, safe, real, sure.*

Words of more than two syllables average about one in 5.25 lines, and most are not difficult; her first ten (apart from proper nouns) are typical of all but a very small number that she uses: *seventeen,* [church's] *register, laughable, omitting, stranger-like, particular, ominous, remembers, twenty-two, dagger-wounds.* Moreover, her very simplest words tend to be those which she repeats, so that she really has, as it were, three vocabularies: one consisting of common terms that a child might use, and that she draws on most frequently, even to the point of repeating certain ones again and again; a second consisting of terms only slightly more complex in structure but not so rare or technical as to be beyond the scope of an intelligent seventeen-year-old, and which she does not repeat; and a third consisting of a very few terms well beyond the scope of an adolescent's speaking vocabulary. These few complex terms are the ones that suggest Pompilia is more than the young girl she appears to be. In meaning, some of them seem to reflect her own spiritual transcendency: *quintessence, pellucid, immeasurable, inimitable, extremity, estrangement, exultingly, invincible, evanishment.* Others she merely remembers from what people have said to her; she quotes Paolo as having used *syllabub* and *embittered,* Violante as having used *volatile* and *unperverse,* Don Celestine as having used *traditionary,* the Archbishop as having used *perquisite,* Margherita as having used *imposthume,* the citizens of Arezzo as having used *turbidity.* Pompilia is remembering these relatively complex and rare words from conversations that took place months ago, however, and so the words would seem to be part of her own third vocabulary, composed of words small in number, but too difficult to have been mastered by a mere girl. These terms and particularly the ones that she does not quote from other speeches in effect transcend her own mentality. They hint of wisdom that has not come directly from experience. And in so doing they suggest that some quality in Pompilia is a transcendent and inexplicable one: she is part adolescent—no stupider or wiser than Lucia, Maria and Sofia who blush and titter, perhaps—but partly something timeless and special and rare: part Virgin and saint.

We should at least suspect at this point that many of the so-called "Browningisms" of Browning are nothing more nor less than verbal devices for the revelation of character, and that special kinds of words (a-prefixed words or colloquialisms, for example) may be resorted to by Browning again and again to fill slightly different requirements of character delineation in different monologues, just as the devices of rhyme or alliteration may be resorted to by a poet for different effects. Certainly it is incorrect to ascribe the repeated use of special kinds of words to a poet's personal idiosyncrasy, to his lack of interest in diction, or to his carelessness, without first carefully examining the poems in which these words occur and trying to find out what the poet was attempting to do in them. It is worth looking hard—even at the risk of looking too hard—to see why Browning used words as he did; after the close examination of any one poem we shall always have time to condemn its diction, if we must. But the close and imaginative examination must come first. The present writer is aware that his own survey has only touched the surface. The diction of each of the twenty poems at hand when further examined in the light of character requirements should yield new information about Browning's artistry and the poems themselves.

8. Sound and the Sentence

RHYTHM

WE shall probably do well to begin with a warning from I. A. Richards. The warning is similar in import to several of Richards' remarks about diction, and it has the virtue of suggesting what we can and what we cannot expect to find in an investigation of rhythm, alliteration, sound quality, and even syntax and punctuation, as these relate to character delineation in twenty of Browning's monologues. Sound in verse, Richards has said,

> gets its character by compromise with what is going on already . . . The way in which the sound of a word is taken varies with the emotion already in being. But, further, it varies with the sense. For the anticipation of the sound due to habit, to the routine of sensation, is merely a part of the general expectancy. Grammatical regularities, the necessity for completing the thought, the reader's state of conjecture as to what is being said, his apprehension in dramatic literature of the action, of the intention, situation, state of mind generally, of the speaker, all these and many other things intervene. The way the sound is taken is much less determined by the sound itself than by the conditions into which it enters . . . To say this is not in the least to belittle the importance of the sound; in most cases it is the key to the effects of poetry.[1]

Sound may be the key to poetic effects, but sound itself does not seem to comprise meaning, as has sometimes been claimed,[2] nor

1. *Principles of Literary Criticism*, pp. 136–37.
2. Owen Barfield for example has said that "Music [i.e. sound in verse] . . . may comprise perhaps as much as half the *meaning* of a modern lyric." See *Poetic Diction: A Study in Meaning* (2d ed. London, 1952), p. 150. Such a statement seems questionable as, if sound does comprise meaning, one should be able to analyze the kind

243

is it really expressive by itself.[3] If, as Brander Matthews has suggested, blank verse is able to convey "the subtlest revelation of human psychology," [4] then this is due to the possibility the poet has in blank verse for achieving a "compromise," to use Richards' term, between sense and sound to produce the subtle revelatory effect that he wants. Far from limiting any study of Browning's techniques in character delineation to a consideration of those elements that might be said to convey some meaning by themselves—dramatic situation, imagery, or diction, for example—such a view challenges us to consider every scrap of Browning's technique down to the relatively miniscule matter of punctuation.[5] We run the risk, as Richards has warned, of joining "the army of critics who have attempted to analyse the effects of passages into vowel and consonantal collocations" [6]—or, unforgivably worse, into collocations of punctuation marks—if we forget that the effects of sound and syntax are largely conditioned by "what is going on already," or by the emotion and the sense of a passage. Sound and syntax in the monologues in fact modify the character-revealing elements of thought, feeling, situation, imagery and diction; they are partly responsible for many of Browning's more subtle psychological effects; but they are not part of the meaning

---

of meaning that it comprises. Barfield has not been able to do this and neither, to my knowledge, has anyone else. For purposes of the present study, at any rate, it has seemed more reasonable to assume that music (or rhythmic and phonetic elements) may considerably influence or modify meaning that is conveyed through language considered apart from its sound in a poem.

3. Leonard Bloomfield did find a "vague signification" in certain sounds in his study of morphologic types; see *Language* (New York, 1933), p. 245. But Richards' comment upon the evidence seems fair, namely that "sound by itself either means nothing at all—as with (fl) in *flame, flare, flash, flicker*—or as with (-ɛə) in *blare, flare, glare, stare* it has by itself only an irrelevant meaning . . ." I. A. Richards, *The Philosophy of Rhetoric* (New York, 1936), p. 60. Sound however may in certain ways imitate or symbolize some of the meaning conveyed; see, e.g., the discussion of "sound-imitation," "sound-painting," and "sound-symbolism" in René Wellek and Austin Warren, "Euphony, Rhythm, and Meter," in *Theory of Literature* (New York, 1949), pp. 163–64.

4. See *A Study of Versification* (New York, 1911), p. 226.

5. This is not to say that we shall necessarily find significance in the smallest matters of a poem. But we may; and if the poem is an effective one we are obliged to look closely even at its pointing—as we shall with a few of the monologues later on in this chapter.

6. *Principles of Literary Criticism*, p. 137.

itself; they modify meaning—or delineating elements—that are already in being or coming into being.

The rhythmic basis of all twenty monologues at hand is that of blank verse—the "decasyllabic line on a disyllabic basis and in rising rhythm," as Robert Bridges has defined the archetypical pattern of it.[7] In Browning's blank verse there are many lines that conform precisely to a decasyllabic, rising (or iambic) rhythm pattern,

> We both have minds and bodies much alike: (*BBA*, 902)

—but probably in the blank verse of few other writers since Surrey can there be found such range in variation from this pattern as there exists in Browning. Hatcher's work on the poet's versification is instructive at this point. "A close and sometimes painful study" of Browning's blank-verse practice, he concluded in part, "reveals but two metrical rules from which he is never known to depart:

> 1—A blank verse line must contain not less than nine, nor more than fifteen syllables
>
> 2—It must not have less than two heavily stressed syllables nor more than ten." [8]

Browning employed some eighty combinations of stresses which differ in some way from the iambic-pentameter pattern, or "close to the mathematical limit of possible variations" according to Hatcher;[9] and frequently in Browning the use of hypermetric syllables and triple measures is such that new rhythmic movements are set up in the iambic pattern, dulling or even replacing the normal rhythm.[10] There is no doubt that a poet who considers that lines of from two to ten stresses are admissible variations on a pattern of five stresses and that lines of from nine to fifteen syllables are admissible variations on a pattern of ten syllables,

7. *Milton's Prosody, with a chapter on Accentual Verse & Notes* (Oxford, 1921), p. 1.

8. Harlan Henthorne Hatcher, *The Versification of Robert Browning* (Columbus, 1928), p. 41.

9. Ibid., p. 45.

10. Ibid., pp. 45–53.

is in fact one who is either excessively fond of rhythmic variation
for itself, or who relies upon this device to an unusual degree to
create the effects that he desires. Probably Browning's blank verse
is to be explained in both ways. He seems to have delighted in
rhythmic variation—and the cause for this is perhaps to be found
in his own temperament and explained in terms of it; but he also
used it rather consistently to aid in the creation of desired effects.
While it would be presumptuous to undertake a general examination of these effects even in a few poems in less than a full-length
study, it will be of interest now to consider a sample of the ways
in which rhythm is used to aid in character delineation. The survey that follows should at least indicate that many of Browning's
rhythmic variations appear to have utility just when we view them
in the light of his character requirements.

Marked variation in stress in the monologues very often helps
to reveal a change of feeling or attitude in the speaker, and often,
in doing this, helps to suggest the presence of a new and unexpected character trait. Lippo's opening lines tell several things
about Lippo, and rhythmic variation underlines them:

> I am poor brother Lippo, by your leave! (*FLL,* 1)
> You need not clap your torches to my face.

So far there is no real departure from the iambic pattern; in line
1, Lippo's first foot may be read as pyrrhic (with a stress following on *poor*), but the whole line may also be read as iambic, with
a light stress on *am;* Lippo at this moment is on the defensive.
But there is an abrupt change with the next few verses:

> Zooks, what's to blame? you think you see a monk! (*FLL,* 3)
> What, 't is past midnight, and you go the rounds,
> And here you catch me at an alley's end
> Where sportive ladies leave their doors ajar?

Rhythmically, the direct attack of lines 3 and 4 is heightened by
caesuras after both initial stresses, and the vigor of the lines is increased through second caesuras (a particularly strong one after
blame, where the line is halted by the question) and the extra
stress as well in line 3. After these two extraordinary verses, Lippo
subsides into the familiar iambic pattern in lines 5 and 6. But

his variations have already helped to tell something about him; their rhythmic boldness emphasizes the boldness of their content; Lippo does not take his arrest lightly—he barks back at his captors right away. His rhythmic variations emphasize indignation, characteristic energy and that superabundance of life that the sense of these lines (and others in the poem) convey. The rest of Lippo's discourse is filled with exceptional rhythmic excursions from the norm. At the peak of his satirical attack on the police the rhythm becomes heavily spondaic:

> Whatever rat, there, haps on his wrong hole, (*FLL*, 9)
> And nip each softling of a wee white mouse,
> *Weke, weke, . . .*

The accented *rat, there, haps,* and *wee white mouse,* / *Weke, weke,* prepare the way for one of the most exceptional rhythmic passages in Browning. Recalling—and, in a sense, reliving—the moment of his temptation at the window when, sick of his saints, he heard and saw three irresistible ladies in the moonlight, Lippo speaks in a rhythm that is duple-triple and heavily spondaic almost at once. If the alternating intensity and rapidity of the movement is unusual, so is the dramatic moment, for it is just here that Lippo's sensuality is seen to take command of him; it fairly bursts into being and carries him off:

>   . . . when a titter   (*FLL*, 58)
> Like the skipping of rabbits by moonlight,—three slim shapes,
> And a face that looked up . . . zooks, sir, flesh and blood,
> That's all I'm made of! Into shreds it went,
> Curtain and counterpane and coverlet,
> All the bed-furniture—a dozen knots,
> There was a ladder!

Rhythmic variation of the kind that helps to underline the vigor and passion of Lippo is comparatively rare in *Andrea del Sarto*. The majority of Andrea's lines may be read as fairly strict iambic pentameter:

> I do not boast, perhaps: yourself are judge, (*AdS*, 64)
> Who listened to the Legate's talk last week,

> And just as much they used to say in France.
> At any rate 't is easy, all of it!
> No sketches first, no studies, that's long past:
> I do what many dream of, all their lives . . .

Even Andrea's exclamations are muted as a result of the even-
ness of his rhythm, as in line 67 above. When variations do occur
their force is diminished through sound, as when, remembering
his feeling for Lucrezia at Fontainebleau, Andrea uses two very
light spondee feet for what would be the third and fourth iambs
in the line,

> And, best of all, this, this, this face beyond, (*AdS*, 162)

The short vowel in *this* keeps the two extra stresses unemphatic.
The regularity and mutedness of Andrea's rhythm have the effect
of toning down most of the feelings evoked as he speaks; his lack
of feeling, his placidity, is felt throughout the poem.

Two basic rhythmic patterns run through the verses of *Karshish*.
Many of his lines have only four natural stresses—or, sometimes,
a fifth stress that is considerably weaker than the others. Often
the weak or missing stress occurs at the last foot, giving the line
a feminine ending:

> A viscid choler is observable   (*EK*, 42)
>
> His service payeth me a sublimate   (*EK*, 50)
>
> There set in order my experiences,   (*EK*, 53)
>
> Or I might add, Judæa's gum-tragacanth   (*EK*, 55)
>
> Cracks 'twixt the pestle and the porphyry, (*EK*, 57)
>
> Confounds me, crossing so with leprosy—(*EK*, 59)

In all instances the weak ending occurs when Karshish is either
writing about scientific facts that have nothing to do with Lazarus,
or discussing the Lazarus case from a scientific viewpoint. When
he writes of Lazarus from the non-scientific—or religious viewpoint—the rhythm changes. Not only are there usually five beats
in these verses, but the final measure is very strong, the ictus often
falling on a monosyllable:

> The man is apathetic, you deduce? (*EK*, 226; italics mine)
> Contrariwise, he loves both old and *young,*

Able and weak, affects the very *brutes*
And birds—how say I? flowers of the *field*—
As a wise workman recognizes *tools*
In a master's workshop, loving what they *make*.
Thus is the man as harmless as a *lamb:*

The nine verses of his peroration about the "very God" have masculine endings, all but one a monosyllable:

So, through the thunder comes a human *voice* (*EK,* 306; my italics)
Saying, "O heart I made, a heart beats *here!*

Contrasting rhythms thus reinforce Karshish's duality. Many of his scientific verses lack full emphasis rhythmically, and so, operating through the factual nature of the sense that they convey, the rhythm helps to suggest a lack of emotional force behind the sense; most of the verses having to do with religion are masculine or rhythmically strong—the rhythm helping to convey in contrast Karshish's special reaction to the message of Lazarus.

Many of *Cleon's* lines carry the former tendency to an extreme. Cleon employs four-stress lines, but he may even use those with three stresses, or even two:

Thou wonderingly dost enumerate.	(*C,* 46)
Intended to be viewed eventually	(*C,* 76)
Which not so palpably nor obviously,	(*C,* 103)
If, in the morning of philosophy,	(*C,* 187)
Of his own life's adaptabilities,	(*C,* 218)
That there's a world of capability	(*C,* 239)
Our bounded physical recipiency,	(*C,* 246)
Unlimited in capability	(*C,* 326)

The effect is to enhance a certain dryness and intellectual detachment in Cleon's discourse, as such prosaic lines occur rather evenly throughout the poem.[11] Rhythmic variation beyond this is not a

11. C. E. Andrews has cited certain lines of Browning in a general study of versification to illustrate the proposition that, "If blank verse has too large a proportion of light stresses the effect may be [in some cases] . . . prosaic . . ." See *The Writing and Reading of Verse* (New York, 1918), pp. 201–2. Whether this effect occurs depends of course partly upon the meaning and the whole poetic context of such lines, as it does in Cleon's philosophic letter to Protos.

marked feature of his monologue. Browning's Pope Innocent employs many lines of less than five stresses, too, but the vigor of his character is partly achieved through dramatic contrasts in the rhythm of succeeding verses:

> And is this little all that was to be? (*TP*, 1613)
> Where is the gloriously-decisive change,
> The immeasurable metamorphosis
> Of human clay to divine gold, we looked
> Should, in some poor sort, justify the price?

Rhythmic variation is by no means wholly responsible for the strength of these lines, which depend for their effect mainly upon the whole sense of the passage in context, but also upon the nature of its diction, imagery, syntax and sound quality. Yet the rhythm—moving from five stresses, to four, to only two, and at once back to the normal five—is exceptional; it is appropriate to the movement of the thought, which builds up to the abstract grandeur of the phrase, "immeasurable metamorphosis," before returning to the more ordinary images of the fourth and fifth lines to complete its expression. Successive lines of five, four and two stresses emphasize the range of the thought conveyed, which in turn helps to reveal the Pope's formidable and far-ranging intellect.

Caponsacchi's verses tend to have extra stresses; very often the extra ones are "optional"—that is, unaccented syllables are often strong enough to receive light stresses of their own:

> Answer you, Sirs? Do I understand aright?   (*GC*, 1)
> Have patience! In this sudden smoke from hell,—   (2)
> So things disguise themselves,—I cannot see   (3)
> My own hand held thus broad before my face   (4)
> And know it again. Answer you? Then that means (5)
> Tell over twice what I, the first time, told   (6)
> Six months ago: . . .

Lines 4–6 here must certainly be read with six accents (stresses on *own, hand, held, broad, -fore, face; know, -gain, Ans-, you, that, means;* and *Tell, twice, I, first, time,* and *told*). Moreover, even if the previous lines (1–3) are read as five-beat ones, several of their "unaccented" syllables must receive light stresses; but, too, all three of the first three lines might even be read with full extra stresses. The hypermetric line 1, for example, might be scanned as:

> *A*ns*w*er you, *Sirs? Do* I under*stand* a*right?*

but also as:

> *A*ns*w*er you, *Sirs? Do* I under*stand* a*right?*

or, conceivably, even as:

> *A*ns*w*er *you, Sirs? Do I* under*stand* a*right?*

All six opening lines—as well as many other similar rhythmic passages in *Caponsacchi*—might be read with six stresses or more each. The effect is to give the content strong emotional emphasis, to help reveal the passion and intense conviction of the priest. No other monologue among those at hand displays this feature: six- and seven-stress lines are to be found elsewhere, but never in a considerable series and never so numerously as in *Caponsacchi*.

A great deal may be accomplished through the arrangement of stresses. Extra accents are not common in the rhythm of *The Bishop at St. Praxed,* but when they do occur they give unusual emphasis through their appearance in a larger rhythmic context, as when the Bishop expects to

> . . . see God made and eaten all day long, (*BSP,* 82)
> And feel the steady candle-flame, and taste
> Good strong thick stupefying incense-smoke!

Numerically the last five-foot line has merely one extra stress and one less unaccented syllable; but its arrangement of four consecutive stresses after half a dozen fairly regular iambic lines (78–83) gives it rhythmic emphasis, so that its cadence and phonetic quality reinforce its effect. Sound supports the image of thick, choking smoke, and the departure from normal cadence heightens the importance of the image, so that the incense smoke seems to be more vital to the Bishop than his own argument; he is carried away by the mere thought of it. The line reveals his

character largely because the sensuousness of its content is so
vigorously and dramatically emphasized through rhythm.

Rhythmically, *Caliban* is a monologue of particular interest
among the twenty at hand—the speaker himself is grotesque, and
his rhythms, while aesthetically satisfying, are also instrumental in
exposing the grotesqueness of the figure who uses them. The
poem begins with a strong spondaic movement within the iambic:

> ['Will *sprawl, now* that the heat of day is best, (*CUS,* 1;
> italics mine)
> Flat on his belly in the *pit's much mire,*
> With elbows *wide, fists clenched* to prop his chin.
> And, while he *kicks both feet* in the *cool slush,*
> And feels about his *spine small eft-things course,*
> Run in and *out each arm* . . .

Shortly thereafter, at the beginning of his homily on Setebos, Caliban abandons his iambic cadence for a new, duple-triple rhythm
(it is almost dactylic-iambic):

> Setebos, Setebos, and Setebos!   (*CUS,* 24)
> 'Thinketh, He dwelleth i' the cold o' the moon.
> 'Thinketh, He made it, with the sun to match . . .

The rhythm contributes to a grotesque effect at this point precisely because there is no clear emotional cause for it; Caliban is
not recounting a moment of well-remembered passion as Lippo is
when he lapses into a somewhat similar movement (*FLL,* 58–64);
his situation is, instead, similar to that of *A Death in the Desert:*
he is discoursing upon his God. But the duple-triple rhythm is not
merely pointless for Caliban himself has been established by this
time as being a monster: he is a grotesque or mimic St. John, and
the strange rhythm is part of his sheer wilfulness. Duple-triple
rhythm and particularly the spondee effect echo throughout his
descriptions of nature—lending them intensity and strangeness:

> '*Say, this bruised fel*low shall receive a worm, (*CUS,* 106;
> italics mine)
> And *two worms he* whose nippers end in red;
> As it *likes me each time,* I *do: so He.*

Caliban even makes up a grotesque little song with a rhythm of its own; [12] his terror at the end of the poem when Setebos wreaks vengeance with storm and lightning elicits a movement of ten strong stresses almost in series:

> . . . *White blaze—* (*CUS,* 289; italics mine)
> A *tree's head snaps*—and *there, there, there, there, there,*
> His thunder follows! . . .

An unusual number of lines with direct attack is another rhythmic feature that serves to reinforce the effect of grotesqueness in context. [13]

Another kind of grotesqueness may be seen in *Mr. Sludge.* Of all Browning's monologues Mr. Sludge's has the closest affinity rhythmically to *Strafford,* where the explosive movement with its frequent caesuras and excessive punctuation mark the verse of that play. In *Mr. Sludge* these features serve another purpose:

> Now, don't, sir! Don't expose me! Just this once! (*MSM,* 1)
> This was the first and only time, I'll swear,—
> Look at me,—see, I kneel,—the only time,
> I swear, I ever cheated,—yes, by the soul
> Of Her who hears—(your sainted mother, sir!)

.   .   .   .

12. I.e. in *CUS,* 276–78. This song seems to be composed of dimeter and monometer verses, the rhymes causing them to be read less as belonging to a pentameter framework and more nearly as they would be if arranged:

> What I hate,
> be consecrate
> To celebrate
> Thee and Thy state,   [Browning's quotation
> no mate   marks and italics
> For Thee;   omitted here]
> what see
> for envy
> in poor me?

13. By my own count, 41 lines with direct attack occur in the first 100 lines of *Caliban,* and 24, 28, and 32, in the first 100 lines of *Cleon, Bishop Blougram,* and *Andrea del Sarto* respectively, for example. Moreover, *Caliban's* direct-attack lines often begin with a whole spondaic foot (the second syllable accented) or an unusually emphasized first stress.

>   . . . Aie—aie—aie!   (*MSM,* 16)
> Please, sir! your thumbs are through my windpipe, sir!
> Ch—ch!
>   Well, sir, I hope you've done it now!
> Oh Lord! . . .

Although rhythm is chopped and minced in these lines by phrasing, punctuation, diction (*Ch—ch!*), and even paragraphing (a
typographical device that breaks no less than thirty-eight of the
pentameter lines of *Mr. Sludge*), the iambic movement of the feet
is not greatly varied. Even later, when stress variation does occur,
its effect upon the rhythm is usually less felt than that of caesura
variation. Tempo in *Mr. Sludge* is of primary importance. Sequences of accented syllables, far from slowing down lines—as they
usually help to do in Browning—more often help to speed them
up:

>   "Sirrah, you spirit, come, go, fetch and carry, (*MSM,* 301)
>   "Read, write, rap, rub-a-dub, and hang yourself!"

In this case the speed of the lines is managed through phonetic
quality and particularly through the alliteration of stressed words;
the stresses themselves impart little emphasis. Mr. Sludge speaks
in a rhythm which is mainly one of quick tempo interrupted frequently by abrupt pauses (which may, in fact, occur at the rate of
three or even four per verse: "Forgiveness? There now! Eh? Oh!
'T was your foot," *MSM,* 50). The effect is to bring out glibness
and lightness in the Medium's own character; he himself is quick,
carefree, gaily explosive. Despite the length of his monologue, and
even the amount of time that he devotes to various topics, he
seems to dwell upon nothing for very long and everything superficially. While always achieving its effects through the content of
the verse, his rhythm peculiarly fits his personality. The ineffectual
and dramatically inexplicable rhythms of *Strafford* are in this
monologue approximated but now controlled for the purposes of
character revelation. The swiftness and brokenness of Mr. Sludge's
rhythm may be partly responsible for depriving the verse of a
certain poetic intensity so that we feel that *Mr. Sludge* is a less
finely-wrought poem than *The Bishop at St. Praxed* or *Fra Lippo*

Lippi; its verse has a more prosaic quality than the verse of the earlier monologues; but the rhythm is at least partly responsible as well for the truth of the portrait—helping to expose Mr. Sludge for what he is.

ALLITERATION AND RHYME

Alliteration in Browning has not been entirely condemned, although—apart from Roma King's close study of it in two or three instances in 1957 [14]—about the best that has been said for his use of it is that it "enforces the emphasis" on certain words in the later poems with "remarkable vigour." [15] It will be of special interest to review a few of the ways in which alliteration is used to implement character delineation in several of the monologues.

In *The Bishop at St. Praxed* alliteration is used, in one sense, exactly as a structural device. The Bishop speaks at a time when his mind is not entirely clear so that his thoughts follow in an order which is not precisely logical but psychological. Setting out to "order" his tomb, he is carried away by considerations of his dead mistress, his dead rival, his sons, life and the world itself, and even by sensuous visions of the materials and ornaments that may glorify his tomb. His reverie is linked by alliterated words:

What's *d*one is *d*one, and she is *d*ead beside, (*BSP*, 6; italics
                                                                    mine)
*D*ead long ago, and I am Bishop since,   (7)
And as she *d*ied so must we *d*ie ourselves,   (8)

14. *The Bow and the Lyre,* pp. 18–19, 36–38; alliteration is treated incidentally elsewhere in King's work.

15. See Groom, *On the Diction of Tennyson, Browning, and Arnold,* p. 132. Browning's alliteration has been criticized recently in Henry Charles Duffin, *Amphibian. A Reconsideration of Browning* (London, 1956), p. 280. That few critics before King in 1957 have commended alliteration in the monologues or discussed it for any of its possible functions may owe in part to the possibility that much too narrow a view has been taken of poetic alliteration by modern critics. C. E. Andrews' opinion, that structural alliteration "had a revival in the fourteenth century but since then has been obsolete" (p. 111) so that alliteration has been used principally as an embellishment ever since, is certainly a misleading one when we turn to Browning. Alliteration may indeed operate as a structural feature in some of the character-revealing dramatic monologues—as it does, for example, in the first one discussed below.

And thence ye may perceive the world's a *d*ream.   (9)
*L*ife, how and what is it? As here I *l*ie   (10)
In this state-chamber, *d*ying by *d*egrees,   (11)
Hours and *l*ong hours in the *d*ead night, I ask   (12)
"*D*o I *l*ive, am I *d*ead?" Peace, *p*eace seems all.   (13)
Saint *P*raxed's ever was the church for *p*eace;   (14)
And so, about this *t*omb of mine. I fought   (15)
With *t*ooth and *n*ail to save my *n*iche, ye *k*now: (16)
—Old Gandolf *c*ozened me, despite my *c*are;   (17)
*Sh*rewd was that *s*natch from out the *c*orner South   (18)
He graced his *c*arrion with, God *c*urse the *s*ame!   (19)

The passage begins with an alliterated movement of (d)-words,
done, dead, died, die, dying, dream, degrees, and *do,* which by line
13 has been supplemented by an (l)-word one: *Life, lie, long, live.*
Lines 13 and 14 are linked by *Praxed's* and the thrice-occurring
peace; and movements of (t)- and (n)-words combine in the next
two lines. Words beginning with sibilants and the phonetic (k)
link lines 17–19: *cozened, care, Shrewd, snatch, corner, South,
carrion, curse,* and *same.* The progression—from (d) and (l), to
(p), to (t) and (n), and then to (k) and the sibilants—in part re-
places the structural element of thought that is missing. In this
way alliteration helps to expose the Bishop's mind, for the sound
of his words to some extent guides what he says, reflecting the sub-
ordination of intellect to feeling in his character. Sound in the
monologue—sound, a sensuous element in itself—becomes a mark
of the Bishop's extreme sensuousness, helping even, in the context later on, to deliver to us an impression of the Bishop's sensuality.

Alliteration in *Bishop Blougram* is used to reinforce rhetoric,
and the alliterated words almost always represent concepts or acts
that Blougram wishes Gigadibs to see as being similar to one another, or logically connected. At its simplest, Blougram's alliteration may link nouns or verbs in close series:

Accordingly, I use heart, head and hand   (*BBA,* 249)
All day, I build, scheme, study, and make friends . . .

But alliterative linkage of this sort may be particularly revealing.

"I know the special kind of life I like," he declares (*BBA*, 234),
that which "bears me fruit"

> In power, peace, pleasantness, and length of days. (*BBA*, 237)

The alliteration of the nouns suggests that they represent equivalent concepts for Blougram: power, peace and pleasantness in life
are equally to be desired, equal goods. The linkage or equation of
power and *pleasantness,* which represent worldly desirables, with
peace, which in context represents a spiritual state of being, as
desirables, reflects that ironic compromise in the speaker's character between worldly and spiritual leanings. Only Blougram
could associate the three nouns through alliteration.

Mr. Sludge uses alliteration rhetorically—and often as an implement of sarcasm and satire. He may characterize Horsefall's
mount as a "hot hardmouthed horrid horse" (*MSM*, 1252), or a
seance participant as "the soft silent smirking gentleman" (*MSM*,
763), or "Miss Stokes" as a young lady who might be pitched
"Foolish-face-foremost" (*MSM*, 713). Often he ridicules himself
indirectly with alliterated words while lampooning society:

> I've felt at times when, cockered, cosseted   (*MSM*, 387)
> And coddled by the aforesaid company,
> Bidden enjoy their bullying,—never fear,
>
> .   .   .   .
>
> I've felt a child; only, a fractious child . . . (*MSM*, 391)

Or:

> "Doubt posed our 'medium,' puddled his pure mind;
>   (*MSM*, 361)

but most frequently his alliteration implements the quick, gay,
irresponsible quality of utterance. It lends his lines added vigor
and often, speed, as in:

> . . . thenceforth he may strut and fret his hour, (*MSM*, 654)
> Spout, spawl, or spin his target, no one cares!

Or:

> Why, take the *q*uietest hack and stall him up, (*MSM*, 294;
>   italics mine)

Cram him with corn a month, then out with him
Among his mates on a bright April morn,
With the turf to tread; see if you find or no
A caper in him, if he bucks or bolts!

In the latter cases, as an implement of rhythm, the device helps to suggest that frivolity which is one of the keynotes of Mr. Sludge's character.

Alliteration is common in *The Ring and the Book,* but its uses vary from monologue to monologue with respect to character requirements. Probably the speaker in *Half-Rome* alliterates the most frequently, employing a simple alliterative pattern that has certain echoes in the monologue following it. Half-Rome joins substantives with a conjunction (usually *and*): *rhyme and reason, stay nor stint, brow and breast, fault and fall, rottenness and ruin, Service and suit, Kith and kin, Dragon and devil, Peter and Paul, pillar and post, foes and friends.* Or predicates: *flocked and filled, ducks and defers, stopped and stilled, win and wed, Pinching and paring, stand and stiffen, find and feel, cursed or kicked, stand or step.* Or, less often, adjectives or adverbs: *gay and galliard, thick and three-fold, safe and sound, Well-famed and widely-instanced, Where and when.*

Approximately 55 instances of such simple linkage occur in the speaker's 1547 lines, or 1 in 28 verses on an average, a frequency great enough to lend *Half-Rome's* verse a special quality. Browning introduces the speech in Book I as "Gossip in a public place," [16] and Half-Rome, the gossiper, is only an incidental figure at the periphery of the murder-story. His easy and frequent alliteration lends casualness to what he says. Many of his linkages are parts of common aphorisms or patterns of speech: *Kith and kin, Peter and Paul, pillar and post, safe and sound.* Like his thought, his alliteration is never subtle. His couplings are simply a verbal convenience, reflecting superficial concern with the subject at hand and that more inherent superficiality which marks Half-Rome's character. The simplicity and carelessness of his judgments is underlined again and again through alliteration: Violante is that "mock-mother" and Pompilia her "child-cheat" (*H-R,* 61); the baby Pompilia, strangled, would simply "soar to the safe" (*H-R,* 236);

16. *The Ring and the Book,* I, 865.

Pietro and Violante in Arezzo reduced Guido's life to "cat-claw, curse and counterblast" (*H-R,* 505). In every case alliteration facilitates the easy and unreflecting flow of his thought; Half-Rome is morally obtuse, merely vocal, basically unconcerned with human affairs beyond his own.

Simple alliteration of this kind is not striking enough to create special effects in a long poem when used sparingly; and Browning employs it elsewhere, but only extensively in one other speech in *The Ring and the Book,* that of Other Half-Rome. Here, on an average, the device occurs only once in 48 lines. Alliterated pairs seldom initiate verses, as they may in *Half-Rome.*[17] And many of Other Half-Rome's pairings are structurally more complex: *gentle face and girlish form, sealed eyes and stopped ears, Coached her and carried her, gnawn lip and gnashed teeth, blind cuts and black turns.*

He may even use consonantal repetition and inversion in the alliterative pattern: *obscure and scorned* or *tame and mute,* for example, and occasionally an alliterated sound may run through consecutive verses. In this way his monologue is an echo of the preceding one; he is, indeed, the first speaker's "other half." Yet Other Half-Rome's character is the more reflective; although he glosses over reality with a smooth summary of the murder, and is no less morally obtuse than Half-Rome, he speaks of the tragedy with some refinement. In context his alliteration reflects his sentimental preoccupation with the facts as he sees them: a sentimentality that prevents him from seeing clearly, deeply, patiently, but which leads him to express what he does see with a certain delicacy that his counterpart does not manifest or possess.

Alliteration is used in several of the monologues in the manner of the key words discussed in Chapter 7 above. In Caliban's description of a magpie,

> . . . and the pie with the long tongue (*CUS,* 50)
> That pricks deep into oakwarts for a worm,
> And says a plain word when she finds her prize,

the words *pricks, plain,* and *prize* become, in effect, key words with respect to the pie's character; its peculiar foraging habit (*pricks*), its cry (*plain word*), and the reason for its actions (*prize*) are identi-

17. See, e.g., *H-R,* 286, 423, 459, 491, 572, 944, and 996.

fied with the bird through alliteration, and these words are key ones in explaining what the pie is like and what it does. Similar "key" alliterations may run throughout a monologue, and when they do, they often tie together words of special significance in describing or revealing the speaker. Mr. Sludge repeats his own name so often that it becomes identified with many (s)-words— particularly those that occur near an instance of the word *Sludge:*

> . . . He's a means,   (*MSM*, 332)
> "Good, bad, indifferent, still the only means [18]
> "*Spirits* can *speak* by; he may misconceive,
> "*Stutter* and *stammer,*—he's their *Sludge* . . .

> . . . 't was crusted o'er with creatures—*slick,*
> (*MSM,* 542)
> Their juice enriched his palate. Could not *Sludge!"*

And thenceforth he may *strut* and fret his hour, (*MSM*, 654)
Spout, spawl, or *spin* his target, no one cares!
Why hadn't I leave to play tricks, *Sludge* as *Sludge?*

> . . . He's the man for muck;   (*MSM*, 755)
> *Shovel* [(ʃ) for (s)] it forth, full-*splash,* he'll *smooth* your
>   brown

I' the *slime* o' the *slough* . . .   (*MSM*, 769)

The Name comes close behind a *stomach-cyst,* (*MSM*, 1117)
The *simplest* of creations, just a *sac*

The *small* becomes the dreadful and immense! (*MSM*, 1122)
Lightning, forsooth? No word more upon that!
A tin-foil bottle, a *strip* of greasy *silk* . . .

The 84 occurrences of *sir,* and many other words, *smiles, submits, soft smiler, serves, smut, siphon, sweet, spark,* for example, are

18. The (m)-words in this passage, *means, means, misconceive,* similarly echo Mr. Sludge's professional "name," *Medium.* Italics in this and the following six excerpts are mine.

linked through alliteration to Sludge's name, so that many of the (s)-words in the poem (and occasionally other sibilants) which are of particular importance in suggesting his moral quality or his characteristic traits or habits help to intensify our impression of him. Alliteration and phonetic quality may combine to reveal character in a "key" manner as well, as we shall see presently in the case of *Caliban*.

In *Fra Lippo Lippi*, (m)-word alliterations seem to serve two purposes. The words *monk* and *man* (sometimes in different forms, e.g. *monk's-things, man's*) occur 11 and 12 times respectively throughout the poem, and the terms in context are important enough to function in a key-manner in Lippo's portrait: they epitomize the duality and tension between man and monk, sensuality and piety, in his make-up. But (m)-words as a whole have a structural function in the poem; at every stage of Lippo's argument an (m)-word occurs in a significant phrase, so that, in fact, a simple listing of (m)-words and their phrases actually provides a fair outline of the poem:

monk

midnight

wee white mouse

Master–a . . . Cosimo of the Medici

munificent House

shut within my mew

moonlight

If I've been merry, what matter who knows?

Mum's the word

mother died

munching my first bread that month

". . . you're minded,"

Wiping his own mouth

miserable world

mouthful of bread

men's faces

music-notes

the mark [of painting]

any sort of meaning looks intense

I'm grown a man

I'm my own master

You keep your mistr . . . manners, and I'll stick to mine!

The old mill-horse [image for Lippo]

It makes me mad

[the world] means intensely, and means good:

To find its meaning is my meat and drink.

remember matins

mind you fast

mistake an idle word

to make amends

God in the midst, Madonna and her babe

Mazed, motionless and moonstruck—I'm the man!

I, caught up with my monk's-things by mistake

six months hence!

The effect—which is aided by what appears to be an abnormally high frequency of the phonetic (m) in Lippo's language in general [19]—is to emphasize the key words *monk* and *man* throughout the monologue; their initial sounds become Lippo's characteristic sound; his speech is at once unified through the (m)-alliteration, and the impression of duality in oneness, of Lippo's being pious monk and sensual man—and yet the integrated artist, effective, functioning, intense, complete as he is—is reinforced by it.

Rhyme is a less important intrusion in Browning's blank verse than it is in the speeches of *Paradise Lost*, for example.[20] Part

19. As in words such as *blame, company, remember, comes, amends, comrade, thyme, scrambling, to-morrow, remarks, Camaldolese, crammed, simple, time, smallish, somewhat, palm,* among many others of the same sort, where rhythmic stress falls on the syllable containing the (m)-sound, and a host of incidental words in the monologue beginning with the letter *m:* e.g. *must, many, more, may, mayn't, met, make, made, me, my,* several of which are repeated often.

20. For several prominent uses of it in the blank-verse speeches of *Paradise Lost,* see John S. Diekhoff, "Rhyme in *Paradise Lost,*" *PMLA, 49* (1934), 439-43.

of the reason for this would seem to be that Browning's speakers, who are often self-consciously aware of their own diction and imagery, are aware of their own rhyming as well and regard rhyming as, in fact, a poetic act. "Bless us, I'm turning poet!" Mr. Sludge declares after two lines in which *Fine, line,* and *mine* occur (*MSM,* 1182–83), and later, after a couplet rhyming *act* and *fact:* "(There's verse again, but I'm inspired somehow")" (*MSM,* 1285). No monologuist is aware that he is actually speaking in verse all of the time, of course; but rhyme is avoided for the most part by Browning simply because it is in his view an unmistakable feature of poetry—no speaker, in other words, could be allowed to use rhyme (and indeed is allowed to use rhyme) without showing himself to be perfectly aware of the fact that he is rhyming. Browning's people, on the whole, are a good deal more aware of poetic device itself than Satan is, or than Adam is. Sludge, Caliban, Hohenstiel-Schwangau, Tertium Quid, Bottini, and Arcangeli use rhyme sparingly *as* rhyme.

It is most common in *Archangelis*.

> . . . What, to-day we're *eight?* (*HdA,* 2; my italics)
> Seven and one's *eight,* I hope, old curly-*pate!*
> —Branches me out his verb-tree on the *slate* . . .

Arcangeli begins, the rhyme underlining not only his mood as he contemplates Giacinto's birthday and the coming family banquet, but his basic lightheartedness. He sings out variants of a favorite proverb,

> Dispose, O Don, o' the day, first work then play! (*HdA,* 18)

—and ends his speech in rhyming and alliterating song,

> Off and away, first work then play, play, play! (*HdA,* 1803)
> Bottini, burn your books, you blazing ass!
> Sing 'Tra-la-la, for, lambkins, we must live!'

He even relieves his prodigious labors upon Latin from time to time with bits of rhyme: *ermine-vermin, soar and pour, name and fame, round and sound,* and *landed and stranded.* Although the device is not employed extensively in his portrait, it has the effect of emphasizing his obtuse and carefree nature as he conjures up a defense for Guido. Caliban uses rhyme only in his grotesque song (*CUS*, 276–78), and Hohenstiel-Schwangau, apart from a few moments of levity, employs it conspicuously only once—to satirize poetry itself: [21]

> The novel thought of God shall light the world? (*PH-S*, 1972)
> No, poet, though your offspring rhyme and chime
> I' the cradle . . .

For the Prince, rhyme epitomizes poetry. As with the other monologuists, he is too conscious of the lyric nature of the device to use it frequently and freely as a natural means of self-expression.

PHONETIC QUALITY

Phonetic quality in the monologues at hand seems to aid in character revelation in one of two basic ways. Quality may influence rhythm, particularly tempo, and thereby influence the whole effect of a passage, making it more revelatory than it would be if it had other phonetic components. And phonetic quality also seems to operate at what Wellek and Warren have called the levels of sound-imitation and sound-metaphor or -symbolism.[22] The latter is a level at which a good deal seems to happen in almost any fine poem, but it is also a level at which the student of poetry, in attempting to discover and to explain exactly what does happen, may well open himself up to the charge of subjectivity; and there can be no doubt that we are at present in need of more information about the symbolic effects of sound in language, and a methodology, a way of ascertaining the precise nature of these effects, and a way of discussing them, that will, at least, lessen the subjective element.

We shall treat whatever sound-symbolism there seems to be in the character-revealing monologues warily and conservatively here—but we shall also attempt to point out a few evident ex-

---

21. Hohenstiel-Schwangau has previously made clear what he thinks of poets and poetry, incidentally exposing his own Philistinism. See *PH-S*, 517–55.

22. See René Wellek and Austin Warren, *Theory of Literature* (New York, 1949), pp. 163–64.

amples of it, if only to show that it does exist, and that it has an important bearing on Browning's treatment of character.

The most obvious effect of quality in the monologues seems to be that which it has upon rhythm. Near the climax of his diatribe on Guido, in which he pictures the slayer of Pompilia as sliding into hell to join Judas, Caponsacchi says,

The cockatrice is with the basilisk! (*GC*, 1950)

Imagery—*cockatrice* for Guido and *basilisk* for Judas—combines with rhythm to reveal the obverse of the priest's capacity for passionate love: he hates passionately, as well. The feeling behind the words is suggested through the exceptional rhythm in which they are delivered: the line has only two full stresses. And the light stresses are modulated by the phonetic quality of the consonants: the dental stop, dental continuants, and guttural stop in *-trice*, *with* and *-lisk* [(t), (s), (o), again (s), and (k) respectively] are unvoiced sounds, and all occur in syllables that would normally be stressed in the iambic pattern; in addition, the repeated vowel is a short one: (i), further decreasing the weight of stresses on all three syllables. Yet the phonetic quality of the line does more. The repeated sibilants and unvoiced dentals and guttural suggest the intensity of Caponsacchi's hate in the context of the imagery. The fabulous serpent and lizard seem to hiss; and the hissing conveys Caponsacchi's actual feeling for the human creatures that they represent. Caponsacchi hisses at the two men through the phonetic quality of his images, so that sound helps to convey hatred, the hatred in turn reflecting characteristic passion in his nature. Phonetic quality in this case is only effective through rhythm and imagery, but it adds unmistakably to the revealing effect of a superb line.

Euphony, as Lascelles Abercrombie has said, "may be deliberately violated in poetry, if something expressive is to be gained," [23] and character requirements in the monologues frequently necessitate difficult sound patterns. *Karshish*, of course, is an obvious example. But let us look at the verse for a moment. The most difficult lines occur early:

23. Lascelles Abercrombie, *The Theory of Poetry* (New York, 1926), p. 156.

> Karshish, the picker-up of learning's crumbs,   (*EK,* 1)
> The not-incurious in God's handiwork
> (This man's-flesh he hath admirably made,
>
> .   .   .   .
>
> —To Abib, all-sagacious in our art,   (*EK,* 7)
> Breeder in me of what poor skill I boast,
> Like me inquisitive how pricks and cracks
> Befall the flesh through too much stress and strain,
>
> .   .   .   .
>
> And aptest in contrivance (under God)   (*EK,* 13)
> To baffle it by deftly stopping such:—
> Sends greeting (health and knowledge, fame with peace)

Although verses that contain not one of the four sibilant sounds, (s), (z), (ʒ), and (ʃ), are comparatively rare in Browning, there are fewer of these—less than half as many—in *Karshish* than in other monologues of similar length; [24] and the tempo of Karshish's lines is considerably slowed through sibilancy. The (ʃ)-sound, of the speaker's own name, and the (s)- and (k)-sounds used together, are relatively difficult to pronounce, and the effect of such sounds used in series is a particularly retarding one; in the passage above, Kar*sh*i*sh,* learning'*s* *c*rumb*s,* man'*s*-fle*sh,* all-saga*c*iou*s,* *sk*ill, in-*qui*s*i*tive, pri*cks* and cra*cks,* and fle*sh,* slow the movement. Karshish's phonetic stops in the first sixteen verses average 6 per line —as against, for example, 4½ and 4 per line in the sixteen opening verses of *Cleon* and *Andrea* respectively; [25] and many of the stops

24. In *Karshish* there are only eight lines that contain no sibilants at all (113, 157, 168, 177, 198, 255, 261, and 279) and none among the first 112 lines. There are over twice as many of these in *Fra Lippo Lippi* (19) and in *Andrea* (22). Even so, the statistics do not reflect the fact that many of *Karshish's* lines contain as many as three and four sibilants—more of a rarity in the other monologues.

25. My counts for six phonetic stops in the first 16 lines of the three poems gives:

	(p)	(b)	(t)	(d)	(k)	(g)	
Karshish	16	14	24	15	18	5	total: 92
Cleon	10	2	27	10	15	7	total: 71
Andrea	5	8	28	9	9	1	total: 60

It is interesting that as the total number of stops decreases the most sharply articulated one, (t), increases in frequency. I am not at all sure that this is generally the rule in Browning. My object here is simply to show that *Karshish's* opening verses contain an unusually large number of stops when compared with those of two other monologues picked at random.

occur in relatively difficult combinations: *picker-up, not-incurious, aptest, deftly stopping,* for example. Still the rhythmic movement is not broken or "explosive" as it is in *Mr. Sludge.* The Arab's first twenty lines are a syntactical unit and a quarter of the lines are enjambed. The effect is to give what he says a continuous but laborious movement which reflects the manner in which Karshish's mind operates—professionally pausing over the minutest anomalies in nature, picking up crumbs, being slow, careful, thorough. Yet the high frequency and cacophonous combinations of his phonetic stops help to suggest something else about his nature, too, for Karshish as physician is a troubled and incomplete Karshish. He is susceptible to the lesson of Lazarus precisely because science, for him, has not provided a unified and fully satisfying answer to life as he sees it. In the postscript lines 304–12 there is a stress-pattern different from the pattern that he uses in many lines of scientific import, as we have seen. But, too, the lines in which he discusses God have different phonetic qualities:

> So, through the thunder comes a human voice (*EK,* 306)
> Saying, "O heart I made, a heart beats here!

There are fewer stops in these lines, no cacophonous combinations, and fewer short-vowel sounds. The religious discovery of Karshish (including all of the lines in which he writes of Lazarus from a non-scientific viewpoint) is expressed in verse that is contrastingly euphonic. Sound quality here seems to suggest what it is that Karshish discovers in religion but could not discover as a scientist —namely, harmony. Religion provides an aesthetic and unified view of the world, as science did not, and his religious pronouncements alone are phonetically harmonious.

Caliban's verse, though marked by stress variations that help to establish the grotesqueness of his character, is not cacophonic in the way that Karshish's verse often is. Nevertheless, the guttural stop, (k), which seems to require more effort to pronounce than most other consonantal sounds,[26] is one of Caliban's fairly constant sounds—so common in his monologue that it becomes identi-

---

26. "The effort to produce a particular sound is greater the earlier the check is applied to the breath, greatest at the throat (gutturals) . . ." Joseph B. Mayor, *A Handbook of Modern English Metre* (Cambridge, England, 1903), p. 101.

fied with him. Many of his verbs begin with the (k)-sound: *clench,
kicks, course, creep, catch, crunch, cross, kiss, conceiveth, continue,
cower, crawl, caught, careth, cannot, compared, could, curl, kill,
cut, curse, call,* and *cry.* Other verbs contain it: *tickle, look, talk,
vex, 'scape, thinketh, sicken, prick, pluck, work, mislike, drink,
mock, lick, scatter, knock, chuckle, misconceive, scream, scratch,*
and *skud,* for example. References to animals and plants often include it: *snake, auk, oakwart, creature, scale, crab, comb, skull,
honeycomb, squirrel, crane, quail, cuttle-fish, orc, cricket,* and
whelk. Adjectives—*cool, rank, dark, cruel, crafty, second, sleeker,
cold, crystal, sleek-wet*—and other words contain it; [27] even Caliban's supreme deity (over Setebos) is the *Quiet,* residing in its
spatial *couch* (*CUS,* 137–38). Alliteration of (k)-words and the
repetition of (k)-sounds have the structural effect of linking the
various stages of his discourse, as (m)-words and -sounds do in *Fra
Lippo Lippi;* and the sound is associated with Caliban himself not
alone through frequency but through links with his thrice-
repeated name:

> Put *c*ase, unable to be what I wish, (*CUS,* 75; my italics)
> I yet *c*ould make a live bird out of *c*lay:
> Would not I take *c*lay, pinch my *C*aliban
> Able to fly?—for, there, see, he hath wings,
> And great *c*omb . . .
>
>   . . . and now pens the drudge (*CUS,* 165;
>   my italics)
> In a hole o' the ro*c*k and *c*alls him *C*aliban . . .

In context, this unvoiced guttural stop is particularly appropriate
to the speaker; it is relatively difficult to pronounce and it origi-
nates at the back of the mouth, so that, particularly through its association with words such as *crunch, clench,* and *chuckle,* it helps
to symbolize the bestiality and even mimic the grunting noise of
the animal-like Caliban. More importantly, it retards the tempo of
many lines enough to suggest the effort that a brute speaker must
make in order to put his thoughts into language.

27. I have not attempted to supply a complete list of verbs, nouns or adjectives
containing (k); I have omitted third-person endings (-s, -es) and plurals (-s) here in
several cases.

Certain sounds need not permeate a speech evenly, or with equal intensity, in order to assist in characterization. Arcangeli's nature is revealed through the sense, the diction, and the phonetic quality, of a passage in which he pictures himself in action physically:

> Oh, I was young and had the trick of fence, (*HdA*, 270)
> Knew subtle pass and push with careless right—
> The left arm ever quietly behind back
> With the dagger in't: not both hands to blade:
> Puff and blow, put the strength out, Blunderbore!
> That's my subordinate, young Spreti, now,
> Pedant and prig,—he'll pant away at proof,
> That's his way!

Phonetic quality imitates physical sound, the very puffing and blowing of the obese Arcangeli, in the labial explosives in *pass, push, back, both, blade, Puff, blow, put, Blunderbore, subordinate, Spreti, Pedant, prig, pant,* and *proof,* and in several of the long vowels (e.g. *blow, -bore*). In the monologue context the six lines help to suggest the lawyer's pomposity as well as his physical awkwardness, achieving the effect partly through their phonetic quality. When used in frequency throughout a monologue explosive consonants often have the effect of emphasizing the speaker's energy, vivacity, or physical agility, as they do in the verbs of *Mr. Sludge* and *Fra Lippo Lippi*. The symbolic functions of such sounds are dependent upon the contexts in which they occur—they work through the sense and emotion conveyed—but their effects are felt.

Sound quality may condition the effect of words and passages by mitigating the force of rhythmic stresses. Other Half-Rome's exclamatory lines, in contrast to Half-Rome's or Sludge's or Lippo's, are toned down by quality. Liquid, nasal, or aspirated sounds tend to be used in his exclamations, modifying the force of phonetic stops that may also be present:

> A miracle, so tell your Molinists! (*OH-R*, 34)
>
> For Christ's particular love's sake! (*OH-R*, 90)
>
> No sparing saints the process! (*OH-R*, 112)

. . . See the girl!	(*OH-R*, 205)
Words to the wind!	(*OH-R*, 503)
All at an impulse!	(*OH-R*, 921)
As in romance-books!	(*OH-R*, 922)
. . . Lies!	(*OH-R*, 1106)

The effect is to deprive the speech of intellectual vigor. Other Half-Rome indeed sees the world through a cloud of sentimentality and self-pity, dominant traits that have fairly emasculated his character.[28]

Andrea del Sarto, as he himself realizes, is muted "at every point":

> My youth, my hope, my art, being all toned down (*AdS*, 38)
> To yonder sober pleasant Fiesole.

The "toned down" quality of his character, his spiritual and physical deficiency, is reflected in the phonetic quality of his verse in two ways. A great many of his lines contain two or more long, back vowels, usually (o) (ɔ), (a), or the diphthong (au), as in the two lines above, or:

> And that long festal year at Fontainebleau!   (*AdS*, 150)
> I surely then could sometimes leave the ground,
> Put on the glory, Rafael's daily wear,
> In that humane great monarch's golden look,—

> I dared not, do you know, leave home all day, (*AdS*, 145)

> You called me, and I came home to your heart. (*AdS*, 172)

> Upon a palace-wall for Rome to see,   (*AdS*, 187)

> I am grown peaceful as old age to-night.   (*AdS*, 244)

These sounds, often occurring in the stressed syllable, retard tempo in a different way from that of the consonants of Karshish: the effect is that of a slow but unlabored movement: the verse is

---

28. For his self-pity see esp. *OH-R*, 1674–94, where the speaker's identification of Pompilia's grievance with his own finally causes him to burst into outright anger. His sentimentality is apparent with the first:

> Little Pompilia, with the patient brow (*OH-R*, 2)
> And lamentable smile on those poor lips . . . etc.

euphonious, remarkably even in tempo, and more uniform in its vowel sounds than that of most of the other nineteen monologues. Moreover, it is deficient in phonetic stops, particularly the labial plosives (p) and (b). It has a high frequency of liquids, (l) and (r), and the fricatives (f) and (v), which deprive the verse of energy—a comparison of the first 50 lines in *Lippo* and *Andrea* reveals that Andrea's lines have substantially more liquids than do Lippo's, and nearly twice as many fricative (f)'s and (v)'s.[29] Phonetic quality is thus greatly responsible for creating a rhythm and tone in Andrea that emphasize the speaker's "low-pulsed," dispirited, weary condition. The quality of Andrea's vowels and consonants lend the verse a slow, even, uninterrupted movement, deprived of the rhythmic surprise and vigor that mark Lippo's and to some extent most of the other monologuists' verse. The effect is not dependent upon sound-symbolism in *Andrea,* although the quality of the speaker's typical vowels, the recurring (o) and (ɑ) and (ɔ), for example, with their low, sustained, hollow tones, seems to reflect that quiet despair of Andrea's that comes to us through the sense, the imagery, and the verbal symbolism of his lines.

SYNTAX

"Browning," wrote Oliver Elton, "is one of the few English poets since Milton who may be said to have a grammar of his own. . . . But the grammar is much the same throughout; it is a deliberately practised idiom that soon becomes second nature."[30] In the last ten years several of the monologues have been subjected to careful scrutiny for their grammar, and the result has been to confirm at least the first half of Elton's opinion—and, in a way, to enlarge upon it. E. K. Brown for example in a brilliant paper, "The First Person in 'Caliban upon Setebos,'" found that even so minute and special a grammatical irregularity as Caliban's shifting to the first person and back again to the third served to

29. The first 50 lines of *FLL* contain 133 liquids [88 occurrences of (r) and 45 of (l)] and 32 fricatives [18 of (f) and 14 of (v)] whereas the first 50 lines of *AdS* contain 153 liquids [92 occurrences of (r) and 61 of (l)] and 57 fricatives [31 of (f) and 26 of (v)]—by my count. Liquids and fricatives seem to occur with high frequency throughout *Andrea del Sarto.*

30. *The Brownings* (London, 1924), pp. 66–67.

"enrich the characterization and heighten the drama" of *Caliban*.[31]
Browning had a grammar of his own and it could be a delicate
instrument. However, a survey of syntax as an instrument of character revelation in a number of monologues suggests a careful
consideration of Elton's second point, or of what it implies—that
there is a sameness in Browning's grammar, and that the monologuists speak in a Browningesque idiom. To what extent is this
true?

Two syntactical features of the twenty monologues considered
together do seem to stand out as being particularly Browningesque
—the occasional omission of parts of speech (chiefly relative and
possessive pronouns, and articles), and certain idiosyncrasies of
punctuation. Both of these have a special bearing on Browning's
treatment of character. We shall deal with the problem of syntactical omissions here—before taking up other matters of syntax,
and punctuation in the next section.

Significant omissions of parts of speech began with *Sordello*.[32]
That poem became, as we have seen, a poetic laboratory for Browning; but comparatively few of the more radical syntactical experiments were actually carried over into the early character-revealing
monologues. In *The Bishop at St. Praxed* there are lines such as

> Bedded in store of rotten fig-leaves soft, (*BSP*, 40)

or

> There's plenty jasper somewhere in the world— (*BSP*, 72)

where the solecisms, if they are to be considered solecisms at all,
are not striking. The Bishop might have said "*a* store" or "plenty
of," but the omissions are easily justified artistically and even, to
an extent, grammatically.[33] In the *Men and Women* monologues

---

31. *Modern Language Notes, 66* (1951), 392–95, esp. 395.

32. The frequent obscurity of *Pauline* often seems to be due to the obscurity of
its syntax as in lines 79–87, but not to omitted parts of speech; there are a few
almost equally complicated sentences in *Paracelsus*. In *Strafford* many parts of speech
are omitted, but the sentences follow colloquial or normal speech patterns.

33. As H. W. Fowler mentions in his entry after *plenty*, the omission of "of" in a
sentence such as "There is plenty wood." is easily paralleled in constructions such
as "a little brandy," "a dozen apples," "more courage," "enough food"; see *A*

there are similar judicious omissions. Fra Lippo Lippi, describing an angel in his contemplated "Coronation of the Virgin" painting, says,

> Then steps a sweet angelic slip of a thing (*FLL*, 370)
> Forward, puts out a soft palm— . . .

carefully keeping all three of his articles; but a little earlier in,

> Ouf! I leaned out of window for fresh air. (*FLL*, 50)

—an optional article is omitted. In the latter case Lippo is recounting a real, not an imagined, experience, one that causes him even now to become breathlessly excited, and the omission appropriately speeds the line.

It is not until the *Dramatis Personae* monologues of 1864 and *The Ring and the Book* of the same decade that syntactical omissions become more noticeable. There are very few in *A Death in the Desert*, but many in *Caliban*, where the omissions serve a character-revealing purpose, as we shall see. It is really in *Mr. Sludge*, the monologues of *The Ring and the Book*, and *Hohenstiel-Schwangau*, that syntactical omissions seem to be rather obtrusive:

> Why, you can double fist and floor me, sir! [your] (*MSM*, 1251)
> 'This is indeed a business' law shook head: [its]   (*H-R*, 1091)
> Nor, in Arezzo, knew her way through street [the] (*OH-R*, 1070)
> Do I deserve grace? For I might lock lips, [my]   (*GC*, 1623)
> We don't card silk with comb that dresses wool. [a] (*HdA*, 324)
> Ay, and enliven speech with many a flower   (*JDB*, 3)
> Refuses obstinately blow in print [that; to]

However, in no monologue but *Hohenstiel-Schwangau* are there inconsistencies of omission within the same line, as when the Prince says:

Dictionary of Modern English Usage (Oxford, 1940), art. *plenty*. The use of *store* without an article (as a n.) also has its parallels, and both lines seem to be appropriately colloquial for a Bishop who is talking informally (using the familiar form of pronoun address, *ye*, for example) to his sons.

In goes the shovel and out comes scoop—as here! (*PH-S,* 110)

—where "shovel" but not "scoop" takes an article, or:

By soul,—the lust o' the flesh, lust of the eye, (*PH-S,* 2118)

—where only one "of" is contracted. Actually, in the case of most omissions in *Mr. Sludge* and *The Ring and the Book* there is a grammatical parallel within the line to support the dropping of an article or a pronoun. For example, Mr. Sludge says "double fist" and "floor me," above, the exceptional verb-noun sequence paralleling the normal verb-pronoun one. Half-Rome, in line 1091, personifies "law," so that it need not take an article, and parallels this in omitting the pronoun before "head." Caponsacchi, in the line above, says "lock lips" after "deserve grace," "grace" being one of those nouns that does not need an article when used in one of its senses; he parallels the normal omission when he comes to his next noun, leaving out a normally included word. Similar grammatical parallels may be found in most other cases of pronoun and article omission in the later monologues.

But there is a more important general justification for Browning's practice. Save *Caliban*—which is a special case—all of the monologues in which syntactical omissions are common are particularly long ones. *Mr. Sludge* contains 1525 lines, *Hohenstiel-Schwangau* 2155, and *The Ring and the Book* monologues between 1547 and 2425 lines each. The omission of certain smaller parts of speech in these poems is functional. For, no matter how expertly employed to enhance rhythm, to implement special sound effects, or to modify the effects of other words, relative and possessive pronouns and articles in poetry serve mainly to link more important words together: they carry little meaning themselves. In poems of even several hundred lines, such as *Fra Lippo Lippi,* the "dead weight" of such words is not apt to be felt; but in poems of 1,500 and 2,000 lines, where the poet's interest is in delineating a single human character with the utmost intensity, the accumulated effect of smaller words, *my, his, the, a,* and *that,* necessarily iterated again and again, is apt to mitigate the effect of more functional words—to lower intensity. Browning of course is not the first poet to have taken liberties with the English article.

And if we are able to accept the rules of elision that enabled Milton to write, "Fair Consort, th' hour / Of night," or Pope to write,

> The sick'ning stars fade off th' ethereal plain,

in reading these poets, we should also be able to accept certain practices of omission in Browning's lengthier monologues—without letting the omissions themselves blind us to the very evident fact that Browning was sensitive to sentence structure. These omissions, often paralleled in similar, accepted constructions within the same line or passage, are rarely so obtrusive that they stand out as solecisms; instead, the practice almost invariably serves to increase the intensity of his longer portraits.

Syntax in the twenty monologues at hand most often reflects the mental processes or the mental condition of the speaker and so helps to reveal him. In *Caliban*, the abruptness of the syntactical movement itself, with its very high frequency of omissions, reflects the nature of Caliban's mind:

> 'Conceiveth all things will continue thus,   (*CUS*, 241)
> And we shall have to live in fear of Him   (242)
> So long as He lives, keeps His strength: no change, (243)
> If He have done His best, make no new world   (244)
> To please Him more, so leave off watching this,— (245)
> If He surprise not even the Quiet's self   (246)
> Some strange day,—or, suppose, grow into it   (247)
> As grubs grow butterflies: else, here are we,   (248)
> And there is He, and nowhere help at all.   (249)

He omits a personal pronoun in line 241, as he does in 42 other places in the poem where the pronoun is indicated by the apostrophe.[34] He omits an optional conjunction in line 243 and words to the effect of "there will be" before *no change*. In line 244, he switches to the future tense with *make,* omitting a subject pro-

---

34. As in *'Thinketh* (5 times), *'Am, 'Let, 'Esteemeth, 'Saith,* e.g. The omission of the personal pronoun standing for Caliban's own name seems best explained psychologically as part of his attempt to trick Setebos into believing that it is not Caliban who is speaking. Cf. Stopford A. Brooke, *The Poetry of Robert Browning* (London, 1905), 2, 79, and E. K. Brown, "The First Person in 'Caliban upon Setebos,'" *Modern Language Notes*, 66 (1951), 393.

noun and future auxiliary verb: "He will." In line 245 he again omits the auxiliary "will" before *leave,* and in the next line omits the auxiliary "should" before *surprise.* In line 247 he uses *it* for the whole meaning, "being the Quiet Himself," and in line 248 omits "into" after the verb *grow.* Finally in line 249 he omits an optional verb before the subject *help,* making the first verb in the line serve twice. No other speaker in Browning clips so many parts of speech, particularly so many auxiliary verbs, and the curtailment serves to reflect the bluntness and crudity of Caliban's mind. His typical sentences are composed of short phrases and clauses that follow one another abruptly, often with a colon or simply a comma linking two independent clauses. Frequently the syntax combines with thought, imagery, and sound quality to expose the gruff, ruthless nature of his being:

Put case such pipe could prattle and boast forsooth (*CUS,* 122)
"I catch the birds, I am the crafty thing,
"I make the cry my maker cannot make
"With his great round mouth; he must blow through mine!"
Would not I smash it with my foot? So He.

In *Archangelis,* there are mainly three types of sentences: short and often exclamatory ones, expressing Arcangeli's generally high spirits:

Why, work with a will, then! Wherefore lazy now? (*HdA,* 60)
I defend Guido and his comrades—I!　　　　　　(*HdA,* 92)
　　　　. . . Mum, mind business, Sir!　　　(*HdA,* 138)
Curb we this ardour! . . .　　　　　　　　(*HdA,* 146)
　　　　　　　　. . . Boh!　　　(*HdA,* 172)

—as well as a second type, frequently studded with alternating short Latin and English phrases, which the lawyer uses when he is deep in the middle of his literary labors; and a third type, which might best be described as an incremental sentence in which clauses and phrases often have an interlocking connection with one another, the object of one clause becoming the subject of the next, and so on. The structures are psychologically revealing. From explosive bursts, Arcangeli lapses into plodding

sequences of phrases when he is hard at work, or into long, addi-
tive sentences with interlocking parts when he is not. One of his
earliest sentences establishes the pattern of the latter: "For too
contagious grows the mirth," he begins, thinking of the evening's
birthday feast to come,

> the warmth (*HdA*, 23)
> Escaping from so many hearts at once— (24)
> When the good wife, buxom and bonny yet, (25)
> Jokes the hale grandsire,—such are just the sort (26)
> To go off suddenly,—he who hides the key (27)
> O' the box beneath his pillow every night,— (28)
> Which box may hold a parchment (some one thinks) (29)
> Will show a scribbled something like a name (30)
> 'Cinino, Ciniccino,' near the end, (31)
> 'To whom I give and I bequeath my lands, (32)
>
> .   .   .   .
>
> Wherefore—yet this one time again perhaps— (35)
> Sha'n't my Orvieto fuddle his old nose! (36)

Arcangeli is daydreaming here, his mind moving from one pleas-
antly sensuous picture to the next: a vision of Giacinto's banquet
with its contagious merriment leads to a vision of his plump wife
teasing the rich old grandfather, which leads to a vision of what
these two will do together, which in turn produces a vision of the
grandsire's miserly habits with his treasure box, which leads to a
vision of the parchment that must be contained in the box, and
then the happy words contained in the parchment, which at last
leads to a conclusion: Arcangeli must prime the old man with
his best Orvieto. The nature of the daydream is emphasized
through syntactical parts joined in a simple chain-like pattern:
the object *grandsire* in line 26, for example, becomes the subject
of the new clause in line 27 through the pronoun *he*; *box*, part
of the object in line 28, becomes the subject of the new clause
in line 29; and '*Cinino, Ciniccino*', nicknames for Arcangeli's son,
become the antecedents for *whom* in line 32, the indirect object
of the next three lines in which the grandsire's will is quoted.
Separation between the links is emphasized through heavy punctuation: dashes or double stops (,—) instead of single commas.

This type of sentence, especially as it contrasts with the other two types in the monologue, exposes Arcangeli: erupting in exclamations, plodding wearily through sequences of short phrases, or lapsing into long, meandering, incremental periods, he seems to lack intellectual vigor and discipline. His mind explodes, plods, or wanders. He is lazy. His exclamations are not offset by those complex but vigorous constructions in which Mr. Sludge or Fra Lippo Lippi commonly express their arguments. Moreover, the very fact that his basic syntactical patterns are relatively few in a monologue of 1805 lines is indicative of his lack of complexity and depth. The Pope's speech *seems* to us in every way the product of a formidable, widely-ranging intellect—it comes just after Arcangeli's—whereas Arcangeli's seems the product of a very average, albeit delightfully pompous, civil servant; but we receive these two different impressions not alone through the sense of the words in both speeches but through the contrasting patterns in which those words occur, and even through the relative range in structural pattern within both monologues.

Tertium Quid is "neither this nor that," as Browning introduces the monologue, neither typical of one half of Rome nor the other, but something elaborate "bred of both," [35] and Tertium Quid does indeed go to great lengths to convince his auditors of the neat and discriminating balance of his mind. His syntax reflects artificiality, on one level, for it is excessively balanced, marked with parallels and recurring patterns that betray his lack of concern for what he says and considerable concern for how he says it:

> True, Excellency—as his Highness says,   (*TQ*, 1)
> Though she's not dead yet, she's as good as stretched
> Symmetrical beside the other two;
> Though he's not judged yet, he's the same as judged,
> So do the facts abound and superabound:
> And nothing hinders, now, we lift the case
> Out of the shade into the shine, allow
> Qualified persons to pronounce at last,

35. See *The Ring and the Book,* I, 912–13. Tertium Quid is also one who "Harangues in silvery and selectest phrase" (I, 933).

Nay, edge in an authoritative word
Between this rabble's-brabble of dolts and fools
Who make up reasonless unreasoning Rome.

The speaker is pleased to think of Pompilia's being "Symmetrical" beside her parents, and he uses every device at hand, particularly syntax, to achieve symmetry in his discourse. These lines are filled with phonetic, verbal and syntactical parallels:

Excellency	Highness
Though she's not dead yet,	Though he's not judged yet,
she's as good as stretched	he's the same as judged
abound	superabound
we lift	[we] allow
Out of the shade	into the shine
Qualified persons	authoritative word
rabble's-	brabble
dolts	fools
reasonless	unreasoning

Tertium Quid achieves symmetry in a host of ways. Instead of linking a compound subject with a conjunction, he does it with a comma, repeating a demonstrative: "This Pietro, this Violante" (*TQ*, 70); he implores two of his auditors in turn, then together, thus:

. . . Excellency, your ear!   (*TQ*, 68)
Stoop to me, Highness,—listen and look yourselves!

He uses verbal phrases so that the verb falls on the same stress in successive lines:

And so, deliberately snaps house-book clasp, (*TQ*, 146)
Posts off to vespers, missal beneath arm,
Passes the proper San Lorenzo by,
Dives down a little lane to the left . . .

He uses other parallel constructions, emphasizing the parallels alliteratively or through word repetition:

What banker, merchant, has seen better days, (*TQ*, 347)
What second-rate painter a-pushing up,
Poet a-slipping down, shall bid the best . . .

Having, he, not a doit, they, not a child . . . (*TQ*, 525)

Daughter o' the couple we all venerate,   (*TQ*, 873)
Wife of the husband we all cap before,
Mother o' the babes we all breathe blessings on . . .

The effect implements the structure of *The Ring and the Book,*
for *Tertium Quid* concludes the three introductory Roman monologues in a virtual coda of summarizing parallels. Yet character
is also revealed in the process. Excessive symmetry marks the expression of every thought Tertium Quid has; he never relents,
so that even the tragic details of the murder are reported in sentences that reflect obtuseness and depravity in their very balance.
Motivated only by social insecurity and a desire for advancement,
he reveals himself through the elaborate syntax, diction and alliteration that he uses to impress the fashionable people around
him.

Caponsacchi's syntax is contrastingly simple and direct, reflecting strength and sincerity. He uses more short sentences, in normal subject-predicate word order, than any other speaker in *The
Ring and the Book,* many beginning with the first person pronoun: "I want no more with earth." (*GC*, 169); "I begin." (*GC*,
220); "I stopped short awe-struck." (*GC*, 268). When he harangues the court, as in lines 5–63, sentence structure becomes
more complex, but when he tells Pompilia's story, or recounts
his own experiences in Arezzo or on the road to Rome, his sentences tend to be either brief and simple, or composed of short
independent clauses joined by colons and double punctuation:

So, I went home. Dawn broke, noon broadened, I—(*GC*, 1022)
I sat stone-still, let time run over me.
The sun slanted into my room, had reached
The west. I opened book,—Aquinas blazed
With one black name only on the white page.
I looked up, saw the sunset: vespers rang:
'She counts the minutes till I keep my word
'And come say all is ready. I am a priest.
'Duty to God is duty to her: I think
'God, who created her, will save her too

'Some new way, by one miracle the more,
'Without me. Then, prayer may avail perhaps.'
I went to my own place i' the Pieve, read
The office: I was back at home again
Sitting i' the dark . . .

Short independent clauses and simple sentences increase the dramatic intensity of such a passage, so that Caponsacchi's own narrative of the murder-story seems to be more deeply felt than any of
the preceding ones. His sentences are declarative ones, as a rule,
unmarked by qualifying phrases and dependent clauses. He has
the courage to state facts simply, letting them stand as they are.
His syntax thus directly reflects passion, courage, and spiritual
simplicity. Caponsacchi is capable of subtle thought—as not only
his meaning but the syntax of a minority of his sentences seems
to attest, but he takes no refuge in intricate constructions when
boldness and plainness are required, as they are when he speaks.

As a final instance of Browning's use of syntax to differentiate
and to reveal the various speakers in the poems at hand, we might
consider briefly together the portraits of the two Catholic bishops
—the one who is said to order his tomb, and Blougram.

Despite its short length, *The Bishop at St. Praxed* contains sentences that vary considerably in structure. One of the reasons for
this is that the speaker's state of mind varies: he starts briskly and
lucidly, approximately quoting a verse in Ecclesiastes, and issu-
ing a brief command that turns into a query:

> Vanity, saith the preacher, vanity!   (*BSP*, 1)
> Draw round my bed: is Anselm keeping back?

But then he begins a sentence that is not finished:

> Nephews—sons mine . . . ah God, I know not! . . . (*BSP*, 3)

He breaks off because the implication of "Nephews—sons mine,"
once the words are uttered, suddenly strikes him as an unallowable one; he hastens to cover up his mistake and even to excuse
himself in the rest of the line, as we have seen in a consideration
of the key word *God* in the poem.[36] A number of other sentences

36. See above, pp. 218–19.

in the poem are incomplete; the dying Bishop struggles constantly with two sets of conflicts that he can scarcely control: first, the conflict between facts (that his "nephews" are his sons, for example, or that, as in lines 36–44, he has actually secreted a lump of *lapis* in the vineyard for his tomb) and his awareness of the impropriety of the facts; and second, the conflict between sensuous visions connected with his tomb, which lead him to dwell excessively on certain details, and his awareness of the purpose of his talk, to persuade his sons to carry out an order for the monument. In contrast, Bishop Blougram's sentences are always fully controlled by the speaker: rhetorically they take him exactly where he wishes to go, for Blougram to a far greater extent realizes the implications of what he is saying, and realizes them in advance. Thought, in *Bishop Blougram,* precedes expression. In *The Bishop at St. Praxed* feeling in general leads and dictates the thought. There are few interruptions in Blougram's sentence patterns, apart from frequently intricate qualifying clauses and phrases that elaborate upon his meaning. Moreover, many of Blougram's sentences are periodic, the meaning often revealing itself with a surprise at the conclusion:

> So, drawing comfortable breath again, *(BBA,* 78)
> You weigh and find, whatever more or less
> I boast of my ideal realized
> Is nothing in the balance when opposed
> To your ideal, your grand simple life,
> Of which you will not realize one jot.

Few of the dying Bishop's periodic sentences are completed, and one of his most common constructions is marked by the presence of an absolute-type element. Roma King has explained this and other syntactical features of the poem in terms of the "sterility" of the Bishop's mind and his "lack of ingenuity and his subservience to established pattern," [37] but surely this rather ingeniously misses the point. The Bishop's typical constructions attest to the prevailing sensuousness of his character—sensuousness that leads and dominates the thought:

> . . . Well—   *(BSP,* 3)
> She, men would have to be your mother once,

37. *The Bow and the Lyre,* pp. 59–60.

Old Gandolf envied me, so fair she was!

—Old Gandolf with his paltry onion-stone,   (*BSP*, 31)
Put me where I may look at him! True peach,
Rosy and flawless: how I earned the prize!

One block, pure green as a pistachio-nut,   (*BSP*, 71)
There's plenty jasper somewhere in the world— . . .

His dead mistress, or the delicious picture of his rival's paltry
headstone, or the color and quality of the stone that he contemplates for his own tomb, all press upon the Bishop's imagination
so that he expresses these visions without regard to the way in
which they will fit into his argument or impress his auditors; the
cool logic of Bishop Blougram is utterly missing here, for the
Renaissance Bishop struggles with heady delights even as he
speaks. Again and again his visions carry him off from the purpose at hand. As delirium comes upon him at the end of the poem
he does not speak in sentences at all, but in fragments which express only the horror before his eyes:

. . . Stone—   (*BSP*, 115)
Gritstone, a-crumble! Clammy squares which sweat
As if the corpse they keep were oozing through— . . .

Blougram, on the other hand, not infrequently speaks in sentences so neatly balanced that they reflect the very finest control
of rhetoric. Some approach the symmetry of Tertium Quid's:

Men are not angels, neither are they brutes: (*BBA*, 864)
Something we may see, all we cannot see.

Stood you confessed of those exceptional   (*BBA*, 934)
And privileged great natures that dwarf mine—
A zealot with a mad ideal in reach,
A poet just about to print his ode,
A statesman with a scheme to stop this war,
An artist whose religion is his art—
I should have nothing to object: such men
Carry the fire, all things grow warm to them,
Their drugget's worth my purple, they beat me.

Blougram's sentences on the whole are not excessively patterned,
so that they do not reflect artificiality; balance attests rather to

his complete presence of mind and full awareness of his auditor. Blougram's details are almost always subordinated syntactically. They illustrate meaning: they are not emphasized as the Bishop at St. Praxed's details are, as when, for example, Blougram mentions "man, woman, child" or "cosmogony, / Geology, ethnology" in *BBA*, 676–80. Syntax, rhythm, diction, and phonetic quality often combine to heighten the effect of enumerated details in *The Bishop at St. Praxed,* as in the sentence beginning, "And then how I shall lie through centuries," (*BSP*, 80), or in the incomplete periodic beginning, "The bas-relief in bronze ye promised me," (*BSP*, 56), so that the dying Bishop's details—ostensibly uttered to illustrate his argument—assume far more importance than the argument itself. Neither bishop, certainly, has a sterile mind, and both have worldly and spiritual affinities. But beyond this their differences are enormous and are reflected in no way more tellingly than through the syntactical patterns they employ.

PUNCTUATION

"I attach importance to the mere stops," Browning wrote to Edward Chapman of Chapman and Hall on October 31, 1855, on finding "a few errors" in copies of the new *Men and Women* volumes which the publisher had just sent him; [38] and a year later, somewhat facetiously, but no less truly, he wrote to Chapman concerning possible corrections to be made in Elizabeth's *Aurora Leigh:*

> And for the rest, there would seem to be no verbal errors to signify; however we will look to that, and let you know or not, as it may seem worth while. But the principal thing is to pray you not to keep people waiting a moment in waiting for further notice from us (*Us*—I am the church-organ-bellows' blower that talked about *our* playing, but you know what I do in the looking after commas and dots to i's).[39]

It is possible that Browning's name will occupy an interesting place in the history of English poetic punctuation when such a

38. *New Letters,* ed. DeVane and Knickerbocker, pp. 83, 82.
39. Ibid., p. 97. Letter dated December 2, 1856.

history is written.[40] Browning's artistic techniques matured during several decades in which a major upheaval was occurring in the field of English punctuation theory,[41] and it is clear that Browning took an unusually keen interest in pointing. *Pauline* (1833) reflects Shelley's loose practice with the dash and the comma and displays nothing particularly new in its punctuation, but by the time of *Dramatic Romances and Lyrics* (1845), Browning had worked out a practice of his own. Like Matthew Arnold,[42]

40. Apart from some work that has been done on the classical backgrounds of punctuation theory and on Elizabethan punctuation (interest in the latter probably dating from Percy Simpson's valuable *Shakespearian Punctuation,* Oxford, 1911), we know relatively little about the history of English punctuation itself and still less about the history of poetic punctuation. I have drawn for some background in what follows on my "Eighteenth and Nineteenth Century English Punctuation Theory," *English Studies, 41* (1960), 92–102.

41. By the beginning of the eighteenth century the traditional system of elocutionary pointing had been supplemented by a crude syntactical system, and some acknowledgment is paid to the dictates of both syntax and elocution alike in most grammars and pointing treatises until the 1780's. In his *Elements of Elocution* (London, 1781) and *A Rhetorical Grammar* (1785), John Walker pointed out the distinctions between elocutionary and syntactical systems; J. Robertson drew up an elaborate system of syntactical rules in *An Essay on Punctuation* (London, 1785); and the next year, partly in replying to Robertson, David Steel strongly argued against the elocutionary basis, maintaining that grammar alone should become the basis for pointing; see Steel's *Elements of Punctuation* (London, 1786), pp. 4–25, 88–89, 164, especially. Steel's book is cited often in pointing treatises of 1800–1830; grammarians generally either aligned themselves on Steel's side, arguing in favor of the grammatical basis, or opposed him in favor of the old elocutionary one. Pointing practice became more anarchical in general, and complaints over the status of punctuation more vociferous, until in the decade of the 1840's several factors combined to bring about a triumph for syntactical theory. John Wilson's *A Treatise on Grammatical Punctuation* (Manchester, 1844), a systematic, elucidating, and detailed guide written by a professional printer who denied the value of the elocutionary basis, became quickly popular; after 1848 few grammars or pointing treatises vouched for the elocutionary system, although some continued to include rules for punctuation reflecting the older basis. It is likely that few periods in English history have witnessed such widespread interest in punctuation theory and practice as the period between 1820 and 1844 or 1848, when the "battle" between those favoring the syntactical and those favoring the elocutionary bases was at its height, the main issue unresolved; and it is during these years that Browning received his "formal" education (largely from scholarly tutors and a book-loving and well-informed father), read widely, explored the uses of language—significantly experimenting with syntax—in *Sordello,* and perfected the techniques of the character-revealing dramatic monologue.

42. For Arnold's "addiction" to punctuation see, e.g., *The Poetical Works of Matthew Arnold,* ed. C. B. Tinker and H. F. Lowry (London, 1950), p. v.

he continued to revise the punctuation of almost all of his poems
in successive editions until the time of his death, but unlike many
previous poets Browning seems to have ensured that his own
punctuation—rather than the printer's—be followed; moreover,
there is evidence that those who printed his mature poems followed his own punctuation short of the inevitable commission
of occasional typographical errors.[43]

In the monologues, the basis of Browning's pointing practice
seems to be the elocutionary one, in which stops are used to indicate pauses of varying lengths; but superimposed upon this,
or partly modifying it, is a system which generally takes account
of grammatical considerations. Stops are very rarely omitted where
they are grammatically called for. But added stops are used when
pauses are required to indicate the speaker's slower enunciation,
or the letter-writer's more intense consideration, of a passage:

> The very God! think, Abib; dost thou think? (*EK*, 304)
> So, the All-Great, were the All-Loving too—   (305)
> So, through the thunder comes a human voice   (306)
> Saying, "O heart I made, a heart beats here! [44]   (307)

Karshish omits no punctuation required by the syntax of these
lines; but the expression of his important discovery—that the
deity of power is also the deity of love—is considerably slowed
by both of the commas in line 305. The second comma in the line
separates the clausal subject "All-Great" from the verb "were"

43. See Browning's letter of October 31, 1855 to Edward Chapman in *New Letters,*
ed. DeVane and Knickerbocker, pp. 82–83. I have compared Browning's MSS of *The
Ring and the Book* (B.M. Add. 43485–86) with the text of the first edition and
have found, in a close inspection of punctuation in Books I, V, VII, and XI, no
changes beyond a very few incidental ones that Browning himself probably made
when he revised the text slightly from proof sheets. Specifically, marks of double
punctuation, e.g. (,—), (;—), which might easily have been altered by the compositors if they had been in the habit of altering his points, were not altered. It
seems reasonably clear from this, and the evidence of Browning's letters of 1855–56
to his previous publisher, Chapman, that Browning insisted that his own punctuation be followed—at least by the time of the *Men and Women* volumes—and that
his compositors did follow it with some care.

44. Karshish's lines stand as such in *Men and Women* (1855), where the poem
first appeared, and in all subsequent editions of the poem published during the
poet's lifetime. Curiously, the original punctuation of *Karshish* remained generally
untampered with, while the punctuation of the epistolary *Cleon,* the poem most
like it in *Men and Women,* underwent quite a few changes in subsequent editions.

and is thus purely an elocutionary device. The commas after "So" in lines 305 and 306 are at least unnecessary in marking out the syntax, too, and are injected to slow the tempo of the passage. In line 304, another type of elocutionary device occurs that was used frequently by Browning in the monologues before *The Ring and the Book;* the exclamation point is employed not as a terminal stop but as a coordinating one: "The very God! think, Abib." The effect is to accentuate the stress on *God,* increasing the quantity and raising the pitch of its vowel sound, without bringing about such a marked pause that the next word, *think,* is deprived of due stress. A colon or semicolon would not affect the quantity or pitch of the first word, and a capitalized "Think" would actually deprive Karshish's *think* of some of the stress that it now has. The question mark is also frequently used as a coordinating point in the earlier character-revealing monologues:

Zooks, what's to blame? you think you see a monk! [45] (*FLL,* 3)

Here the pitch is raised in the vowel of *blame,* heightening the audacity of Lippo's early rhetorical thrust at his captors, but the line is not excessively retarded as the next word, *you,* is not capitalized—Lippo's energetic pace is not unduly slackened. Browning uses one other type of punctuation primarily for its effect upon sound (and therefore, in most cases, for its assistance in characterization), rather than for its clarification of syntax. He employs the dash and comma together (,—) and less often the dash with other marks (!—), (?—), (:—), or (;—), in order to indicate pauses of greater duration than any one of these marks would suggest if used alone, but of less duration than the ellipsis or the terminating full stop necessitates. Such double punctuation, although not in fashion now, was in common use throughout the nineteenth century and seems to be a legacy of elocutionary pointing.[46] Browning uses it somewhat sparingly in the early mon-

45. The line appeared as such in *Men and Women,* and was never altered by Browning.

46. Justin Brenan criticized the widespread use of (,—), (;—), and (:—), in particular, in his *Composition and Punctuation Familiarly Explained* . . . (London, 1829), p. 95. Grammarians and others continued to use the double mark (,—) and other combinations throughout the nineteenth century, however. See, e.g., the practice in Hugh Doherty, *An Introduction to English Grammar, on Universal Principles* (London, 1841), and James Stormonth, *Punctuation Based on the Analysis of Sentences* (London, 1877), passim.

ologues and more frequently in *The Ring and the Book,* where
the average ratio seems to be approximately one mark of double
punctuation per 10 lines.[47] Several of these marks used together
may have a decisive effect upon the tempo of a passage—as when
Pompilia, speaking of Guido's attempt to lure Caponsacchi to
the house in Arezzo, momentarily falters:

> He ought not to have wished me thus act lies, (*P,* 700)
> Simulate folly,—but,—wrong or right, the wish,—
> I failed to apprehend its drift.

The act of luring Caponsacchi is in fact the one good act that
Guido has committed, and Pompilia's apprehension of this irony
—Guido's very evil resulted in bringing about her own salvation
—is registered through a line in which the strongest possible
pauses interrupt the rhythm without bringing the flow of thought
to a complete halt. In *Andrea del Sarto* the device occurs less
often, but is useful. Browning employs it only once in the opening 34 lines of the poem:

> Oh, I'll content him,—but to-morrow, Love! (*AdS,* 10)

The comparatively long pause separates too very different feelings: Andrea's tired resignation (he has agreed to paint for
Lucrezia's "friend's friend"), and his momentary joy (he has won
Lucrezia's company in the bargain and will not have to begin
painting until tomorrow). Syntactically the two expressions of
feeling are related because they both spring from the same cause,
the bargain Andrea has struck. Rhythmically they are separated
because the two feelings are in fact quite different, and the effect
of double punctuation in this case—preserving the syntactical
unity of the line while disrupting the rhythm with an unusually
strong caesura—helps in its small way to emphasize the tragedy
of Andrea's situation: what pitiful joy that he has is caused by
an act that also, typically, wearies and emasculates him. It is primarily through its operation upon rhythm that pointing becomes
a useful device in helping to expose character.
  In several of the monologues particular stops occur more often

---

47. Based on random 100-line counts of mine in ten monologues of *The Ring
and the Book.*

than others, and these may, in addition, have a cumulative effect that helps to tell something about character. In *Mr. Sludge's* opening 180 lines, for example, there are over four times as many exclamation points as there are full stops. The ubiquitous exclamations, beginning in the first line,

Now, don't, sir! Don't expose me! Just this once! (*MSM*, 1)

—have the rather subtle effect of raising the pitch of many of Mr. Sludge's vowels as well as the more obvious one of lending his verse an abrupt and explosive quality. Mr. Sludge himself thus soon becomes identified with explosive rhythms and shrill sounds (indeed we think of him as being explosive and shrill)— the one, in context, reflecting his vivacity and the other his crudity and sheer unpleasantness. In *Caliban* a quieter mark of punctuation is employed with frequency: the colon. Caliban uses this point 37 times in less than 300 lines, or approximately twice as often as Bishop Blougram and Cleon do, and three times as often as Fra Lippo Lippi does. In *Caliban* it is used not only to set off appositive clauses and phrases, as in,

'Thinketh, it came of being ill at ease: (*CUS*, 31)
He hated that He cannot change His cold,

or in,

As it likes me each time, I do: so He. (*CUS*, 108)

but to separate syntactical parts that might ordinarily be separated by a semicolon or a full stop, as in,

'Wove wattles half the winter, fenced them firm (*CUS*, 205)
With stone and stake to stop she-tortoises
Crawling to lay their eggs here: well, one wave,
Feeling the foot of Him . . . ,

or that might be separated by a comma, or even, as in the case of the colon that follows "taste" in line 274, that need no punctuation at all. The colon is thus used more often than syntactical requirements actually dictate in *Caliban*. Its excessive use is not entirely to be explained by the needs of rhythmic pause, for in many cases approximately the same caesura might have been indicated by another point. Browning's excessive use of it more nearly parallels that of the Elizabethans, in particular that of Shakespeare, or Shakespeare's printers, than it does his own practice elsewhere. But the point does more than simply reflect an element of "style" in *The Tempest*.[48] It occurs frequently enough in the appositional pattern, in which the second clause or phrase appears to be a consequence of the first, that it seems to heighten *consequence* throughout the discourse. For Caliban nature has consequences, and the consequences follow abruptly:

> There is the sport: discover how or die! (*CUS,* 218)
>
> . . . 'Sees, himself, (*CUS,* 257)
> Yonder two flies, with purple films and pink,
> Bask on the pompion-bell above: kills both.

The colon thus helps to reflect a peculiarity of Caliban's mind. To the savage, nature itself seems fierce, sudden, filled with abrupt and illogical events. All things are paralleled for Caliban; relatively few of his constructions subordinate one thing to another. As he is savage: so is Setebos. If Setebos sees two flies: He kills them both. If Caliban happens to spare a squirrel he may also spare a cub: he may also smash them both. In its particular qualities as being a mark that reflects consequence, that suggests that what is to follow is equal or parallel to what has preceded, and that arrests the rhythmic movement sharply, the colon helps to express the animality of Caliban in its various contexts.

The cumulative effect of a stop depends, of course, upon its excessive use in a context, but the cumulative effect may be felt in passages that are shorter than a whole monologue. In *Guido,* for example, the use of the isolated dash (—) becomes more frequent, generally, as the speech continues, until in the final few lines it becomes a characteristic mark. With double punctuation (,—) and the now equally frequent exclamation point, it helps to indicate the speaker's complete mental disintegration:

48. No one can be sure at this time to what extent Shakespeare's punctuation is Shakespeare's own, of course. Browning certainly endeavored in *Caliban* to incorporate other technical features of Caliban's speeches in *The Tempest* (see, e.g., above, p. 226, n. 22, for diction), and *Caliban's* colons may have been suggested by those in the play. But Browning's portrait is not an imitation of its "model." The colon here does something very different from what it does in Shakespeare's play.

. . . All was folly—I laughed and mocked! (G, 2417)
Sirs, my first true word, all truth and no lie,
Is—save me notwithstanding! Life is all!
I was just stark mad,—let the madman live
Pressed by as many chains as you please pile!
Don't open! Hold me from them! I am yours,
I am the Granduke's—no, I am the Pope's!
Abate,—Cardinal,—Christ,—Maria,—God, . . .

But the great resolving verse of the monologue significantly contains none of these stops. Guido's disintegration is now complete. In the final line he finds spiritual integration, and salvation:

Pompilia, will you let them murder me? [49] (G, 2425)

49. It would, admittedly, be the height of folly to suggest that very much of the effect of these verses—or of any verses in Browning—is to be explained through an analysis of punctuation. My object has been to suggest that punctuation in its small way influences the effects in the dramatic monologues, and that Browning used the points consciously as devices (among many more important devices) to aid in the delineation of his speakers.

9. The Arch-Villain

"Yet here is the monster! Why, he's a mere man—"
(*TQ,* 1603)

IN the last few chapters, we have been examining a number of
the ways in which dramatic, prosodic and verbal elements are related to character delineation in twenty of Browning's monologues. We are aware of at least a few of the special uses Browning made of these elements in creating impressions of character,
and we should now be able to analyze a passage rather closely in
order to see how different elements of technique may combine in
a character-revealing monologue to produce an intense central
impression.

We shall take up two: a passage of 19 lines from *Count Guido
Franceschini,* and another of 21 lines from *Guido.* Both passages
comprise a mere one percent of the monologues from which they
are excerpted; both have, of course, specific functions in the contexts of Guido's two portraits—and we must be careful not to
think of the excerpts as whole little poems in themselves. But
both, selected on the basis of their somewhat self-explanatory and
self-contained meanings, not only shed light on specific traits and
attitudes of the speaker when they occur, but, like most of the
lines that immediately precede and follow them, illumine equally
the central black villainy of his nature—the unifying element of
Guido's being.

From the uncertain evidence as to the real Guido's character,
Browning created in *The Ring and the Book* a highly individualized villain.[1] It is clear that Browning felt his own conception

1. See Browning's chief historical source for *The Ring and the Book,* reproduced
and translated, in Charles W. Hodell, *The Old Yellow Book* . . . , Baltimore, 1908.
Although Browning's Guido resembles the original Count Guido in many circum-

to be perfectly consistent with the historical facts. He defended *Count Guido Franceschini* and what was "worse" to come, *Guido*, in his letter of November 19, 1868 to Miss Wedgwood in this manner:

> But here,—given the subject, I cannot but still say, given the treatment too: the business has been, as I specify, to explain *fact*—and the fact is what you see and, worse, are to see. . . . Before I die, I hope to purely invent something,—here my pride was concerned to invent nothing: the minutest circumstance that denotes character is *true:* the black is so much— the white, no more.[2]

"Think," he wrote two months later,

> . . . of six people, that do any remarkable thing: there will be nobody to match Guido, whose wickedness [in Book V] does . . . or rather, by the end [in Book XI], *shall* . . . rise to the limit conceivable . . .[3]

Guido, in Browning's conception, is not a devil but he is diabolic: his black is the deepest black. He admitted to Miss Wedgwood that he did "unduly like the study of morbid cases of the soul," and enjoyed depicting Guido, whose

> curious depth below depth of depravity . . . might well have warned another [off] . . . but I thought that, since I could do it, and even liked to do it, my affair it was rather than another's.[4]

---

stantial ways, there is little basis for Browning's conception of his psychological nature in the court records of the Old Yellow Book. The Count does not speak at all in them—and, given these facts, one might deduce, as it were, any number of interpretations as to the psychology of his character.

2. *Robert Browning and Julia Wedgwood: A Broken Friendship as Revealed by Their Letters*, ed. Richard Curle (New York, 1937), pp. 143–44.

3. Ibid., p. 153 (interior ellipses are Browning's, not mine). Letter of January 21, 1869. At this time Julia Wedgwood had only read Books I–VI of *The Ring and the Book;* Browning delayed in sending her the rest. Interestingly, his treatment of evil in *The Ring and the Book*—and especially his treatment of Guido's character— strongly criticized by Miss Wedgwood, became one of the reasons for the rupture in Browning's friendship with her, or, at least for Miss Wedgwood, a pretext for the rupture. See their correspondence in the work cited, pp. 126–96.

4. Ibid., pp. 143, 145. Letter of November 19, 1868.

Guido is presented from the beginning of *The Ring and the Book* as the villain of the piece, so that we are never really left in doubt as to what to think of him. Considerable preparation for his two speeches precedes them. He is introduced as a murderer in a translation of the Old Yellow Book's title-page—and is thus the first speaker to be mentioned by name in Book I:

> 'Romana Homicidiorum'—nay,   (I, 120)
> Better translate—'A Roman murder-case:
> 'Position of the entire criminal cause
> 'Of Guido Franceschini, nobleman,
> 'With certain Four the cutthroats in his pay,
> 'Tried, all five, and found guilty and put to death . . .

In Browning's summary and quotations of the arguments of the Fisc (I, 165–76), the Patron of the Poor (I, 175–97) and their legal adjuncts (I, 200–13), Guido appears in a guilty light, and soon after, in a short denunciatory speech of the Pope (I, 328–43), Guido is conclusively damned by Browning himself, who has introduced the Pope as just, merciful, humble, great and good (I, 300–26): it is impossible, we are led to believe, that the Pope's opinion of Guido could be wrong.

Thus by the time Browning announces, "This is the bookful . . ." (I, 364) and "You know the tale already . . ." (I, 377), we have a picture of Guido as a guilty murderer. From now on the picture progressively darkens. At line 502 there is a hint that the murderer was a torturer: Guido's Arezzo is Pompilia's "trap and cage and torture-place" (I, 502). A few lines later the torturer becomes a "monster": Paul and Girolamo Franceschini are

> Two obscure goblin creatures, fox-faced this, (I, 549)
> Cat-clawed the other, called his next of kin
> By Guido the main monster . . .

And then the monster becomes the wolf. This "staunch image," as Guido later calls it, runs like a leitmotiv throughout *The Ring and the Book* and is used by Guido to depict himself in his second monologue.[5] He and his accomplices are now linked to it:

5. See *Guido*, 1177. Also see the discussion of animal imagery in *The Ring and the Book* in Chap. 6 above.

> Glimmeringly did a pack of were-wolves pad (I, 611)
> The snow, those flames were Guido's eyes in front . . .

The wolves see the Comparini, Comparini the wolves, and then, "the wolves, their wolf-work done," (I, 628), are embosomed in the night again. Apprehended, Guido is defended by men who turn "wrong to right," prove "wolves sheep and sheep wolves" (I, 646)—Guido becoming the wolf-in-sheep's-clothing as he feigns innocence that truly distinguishes Pompilia alone. Even after the Pope's judgment, we are told, "tarriers" looked to find in Pompilia and Guido

> A touch of wolf in what showed whitest sheep, (I, 656)
> A cross of sheep redeeming the whole wolf . . .

Following this, Guido is described physically,

> A beak-nosed bushy-bearded black-haired lord, (I, 782)
> Lean, pallid, low of stature yet robust,
> Fifty years old,—

before the two lengthy, formal introductions to his monologues (I, 949–1015, 1272–1329), in which the settings of these speeches, as well as Guido's appearance, tone of voice, and general manner at both times, are described. In the second passage Guido's monstrosity and bestiality are further underlined; he is "the part-man part-monster" (I, 1294), and the "tiger-cat" who

> . . . screams now, that whined before, (I, 1296)
> That pried and tried and trod so gingerly,
> Till in its silkiness the trap-teeth join;
> Then you know how the bristling fury foams.

By the end of Book I we have met exactly the Guido that we are to know intimately in Books V and XI. Our basic impression of him in the monologues will not be different from the one that we now have—save that, as his villainy is reflected and established in intricate detail, that impression will be enriched many times over. We have yet to experience the artistic impact of his portrait. Book I has enumerated and described the canvases to come.

Guido has, of course, been discussed thoroughly by the speakers of *Half-Rome, Other Half-Rome,* and *Tertium Quid* before
we hear his own voice. Not one of these speakers has seen him
clearly. Half-Rome's judgment is farthest wide of the mark; his
epithets and images for Guido are false, as are all of his explanations for Guido's actions. Other Half-Rome echoes the wolf-im-
agery of Book I (as in *OH-R,* 991) and, for the wrong reasons,
sometimes expresses Browning's opinion of Guido's character,
but the Guido who emerges from his speech is more nearly the
villain of a sentimental melodrama. Tertium Quid's contributions to the portrait that follows his own are principally to supply a more elaborate description of what Guido looks like (*TQ,*
717–19), echoing Browning's own in Book I, and to mention the
torture that has been administered to Guido prior to his first address (*TQ,* 1621–30).

Nevertheless Guido's situation is clear in the opening lines of
Count Guido Franceschini. Attempting to win the sympathy of
the Court, Guido exploits at length the fact that he has just come
from the rack, feigning surprise over the glass handed to him that
contains "Velletri,—and not vinegar and gall" (*CGF,* 5), but de-
clining more than a single sip of the wine, for, as he states,

> . . . I want my head (*CGF,* 7)
> To save my neck, there's work awaits me still.

His auditors, Judges Tommati, Venturini and others,[6] are all
members of the clergy, a fact that Guido acknowledges not only
in his use of "reverend" when addressing them, but in invoca-
tions ("I' the name of the indivisible Trinity!" *CGF,* 121), in references to the saints, the heretical Molinists, and ecclesiastical
affairs. They have ordered him to speak in his own "defence /
Plainly," as he repeats later (*CGF,* 918–19), and Guido knows
that life hangs on the balance of what he says. In this, the moment

6. Guido does not mention their names. Browning describes them as "Tommati,
Venturini and the rest," in his introduction to *Count Guido Franceschini* in I, 952,
and Caponsacchi rather daringly singles out Tommati to scold him in *GC,* 34–48,
132–36. It is likely that Guido has heard the names of his auditors, but refrains from
mentioning them as he does not wish to appear impudent or, above all, to be
taking special advantages.

of his address is a more "climactic" one than is usual in Browning's monologues, but the moment is one of the very few in which Guido might be expected to reveal himself at all; the liar is here confronted with circumstances that prevent him from lying unmitigatedly about himself, as he might on more normal occasions, for the Court already knows the salient facts of the case, and these Guido cannot avoid. Guido does not know his auditors personally, but he has, as he says, spent thirty years of his life as a minor and unrewarded cardinal's attendant in Rome (*CGF*, 242–92, 336–67) and so knows the type of men to whom he now speaks. In fact the reverend Court represents, in one sense, a certain psychological extension of Guido. For thirty years he has masked himself as a little element of the Catholic clergy itself. In Rome he

. . . assumed (CGF, 269)
Three or four orders of no consequence,

he admits, which gave "clerical savour" to his existence and facilitated his "claim to loaf and fish" (*CGF*, 273–74), so that, in "the train of Monsignor and Eminence" (*CGF*, 338), he partook of the best of the city's life. For thirty years he has tried to *appear* to be what his present auditors are—but without in any sense abandoning his gaming habits, fencing, riding, dancing, the old expressions of his personality. Now he takes up a similar mask. He no longer pretends to be a member of the Roman hierarchy, but presents himself as one who earnestly tried to uphold his family's name in following the Church for as long as he was able; he has failed only through bad luck. Thus he establishes himself as being the moral equal of his auditors, and this gives him leave to blame, cajole, flatter, and snap at them by turns.

Yet he needs primarily his auditors' sympathy if he is to win acquittal, and to this end most of his lines are directed. In his preliminary (1–139), he emphasizes the condition of his tortured body and the misfortune of his present state, and then disarmingly admits that he has indeed murdered Pompilia and the Comparini. Next he sketches in his family history and the personal difficulties that led to his meeting with the Comparini (140–412), after which he recounts the circumstances of the pact with Pompilia's foster parents, the marriage itself, and his own attitude toward the pact

(413–606). This brings his narrative to the point of his married life with Pompilia in Arezzo.

In the course of picturing his young wife's coldness and quiet obstinacy, Guido utters the following lines—and these we may examine in some detail:

Count Guido Francéschini (701–19)

Pompilia was no pigeon, Venus' pet,	(701)
That shuffled from between her pressing paps	(702)
To sit on my rough shoulder,—but a hawk,	(703)
I bought at a hawk's price and carried home	(704)
To do hawk's service—at the Rotunda, say,	(705)
Where, six o' the callow nestlings in a row,	(706)
You pick and choose and pay the price for such.	(707)
I have paid my pound, await my penny's worth,	(708)
So, hoodwink, starve and properly train my bird,	(709)
And, should she prove a haggard,—twist her neck!	(710)
Did I not pay my name and style, my hope	(711)
And trust, my all? Through spending these amiss	(712)
I am here! 'T is scarce the gravity of the Court	(713)
Will blame me that I never piped a tune,	(714)
Treated my falcon-gentle like my finch.	(715)
The obligation I incurred was just	(716)
To practise mastery, prove my mastership:—	(717)
Pompilia's duty was—submit herself,	(718)
Afford me pleasure, perhaps cure my bile.	(719)

We may note first of all that this passage has a special unity: it consists of a single, elaborated image. Imagery itself is an excellent rhetorical instrument for the liar who is troubled by the knowledge that his auditors are already apprised of the true facts, and Guido depends upon images to an extent that no other speaker in *The Ring and the Book* save Bottini does: he uses them consistently to express rather than merely to illustrate or to embellish his meaning. He knows, for one thing, that when he calls Pompilia "a hawk" he is on somewhat safe ground: a certain leeway with the facts must be granted to anyone who uses metaphor, for no metaphor is in a factual sense entirely true. Indeed the test of whether a metaphor is a true and fitting one at all is a difficult one to make in a court of law; a witness permitted to speak metaphorically might succeed in perpetrating the most outrageous falsehoods just because metaphor itself takes leave of factually demonstrable relationships and communicates meaning implicitly or symbolically. Legally, then, Guido is safe here: his judges could not accuse him of perjury. But there is also a good deal of implicit truth in what he says. He has indeed purchased Pompilia from the Comparini as one might purchase a bird at the Santa Maria della Rotonda in Rome, paying instead of cash his own noble title, his "name and style"; the Comparini agreed to it, and so did Pompilia. Further, he has found that the callow nestling he selected possessed a will of its own: the girl was no pigeon fluttering from the breast of Venus: she did not come to him submissively with love, but obstinately, with coldness, self-possession and even hate for her purchaser. If so, why, he asks, should he not "properly train" his bird—even as one trains a hawk? One fondles the pigeon, but the hawk must be treated more severely if it is to become useful, unless it should prove to be a "haggard," [7] in which case, if it is disobedient, untractable, and vicious, why, indeed, not kill it? [8] The image is a brilliant one for Guido because he has established at length the fact that Pompilia was acquired through a bargain, as well as the fact that the self-possessed Pompilia in Arezzo turned out to be quite different from the timid Pompilia he had parleyed for in Rome.[9] One bargains for possessions—such as pigeons and hawks. If one owns a bird and it

7. The *OED* gives the following for *haggard, sb²*: "I. A wild (female) hawk caught when in her adult plumage. (With some, in 17–18th c. = peregrine falcon.)" Cook in his excellent commentary supplies the gloss: "The haggard is a hawk which has fully moulted at least once before she is trained . . . [and may] prove 'untrainable, or be more trouble to reclaim than she is worth'; and Shakespeare, like Browning here, uses the word with this fact in view, *e.g.* in *Othello*, 3.3. 260–63 . . ." A. K. Cook, *A Commentary upon Browning's The Ring and the Book* (London, 1920), p. 101.

8. Browning's MS shows an earlier version of line 710: "And should she prove a haggard,—twitch her beak"; "twitch" and "beak" are crossed out and "twist" and "neck!" substituted. It is apparent that Browning wanted not only to emphasize Guido's cruelty in the latter phrase but to suggest his murderousness: the unruly haggard not only may be punished but, in Guido's view, may be eliminated—as one kills a chicken by twisting its neck. See B.M. MS Add. 43485, p. "257."

9. See *CGF*, 415–516, 567–664.

proves unruly, one may with perfect legality chastise it, or even kill it. Guido's metaphor in the context of his situation reveals on one level wit, shrewdness, and audacity.

On another level it reveals the very depths of villainy. And it is in picturing Guido's unrelieved blackness that Browning draws upon a host of technical elements simultaneously.

The falsity of the hawk image is suggested through the operation of poetic devices that serve, in effect, to contradict the set of relationships that Guido strives to establish. In this sense, there are in his talk what we might call elements of negative rhetoric that belie Guido's intention. Let us consider the effect of his alliteraton. *Pompilia,* the first word in line 701, is followed by a strong movement of alliterated terms in the first eight lines: *pigeon, pet, pressing paps, pick, pay, price, paid, pound,* and *penny's.* All of these words, in fact, truly pertain to Pompilia or to Guido's real attitude toward Pompilia. The Pompilia-pigeon relationship is flatly denied, but at the same time the two nouns are phonetically associated through their initial sounds, so that the truth Guido endeavors to cover up is at least hinted despite his attempt to deny it: if Pompilia resembled any bird, that bird was the pigeon. Guido denies the appropriateness of the Venus-metaphor for Pompilia, but alliteration again links *Pompilia* with Venus' *pet* and *pressing paps,* reflecting a true metaphorical relationship: Pompilia came to Arezzo with Venus' attribute, love—love that Guido, the "devil and no man" (*CGF,* 613) could not receive and did not want; the monster was in fact insusceptible to the humanity that was offered him. Guido did really "pick" Pompilia and "pay the price" of his name to the Comparini in return for her; his noble title was his "pound" and he expected his "penny's worth" in return—except that Pompilia refused to be considered and treated as an object in a purely mercenary bargain. Thus a true image for Pompilia emerges in conflict with Guido's actual meaning and intention: Pompilia was Venus' pigeon, picked out and paid for by Guido, and unsatisfactory to him only because she refused to assume the status of a possession.

His false image for Pompilia is the *hawk.* This word is repeated twice and linked to other aspirates so that the series, *hawk, hawk's, hawk's, home, hoodwink* and *haggard* (lines 703–10), is set up in contrast to the (p)-series. These terms have nothing to do with Pompilia and are unrelated to the (p)-words in sound as in meaning; they have, instead, the effect of reflecting Guido's own character. The word *home* (signifying Guido's estate in Arezzo) is linked with *hawk's* in the same line, and *hawk* and *hawk's* before and after it:

> —but a *hawk,*   (703)
> I bought at a *hawk's* price and carried *home* (704)
> To do *hawk's* service—   (705)

The subject of the dependent clause in lines 704–5 is *I,* and the proximity of this pronoun reinforces the identity between Guido and the hawk that he stresses; the subject of the whole sentence, *Pompilia,* occurs three lines before, so that the Pompilia-hawk identity is again minimized. Alliteration and syntax both underline the Pompilia-pigeon and Guido-hawk relationships, the true ones. Punctuation and sound quality contribute as well. When Guido says,

> Pompilia was no pigeon, Venus' pet,   (701)
> That shuffled from between her pressing paps (702)
> To sit on my rough shoulder,—but a hawk,   (703)

the mark of double punctuation induces a strong caesura after *shoulder,* separating the *hawk*-phrase that follows from the *Pompilia-pigeon-pet-pressing paps* alliteration, which occurs in a more closely knit rhythmic unit. Moreover the falsity of the Pompilia-hawk identity is even more strikingly reinforced through the phonetic quality of accented vowels in the alliterated words and *hawk.* Phonetically, the accented vowel sounds, (i) in *Pompilia,* (I) in *pigeon,* (ε) in *pet* and *pressing* and (æ) in *paps,* are all front vowels, similar in their being articulated forward in the mouth; in considerable contrast the (ɔ) of *hawk* is an open back vowel, articulated in the throat, and the effect of *hawk,* terminating in the only guttural stop in the three lines, is to disrupt markedly the series of accented vowel sounds in the alliterated words. The sound, *hawk,* is thus in all of its components (initial aspirate, open back vowel, and guttural stop) out of harmony with the sound of the (p)-words. The image is dissociated from Pompilia through alliteration, punctuation, phonetic quality, and even through syntax, so that all of these elements help to expose the nature of Guido's lie. Moreover, in emphasizing the true application of the hawk image to Guido's own character, these devices help to characterize Guido not only as a liar but as the vicious and predatory animal that *hawk* stands for in context.[10]

Diction further emphasizes this viciousness. The words Guido actually uses with reference to himself are revealing. His verbs include *bought, pick, choose, pay, paid, hoodwink, starve, train, twist, incurred, practise, prove, submit,* and *afford.* These fall principally into two groups, denoting in the senses used either acts that have to do with market transactions, or with discipline, pain or violence. His nouns as he uses them tend to reflect transactions, *price, pound, penny's worth,* or somewhat vague abstract concepts, *name, style, hope, trust, all,* or abstract concepts with specific implications, such as *mastery, mastership,* and *pleasure.* As a whole these words help to picture Guido's mask, which itself is an inhuman one: he appears to have regarded Pompilia strictly as an economic object. But beneath this the real Guido shows: he has in fact regarded her not even as an ordinary bought object, but as a thing to torture and to master. He refers to his own physical condition twice, in mentioning his "rough shoulder" upon which a pigeon might sit (line 703) and his "bile" which he expected Pompilia to cure (line 719), and both of these help to expose the true Guido. His "shoulder" reference is a seemingly accidental reminder to the Court of the rack-torture that he has just endured; Guido refers to his wrenched shoulder-blade no less than seven times in the monologue, calling particular attention

10. Guido, it should be added, is no fool. Part of his own object is to imply that the truth about Pompilia, which he alone has understood, contrasts sharply with received opinion. Thus his "negative" rhetoric is part of his intentional rhetoric. However, this rhetoric carries him too far. We are led to feel that "hawk" and "Pompilia" have no natural or self-evident relationship with one another. Moreover, unwittingly, Guido seeks to condemn his wife with a metaphor that all too appropriately applies to himself—and, still more disastrously, he associates himself with the hawk in line 704 through alliteration and, indirectly, through syntax. Other Half-Rome has already associated Guido with *hawk* in *OH-R,* 1533–39; Caponsacchi, and then Pompilia, in the two monologues that follow this one of Guido's, will in turn characterize him with the same image. See *GC,* 109–10, and *P,* 443–44.

to it earlier by using the osteological term *omoplat*.[11] His object
is to elicit the Court's compassion and so to increase the effectiveness of his argument at key points; but his sheer wiliness is revealed in indirect references to it, as in the pigeon [12] context of
lines 701-3. His use of *bile* is intended to elicit sympathy, as well,
but it does something else. The revealing effect of the word in
context is partly due to rhythm and sound:

> The obligation I incurred was just   (716)
> To practise mastery, prove my mastership:— (717)
> Pompilia's duty was—submit herself,   (718)
> Afford me pleasure, perhaps cure my bile.   (719)

Browning's MS reveals an earlier version of line 718,

> Pompilia's duty,—to submit herself,[13]

11. Browning's use of *omoplat* (in *CGF*, 118 and 248) has been parodied by
Calverley (see the quotation from *The Cock and the Bull* on p. 209 above) and
criticized by others. However, the word is not only functional and effective but part
of his legitimate vocabulary. In *Guido* he indicates that he has studied anatomy in
order to improve the deadliness of his fencing (G, 282-9) and uses kindred terms
(e.g. *Atlas, Axis, symphyses, arachnoid*). He does not explain how it is that he
knows such a word at the present time because its rhetorical effect depends
upon its apparently casual use. Its advantage lies precisely in its being a very
unusual word that serves to call attention to a matter he must strongly emphasize
without seeming to do so.

12. In line 715 Guido mentions two other birds: *falcon-gentle* and *finch*. Cook
mentions that the term "falcon-gentle" was applied in Elizabethan England "to the
whole species of peregrine hawks." See his citation from Gerald Lascelles' essay on
Elizabethan falconry in A. K. Cook, *A Commentary* (London, 1920), p. 102. Guido's
falcon-gentle is thus in context a synonym for *hawk* and, of course, intentionally
another reference to Pompilia. Guido's *finch*, on the other hand, is a careful
reference to his maid-servant, Margherita, whom Pompilia later intimates was
Guido's mistress:

> . . . There may have elapsed a week,   (P, 1051)
> When Margherita,—called my waiting-maid,
> Whom it is said my husband found too fair— . . .

Guido's vicious inhumanity is thus further underlined in the finch reference, as
the two women in Arezzo become either the (haggard-) *hawk* (a useless bird that
may be killed) or the *finch* (a gentle bird that may be petted) depending primarily
upon their submissiveness to him.

13. See B.M. MS Add. 43485, p. "257." The line stands as such in the MS.
It was probably revised in proof.

which is decasyllabic but which minimizes one stress, and in changing this to the present version, a line of five regular iambs but with a caesura after the third foot, Browning greatly emphasized the rhythmic variation of the next line (719), which imparts a strange emphasis to the word *bile*. In fact the rhythm of all four lines, 716–19, now contributes to the effect of this one word, for the rhythm follows a balanced pattern until the last half of line 719. The tempo of 716 is quickened by light stresses; the tempo of 717 is slightly reduced through the mid-line caesura dividing the verse into parallel components ("*prac*tise *mas*tery, *prove* my *mas*tership"); and the tempo of 718 is still a bit slower due to its five even stresses and again the mid-line caesura. Line 719 begins by following the now established pattern; there is a mid-line caesura, but after the caesura the tempo is reduced markedly:

> . . . , perhaps cure my bile. (719)

Four effectual stresses occur together here.[14] The tempo of "my bile" is further slowed by the repetition of the vowel sound, which is one of considerable quantity: the full diphthong, (aɪ). Thus the rhythm of four lines and the phonetic quality of its own vowel and the vowel preceding it set off the word *bile*. With *hawk, bile* becomes one of the two most emphasized words in the passage, and the heightening that it receives has the effect of conditioning its meaning and the implications of its meaning in context. Guido uses *bile* in the figurative sense of anger, ill-temper, or peevishness.[15] Now the latter are somewhat indefinite qualities of mood, for anger or ill-temper may imply anything from mild irascibility to sheer murderousness. As Guido himself has admitted that he is a murderer at the outset of his argument, and as *bile* is greatly stressed, the effect is to suggest the most intense and the worst of its possible implications here, and as it occurs in the context of his bird image for Pompilia, in which Guido has unwittingly characterized himself as a hawk, it also has the effect of belying

14. Strictly, *my* seems to take a lighter stress than -*haps, cure* and *bile,* but the whole line cannot be read without imparting some stress to *my*—a syllable that at least takes more stress than any of the unaccented syllables in the line. The quantity of its diphthong is partly responsible; contrast the complete lack of stress that "a" or "the" would have in its place.

15. Cf. *OED,* art. *bile,* 2. *fig.*

Guido's whole intention in this passage: he has not treated Pompilia harshly because she failed to please him as a purchased bird might, but because harshness and villainy are at the root of his nature. A variety of technical devices serve to accentuate *hawk* and *bile* exactly because these two words tell the most about the real Guido.

The voices of Caponsacchi, Pompilia, Arcangeli, Bottini, and the Pope are heard before we hear Guido's voice again. In contrast to the speakers of *Half-Rome, Other Half-Rome* and *Tertium Quid,* three of these see Guido clearly—only the two lawyers presenting burlesque versions of his character. In *Caponsacchi* Guido's villainy is outlined in an impassioned narrative and condemned; in *Pompilia* his villainy comes newly to light in an intimate account of the Arezzo days; and in *The Pope* Guido's whole career and character are summarized and carefully judged. But Guido has yet to speak in his own "wolf's" voice: in Book V his shag has appeared in dark flashes through the outer disguise of sheep's clothing, but the wolf itself has remained unexplained.

He does not, in this sense, speak quite freely in his own voice until line 443 in *Guido,* when he acknowledges his sheep's disguise and figuratively casts it off his back; from approximately this point on true motivations are not concealed and depths of viciousness come progressively to light as Guido harangues Acciaiuoli and Panciatichi with denunciations of civilization, a new account of his meeting with the Comparini, his marriage, life in Arezzo, the murder, and his attitude toward his son Gaetano and toward life itself (462-2411). The lines before 443 are primarily important for their function in leading the speaker to a point at which he is willing to doff his disguise.

> You are the Cardinal Acciaiuoli, and you, (G, 1)
> Abate Panciatichi—

he begins in *Guido,* and a little later mentions the time as "ere break of day" (G, 24), indicates that he knows he may die "at sunset" "twelve hours hence" (G, 25, 32), and refers to his "gaoler" and "straw-truss" (G, 33, 34). The scene is again set in Guido's opening lines. Guido knows why the Abate and Cardinal have come to his cell, but wildly hopes that their visit may be

> . . . a well-intentioned trick, (G, 22)
> That tries for truth truer than truth itself,

and not one for the purpose of obtaining a last confession. The Abate and Cardinal linger quietly on. It is their failure to respond to any of his overtures—beyond crossing their breasts or fingering their beads—that drives Guido to desperation in the light of his predicament; by line 130, having elicited no response, he tells them in a bitter burst of irony to keep quiet:

> . . . let me talk,   (G, 130)
> Or leave me, at your pleasure! talk I must:
> What is your visit but my lure to talk?
> You have a something to disclose?—a smile,
> At end of the forced sternness, means to mock
> The heart-beats here? I call your two hearts stone!
>
> .   .   .   .
>
> Be tacit as your bench, then!   (G, 137)

But Cardinal and Abate have come solely to fulfill a priestly mission: in attempting to obtain a confession from Guido and so to prepare his soul for Judgment, they represent not only the Pope and the Church but officially the power of God on earth. Ironically, it is just in this sense that Guido's character dramatically includes the characters of his auditors and what they stand for.[16] For all his villainy, Guido still has the power to confess. This power is his spiritual potential, and in the act of confession, and only in this act, Guido may still align himself with righteousness; he may still, in other words, become spiritually one with his auditors. Dramatically he is much larger than they are because he is in fact the ultimate villain: liar, schemer, torturer, and killer. The holy mission of the Abate and Cardinal is to draw out the one potential for good that still remains underneath layer upon layer of villainy, to cause him to abandon not only his sheep's disguise but the wolf's shag itself—his worldly personality—and to

16. Cf. above, pp. 155–56. In *Guido,* as in all of the monologues discussed, the audience element represents dramatically one part of the speaker's own being.

throw himself nakedly upon the power of the Cross. Though they are quiet, they succeed, for as each of Guido's frantic pleas for assistance is met with nothing but the raised crucifix or the mumbled prayer, his despair is increased, and he is driven to give up not only the pretense of innocence but one secret after another of his monstrous consciousness until, divested of all other hope, he turns to the dead Pompilia in order to save himself—thereby acknowledging the power of spiritual goodness. As the Venetian letter-writer of Book XII reports, Guido's full confession followed (XII, 120–28).

We may consider in some detail a pivotal point in this unmasking—lines 433–54, in which Guido abandons his outer disguise and begins to talk freely in his own voice to Panciatichi and Acciaiuoli.

Guido (434–54)

. . . I end,	(433)
Telling the truth! Your self-styled shepherd thieves!	(434)
A thief— and how thieves hate the wolves we know:	(435)
Damage to theft, damage to thrift, all's one!	(436)
The red hand is sworn foe of the black jaw!	(437)
That's only natural, that's right enough:	(438)
But why the wolf should compliment the thief	(439)
With the shepherd's title, bark out life in thanks,	(440)
And, spiteless, lick the prong that spits him,—eh,	(441)
Cardinal? My Abate, scarcely thus!	(442)
There, let my sheepskin-garb, a curse on 't, go—	(443)
Leave my teeth free if I must show my shag!	(444)
Repent? What good shall follow? If I pass	(445)
Twelve hours repenting, will that fact hook fast	(446)
The thirteenth at the horrid dozen's end?	(447)
If I fall forthwith at your feet, gnash, tear,	(448)
Foam, rave, to give your story the due grace,	(449)
Will that assist the engine half-way back	(450)
Into its hiding-house?—boards, shaking now,	(451)
Bone against bone, like some old skeleton bat	(452)
That wants, now winter's dead, to wake and prey!	(453)
Will howling put the spectre back to sleep?	(454)

The passage is similar to Guido's Pompilia-pigeon utterance—
for here, too, the thought is expressed in a single complex image.
Similarly, it is an animal image. Guido is the *wolf*. The enormous
difference is that the present metaphor is a true one, and it becomes intensely revealing of Guido's character through the operation of elements that make it seem even more pertinent than
Guido intends.

Guido calls himself a wolf because he has fallen victim to his
own rhetoric. A few lines earlier, railing against the Pope, he has
referred to "this Vicar of the Lord, / Shepherd o' the flock" (G,
400–1) who has failed to act as shepherd should; instead of saving
Guido with his crook, the Pope has

> . . . thrust the shuddering sheep he calls a wolf, (G, 405)
> Back and back, down and down to where hell gapes!

Now, in lines 434–41, the earlier image is pursued: far from being
a shepherd, we are told, for shepherds save their flocks, the Pope
is a thief. Guido's Pope has assumed "the shepherd's title" only
to rob.

Guido has now developed a personally satisfying image for the
Pope except that, quite unwittingly, he has forced one side of his
earlier comparison too far: if the Pope is not merely a bad shepherd but a shepherd thief, why is it that he hates Guido? The
words,

> Your self-styled shepherd thieves! (434)
> A thief—   (435)

force the shepherd image to a critical point, for it will collapse
unless the Pope as *thief* can be shown to have had a good reason
for condemning Guido to death. In this rhetorical predicament
Guido brands himself with the name of the animal he imagines
that the Pope has called him earlier—the *wolf*, for Guido's Pope
has indeed an excellent reason for hating wolves. Wolves and
thieves are enemies: both prey on the same innocent beings. The
new complex Pope-thief Guido-wolf image is a strong and useful
one, for Guido may turn it savagely against his auditors:

> But why the wolf should compliment the thief   (439)
> With the shepherd's title, bark out life in thanks,   (440)

And, spiteless, lick the prong that spits him,—eh, (441)
Cardinal? My Abate, scarcely thus!   (442)

If the Pope is a *thief*, and Guido a *wolf*, it would be mere self-mockery for Guido to "compliment" his rival by repenting. Moreover—Guido is able to imply—the Cardinal and Abate are here on a fool's mission, for no moral difference exists between the Pope-thief and the Guido-wolf; the holy men would do well to give up the thief's mission and help Guido to escape destruction. Guido does not pick up his "sheepskin-garb" after this, but instead identifies it for what it is, curses it, and figuratively drops it (443–44), because, as *wolf*, he is able to maintain a position which makes that of his auditors untenable (Abate and Cardinal cannot expect a wolf to confess its sins), and which also lends force to the pleading that follows in the monologue (Abate and Cardinal cannot deny that Guido is now speaking frankly in his own voice). Yet it is a desperate concession, too, for he can no longer claim to be innocent. From now on he must rationalize pure villainy.

Thus Guido's rhetoric leads him inadvertently into the wolf metaphor for himself. Once he adopts it, he keeps it for its further usefulness. But how, we may then ask, does its expression in this passage help to reveal Guido's character?

The wolf metaphor becomes in fact excessively vivid. Guido gives greater force to the picture of himself as a wolf than he needs to do or even intends to do for the purposes of his argument, and it is through the combined operation of a number of verbal, prosodic and syntactical elements that Browning is able to make Guido's ferocity and rapacity appear as fundamental character traits by intensifying the effect of the image so greatly that wolf and speaker seem to be truly one.

Guido in the first place uses more animal terms, or words that are associated with animality in context, than he must in order to establish his point. His verbs and verbal nouns include: *bark*, *lick*, *spits* [in the sense of impaling a carcass], *hook* [as with a claw], *gnash*, *tear*, *foam*, *prey*, and *howling*. He characterizes himself not alone with the noun *wolf*, but with the terms, *black jaw*, *wolves*, *teeth*, *shag*, and indirectly with *bone* [twice], *skeleton*, *bat,* and *spectre.* The latter four are involved in a simile within the main image in which Guido likens the machine that is to end his life with another animal—again, an animal whose deadliness is emphasized:

> —boards, shaking now,   (451)
> Bone against bone, like some old skeleton bat   (452)
> That wants, now winter's dead, to wake and prey! (453)

Syntax and even punctuation emphasize the wolfishness of Guido, for his sentences are short, abrupt, and, in every case here, they end with words whose pitch is raised. The effect, operating through the meaning conveyed, is to give Guido's utterance a snapping, savage quality. Verbs are omitted, as in lines 434, 442, 445, and the absolute construction is employed. This type of construction had been used in *The Bishop at St. Praxed* to emphasize the Bishop's sensuality, where syntactical fragments embodying sensuous images had seemed to lead the Bishop's thought. Here the effect is again to indicate the ascendency of feelings, but feelings of brutish hate and brutish fear:

> Your self-styled shepherd thieves!   (434)
> *A thief*—and how thieves hate the wolves we know: (435)
>
> Will that assist the engine half-way back   (450)
> Into its hiding-house?—*boards, shaking now,*   (451)
> *Bone against bone . . .*   (452)

Guido's utterance, moreover, is broken by frequent short rhythmical units that take on an explosive quality due to their terminal stops. In this, his verse is reminiscent of *Mr. Sludge,* except that the meaning here helps to suggest the presence of vicious, animal energy behind the explosions rather than simple high spirits: "I end, / Telling the truth!" (433–44); "The red hand is sworn foe of the black jaw!" (437); ",—eh, / Cardinal?" (441–42); "Leave my teeth free if I must show my shag!" (444); "Repent? What good shall follow?" (445). Sound contributes to rhythm in helping to impart through meaning this same savage energy. When Guido says, for example,

> If I *fall forthwith* at your *feet, gnash, tear,*   (448)
> *Foam, rave,* to *give* your *story* the *due grace,* (449)

extra stresses in both lines and the presence of first three and then
five consecutive stresses—a strong spondaic movement—give the
verses unusual emphasis. But at the same time the tempo is not
markedly reduced from that of preceding lines, as both alliteration, in *fall, forthwith, feet, foam, give* and *grace,* and the repetition of consonant sounds, chiefly (r) and (ө), impart speed. Strong
rhythmic emphasis and unslackened speed combine with the
meaning to convey the impression of quick, savage force. Guido's
mode of expression throughout the passage is thus conditioned by
factors of diction, sound and syntax so as to intensify the over-all
effect of the image: he seems to speak with the voice of the wolf
and so in effect assumes the wolf's total character.

Guido's fear, which comes over him in a terrifying wave in the
last half of this passage, is one other manifestation of wolfishness.
Neither faith nor philosophy stand between the beast and the
terror awakened by its awareness of approaching destruction, and
Guido, in fact, displays a morbid obsession with death throughout
his monologue. He uses the words *die, dies, died, dying, dead,
death, death's* and *death-hour* no less than 64 times in all, refers
repeatedly to his *neck* or the *cord* [17] that will be sliced by the
axe of the Mannaia machine, which he gives an elaborate account
of (G, 179–249), and in the passage above harps on his death in
almost every line.

In context, all of the following words directly reflect the death
obsession: *end* (2), *hate, red, prong, spits, thirteenth, horrid, en-
gine, hiding-house, boards, bone, skeleton, bat, dead, prey,* and
spectre. The simile of the bat, which we have noted as a mark
of Guido's viciousness, also becomes a mark of his terror. The
word *bat* is alliterated with *boards, bone, bone,* other elements of
the bat-simile in lines 451–52, and the repeated vowel sound of

17. In *Guido, neck (neck's, necks)* occurs 12 times and *cord* (as of the spine)
5 times. Many other words suggest his preoccupation with decapitation and death,
even when considered out of context: *murder (murder's, murdered, murderer,
murderous)*—9; *kill (kills, killed)*—6; *slay (slays, slaying)*—5; and *death-damp, death-
bed, 'Sdeath,* for example.

these three stressed words, (o), represents a marked fall in pitch from the vowel sounds of the stressed syllables that have preceded them in lines 450–51. The fall in pitch from sounds such as (æ), (ɪ), (ɛ), (ɑ), and (aɪ), in

> Will that assist the engine half-way back (450)
> Into its hiding-house?   (451)

—to the (o) sounds that follow, in

>   —boards, shaking now, (451)
> Bone against bone,   (452)

emphasizes the emotional change that occurs in the middle of line 451, as does the grammatically absolute nature of the new movement. But the fall in pitch to (o) also suggests the psychological quality of the vision of the Mannaia-bat: it is a terribly real vision of death in Guido's mind, a vision filled with despair and horror. The (o)-sound is "hollow" in this special context; it is out of harmony with the sounds that have preceded; it helps, indeed, to reflect that all-consuming fear in the face of death that only the animal quite experiences. For by the time that Guido utters these lines the tables have truly turned against him. The voracious wolf has had its day, and we see now the wolf's true mettle just in the way that it faces certain death.

CONCLUSION

We have seen that Browning's mature techniques in the treatment of character were developed rather slowly, through trial and error, in a series of long poems, stage plays, and experimental dramas—dating from the time of *Pauline* (1833) to the year of the *Dramatic Romances and Lyrics* (1845). In a series of twenty character-revealing dramatic monologues, composed between 1844 and 1871, Browning richly exploited the lessons that he had learned in his early experiments and stage dramas. Various dramatic, imagistic, verbal, syntactical, and prosodic devices are employed in these twenty poems to create impressions of character; the devices tend to work coordinately, and to achieve intense effects. We have surveyed a number of the ways in which these individual devices seem to operate in the poems, and we have attempted to suggest, in two analyses of passages from *The Ring and the Book,* several of the ways in which these devices may combine to achieve central impressions. We may bring the present study to a close by drawing two conclusions.

First, it would seem to be clear that Browning himself was a poet who paid the utmost attention even to the minutiae of his artistry, and that he was able to fuse the complex elements of his art again and again to create desired effects in his finest poems.

Second, it would seem to be equally clear that character itself is of key importance in Browning's art in the dramatic monologue form. This is not to say that all of the poet's monologues are of equal importance as character portraits, or indeed that any one monologue need be viewed as a character portrait alone. But much of Browning's true achievement becomes clear when we consider certain monologues in the light of his treatment of character—and it is in this light, and in rereading these monologues with close attention to their details, that we may come to a new understanding of them.

Index

Titles are indexed under author, and characters in poems and plays are treated under title. Numerals in italic type indicate a main entry.